Frontline HR

A Handbook for the Emerging Manager

Jeffrey S. Hornsby

Donald F. Kuratko

THOMSON

Australia · Canada · Mexico · Singapore · Spain · United Kingdom · United States

THOMSON
™

Frontline HR: A Handbook for the Emerging Manager

Jeffrey S. Hornsby & Donald F. Kuratko

ISBN: 0-324-20323-3
Printed and bound in the USA by R.R. Donnelley, Crawfordsville, IN
1 2 3 4 5 6 7 8 9 07 06 05

For more information, contact Texere at Thomson Higher Education, 5191 Natorp Boulevard, Mason, Ohio, USA 45040. You can also visit our website at www.thomson.com/learning/texere.

This publication is designed to provide accurate and authoritative information in regard to the subject matter covered. It is sold with the understanding that the publisher is not engaged in rendering legal, accounting or other professional services. If legal advice or other expert assistance is required, the services of a competent professional person should be sought.

Cover Designer: Lisa A. Albonetti

The names of all companies or products mentioned herein are used for identification purposes only and may be trademarks or registered trademarks of their respective owners. Texere disclaims any affiliation, association, connection with, sponsorship, or endorsements by such owners.

This book is printed on acid-free paper.

Library of Congress Cataloging-in-Publication Data
HF5549.H52987 2005
658.3--dc22
2004028007

Asia (including India)
Thomson Learning
5 Shenton Way
#01-01 UIC Building
Singapore 068808

Canada
Thomson Nelson
1120 Birchmount Road
Toronto, Ontario
M1K 5G4
Canada

UK/Europe/Middle East/Africa
Thomson Learning
High Holborn House
50/51 Bedford Row
London WC1R 4LR
United Kingdom

Australia/New Zealand
Thomson Learning Australia
102 Dodds Street
Southbank, Victoria 3006
Australia

Latin America
Thomson Learning
Seneca, 53
Colonia Polanco
11560 Mexico
D.F. Mexico

Spain (including Portugal)
Thomson Paraninfo
Calle Magallanes, 25
28015 Madrid, Spain

Contents

CHAPTER 1

The Human Resources Role for Emerging Managers

Perhaps one of the most difficult challenges a frontline manager must confront is defining the true value of human resources (HR) for other managers. It can take several months, even years, to change the minds of executive officers, but it will ultimately be the floor supervisors and frontline managers whose daily practices will be affected the most by this extreme change in business attitudes. Once a culture that respects the importance of HR pervades the board room, much more may be expected of both HR professionals and the frontline managers who support the work force. As the bottom-line-only orientation of so many recent CEOs is disappearing into oblivion, the new focus for future success is becoming people, rather than merely numbers.

Richard Pinola, chair and CEO of Right Management Consultants, Inc., has identified what executive officers require from frontline professionals in terms of human resources.[1] He believes that to add real value to a company, HR must relate to the organization's overall strategy. Once this is accomplished, positive changes can occur in:

- **Talent management:** Attract, select, develop careers, manage performance, retain talent, and manage succession.

[1] See Sandler, Susan F., ed. 2002. "What CEOs Want from HR." *HR Focus* (September), pp. 1, 14-15.

1

- **Leadership development:** Assess, coach, and build leaders and teams.
- **Organizational performance:** Assess, strategize, and manage change.

Clearly, if employees do not feel part of the team, low morale can negatively affect their work experience and work ethic. Disillusionment is inevitable if people feel ignored. Too little time and effort are spent on helping new hires. Even if there's lots of work for them, they don't know the business, so they can feel isolated. This type of employment experience critically undermines the prestige equated with a company's name in the eyes of current employees and applicants. To create a solid employer brand, create an employee value proposition (EVP):

- **Define:** Create a distinctive employment identity (the EVP).
- **Declare:** Make an effort to market the EVP. Brand yourself to both current and potential workers—and deliver on what you promise.
- **Demonstrate:** Deliver on the EVP.

Front-line managers often take the EVPapproach to create an environment where employees feel more empowered and important, but it appears that among the benefits are not only improved morale but also improved profits—perhaps only in the long term, but profits nonetheless.

THE MANAGER'S CHALLENGE

For far too long, the line manager's role in human resources has been one of confusion and avoidance. Many managers don't understand the role of the HR professional in their organization, if indeed there is an HR professional. And even though a majority of the tasks that are part of managing require planning for, selecting, training, evaluating, and disciplining employees, too many managers still don't see any link between these activities and the HR role.

At the same time, many organizations are changing the strategic positioning of HR activities. HR professionals are being challenged to break out of their functional activities and act as internal consultants to managers. Meanwhile, increased outsourcing of activities and downsizing in HR departments, coupled with the change in HR strategy, place ever-growing pressure on line managers and supervisors to take on the role of HR professional. Managers at all levels must take increasing ownership of the HR function by increasing their HR knowledge and skills. Organizations must support these initiatives with training and mentoring.

A comment by Abraham Zaleznik pinpoints the critical importance of HR activities in any organization: "The work of human resources is to identify and develop people who have the talents and imagination companies need to compete in a changing, complex, competitive environment. That means that HRM ought to be the most important job in every business."[2]

HR management doesn't necessarily require an HR department, and even where there is one, responsibility for identifying and strengthening key personnel doesn't rest solely with the department. Managers play a crucial role in these and other human resource activities. In fact, managers actually implement most functions while any HR representatives simply administer and coordinate them. Specifically, managers are responsible for interviewing, training, appraising, and disciplining their subordinates. They also play important roles in compensation, safety, job analysis, and planning. That means every manager is a first-line HR manager.

This is especially true in smaller and growing firms that are less likely to have an HR department. Well over 99 percent of all businesses in the United States have fewer than 500 employees, and close to 80 percent have fewer than 10.[3] However, most of the research in HR management has tended to focus on larger, more established companies; most HR management books assume that a firm has at least one HR professional who is competent to carry out the practices they describe in their publications. Because smaller firms aim to grow larger, they need guidance on how to deal effectively with HR resource issues as they begin to deal with the challenges presented by larger employee groups. In support of this argument, a study of young entrepreneurs found that HR topics ranked highest among the areas where they thought they needed more learning.[4]

[2] Zaleznik, A. 1988. "What's Wrong with HRM," *Harvard Business Review*, 66: 170-71.
[3] United States Small Business Administration Office of Advocacy. 1997. "Characteristics of Small Employers and Owners." *www.sba.gov/advo/stats/ch_em97.pdf.* Last accessed 18 May 2004
[4] Heneman, R. L., J. W. Tansky, and S. M. Camp. 2000. "Human Resource Management Practices in Small- and Medium-sized Enterprises: Unanswered Questions and Future Research Perspectives." *Entrepreneurship Theory and Practice*, 25: 11-26.

Over the last decade numerous pressures have stimulated the emergence of HR as a general management responsibility. Eight critical managerial issues affect growing firms:[5]

1. *Increasing international competition.* Global competition from areas like the Far East means that domestic companies need more skilled employees and greater employee commitment.
2. *Increasing company complexity.* Though challenged by the need to reduce bureaucracy, companies at the same must time deal with a more geographically dispersed work force. Managers must understand how employment laws and customs vary from country to country.
3. *Organizational downsizing.* As organizations tighten and downsize, their ability to offer career advancement becomes limited.
4. *Greater government involvement in HR management.* Equal employment practices, most recently the Americans with Disabilities Act (ADA) and the Family and Medical Leave Act (FMLA), make functional managers responsible for compliance.
5. *A better-educated work force.* Managers must now think about how much responsibility employees want.
6. *Changing employee values.* Employees are demanding more involvement in management. Managers need mechanisms for more employee participation.
7. *More concern with balancing career and life satisfaction.* Traditional assumptions about career paths no longer hold true. The lifestyle choices of their employees will increasingly force companies to chart new alternative career paths to keep key personnel.
8. *Work force diversity.* The increased numbers of females and minorities in the work force have forced companies to reexamine their employment policies and practices.

These eight HR issues, combined with all the other issues growing firms must deal with, will continue to challenge managers well into the future.

---

[5] Adapted from Beer, M., B. Spector, P. R. Lawrence, D. Q. Mills, and R. E. Walton. 1985. Human Resource Management: *A General Manager's Perspective.* New York: The Free Press.

THE EVOLVING ROLE OF THE LINE MANAGER IN HR

As business challenges, such as retaining employees, improving customer service, and dealing with the pressures of globalization and increased litigation recur, practices are evolving to help companies become more attuned to meet the challenges. To maintain a competitive advantage in today's business environment, companies are using HR management to reach strategic objectives,[6] and are restructuring and passing routine tasks down to line managers rather than centralizing them in HR departments. Job analysis, recruitment, selection, compensation, rewards, appraisals, and training and development are increasingly being shared between central administration, with or without an HR department, and line managers.[7]

In allocating this new responsibility, companies must train line managers in people management skills if they are to retain their best employees. Yet far too many line managers receive at best inadequate, at worst no, training in the HR functions they have become responsible for. This leads to inefficiencies, high turnover rates, and problems in complying with the law.

In an article in *Business Review Weekly*, it states that "the responsibility of the HR department is to ensure that the policies and procedures are in place to help line managers do their job."[8] One way to do this is to systematically train managers on how to conduct HR tasks and motivate employees. Training programs could be college courses, seminars given by professional associations, on-line courses, in-house training, informal mentoring, project assignments, task forces, case studies, or a combination of these.[9]

Although HR departments recognize the importance of training line managers in HR functions, few companies give them enough training. A

[6] McGinty Weston, Diane. September 14, 2003. "Delivering HR Services: Automation and Outsourcing Strategies." *http://www.sric-bi.com/BIP/DLS2264.shtml.* Accessed 18 May 2004.

[7] Das, J., and K. Shubhra. 2003. "HR Profession in Transition: Role of Line Managers," *India Infoline, http://www.indiainfoline.com/bisc/hrpo.html.* Accessed 14 January 2004.

[8] McColl, Gina. 2003. "Higher Responsibilities." *Business Review Weekly* 8 May 2003, 5 Sept. 2003

[9] Grensing Pophal, Lin. 1999. "Management Development: A Strategic Initiative," presentation to the Society for Human Resource Management. *http://www.shrm.org/hrresources/whitepapers_published/CMS_000455.asp.* Accessed 14 September 2003.

1998 study by the Center for Human Resource Management found that line managers believe they are accountable for HR and that the HR office role is to help them carry out their critical HR responsibilities.[10] However, there is a disconnect between what people in the HR department think they are doing to help line managers and what line managers think HR is doing to help them. HR training for line managers must be improved.

Another research study, this one by McKinsey & Company, reported that 80 percent of corporate officers think it is critical that HR departments be forceful partners with line managers,[11] yet only 12 percent believed that HR is actually playing that role today. *Personnel Today* found 80 percent of organizations planned to invest in training for their line managers over the next year.[12] The quality of the HR training provided to line managers was reported as crucial to helping a company reach its objectives. In addition to more training, regular communication and information sharing are also critical to help line managers handle HR.[13]

There are many benefits to training line managers in HR. When they can handle their own problems without passing the buck upstairs, they build credibility with their employees.[14] Training front-line managers in HR policies and procedures also helps to avoid costly litigation, while training them in routine HR tasks frees up time for administrators to do more strategic, value-added work.[15] A study by Mercer Human Resource Consulting found that one company decreased turnover by 10 percent simply by refocusing HR time from transactional to strategic.[16]

As one author has said, "The more an HR manager can educate line managers and their employees to take responsibility for their own career situations, the more likely they are to develop self-resilient employees who embrace, rather than fear, change in their work world."[17] Clearly, training

[10] McLure, Herb, and Darryl Renett. 1998, Summer. "New Partnerships: Federal Managers and the Human Resources Office." Public Manager, 1998: 44-48.
[11] *wwwmckinsey.com/clientsservice/*
[12] "What HR Can Do to Close the Skills Gap." *Personnel Today*, 13 May 2003.
[13] McLure, Herb, and Darryl Renett. 1998, Summer. "New Partnerships: Federal Managers and the Human Resources Office." Public Manager, 1998: 44-48.
[14] Herrmann, Donald M., Jr. 2002. "Passing the Buck to HR Undermines Your Credibility With Your Staff." Society for Human Resource Management, *http://www.shrm.org/manag - ingsmart/articles/winter02/0102dl.asp*. Accessed 14 September 2003.
[15] Coudron, S. 1999. "HR versus Managers." *Workforce*, August: 32.
[16] Sussman, Marsha. 2003. "Beyond HR Transformation: Sharing the HR Responsibility." Mercer Human Resource Consulting. 28 January 2004.
[17] Stevens, Paul. 2003. "Cost-Effective Human Resource Actions in Medium-Size Firms." *http://hr.monster.com.sg/srticles/5647/*. Accessed 23 September 2003.

front-line managers in HR functions creates a situation that is beneficial to both company and employees.

HR NEEDS OF SMALLER FIRMS

Many smaller firms may be lagging behind in terms of formalizing their HR functions. A comparison of the results of two parallel studies conducted 12 years apart[18] suggests that HR practices in smaller ventures of all sizes had generally stagnated since the first study was conducted. Targeted legislation and the changing dynamics of the U.S. work force have not put enough pressure on small firms to increase their HR emphasis.

The HR issues of concern to owners of smaller ventures did not change significantly over the 12 years between the two studies. Attraction and retention of quality workers, benefits, wages, and government regulation are still critical, regardless of the size of a venture. This may be the most valuable finding of the research, because it reveals that although the sophistication of practices currently used by small ventures is affected by size, concern over the most important future HR issues is not. The same concerns are carrying over into the new millennium.

The purpose of this book is to give both new managers in established firms and managers in growing businesses an understanding of which HR functions are most important and of the practical tools necessary to carry them out. The goal of this chapter is to introduce aspects of HR management with an overview of the different functional HR areas, a brief historical review, a discussion of how HR activities relate to total quality management (TQM), and suggestions for the future practice of HR.

---

[18] Hornsby, J. S., and D. F. Kuratko. 1990. "Human Resource Management: Critical Issues for the 1990s." *Journal of Small Business Management*, 28: 9-18; and Hornsby, J. S. and D. F. Kuratko. 2003. "Human Resource Management in U.S. Small Businesses: Critical Issues for the New Millennium." *Journal of Developmental Entrepreneurship*, Vol. 8 #1, pp. 73-92

THE MAJOR HUMAN RESOURCE FUNCTIONS

Exhibit 1.1 provides a model of how HR resource activities fit together in light of the critical managerial issues already noted. Examination of the model reveals two types of HR activities. The first type, the core HR duties, we refer to as internal challenges. They include:

- Job analysis
- HR planning
- HR information systems
- Employee recruitment
- Performance appraisal
- Training and development
- Discipline
- Compensation

The second type of HR activities confronts external factors that influence the practice of the core activities. These challenges include:

- Legal and ethical issues
- Global challenges
- Labor relations and characteristics of the changing work force
- Health and safety requirements
- Managerial issues

Let's examine types of human resource activities that are internal as well as external.

Internal Factors

Job analysis is the most fundamental human resource activity. Identifying required tasks or duties and assigning them to roles is the foundation for all other HR activities. It is certainly impossible, for instance, to conduct a job-related selection interview without an extensive knowledge of the job

Exhibit 1.1: The Human Resource Process

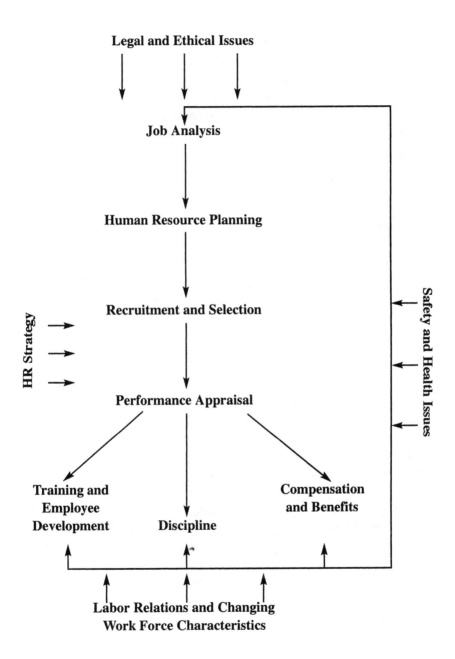

responsibilities. Job analysis information as summarized into a job description is used in recruiting, selecting, training, appraising, and compensating employees. Job analysis information also plays a major role in compliance with equal employment opportunity and other legal requirements. Though managers may view job analysis as tedious, it is essential groundwork for most other employment issues.

Human resource planning links corporate strategy with HR practice. Staffing levels, job requirements, and training needs must be correlated with the goals and objectives of the company; moreover, the company's ability to deal effectively with environmental changes related to the economy and technology is directly related to the success of the human resource planning effort. If the HR planning process is to be successful, top management must view HR management as a strategic function necessary to accomplish organizational goals.

Human resource information systems (HRIS) are important for effective HR planning. They encompass job requirements and data on employee knowledge, skills, abilities, and interests. This type of information, if readily accessible, can accelerate the hiring process and help in succession planning.

Attraction and retention of quality personnel is a consistent problem for all companies, but especially smaller firms looking to grow. This has remained the number one priority for firms with less than 150 employees.[19] Here is where the line manager plays a critical role, with the help of accurate job analyses. Recruitment involves, among other things, finding good sources of applicants, managing recruitment operations, and evaluating recruiting effectiveness. The success of any recruitment effort is its ability to develop a large pool of qualified applicants from which to choose. The larger the pool of applicants, the more likely the firm will make a successful selection.

The selection process involves using procedures like application blanks, interviews, reference and background checks, aptitude tests, and drug tests. The procedures used must relate to job content to meet equal employment requirements. Too often managers over-rely on interviews as their main selection procedure; it's important to use other selection devices as appropriate to increase the likelihood of a successful selection.

---

[19] See Hornsby and Kuratko, n. 18.

Performance appraisal is evaluation of how well employees are doing their jobs. This is a direct responsibility of the manager. It often determines employee-training needs, pay increases, and sometimes discipline. Once again, the standards used must be related to job content. As long as job-relatedness can be substantiated, performance appraisal data can be used to defend any employment decisions that may be challenged.

Training and development covers employee orientation, training employees to perform their current jobs, and helping them build new skills and abilities as jobs change or employees are promoted. Activities specific to designing a training program include needs assessment, selection of training methods, and evaluation. Training should be a critical concern for emerging firms as they attempt to strengthen staff ability to meet increasing demands.

An employee who violates a company policy or cannot do the job acceptably should expect to be disciplined. Companies should identify the types of employee actions that necessitate discipline and create a formal step-by-step procedure for carrying it out. Discipline usually consists of one of three actions: incremental/progressive discipline (verbal warning, written warning, probation, etc.), suspension, and termination. It is important that every step in the discipline process be documented in case an employment decision needs to be justified in court.

Employee compensation usually falls into two categories: direct monetary compensation and benefits like health insurance and retirement. Every company needs compensation systems that are competitive with their competition and are fair to employees based on what each employee brings to the job (education, skill, and effort). Activities like job evaluation, market pricing, and pay-for-performance programs are used to determine direct compensation.

Building an effective benefits package is a complex HR function. Rising insurance costs coupled with changing employee lifestyles has made it necessary for companies to regularly scrutinize their benefit packages. One response to these changes is to use some type of flexible benefit plan.

External Challenges

As we noted earlier, there are a host of legal and ethical issues involved with human resource activities. Most activities have gained importance from one of several pieces of equal employment legislation or a Supreme Court decision. Acts like the ADA and the FMLA, passed in the 1990s, certainly made it necessary for companies to reevaluate their selection and benefit practices. All employment decisions must be made in light of the law protecting the rights of employees, especially "protected classes" identified in discrimination legislation. The two most prominent legal issues defined not by Congress but by the courts, are employment-at-will and negligent hiring or retention.

As the geographic boundaries for businesses expand rapidly, the *glob - al market* is easily accessible. For most professionals who are employees, the likelihood of at least one international assignment during their careers is increasing greatly, and employees from sites in other countries may be transferred to the United States. The exporting and importing of employees raises important recruitment, selection, training, and compensation issues, not to mention the cultural and cost-of-living adjustments that must be addressed for a successful international assignment.

Labor relations and work force diversity will continue to challenge firms. While union membership may be on the decline, union involvement in key industries like auto manufacturing and transportation require managers to have some comprehension of labor relations. A sound understanding of the legal requirements, contract negotiation tactics, and contract administration can help improve labor-management relationships. Moreover, even nonunionized firms often establish employee grievance procedures.

Managing a diverse work force, with increasing numbers of women, physically challenged, ethnically diverse, and aging employees, adds another layer of complexity to recruitment, selection, training, and performance appraisal.

Health and safety issues have always been a concern, especially for manufacturers. The Occupational Safety and Health Act of 1970 mandates that companies maintain a safe and healthy workplace. Regulations established by the Occupational Safety and Health Administration (OSHA) are designed to reduce workplace accidents and illness. Some of better-known regulations apply to handling and use of hazardous chemicals, lockout/tag-out of dangerous equipment, confined space entry, and air quality. OSHA also undertakes investigation and enforcement activities to ensure adherence to the Act. Emerging firms in the manufacturing and medical sectors in particular must attend to OSHA regulations as they expand with additional equipment and employees who may not be properly trained.

THE HISTORICAL DEVELOPMENT OF HUMAN RESOURCE MANAGEMENT

Though HR management originated as very rigid discipline that emphasized record-keeping and payroll systems, it has grown to embrace a very complex set of responsibilities for employee motivation, total quality management (TQM), and strategic planning. This increased complexity has spurred increased demand for HR expertise.

The historical development of the human resource function can be divided into six major periods:

1. **Pre-1910: Production-centered**

   The first period, up to about 1910, emphasized a production mentality; the major concern was to produce products as cheaply as possible. There was almost no need for any HR function. The work did not require any skills and laborers were asked to work long hours at very low wages. Those employees who could not keep up were simply replaced. Employers often took a paternalistic approach with their employees, providing employees with housing and other services to ensure a steady work force.

2. **1910-1930: The birth of the HR function**

   In the next 20 years, the HR function was instituted to perform such traditional activities as employee selection and training. As the skills required grew in complexity, employees started expressing a desire for work that matched their individual abilities. Among the things that spurred such changes were the psychological reform movement in the 1920s and 1930s, the implementation of scientific management principles, and World War I. All these increased demand for efficiency in production and work specialization.

3. **1930-1960: The childhood of HR, a time of expanding responsibilities**

   Major changes that greatly affected the growth and importance of HR management between 1930 and 1960 include:

- Several fundamental pieces of legislation passed that dictated how employers could treat employees. The new laws gave unions the right to exist, established ground rules for union-management relations, specified a minimum wage, limited child labor, and provided guidelines on overtime pay.
- Employee values changed dramatically. Experiences in World Wars I and II, coupled with increasing skill and education, made employees more aware of what they valued about their jobs.
- As a response to new legislation and changing employee values, there was a shift in personnel philosophy. Companies became more oriented towards human relations, directing more of their attention to employee morale and job satisfaction.

4. **1960-1980: HR as a teenager, with increasing awareness of the value of employees**

As an outgrowth of what had happened up to 1960, employers worked to increase employee participation and to redesign jobs to make them more challenging and interesting. During this time employees began to be viewed as a valuable company resource. This new outlook promoted a change in the name of the field from Personnel Management to Human Resource Management. This was also the period when Congress passed the most significant antidiscrimination legislation. Employers were now legally responsible for preventing discrimination in their employment decisions.

5. **1980-2000: The maturing of the HR function and crisis management**

The end of the twentieth century presented many new challenges to the HR function. Employee displacement through downsizing brought about a renewed emphasis on training so that the displaced workers could gain skills to make them more employable in a changing marketplace. The ADA and the FMLA forced employers to take another look at their hiring and benefits policies.

6. **2001 to Date: Changing HR strategic direction; the importance of the line manager**

Today, Professor David Ulrich of the University of Michigan (who has published widely on aspects of strategic HR) says that the strategic role of the HR professional must evolve into activities like being coach, architect, deliverer, facilitator, and leader of line managers and others who deliver front-line HR services to employees.[20] Strategically, Ulrich also recommends that HR departments consider outsourcing such routine tasks as payroll, benefits administration, and temporary staffing to free up time for HR professionals to help line managers with more strategic duties.[21]

HR AND TQM

Improving quality has become a key objective for most managers. Traditionally, the quality movement has been mainly concerned with improvements to technical systems, but Bowen and Lawler[22] believe that while this emphasis is necessary, it may not be the most important variable in enhancing quality. They cite a Gallup survey of senior managers on TQM in which respondent managers cited productivity and quality most frequently as the top competitive issues facing their firms. Asked to rank the most effective approaches to improving quality, the mangers cited:

- Employee motivation
- Change in corporate culture
- Employee education
- Process control
- Expenditures on capital equipment
- More control of suppliers
- More inspections
- Improved administrative support

While some of these approaches to enhancing quality do involve technical improvements, clearly the majority center on effective management of human resources. The Bowen and Lawler study adds further evidence of the importance of HR management to the quality process; it notes that

---

[20] Ulrich, D. 2002. Masters Series Lecture, SHRM Conference. Philadelphia, June.
[21] Ibid.
[22] Bowen, D. E., and E. E. Lawler. 1992. "Total Quality-Oriented Human Resources Management." *Organizational Dynamics*, Spring: 29-41.

utilization of human resources is one of the seven categories evaluated for determining the Malcolm Baldridge National Quality Awards.

A survey of 184 small firms in the U.S. was conducted using the classification scheme for quality systems consistent with the Baldridge Award performance criteria, which are leadership, strategic planning, customer and market focus, information and analysis, human resource focus, process management, and business results.[23] The results support the proposition that small firms tend to employ quality practices that enable change and that position the firm to pursue flexibility as a competitive priority.

The importance of an HR focus was particularly highlighted. The survey findings suggest that quality strategies employing training programs, employee involvement, employee/team recognition programs, and formal education programs were rated as moderate to highly valuable. However, except for training programs, less than half the respondents employed these quality strategies.

How can HR be managed to enhance production quality? We recommend that the same principles of TQM that are applied elsewhere in the organization be applied to HR. The five most basic TQM principles[24] are:

1. Quality work the first time;

2. Focus on the customer;

3. Strategic, holistic approach to improvement;

4. Continuous improvement as a way of life; and

5. Mutual respect and teamwork.

---

[23] Kuratko, D. F., J. S. Hornsby, and J. C. Goodale. 2001. "Quality Practices for a Competitive Advantage in Smaller Firms." *Journal of Small Business Management*, Vol. 39 #4, 293-311. *See also* Hodgetts, R. M., D. F. Kuratko, and J. S. Hornsby. 1999. "Quality Implementation in Small Business: Perspectives from the Baldridge Award Winners." *SAM Advanced Management Journal*, 64(1): 37-47.
[24] Bowen and Lawler, n. 22., 29-41.

`A fairly recent study of small to medium-sized manufacturing firms found that a TQM strategy was most effective when it was supported by significant training and group-based compensation.[25] The same study seemed to contradict the opinions of Deming and other quality experts when it found that goal-setting and incentive compensations systems yielded positive TQM results and did not undermine implementation of TQM. Both HR professionals and managers who perform HR functions should approach their HR work with the same quality emphasis as they do other functions. Quick fixes or quick decisions should be avoided; decision-makers need time and resources to make quality decisions. For example, managers often view performance appraisal as a painful, time-consuming process that is somewhat unrelated to the rest of their activities. Senior management should emphasize the importance of appraisals by integrating them into corporate decisions and making sure managers have the time to perform them effectively. If they are to do this, managers must also be trained to conduct both the appraisal and the appraisal interview. In fact-they should be trained to perform all their HR responsibilities, including job analysis, selection, training, and compensation. If the firm has an HR department, its employees should regularly take the time to evaluate their programs instead of repeating activities without knowing how effective they are in achieving company objectives. HR departments, like line managers, must also be sensitive to employee needs rather than simply focusing on their own special projects.

THE FUTURE OF HR

Over the next decade, HR management faces both challenges and opportunities. The integration of HR management and TQM is one example, even though Jain and Murray claim that the HR function in most companies has very little impact on company performance:

> *"In spite of the strenuous efforts of many wise practitioners, teachers, and researchers over the years, the personnel function has failed to have any significant impact of its own. Rather it has been, and remains today, a reactive function, only responding to problems once they*

---

[25] Chandler, G. N., and G. M. McEvoy. 2000. "Human Resource Management, TQM, and Firm Performance in Small- and Medium-sized Enterprises." *Entrepreneurship Theory and Practice*, 25: 43-57.

arise. Furthermore, it is heavily constrained by forces that effectively work against the adoption of many of the policies that have been advo - cated by leading personnel experts for decades."[26]

Among the facts Jain and Murray cite to support their contention are:
- Job analysis is seldom done; when it is, it is often not done accurately.
- HR planning is rarely integrated into company strategic planning.
- Almost all companies rely heavily on interviews even though they have been proven to be unreliable.
- Less than 20 percent of companies have formal training programs, and even these are seldom integrated into company strategic objectives.
- Performance appraisal policies are seldom put into practice; when they are, their results are seldom used in organizational decision making.
- While open pay systems have been recommended for a long time, most companies fight to keep pay information confidential.
- Very few companies have employee representation on their boards of directors.
- Research and evaluation of HR efforts are rare.

Jain and Murray contend that implementation of recommended HR practices has not been successful. They recommend that the HR function take a more strategic position within the firm so that its activities will be taken seriously. Line managers and supervisors must buy into the importance of effective HR practices. Because HR activities use organizational resources, their impact must be clear to motivate their implementation and continued use.

---

[26] Jain, H., and V. Murray. 1990. "Why the Human Resources Management Function Fails." In Ferris, G. R., K. M. Rowland, and M. R. Buckley, eds. *Human Resource Management: Perspectives and Issues*, 2nd ed. Allyn and Bacon, Needham Heights, Massachusetts p. 25.

WRAP-UP

The next few years represents a challenging time for the HR function. Schuler sums up the challenge when he states that HR departments have a choice: they can continue to be simply functional specialists or they can reorient themselves and see HR issues as business issues and help line managers solve them.[27] Owners and senior executives of growing firms similarly need to empower their managers to perform HR functions in such a way that the firm achieves a sustainable competitive advantage.

---

[27] Schuler, R. S. 1990. "Repositioning the HR Function; Transformation or Demise?" *Academy of Management Executives*, 4: 49-60.

CHAPTER 2

The Legal
HR Challenge

To understand how dangerously the vitality of the American legal system can shake a business, just ask around. Plenty of pessimistic businesspeople have personal horror stories involving unhappy partners, customers, and, perhaps worst of all, employees. Unhappy employees will occasionally go to great lengths to seek revenge against their bosses, or, at the very least, let off steam.

An Inc. Magazine article from the middle of the last decade[1] gives the following examples of employee retaliation:

- Alpha Blouse Corp. (ABC), a seven-year-old apparel maker, hired an elderly woman who claimed she wanted a job just to "finish out" her time. After working for 10 days, she requested a furlough. The furlough was granted and the woman was told to let the company know when she would come back. Instead, her lawyer called, claiming that the woman had double carpal tunnel syndrome as a result of using a duster at ABC for 10 days. He explained she would settle for a mere $20,000 per wrist. Further investigation revealed that the woman had engaged the lawyer before applying for work at ABC.

---

[1] See Mamis, R. A. 1995. "Employees from Hell." *Inc. Magazine*, January: 50-57.

• A $5-million dollar equipment repair service near Philadelphia was served with a criminal charge by an upset employee. The company had been monitoring the employee's behavior as he regularly took unannounced absent periods beyond those acceptable under the company's policy. The worker claimed he was unexpectedly rendered disabled when his bursitis flared up. After this happened a few times, the company's operating officer drove by the employee's home and saw him outside waxing his car with the arm that was supposedly incapacitated. When the employee returned to work the following day, the operating officer and supervisor called him into an office to discuss the situation. To avoid bothering the clerks outside, they shut the door. The employee then immediately left the room. The next day the sheriff served each manager with criminal complaints, including assault and battery, stalking, kidnapping, and interfering with the exercise of civil rights. The employee stated, "I was held in a locked room against my will." Furthermore, the employee claimed "Each time I tried to leave the room the defendant threatened me . . . The defendant pulled my arm so hard that it injured my shoulder permanently." The outcome of this situation is unknown.

• Jay Estes, owner of a new office furniture store in New Jersey called Interior Motives, took great care to follow good employee-relations practices. Before an employee was dismissed, Estes would give a written and an oral review, and then repeat the process a second time. He was confident that his decision to dismiss an unproductive manager was justified after the manager was warned three times within one year. The employee turned in his company credit card and left the company. Four weeks later, when Interior Motives received its statement from American Express, $3,000 more than was expected had been charged on the card. Because the employee sensed that he was going to be fired, he used the card to eat expensive dinners, rent a fancy car, stay in luxury hotels, and party in nightclubs. Estes took the ex-employee to court, charging that he misappropriated funds by taking a vacation on Interior Motives'tab. The ex-employee claimed that such use of the business credit card was "an implied perk."

• A man working for a siding company on the east coast fell from a scaffold; witnesses said the fall was due to his own carelessness and his unwillingness to follow the safety instructions on the scaffold. The incapacitated employee became eligible for medical payments and wages (2/3 of full pay) for up to 160 months (13.3 years). The employer protested about having to shell out $28,000 per year for the employee who, he claimed, was actually malingering and in good physical health. The company president complained that "He'd hobble into the Industrial Accidents Board with some doctor's statement in hand, and the judge found for him every time." To make things worse, when the company advertised an open management position, the disgruntled employee applied. When a person other than himself was chosen for the job, he sued the company, claiming discrimination against the handicapped.

Managers in emerging companies should recognize that though stories like these are certainly not everyday events, they do highlight the need for care in dealing with employees. Besides using the most open communication methods possible, managers should have the HR policies and techniques in place to stop such situations from getting out of hand. While effective HR techniques can never guarantee that such situations could never happen, they certainly minimize the chances that they will.

THE MANAGER'S CHALLENGE

Federal, state, and local legislation is often cited by firms as a major barrier to growth. Compliance with laws on hiring practices, compensation, employee safety, and labor relations is considered a major cost of doing business. The critical role of front-line managers in all these activities, if it does not conform to the law, could cost a firm significantly. HR departments or other administrators may do an excellent job of designing systems that comply with the law, but if the line manager is unaware of policies or ignores them, the company may be held liable.

Too often, managers are promoted or hired with little or no training and asked to conduct interviews and evaluations and to discipline and terminate employees. Most managers lack knowledge of discrimination laws; indeed, they often view these laws as an infringement on their right to run their own operations. However, because of the huge expense related to fighting employee lawsuits or paying government fines, it is crucial that every company makes clear the importance of integrating compliance with the law into daily management practices.

The HR function has been largely reactive to legislation, waiting until a particular law pushes them to meet requirements for job analysis, test validity, selection, compensation, labor relations, and safety. This chapter will review the four major areas where government has intervened, describe in detail the requirements born out of equal employment opportunity (EEO) legislation, and discuss how the law views employment-at-will, negligent hiring and retention, adverse impact, affirmative action, and sexual harassment.

THE MAJOR TYPES OF LAW

HR management has been heavily influenced by legislation and its concomitant regulations in four areas: (1) EEO, (2) compensation, (3) labor relations, and (4) safety. Exhibit 2.1 shows the intent of the law in these areas. EEO legislation, the main concern of this chapter, deals with discrimination against protected groups in recruitment, selection, compensation, training, labor, and employee relations. Compensation law deals with such issues as minimum wage, overtime, child labor, garnishments, retirement, income projection, paying the prevailing wage in the market for federal contract work, and worker's compensation for work-related accidents. Labor relation laws deal with union elections, unfair labor practices, and notifications of plant downsizing or closure. Safety laws regulate employee rights to a safe and healthy work environment, especially as that relates to air quality, safe machine operation and shut-down, plant layout, chemical hazards, and blood-borne pathogens.

This chapter deals primarily with equal employment law. Protected groups are those people who are protected by the discrimination laws described in the next section. The law as it applies to compensation, labor relations, and safety will be discussed in more detail in later chapters.

EEO Law

Because most EEO legislation is directed at illegal discrimination, it is necessary at this point to differentiate illegal from legal discrimination.

Exhibit 2.1: Intent of Major Employment Legislation

Equal Employment
- Prohibit discrimination in employment based on minority/protected group status.
- Establish an enforcement agency, the Equal Employment Opportunity Commission (EEOC).
- Encourage government contractor/subcontractor compliance with EEO legislation and regulations.

Compensation and Benefits
- Establish pay equity among protected groups.
- Establish pay guidelines for government contractors.
- Support the concept of "prevailing wage."
- Give guidelines on minimum wage, overtime, and child labor requirements.
- Provide administrative requirements for pension/retirement plans and other employee benefits.

Employee Safety and Health
- Set requirements for a safe workplace.
- Set up an enforcement agency, the Occupational Safety and Health Administration.

Labor Relations
- Protect employee rights to unionize.
- Establish bargaining rules for management and labor.
- Establish an enforcement agency, the National Labor Relations Board.

By its nature, the HR function is a discriminatory activity: Decisions have to be made on whom to hire, fire, promote, give pay raises to, etc. Only when these decisions are not made according to EEO requirements will a firm find it has problems with the law. Illegal discrimination can be formally defined as "unfair actions towards members of a protected class."[2] A protected class is a group of people who are protected by one or more of the federal laws described below. These laws and relevant executive orders are summarized in Exhibit 2.2.

[2] Fisher, C. D., L. F. Schoenfeldt, and J. B. Shaw. 2002. *Human Resource Management*, 5th ed. Boston: Houghton Mifflin Company.

Exhibit 2.2: Sources of Redress for Employment Discrimination

Source	Purpose	Administration
U.S. Constitution,		
5th Amendment	Protect against federal violation of due process.	Federal courts
13th Amendment	Abolish slavery and "signs" of slavery.	Federal courts
14th Amendment	Protect against state violations of due process and ensure equal protection.	Federal courts
Civil Rights Act, 1866 and 1871	Establish the right of all citizens to enforce contracts and to sue for damages.	Federal courts
Equal Pay Act, 1963	Prohibit sex discrimination in wages and salary: equal pay for equal work.	Equal Employment Opportunity Commission (EEOC)
Civil Rights Act, 1964 (Title VII)	Prohibit discrimination in employment on the basis of race, sex, religion, and national origin.	EEOC; Federal courts
Age Discrimination in Employment Act, 1967, Amended 1978 and 1986 Equal Employment Opportunity Act, 1972	Prohibit discrimination against persons over 40. Extend coverage of the 1964 Civil Rights Act to include both public and private sectors, educational institutions, unions, and employment agencies	EEOC; Federal courts
Pregnancy Discrimination Act, 1978	Require employers to treat pregnancy just like any other illness covered by the benefit package.	EEOC; Federal courts
Immigration Reform and Control Act, 1986	Require verification of right to work in the United States.	Department of Labor
Americans with Disabilities Act 1990	Prohibit discrimination against handicapped persons.	EEOC and the Department of Labor
Civil Rights Act, 1991	Refine coverage of existing EEO legislation and allow for jury trials and punitive awards for intentional discrimination.	EEOC and the Department of Labor
Executive Orders 11246, 11375, and 11478	Prohibit discrimination by contractors or subcontractors of federal agencies and prescribe merit as basis for federal employment policy.	Office of Contract Compliance Programs (OFCCP)
State and local laws	Prohibit discrimination and establish fair employment practice missions.	State and local fair-employment agencies; city and state courts

Congressional Acts

The Civil Rights Act of 1866 prohibits racial discrimination in making and enforcing contracts. For HR management this could include hiring and promotion decisions. *The Civil Rights Act of 1871* amended the 1866 act; it asserts that in any local, state, or federal government unit, all persons must be given the same rights.[3]

The Equal Pay Act of 1963 (EPA) was passed as an amendment to the Fair Labor Standards Act of 1938 (FLSA). The EPA prohibits gender discrimination in the payment of wages to men and women working in the same jobs in the same company. It states that two jobs are equal if they require the same skill, effort, and responsibility, and are performed under the same working conditions. Exceptions may be made when payment is based on a seniority system, a merit system, or any factor other than gender. Another exception is when a system measuring earnings by quality or quantity of production (i.e., piece rates) is used. This act covers private employers engaged in commerce or in the production of goods for commerce that have at least two employees.

Though not incorporated into any federal law, the theory of comparable worth is often associated with the Equal Pay Act. The difference is that the EPA assures equal pay for people doing equal work while comparable worth suggests that jobs equal in value to the employer be paid equally. The problem primarily affects women. Women still earn less than 80 percent of the income that men earn; the big question is why.

Four major reasons for this pay discrepancy can be presented:
1. Women may choose occupations that do not compensate them as well as others (teaching, for instance). They may be attracted to jobs that pay less in monetary compensation but that offer other intrinsic rewards, such as flexible hours or training.
2. Women are subject to a glass ceiling in corporations where very few women are promoted into higher-paying positions.
3. Differences in pay may be the result of our society valuing positions traditionally dominated by women less highly than those traditionally dominated by men. A common example of this problem is the pay for nurses versus engineers.

---

[3] Sovereign, K. L. 1998. *Personnel Law.* Englewood Cliffs, NJ: Prentice Hall.

4. Some organizations intentionally discriminate against women. Comparable worth attempts to stop this discrimination.

The Supreme Court is inconsistent in its stand on the equal pay issue. The justices believe that making decisions in this area would require an expertise in job evaluation that may be found in companies but not in the Court.

Title VII of the Civil Rights Act of 1964 is one of the major laws regulating employer selection of employees. Title VII prohibits employers, unions, and employment agencies from discriminating with regard to any employment decision (selection, compensation, other benefits of employment, or firing) against an employee on the basis of gender, race, color, religion, or national origin.

This act created the Equal Employment Opportunity Commission (EEOC) and gave it the power to investigate and challenge any person or company who is allegedly using any of the unlawful employment procedures identified in Title VII. Though the EEOC was originally established to investigate discrimination based on race, color, religion, gender, or national origin, it now can investigate charges of pay, age, and handicap discrimination.

The EEOC, in other words, enforces the Civil Rights Act. When a charge of discrimination is filed, the EEOC first tries to convince the parties to settle the case themselves through conciliation. If this cannot be accomplished, the case is investigated and the EEOC will issue a statement of "probable cause" or "no probable cause." If the decision is probable cause and the employer refuses to correct the problem, the EEOC either takes the case to court or issues a "right to sue" notice that allows the party making the charges, whether it's an individual or a group, to go to court.

The Age Discrimination in Employment Act of 1967 (ADEA) was passed to provide equal employment opportunity to people of all ages. The law prohibits discrimination against those aged 40 and above unless the employer can show that age is a bona fide occupational qualification (BFOQ) for the job. Age discrimination occurs when, for example, a senior employee is terminated so that a younger employee can be hired at a lower salary even though the new employee has less knowledge, skill, and ability.

To avoid an ADEA charge, an employer must demonstrate that a particular age requirement is "reasonably necessary to the normal operations of the particular business." On January 1, 1987, an amendment to the ADEA took effect that eliminates mandatory retirement at age 70. Organizations covered by the ADEA are private companies employing 15 or more; labor organizations; employment agencies; and state, local, and federal governments. Still, there are exceptions to the law. For example, the act permits mandatory retirement at 65 for highly compensated executives.

The Equal Employment Opportunity Act of 1972 (EEO) was passed as an amendment to strengthen the Civil Rights Act of 1964. Its primary goal is to ensure equal employment for members of protected groups. The EEO also increased the number of organizations affected by the Civil Rights Act by reducing the required number of employees from 25 to 15.

The Vietnam *Veterans Readjustment Act of 1974* applies only to the government, government contractors, and businesses receiving federal funds. It protects disabled veterans seeking employment. Government contractors are required to list all open job positions with the state employment agency.

The Pregnancy Discrimination Act of 1978 amended Title VII of the Civil Rights Act. It states that an employer may not discriminate against applicants or employees because of pregnancy, childbirth, abortion, or planned adoption. Disabilities related to pregnancy or childbirth must be treated like other types of disabilities or medical conditions. Women cannot be forced to go on leave as long as they are still able to work; they are entitled to get their jobs back when they return from their leave of absence. The law also requires that employers may not decline to give unmarried employees pregnancy benefits, and they must offer the same benefits to all spouses.

The Immigration Reform and Control Act of 1986 prohibits employers from employing aliens who are not authorized to work in the United States. An employer must verify authorization by asking for a U.S. passport, certificate of U.S. citizenship, certificate of naturalization, resident alien card, birth certificate, social security card, documents authorizing work in the U.S., driver's license, or other documentation of personal identity. The employer must be sure that the document "reasonably appears on its face to be genuine."[4] If the accuracy of a document is questionable, the employer may require additional documentation.

---

[4] Gatewood, R. D., and H. S. Field. 2000. *Human Resource Selection*, 5th ed. Ft Worth, TX: Dryden.

At least 43 million Americans have a disability. This is one reason the *Americans with Disabilities Act* (ADA) was passed on July 26, 1990. The law covers employers with at least 15 employees. The general premise of the ADA is that "employers may not discriminate against a qualified person with a disability because of the disability in hiring, advancement, discharge, compensation, training, and other terms, conditions, and privileges of employment." A person with a qualified disability is defined as "an individual who, with or without reasonable accommodation, can perform the essential functions of the position that he or she desires or holds." Essential functions are job tasks that are fundamental, not marginal.

The ADA considers seven types of conduct to be discriminatory:

1. The employer may not limit, segregate, or classify a job applicant in a way that adversely affects employment opportunity or status. Individuals cannot be labeled disabled and no mention of disability should be included in an applicant's file.

2. Employers cannot involve themselves in any contractual relationship that has the effect of discrimination. For example, an employer cannot refuse a reasonable accommodation by claiming that the lease on the building prohibits any changes to the structure, such as ramps or handicap-accessible bathrooms.

3. The employer may not use standards, criteria, or methods of administration that have the effect of discrimination. An employer cannot refuse to mail application materials and require an applicant to come in person to pick up an application blank, because that would cause undue hardship on many disabled people.

4. Discrimination is not allowed against an applicant or employee because of a relationship or association with a known disabled person. For example, spouses of disabled persons cannot be turned down for jobs because they might be more likely to need family leave.

5. Employers may not refuse to make reasonable accommodations unless they can prove that the accommodation would impose an undue hardship on the business. Some structural changes, such as adding elevators or widening doorways, may require an expense

that the company cannot finance—a particular problem for smaller firms that have limited capital.

6. Qualification standards, employment tests, or other selection criteria that tend to screen out persons with disabilities may not be used. Using such techniques as timed tests may discriminate against a paraplegic who has limited use of arms. Accommodating disabled persons by providing additional time may be necessary.

7. Retaliation against individuals because of past ADA charges or participation in an ADAinvestigation, proceeding, or hearing is not permitted. As with any federal discrimination law, an employer cannot terminate, demote, refuse a pay raise, etc. to any party to a discrimination suit.

Medical examinations are allowable if they are job-related, required of all employees, and the information obtained is kept confidential. It is usually recommended that such an examination be required only after a tentative decision to hire has been made so that there is no temptation to discriminate if a disability is identified. Medical tests may not be used to determine whether someone has a disability or the severity of a known disability.

People protected by the ADA fall into three categories:

1. Those who have a physical or mental impairment that substantially limits one or more of the person's major life activities. Physical or mental impairment refers to any physiological disorder or condition, cosmetic disfigurement, anatomical loss affecting a vital body system, or mental or psychological disorder. Examples of major life activities are seeing, hearing, breathing, and learning.

2. Persons having a record of such an impairment. This part of the ADA covers those persons who have recovered from a physical or mental impairment that previously limited a major life activity.

3. Persons regarded or perceived as having such an impairment. For example, an employee who for years has complained of a bad lower back and had been given job accommodations for it is perceived to be disabled whether or not medical records support such a disability.

Among people not protected by the ADA are those currently using illegal drugs. An employer may use a test to detect the use of illegal drugs and may take action (refuse to hire or dismiss the employee) if the tests are positive. Drug users may be covered if they successfully complete a rehabilitation program.

Others not protected by the ADA are homosexuals, bisexuals, and people with behavior disorders such as compulsive gambling, kleptomania, and pyromania. The ADA does not prevent religious entities giving preference to people of a particular religion.

Two areas that create confusion are health and safety issues and issues surrounding HIV/AIDS. A significant health and safety issue is whether a person poses any direct threat to the health or safety of others or to property. Each case must be determined on its own facts.

The ADA covers persons infected with HIV or AIDS. For example, since there is no medical evidence suggesting that AIDS can be transmitted through the handling of food, an employer cannot refuse to hire someone who is HIV-positive to work in food-related jobs.

Examples of reasonable accommodation under the ADA are:

- making existing facilities used by employees readily accessible to and usable by disabled persons,
- job restructuring,
- part-time or modified work schedules,
- reassignment to a vacant position that is more accessible,
- acquisition or modification of equipment or devices,
- modification of examinations, training materials, or policies, and
- provision of qualified readers or interpreters.

However, an employer that can show that there would be undue hardship on the business may not have to provide an accommodation. Undue hardship is defined as "an action requiring significant difficulty or expense." That, in turn, is determined by the nature and cost of accommodations in relation to the employer's resources and operations.

A charge of discrimination under the ADA must be filed with the EEOC within 180 days of the alleged discriminatory act or within 300 days in states with approved enforcement agencies. Remedies under the ADA are designed to make the individual or class "whole" and to prevent the employer from practicing further discrimination; they include back pay, hiring or reinstatement, and attorneys' fees and costs.

The Civil Rights Act of 1991 is a major amendment to Title VII. It was passed in response to six Supreme Court decisions rendered in the 1980s that Congress felt adversely affected protection against illegal discrimination. The act:

- Enacted into law the *Griggs v. Duke Power Company*[5] decision requiring employers to prove that an employment practice causing disparate treatment was based on business necessity.
- Amended Title VII by making it possible to prove an unlawful employment practice by demonstrating that race, color, religion, gender, or national origin was a motivating factor even though other legal factors also contributed to the decision.[6]
- Expanded the scope of Title VII and the ADA to employees working in foreign countries if the employer is American-owned.
- Broadened the Civil Rights Act of 1866 to cover cases where the employee was discharged.
- Allowed for compensatory and punitive damages in cases of intentional discrimination.
- Prohibited "race-norming" of candidate test scores, meaning that test scores cannot be adjusted because a person is a member of a protected group.
- Established a "glass ceiling initiative" by setting up a special commission to study problems relating to the promotion of women to management positions.

Executive Orders

Executive Order 11246 of 1965 prohibits federal contractors and the federal government from discriminating on the basis of race, color, religion, and natural origin. It covers all agencies, contractors, and subcontractors associated with the federal government.

---

[5] *Griggs v. Duke Power Co.*, 401 U.S. 424, 3 FEP 175 (1971).
[6] Fisher, Schoenfeldt, and Shaw, op. cit., n. 2.

Executive Order 11375 of 1966 prohibits the same organizations from discriminating against an employee because of gender.

Executive Order 11478 of 1969 requires the federal government to base its employment policies on merit. All government agencies are required to maintain an equal employment opportunity program. Some contractors may be required to have an affirmative action plan on file with the Office of Federal Contract Compliance Programs (OFCCP), the enforcement agency for executive orders.

Employee Rights

Employees also have rights under common law, based on court decisions and precedents. Some of the most important HR concepts that have arisen from the common law are employment-at-will, negligent hiring and retention, and constructive discharge.

The *employment-at-will doctrine* states that employment is at the will of the employer and that either can sever the relationship at any time. Under a pure interpretation of the at-will doctrine, no notice of separation is necessary. Over the years, the courts have defined exceptions to the employment-at-will doctrine, including:

- *The public policy exception.* For example, an employee who informs the Environmental Protection Agency that the employer has illegally dumped hazardous chemicals into a local river can defend termination by claiming the public policy exception, because it is in the best interest of the public to be notified of a potential health and environmental concern.

- Employees may not be terminated if a contract, *either written or implied*, gives some promise of security. The employer's contractual obligation to provide employment, or at least compensation for employment, lasts for the duration of the contract. Employers should be careful in writing employee manuals not to imply that employees will have a job as long as the rules in the manual are followed.

- There is also the *implied covenant of good faith and fair dealing*, which prevents the employer from causing harm without justification. This exception is usually applied on behalf of longer-term employees who may have earned the right to fairer treatment. The exception is controversial because it significantly narrows the meaning of at-will employment. The implied covenant is interpreted very differently from state to state; more liberal states like California and New York are more likely to uphold it than conservative midwestern states.

- At-will separation from employment may not violate any federal, state, or local law; this exception is most often applied in the context of discrimination law, but other laws may apply, such as the federal Workers' Readjustment Retraining and Notification Act (WARN), which states that a company must give terminated employees 60 days notice in writing if it plans to reduce its force by 50 or more employees.

The common law doctrine of *negligent hiring and negligent retention* holds employers responsible for exercising reasonable care in hiring employees. Reasonable care includes, but is not limited to, such activities as reference and criminal background checks, skills, and psychological testing. The courts have especially held employers liable for the actions of employees who are in occupations where they have access to dangerous equipment or where their incompetence in operating equipment may cause harm to others.

Negligent retention is similar to negligent hiring. It applies when an organization knowingly retains someone they know poses a high risk of injuring themselves or others. For example, an employee physically assaults another employee but is merely suspended, not terminated. If this employee should assault another employee, client, or visitor, the company can be held liable for negligent retention.

The common law doctrine of *constructive discharge* is based on the behavior of employers who force employees to resign by creating intolerable working conditions. These might be reassignment to an inappropriate job, changing work hours or shifts, and countenancing harassment of the employee by other employees. If an employer is proven to have engaged in constructive discharge, the employee's decision to leave is viewed as a termination and the employer can be held liable for such illegal conduct as employment discrimination.

Constructive discharge of older employees is a common problem. Employers often want to bring in younger workers who will take lower pay, but to avoid an age discrimination suit they try to get the older employee to quit by transferring them to a job they know they cannot handle or a shift they do not want.

PROVING ILLEGAL DISCRIMINATION

The process of proving illegal discrimination starts with a plaintiff, the person charging that there has been an unlawful practice, proving that an organization's employment procedures had adverse impact on a member of a protected class.

Establishing Adverse Impact

Adverse impact occurs when an employment practice has a disproportionate effect on one protected group. Formally, the process of determining adverse impact is known as establishing a prima facie ("on the face of it") case of discrimination.

To prove adverse impact the plaintiff can either use a disparate treatment or a disparate impact argument.

The concept of disparate impact was introduced in the 1971 *Griggs v. Duke Power Company*[7] case, where the Supreme Court determined that adverse impact occurs when the same standards are applied to all employees but have different outcomes for certain protected groups. The plaintiff does not have to prove that the employer had intended to illegally discriminate. *Griggs*, as well as other court decisions, allowed for the use of three types of data for determining disparate impact: (1) comparative statistics, (2) demographic statistics, and (3) concentration statistics:

1. The *comparative statistics* method for calculating disparate impact compares hiring rates or ratios of protected minority groups to the hiring ratios of the majority group. The criterion for comparing the two ratios is known as the four-fifths or 80 percent rule of thumb: If the selection ratio for a protected minority is less than 80 percent of the majority, the impact is adverse. For example, if the selection ratio for males is 60 percent, the selection ratio for females must be at least 48 percent (0.80 x 0.60) or adverse impact is proven.

---

[7] Griggs, op. cit., n. 5.

2. The *demographic statistics* method compares the firm's work force to the "relevant labor market," which is all equally qualified individuals in the population at large. If the firm's employment of protected minorities does not correspond fairly well with their representation in the qualified work force, there may be adverse impact. For instance, the relevant labor market in Arizona or Oklahoma would include many more American Indians than in Pennsylvania or Maryland, so firms in the two western states would be expected to employ more Indians than those in the eastern states.

3. The intent of the *concentration statistics* approach is to prove that protected minority groups are restricted to a particular job or level of jobs. Even though an organization may employ representative amounts of minorities, adverse impact may exist if they are relegated to lower-level positions, such as women to secretarial positions, and blacks and Hispanics to custodial positions. To prove discrimination, the plaintiff must identify a specific practice that has caused this result.

These methods for establishing disparate impact are summarized in *Uniform Guidelines on Employee Selection Procedures*, part of the Code of Federal Regulations.[8] The Uniform Guidelines were written in 1978 to prescribe specific requirements for proving the job-relatedness of employment practices and a specific method for determining adverse impact.

Disparate Treatment

Four criteria for establishing disparate treatment, which occurs when an employer intentionally illegally discriminates against an individual, were set out in *McDonnell Douglas Corp. v. Green* (1973):[9]

1. The individual belongs to a protected minority group.
2. The individual applied for a job for which the employer was seeking applicants.
3. Despite being qualified, the individual was rejected.

---

[8] Uniform Guidelines on Employee Selection Procedures, 29 C.F.R., Part 1607 (1978).
[9] *McDonnell Douglas Corp. v. Green*, 411 U.S. 792, 5 F.E.P. 965 (1973).

4. After the individual's rejection, the employer kept looking for people with the applicant's qualifications.

Defenses to Discrimination Charges

Once the plaintiff has established a prima facie case, the burden of proof shifts to the defendant. At this point, the organization accused of illegal employment discrimination has the opportunity to defend itself by proving that:

- its selection procedures were job-related,
- they represented bona fide occupational qualifications, or
- the action complained of was subject to a seniority system.

Job-Related

An employer who can show that certain qualifications are necessary to perform a job can require that an employee have those qualifications. In other words, as long as its selection procedures are related to the employee's ability to do the job correctly, the company can require those qualifications. Setting up a valid and reliable selection procedure is discussed in Chapter 4.

Bona Fide Occupational Qualifications (BFOQ)

If a company can show that to adequately perform the job in question, the employee must be of a certain gender, race, color, religion, or national origin, it can use a BFOQ defense. This is more likely to be related to gender or religion than to race, color, or national origin requirements.[10]

Seniority System

The use of a seniority system as a defense to an illegal discrimination charge is justified so long as the intent of the seniority system was not to discriminate.[11] This is especially important in layoff situations, where employers can use a "last in, first out" defense for layoff decisions.

AFFIRMATIVE ACTION PROGRAMS

Affirmative action is taken when an employer makes an extra effort to recruit, hire, and promote members of protected groups. While there is some disagreement over just what an affirmative action plan (AAP) should cover, it should at least have the following four parts:

---

[10] Gatewood and Field, op. cit., n. 4,
[11] Teamsters v. United States, 431 U.S. 324, 14 F.E.P1514 (1977).

1. A utilization analysis showing the percentage of protected groups employed in the organization.
2. An availability analysis that shows how many members of protected groups are available in the community, which allows for demographic statistics to be calculated.
3. An identification of problem areas where protected groups are under-represented or under-utilized. Data from the first two analyses can help determine problem areas.
4. An action plan with specific goals and timetables to deal with the problem areas identified.[12]

The three basic reasons for implementing an AAP are that a company is a government contractor, a company has been found guilty of illegal employment discrimination, or a company undertakes the AAP as a voluntary initiative.

Under Executive Order 11246, employers with federal contracts or subcontracts exceeding $100,000 must implement an AAPthat contains the four components described above.

When found guilty of illegal discrimination, a company may be ordered to write and execute an AAP that gives preference to groups that have been discriminated against in its current selection procedures.[13] Its plan should bring representation of those discriminated against up to required standards. Note that during the time a company is under a court-ordered AAP, it cannot be taken to court for reverse discrimination.

If a company finds, after statistical analysis of its selection procedures, that it has discriminated against a particular group, it might choose to employ a voluntary AAP. In *Steelworkers v. Weber* (1979),[14] the Supreme Court ruled that hiring quotas for females were justified because of past discrimination against them. It is recommended that an employer have a temporary plan with distinct steps to be taken that does not unnecessarily ignore the interests of whites or males.

---

[12] Fisher, Schoenfeldt, and Shaw, op. cit., n. 2.
[13] Twomey, D. P. 1999. *Equal Employment Opportunity Law*. Cincinnati: South-Western Publishing Co.
[14] *Steelworkers v. Weber*, 443 U.S. 193, 20 F.E.P1 (1979).

SEXUAL HARASSMENT

One form of discrimination prohibited by Title VII is sexual harassment. Sexual harassment occurs when a hostile, abusive, or intimidating environment is created and when compensation or advancement opportunities are affected.[15] The two types of sexual harassment are:

1. quid pro quo sexual harassment, where a supervisor trades sexual activity for advancement opportunities of some sort; and

2. hostile environment sexual harassment, where an unwelcome environment is created by a supervisor or another employee.[16]

The second type of harassment was recently broadened by a Supreme Court opinion ruling that the plaintiff no longer had to prove physical or psychological harm. Justice Sandra Day O'Connor said, "So long as the environment would reasonably be perceived, and is perceived, as hostile or abusive, there is no need for it to be psychologically injurious."

This ruling, coupled with a 53 percent increase in sexual harassment cases filed since the Anita Hill accusations against Supreme Court Justice Clarence Thomas, suggests that this issue will be a front line topic for many years to come.

Two recent cases, *Fragher v. Boca Raton*[17] and *Burlington Industries v. Ellerth*[18] have helped shape a new foundation for employer liability. In cases dealing with a hostile environment, the employer is liable unless it can prove that it exercised care to prevent an occurrence, took quick and immediate corrective action once an occurrence surfaced, and established policies and training programs to prevent any recurrence. The following activities may help avoid or at least reduce liability:

• Write a policy against sexual harassment with a clearly stated procedure for filing a complaint.

• Once a policy and procedure are in place, make sure everyone knows what they are.

---

[15] Meritor Savings Bank v. Vinson, 106 S. Ct. 2399 (1986).
[16] Guidelines on Discrimination Because of Sex, 29 C.F.R. Sec. 1604.11(a)(1995).
[17] Fragher v. Boca Raton, No. 97-282 (1998) AU: United States Supreme Court
[18] Burlington Industries, Inc. v. Ellerth, No. 97-569 (1998) United States Supreme Court, No. 97-509, decided June 20, 1998

- Be prepared to investigate every complaint in accordance with established procedures.
- Document every employment decision.[19]

WRAP-UP

The legal environment in which the HR function operates can be a huge challenge. Legal issues affect the field of HR management in at least four areas: (1) equal employment opportunity, (2) compensation, (3) safety and health, and (4) labor relations. This chapter looked at specific laws pertaining to equal employment opportunity and the process by which a discrimination claim is proved and defended.

The Civil Rights Act of 1964 is the foundation for discrimination laws. It defined the protected groups covered and established an agency for enforcement. Other laws, like the Equal Pay Act of 1963, the Age Discrimination in Employment Act of 1967, the Equal Employment Opportunity Act of 1972, the Pregnancy Discrimination Act of 1978, the Americans with Disabilities Act of 1990, and the Civil Rights Act of 1991 further elaborate what employment discrimination consists of.

---

[19] Sandler, D. 1998. "Sexual Harassment Rulings: Less than Meets the Eye." *HR Magazine*, October: pp. 136-141

CHAPTER 3

Role Clarification: Effective Job Analysis and Job Descriptions

It may be natural for front-line managers to miss the big picture when it comes to job descriptions. They may agree with HR professionals that updating them periodically is important, but they do not make doing so a top priority. In fact, HR staff members themselves are not very happy with the task. The responsibility that comes with composing good job descriptions turns the assignment into a real monster, one every employee loves to hate. These are some of the major problems related to job descriptions:

- Employees do not take their job descriptions seriously until it immediately affects them in terms of pay or evaluations.
- Employees "fluff up" their responsibilities on questionnaires to improve their status or pay.
- Employees try to add to their job descriptions tasks they are not responsible for.
- An outdated or incomplete job description is used to rationalize disciplining an employee.

As this chapter demonstrates, if only because job descriptions influence employee pay rates, they clearly must be taken seriously. That's why it's important to keep communication channels open before, during, and after the questionnaire stage of updating a description. Although many people are unhappy with the process, try to keep things around the office uplifting and positive. Finally, this is a time when supporting the efforts of the HR department will truly pay off. Managers should help monitor the process because many employees feel more comfortable working with their immediate supervisor to edit job descriptions rather than with an HR supervisor.[1]

THE MANAGER'S CHALLENGE

Documentation is a popular buzzword in HR management. Too often it implies legal necessity to protect the company from an adverse employment lawsuit. While documenting key performance issues is critical, the documentation process should start before employees ever get on the job. Identifying critical job duties and what is needed for successful performance must be done before performance can be managed. Employees can only be held accountable for work they have control over.

The painstaking effort of collecting job information is worth the time it takes to do it effectively, even for the smallest companies. Once the information is collected, it will provide a job-related basis for making selection, promotion, compensation and other HR decisions. Accurate job descriptions define roles for employees, allowing them to be more productive.

It's difficult to overstate the importance of job analysis to HR management. When done thoroughly, job analysis provides a deeper understanding of individual jobs and their behavioral requirements and of how jobs interrelate. A job analysis helps both employer and employee determine what tasks a worker needs to perform and what knowledge, skills, abilities, and other characteristics are necessary to do the tasks satisfactorily.

A job description simply summarizes a job analysis. Job descriptions have many applications—communicating to employees their major responsibilities, determining salaries, anchoring performance appraisals, tracking career development, and helping the company comply with laws like the ADA.[2] This chapter will describe specific purposes for job analyses, methods for analyzing jobs, and the process of summarizing job analysis results into job descriptions.

---

[1] Adapted from Swedberg, J. 2003. "Put it in Writing." *Credit Union Management*, December: 50-53.
[2] Ibid.

JOB ANALYSIS AND JOB DESCRIPTION

Job analysis is often considered the primary building block for human resources. From the many definitions for job analysis, we choose to think of it as a systematic process of collecting and making judgments about all the important aspects of a job.

One problem with this definition, as with others, is understanding the meaning of the word job. A job is a collection of duties and the tasks they consist of that are assigned to be performed by a person. Key definitions relating to a job are:

- Task: One or more elements that combine to achieve a specific purpose, such as cleaning a floor or making a phone call.
- Duty: A collection of tasks that are consistently repeated, such as cleaning offices or making sales calls.
- Job: A collection of related duties, such as custodial or sales duties.
- Occupation: A group of similar jobs that may be found within or across organizations, such as engineer or college professor.
- Job family: Groups of jobs that either call for similar worker characteristics or contain parallel work tasks.
- Job specification: Identification of the knowledge, skills, and abilities (KSAs) needed by an individual to perform a given job.

There are several advantages to grouping jobs into families. Job families make for organizational flexibility, making it possible for workers to perform more than just a single official job. Because many of the characteristics of jobs in a family are similar, if not the same, employees are easily transferred from one job to another. Since these jobs are of similar value to the company, compensation programs are more easily designed. Job families also permit organizations to apply the same work rules and selection procedures, recruit applicants from the same pool, minimize staffing levels, and provide a systematic procedure for promoting employees.[3]

[3] Jackson, S. E., and R. S. Schuler. 2003. *Managing Human Resources Through Strategic Partnerships*, 8th ed. Cincinnati: Thomson-South-Western; Veres, J. G., T. S. Locklear, and R. R. Sims, "Job Analysis in Practice: A Brief Review of the Role of Job Analysis in Human Resources Management," in Ferris, G. R., K. M. Rowland, and M. R. Buckley, eds. 1990. *Human Resource Management: Perspectives and Issues*, 2nd ed. Cambridge, MA: Allyn and Bacon.

Determining the meaning of other parts of the definition of job analysis is also important. Analysis is generally referred to as "the separation of a whole into its parts, with a view to the examination and interpretation of those parts."[4] The important aspects of the definition are:

- Job content, which identifies and describes activities, such as tasks and duties.
- Job requirements, which are the KSAs an employee should have.
- Job context, which incorporates such factors as purpose, responsibility of the employee, supervision, and working conditions.

Exhibit 3.1 presents a logical flowchart for the steps in the job analysis process. All seven steps should be completed for each job analysis.

Exhibit 3.1: Summary of Steps in Job Analysis Process

Step 1: Determine the uses of job analysis data and information
Step 2: Select a method of analysis
Step 3: Inform other managers of the study
Step 4: Inform job incumbents of the study
Step 5: Carry out the study
Step 6: Validate the study
Step 7: Summarize the results

Source: Hills, F. S., T. J. Bergmann, and V. G. Scarpillo. 1994. *Compensation Decision Making*, 2nd ed. Fort Worth, TX: Dryden Press.

The first step is to determine how the information obtained in the job analysis will be used, for instance, to write a job description or conduct a performance appraisal. Those two uses are very different, which is why determining what the job analysis will be used for is crucial.

The next step is to select a method of analysis. The answer found in the first step (the use) will guide the choice of the method. Step three is to inform other managers of the study—management acceptance and cooperation is vital to the effectiveness of the analysis. This is parallel with step four, informing job incumbents of the study, because management buy-in will encourage cooperation from the incumbents. It is important for incumbents to know

---

[4] Veres, Locklear, and Sims, op. cit., n. 3.

the process is taking place so they do not feel as if something is going on behind their backs. Usually, incumbents also know that the job analysis will benefit them.

The fifth step is to actually conduct the study. Allot enough time to do this well. The time needed may be very extensive if there are a number of jobs to be analyzed. Once the work is done, step six calls for the study to be validated to make sure each job analysis contains the information needed for its planned use. Finally, step seven is to summarize and document the information.

USES OF JOB ANALYSIS DATA

Two major forces should be considered when conducting a job analysis: (1) competition and (2) legal concerns, especially equal employment opportunity.[5] As competition continues to increase, managers need to ensure that the most competent and efficient employees are performing the jobs. According to Wayne Cascio,[6] "Job analysis can underpin organizational structure and design by clarifying roles . . . thereby avoiding job overlap and duplication of effort and promoting efficiency and harmony among individuals and departments."

Typical applications of job analysis data are job design, job classification and evaluation, recruitment, selection, training, performance appraisal, and performance management.[7] In each of these applications, there are several examples of how the data can be used. For instance, in job design, job analysis information helps in planning to meet production goals and promoting job mobility, because the firm now knows what tasks each employee must be responsible for and the abilities those tasks demand. With this information, a firm can consider the potential for individuals to rotate jobs in order to increase overall productivity.

Ash and Levine classified six major uses for job analysis:[8]

1. *Job description.* Accounts of the duties and activities associated with a particular job.

---

[5] Ibid.

[6] Cascio, W. F. 2002. *Managing Human Resources: Productivity, Quality of Work Life, Profits*, 6th ed. Boston: Irwin McGraw-Hill.

[7] Bemis, S. E., A. H. Belenky, and D. A. Soder. 1983. *Job Analysis: An Effective Management Tool.* Washington: Bureau of National Affairs, Inc.

[8] Ash, R A., and E. L. Levine. 1980. "A Framework for Evaluating Job Analysis Methods." *Personnel*, 57: 53-59.

2. *Job requirements/specifications.* Descriptions of the characteristics needed to perform the activities identified in job descriptions.
3. *Job classification.* Grouping similar positions into job classes and job classes into families.
4. *Job evaluation.* Assigning a value to a given job classification.
5. *Job design/restructuring.* Redesigning jobs to meet the needs of both employers and employees.
6. *Performance appraisal.* Determining how an employee is performing, given the job description and requirements.

These are only a few of the many uses of job analysis. Exhibit 3.2 is an overview of prominent job analysis applications, many of which help a company to both battle competition and comply with the law.

Exhibit 3.2: Applications of Job-Analysis Data

Job Design
- Enhancing productivity
- Career development
- ADAcompliance

Job Evaluation
- Writing job descriptions and specifications
- Identifying essential job requirements
- Formulating the job/pay hierarchy

Recruiting and Selection
- Clearly stating job content, requirements, and context
- Identifying recruiting sources
- Identifying minimum qualifications
- Choosing or designing valid selection instruments and procedures

Training
- Identifying the competencies needed for successful job performance
- Identifying organization-based competency needs
- Identifying elements necessary for employee orientation

Performance Management
- Identifying critical job elements
- Writing performance standards
- Awarding merit pay
- Promoting employees
- Assessing training needs
- Career development
- Employee feedback on critical behaviors

The law does not actually require organizations to conduct job analyses, but doing so makes it easier for employers to stay out of court. Many laws enacted in the past 40-50 years have spurred use of job analysis, particularly Title VII of the Civil Rights Act of 1964, which prohibits discrimination based on race, color, religion, sex, or national origin. (This and other laws affecting HR management are discussed in detail in Chapter 2.) When an employee can show a personal *adverse impact* from a procedure involved in hiring, promoting, compensating, or another HR functions, a legal case may follow. Adverse impact occurs when an HR decision disproportionately affects a group of people protected by laws.

In these cases, the defendant employer must demonstrate that any tests used were job-related. A job analysis is usually considered a primary display of job-relatedness because it identifies the critical tasks performed in a job. Any selection procedure should be related to the tasks identified in the job analysis study. Unless the defense has done a job analysis, the case is very weak. In 1978, the *Uniform Guidelines on Employee Selection Procedures* confirmed the importance of job analysis in HR management. The *Guidelines* state:

> *"There should be a job analysis, which includes an analysis of the important work behavior(s) required for successful performance and their relative importance, and, if the behavior results in work prod - uct(s), an analysis of work product(s). Any job analysis should focus on the work behavior(s) and the tasks associated with them. If work behavior(s) are not observable, the job analysis should identify and analyze those aspects of the behavior(s) that can be observed and the observed work product(s). The work behavior(s) selected for measure - ment should be critical work behavior(s) and/or important work behavior(s) constituting most of the job."*

One study that reviewed 26 court cases concerned with the requirements for an adequate job analysis came to the following conclusions:

- Results of the job analysis should be in written form.
- The job-analysis process must be described in detail.
- Data should be collected from a variety of sources.
- Information on relevant tasks performed must be included.

• Knowledge, skills, abilities, and other characteristics should be clearly specified and must be operationally defined in terms of work performed.[9]

The first Supreme Court case involving employment discrimination, *Griggs v. Duke Power*, [10] was decided in 1971. Before the 1964 Civil Rights Act was passed, Duke Power had required a high school degree for nearly all jobs within the company except those in the labor pool. When Title VII became effective, the company started using the Wonderlic Personnel Test and the Bennett Mechanical Comprehension Test to select people. To pass these tests, individuals had to score at or above the median of high school graduates. When this passing score was challenged in court, the employer could not show that this job specification was absolutely necessary for many of the jobs for which it was required. Although the requirements were applied equally to all applicants, it had an adverse impact on minority job applicants, and the Supreme Court ruled in favor of Griggs.

In *Albemarle v. Moody*, [11] the plaintiffs challenged a company's use of a verbal intelligence test and, again, the Wonderlic Personnel Test in making promotion decisions. No relationship could be established between the two tests and the skills required for promotion. The Supreme Court ruled for the plaintiff, saying, "[n]o attempt was made to analyze the jobs in terms of the particular skills they might require." This case is particularly noteworthy for its support of job analysis.

SOURCES OF JOB DATA

The three main sources of job data are the job analyst, the job incumbent, and the *supervisor*. Any one, two, or all three may pull together the necessary information. Who does it depends on just what information is needed. Deciding who should do the job analysis depends on the answers to two questions:

1. Who should be responsible for the job analysis program? and

2. Who should provide the job analysis information?

[9] Thompson, D. E., and T. A. Thompson. 1982. "Court Standards for Job Analysis in Test Validation." *Personnel Psychology*, 35: 865-874.
[10] *Griggs v. Duke Power Co.*, 401 U.S. 424, 3 FEP175 (1971).
[11] *Albemarle v. Moody*, Supreme Count of the U.S., No. 74-389. Decided June 25, 1975.

The term *job agent* is generally used to refer to those who collect all the desired job information. The first type of agent is an actual job analyst, a person specially trained to collect, analyze, and interpret job information. These are the people who generally head the job analysis program. Gatewood, Field, and Field[12] state that "job analysts should provide more objective, reliable, and accurate job data" because of their extensive training. As the level of expertise used to analyze jobs has increased, the need for trained job analysts is increasing.

Certain aspects of jobs, however, may escape job analysts because they are not familiar with the work or because a job aspect cannot be observed directly. For this reason, job incumbents and supervisors are often used as agents to collect actual job behaviors, especially in smaller firms where human resource staffs are small or nonexistent.

The job incumbent is an excellent source of information about what is actually done on the job. An advantage to using incumbents is that often there is more than one worker doing the same job, so different points of view are available. When using incumbents as sources of data, though, it's important to realize that workers may inflate or deflate their responsibilities, for different reasons. Responsibilities may be inflated to make a job seem more valuable to the organization. Or a worker may deflate responsibility in hopes of being given more responsibility. Other possible disadvantages to using incumbents is that they may have low motivation to provide information, may not be aware of the job's purpose, or may have inadequate writing or speaking skills. To clarify information from incumbents, a supervisor should verify the information.

Managers and supervisors provide information based on what should be done rather than on what is done as described by the incumbent. Though it's assumed that the supervisor is familiar with a given job, this assumption may not be correct. Despite this problem, the supervisor does add valuable information about the job and required behaviors that can be compared with incumbents' responses. Often, the main role of the supervisor is simply to validate the responses of subordinates.

---

[12] Gatewood, R. D., and H. S. Field. 2000. *Human Resource Selection*, 5th ed. Ft Worth, TX: Dryden, pages 245-267

DATA COLLECTION TECHNIQUES

The technique used to gather data changes depending on the purpose of the job analysis and the job itself; different methods would be used when analyzing the jobs of a secretary, a drill-press operator, and a department manager. The most common methods are:

- Background research
- Actually doing the job
- Direct observation
- Interviews
- Questionnaires
- Diaries

Background research looks at organizational and outside documents. Organizational information could include brochures, training manuals, charts, directions, and past analysis of the job in question, as well as other people in the organization. Professional publications and the *Dictionary of Occupational Titles*[13] (DOT) are examples of outside documents. The DOT is a classification system compiled by the federal government that covers about 20,000 jobs. The system is based on a nine-digit code. Reviewing these documents helps the job analyst to become better acquainted with the job and begin to determine the type of job analysis to use later. Also, training documents and equipment manuals give insight into the tasks performed.

Doing the job is another option for the job analyst. This technique is best used and most helpful when the job involves physical tasks that can be easily learned. Jobs that require substantial amounts of training make the cost of this method prohibitive. Also, since this method is time-consuming, other collection procedures are generally used.

One possible reason to use this method is to buy credibility for the job analyst. Certainly in situations where incumbents have complained that an analyst could never understand the harsh conditions they work under, the analyst should take time to actually perform at least some of the job tasks.

---

[13] Dictionary of Occupational Titles, U.S. Department of Labor, Office of Adminstrative Law Judges, www.oalj.dol.gov, Dictonary of Occupational Titles, 4th ed, Rev. 1991

This symbolic understanding could help win further incumbent cooperation in the project.

Using the *direct observation* technique, the analyst watches incumbents do their jobs and records everything the workers do: tasks performed, how they were performed, how long it took, what the environment was like, and what equipment was used. This is most effective when the work cycle is short (all job tasks performed in a brief period of time) and few of the tasks are mental. For more complex jobs, such as professional and managerial positions, observation is ineffective because of the large amount of time people in these jobs spend on thinking, analyzing, and problem solving. However, observation can be used even here to fill in incomplete information gained from other job analysis methods.

Among the disadvantages to this method are that it is time-consuming and cannot be used to view cognitive activities or those that occur irregularly. For example, a manager might be assigned to a task force that meets only once a month on a project that has a six-month deadline. Analysts must also be careful to make their observation unobtrusive. Otherwise, the worker may feel pressured and may not perform the job in the usual way, so the job observations are not useful. However, direct observation and doing the actual job are good techniques for analyzing jobs that require many manual, standardized, short-cycle activities.[14]

Interviewing is the most common job analysis technique used. Incumbents, supervisors, or both are interviewed to identify job tasks performed and the requirements needed to complete these tasks. The interview may be structured or open-ended. A structured interview is the more desirable because it assures that the analyst will elicit the information desired. Structured interviews are also used to compare different incumbents' responses to questions about the same job.

Whichever interview style is selected, some basic steps should be taken. First, the analyst should develop a rapport with the interviewee and discuss the purpose of the job analysis. Next, the interviewer must not only be a good listener but at the same time keep the interviewee on track. The analyst should never discuss wages because this may cause the incumbent to inflate the job description. Finally, the interview should be verified

---

[14] Cascio, W. F. 1998. *Applied Psychology in Personnel Management,* 5th ed. Englewood Cliffs, NJ: Prentice-Hall, Inc.

with other incumbents and the supervisor. The disadvantages to interviews are their cost and the time they consume.

Questionnaires are the quickest and least expensive data collection technique. They make it possible to study many jobs at the same time. The job analyst distributes the questionnaires to all job incumbents, gives them deadlines for questionnaire completion, and summarizes the results into job descriptions. However, there can be a problem of accuracy because of questions that were misunderstood, incomplete responses, and question-naires that were not returned. Also, it can be expensive to draft the initial job analysis questionnaires.

However, there are already many structured questionnaires available, so that new ones do not always have to be created. One example is the Job Components Inventory, which is appropriate for analyzing jobs that require limited skills. The Occupational Analysis Inventory (OAI) focuses on vocational guidance and occupational exploration. Incumbents may also fill out the Occupational Analysis Questionnaire (OAQ), which determines whether tasks are relevant to their work, and, if so, rate each task on a nine-point rating scale relative to the amount of time spent on that task. The OAQ is particularly helpful for obtaining job descriptions.[15]

Having incumbents keep a *diary* or *log* of their daily activities is use-ful when a job is highly repetitive or involves a high degree of technical knowledge, and for getting specifics of the job. Problems arise, however, when incumbents slack off and stop keeping track of what they are doing. Also, the amount of detail may differ from worker to worker. The diary may contain incomplete or unreliable information. After a diary is turned in, it needs to be verified using other job analysis methods. Thus, this tech-nique can easily become time-consuming and costly.

SPECIFIC JOB ANALYSIS METHODS

Organizations have a choice of creating their own method of analyzing jobs or using one of several standardized methods. There are two types of stan-dardized methods: (1) work-oriented and (2) worker-oriented methods.

Work-oriented methods describe activities performed on the job; they emphasize what is actually accomplished. Examples of work-oriented methods include Functional Job Analysis (FJA), Critical Incidents

---

[15] Ibid.

Technique (CIT), the Management Position Description Questionnaire (MPDQ), and the Guidelines-Oriented Job Analysis (GOJA). The GOJA method is especially suitable for smaller and growing firms because it does not require extensive training and offers a clear progression from job analysis questionnaire to job description to performance standards.

Worker-oriented methods determine what attributes or characteristics an employee needs to perform a job. Worker-oriented methods establish the KSAs. Two of the most popular worker-oriented methods are the Position Analysis Questionnaire (PAQ) and the Physical Abilities Analysis (PAA).

Guidelines-oriented Job Analysis (GOJA): A Tool for the Emerging Firm

GOJA was a response to the publication of the Uniform Guidelines on *Employee Selection Procedures*. There are many steps in this method, each which involve the job incumbents. Before the first step is implemented, incumbents list their names, length of time on the job, experience, and location of the current job. These are the steps they then take:

1. List job domains, which are typically categorized as broad work-related duties.

2. List the critical duties generally performed for successful job performance in each domain.

3. Specify how often each duty is performed.

4. List the skills and knowledge required to perform each duty— specifying only those skills and knowledge that cannot be learned or acquired in eight hours or less.

5. Determine the physical characteristics needed to perform the job duties.

6. Finally, describe other characteristics necessary to perform the job.

The result of these six steps is a job description that is useful for developing performance appraisal forms and analyzing training needs. Selection procedures can also be formulated using GOJA. An example of a GOJA questionnaire can be found in Appendix A.

THE DATA COLLECTION PROCESS

Once a job analysis method is chosen, the analyst must explain to managers and incumbents the purpose of the study so that people are not intimidated by the process. It is important that management be supportive of the study. Without cooperation from management the study can be so difficult to conduct that the process simply stops. In addition, management support encourages incumbents to be generally more helpful. Once everyone is informed, the study process can begin. After the study is completed, it must then be validated.

JOB ANALYSIS STUDY VALIDATION

Validity refers to how well a study measured what it intended to measure. *Supervisory review* is an important component in validating a job analysis study. Supervisors must ensure that specific job requirements are included and that incumbent descriptions do not reflect individual biases—especially when there is only one job incumbent to collect data from.

Another method of validating job analysis results is to compare the findings to comparable jobs in other organizations. While some components of a job may be organization-specific, many traditional jobs do have suitable counterparts in other firms with which they can be compared.

JOB DESCRIPTION AND SPECIFICATION

After validating the study, each job analysis should be summarized in a written *job description* and *job specifications*. The job description is a document that explains the duties, responsibilities, working conditions, and other aspects of a specified job. The first section of it is the *job identity*; it contains such useful information as when and where the job was described (date and location) and by whom (the job analyst). Often a job grade or classification and a supervisor's title or even name is included in this section.

The next item on the job description is the *job title*. The title should reflect actual duties performed and not be inflated to increase job status. Organizations like banks often used inflated job titles (e.g., assistant vice president and vice president) in lieu of pay. This practice is problematic; if these jobs were evaluated as part of the pay determination process, their value could be biased by the job title, resulting in an inflated evaluation.[16]

After the job title comes the *job summary*, a brief paragraph summarizing specific duties performed in the job. This is useful for recruitment advertisements and wage surveys. The writing style, here and elsewhere in the job description, should be concise and direct, using present tense and active statements.

The last part of the job description is the *job duty* or *job task* section, which lists all the tasks required in the job. These are often organized into categories or job domains, which represent important areas of work performed. This categorization process helps when the information is used for training and performance appraisal purposes.

The job analysis not only produces the elements of the job description already listed but also specifies KSAs, working conditions, physical and social environments, physical requirements, and the conditions of employment. Some HR practitioners include these specifications in the job description itself; others put them in a separate document. In any case, the job description should be detailed enough so the reader can understand what is to be done, what products are to be made, what work standards are pertinent, job conditions, and the general outlines of the job design.

Job specifications should not be rigid or inflexible; they are simply guidelines for recruitment, selection, and placement. They state the qualifications an incumbent must possess to perform the job—in other words, these traits are required if the job is to be performed effectively. All these characteristics must be job-related if legal problems are to be avoided. Some individuals, such as the disabled or disadvantaged, may be kept out of certain jobs if the specifications are inflexible, artificially high, or invalid. Job specifications should therefore set the minimally acceptable standards for selection and later performance, so that they comply with the ADA.

Job specifications are valid, then, only to the extent that persons possessing the personal characteristics believed necessary for successful job performance, in fact, do perform more effectively on a particular job than others who lack such qualifications. Often job specifications are included as a component of the job description. See Exhibit 3.3 for an example of a job description that contains job specifications.

---

[16] Smith, B. N., P. G. Benson, and J. S. Hornsby. 1990. "The Effects of Job Description Content on Job Evaluation Judgments." *Journal of Applied Psychology*, 75: 301-309.

Exhibit 3.3: Job Description and Specifications

JOB DESCRIPTION

Title:	Human Resource Manager
Department:	Human Resources
Job Analysis:	January 2004

Note: Statements included in this description are intended to reflect, in general, the duties and responsibilities of this classification and are not to be considered all-inclusive.

Relationships

Reports to:	V.P. Human Resources
Subordinate Staff:	None
Other Internal Contacts:	Manufacturing Managers, Finance Managers and General Public

JOB SUMMARY

Responsible for planning, organizing, directing, and administering the plant personnel program, as well as public relations activities in the community in which the plant is located. Supervises employees engaged in specialized and varied personnel tasks. Work involves matters of a complicated nature where considerable initiative and an extremely high degree of independent judgment are used to make decisions.

Job Domains

A. Negotiate labor agreements and administer labor contracts
  1. Maintains a working relationship with union representatives.
  2. Maintains knowledge of labor agreement history (analyzes problems related to the agreement, communicates management position to the union, analyzes union requests, writes agreement language).

B. Implement policy and procedures
  1. Writes human resources policy.
  2. Communicates this policy verbally.
  3. Makes presentation to groups on this policy.
  4. Answers questions on the policy.

C. Develop policies
  1. Identifies areas for policy development.
  2. Collects input on proposed policy provisions.
  3. Writes new policy.
  4. Presents policy to approval bodies.
  5. Communicates new policy.

D. Management relations
  1. Answers questions from management.
  2. Maintains good relationship with management.
  3. Acquires information at the request of management

E. Compensation administration
  1. Communicates salary and wage guidelines.
  2. Approves salary increase budgets.
  3. Reviews salary and wage changes.

F. Staffing
  1. Finds candidates for specific openings.
  2. Reviews candidate qualifications.
  3. Interviews candidates for specific jobs.

Exhibit 3.3: Job Description and Specifications, *Cont'd*

JOB SUMMARY, Job Domains, *Cont'd*
G. Manage various services
    1. Provides direction to supervisors.
    2. Writes budgets and obtains budget approval.
    3. Solicits feedback about quality of service from customers of Food Services.
    4. Solves problems raised by Plant Security.
    5. Solves problems raised by Plant Safety.
    6. Solves problems raised by Plant Medical.
    7. Solves problems related to Child Care.
    8. Solves problems related to Operations and Relocation.
H. Training and development
    1. Counsels with employees on training plans.
    2. Selects training.
    3. Trains employees.
I. Evaluating employees
    1. Establishes performance objectives for employees.
    2. Observes employee performance.
    3. Prepares documents for formal review.
    4. Provides regular feedback to employees.
    5. Conducts formal review of employee performance.

JOB SPECIFICATIONS
Knowledge and Skills
    1. Oral skills, to convey group presentations, counsel one-on-one, and explain policy.
    2. Math skills, to administer salary and determine budget.
    3. Writing skills, to write policy, correspondence, memos, and presentations.
    4. Reading skills, to study policy, and understand correspondence.
    5. Computer skills.
    6. Knowledge of corporate policy.
    7. Knowledge of labor agreements.
    8. Knowledge of key personnel within the company.
    9. Maintain a high level of group leadership.
    10. Maintain a high level of presentation skills.
Physical Characteristics
    1. See well enough to read, write, type, etc.
    2. Hear well enough to comprehend all forms of communications.
    3. Speak well enough to gain understanding by others through communication within
       the corporation.
    4. Use of hands and fingers to write, type, etc.
Other Characteristics
    1. Must possess strength to work long hours.
    2. Must be adaptable to travel.
    3. Must have mobility to move to other plants and offices.

_____
Employee Signature

_____   _____
Manager Signature   HR Representative or Company Official Signature

WRAP-UP

Job analysis is the main building block of HR management. It can help a company comply with the law and support the success of such HR activities as selection, training, performance appraisal, and compensation. This chapter identified a seven-step approach to completing the job analysis project:

1. Determine the use of the job data.
2. Choose one or more methods of analysis based on the project goals and the budget and time available.
3. Inform managers that there will be a study.
4. Inform and perhaps involve job incumbents, who are the subject matter experts.
5. Conduct the study carefully.
6. Validate the results of the job analysis study to eliminate inconsistencies in information derived from different sources.
7. Summarize the results into a job description listing the essential functions of the job and job specifications that set out the KSAs necessary to perform it.

Clearly, the process must be organized. Because the information that can be obtained is invaluable, the research used to determine the best methods and procedures must be complete. The job analysis function deserves as much attention as the HR functions that rely on it.

Chapter 4

A Quality Employee Team: Effective Recruitment and Selection

Retention is an HR component that is of great value. However, retention can sometimes be given too much value. While management is trying to compensate for dedication, the financial hardships of the last few years have presented decision-makers—particularly those responsible for the budget—with a daunting paradox: on the hiring end of the spectrum there has been an unexpected shortage of valuable applicants, which puts pressure on resources. This is a major challenge to front-line managers.

David Dell of The Conference Board reminds us that, "[e]ven with unlimited funding and resources and the best intentions and programs, HR cannot conquer a turn-over problem alone."[1] A corporate-wide strategy for retention and well-crafted compensation techniques will work wonders instead. Research by Dell and Jack Hickey found a few common, yet avoidable, mistakes that corporations make that hurt retention:

- Failing to make talent supply a long-term strategic priority
- Failing to make the business case for turnover
- Throwing money at the problem
- Practicing organizational denial

---

[1] Adapted from: Sandler, S. F., ed. 2002. "Why Hiring/Retention Is Still a Problem . . . and What to Do About It." *HR Focus*, November: 3-5; and "How to Cut Costs and Improve Retention," *HR Focus*, May: 3-5.

Their survey also found that "today's employees are looking for: organizational stability, opportunities for career and personal development, multilevel involvement and accountability for talent, integrated talent strategies, and a strong employer brand and reputation."

These elements of choice have not changed much over the last five years; what *has* changed is the amount of money top-level executives are willing to put out to keep the best people.

As budgets are slashed, many front-line managers find themselves caught between cost reduction and retention. Managers fear that changes in periodic pay increase percentages could flip preservation the wrong way. Here are some suggested ways to keep things balanced:

- Reduce or eliminate merit pay increases based on yearly percentage increases to base pay
- Institute pay for performance
- Change the base pay/bonus mix
- Benchmark or establish salary levels

Cost-saving measures might include reducing bonuses, altering the pay structure of top executives, and hiring more part-time and temporary workers. Amazingly, by means like these, current employees can be kept happy and managers can use some of that funding for other projects.

THE MANAGER'S CHALLENGE

The care and feeding of quality personnel (better known as *attraction* and *retention* in business terms) is the number one HR issue for emerging managers.[2] Employers, especially smaller ones with limited resources, are often forced to compete for talent in a tight labor market. To deal with the competition, growing enterprises must formalize their recruitment and selection efforts and find ways to attract people away from larger organizations.

---

[2] Hornsby, J. S., and D. F. Kuratko.(2003. "Human Resource Management in U.S. Small Businesses: A Replication and Extension." *Journal of Developmental Entrepreneurship*, Vol 8, #1, 73-92; Heneman, R. L., J. W. Tansky, and S. M. Camp. 2000. "Human Resource Management Practices in Small and Medium-sized Enterprises: Unanswered Questions and Future Research Perspectives." *Entrepreneurship Theory and Practice*, 25: 11-26.

Effective recruitment and selection must be carefully planned and carried out by competent managers, not haphazardly performed. Highly skilled people who might be attracted to a growing firm would surely be turned off by unprofessional procedures.

There are numerous social, legal, economic, and ethical issues to consider when selecting qualified employees. Understanding this process is important for job applicants as well as employers. If actively involved in the search for qualified employees, it is important to have a thorough understanding of this HR activity because it is increasingly important for organizations to have sound selection programs if they are to ensure organizational survival, much less competitiveness.

This chapter discusses how many job applicants experience the selection process, the best possible program for selecting qualified individuals, and an employer's legal responsibilities.

SELECTION AND THE ENTIRE HR SYSTEM

Among the HR activities that relate to the selection system are job analysis, planning, performance appraisal, and compensation.

Job analysis (see Chapter 3) is the foundation of all selection systems.[3] For example, how could a manager select the right employee without knowing the KSAs associated with the job?

Planning for future staffing needs is continuous, given the continuously changing technological aspects of jobs today. For example, managers must decide whether it is more economical to choose people who already have the skills a particular job requires or to train someone already on board or coming in.

Appraising employee performance is a major measure of the success of any selection system. Performance appraisal ratings become the criterion used to assess selection procedures once test validity is established.

Compensation clearly matters for any selection program. Without a competitive and attractive compensation package, organizations cannot recruit highly competent and motivated candidates from whom to make selection decisions.

---

[3] Wernimont, P. F.(1988. "Uses for Job Analysis Results in Human Resource Management: Recruitment, Selection, and Placement." In S. Gael, ed., *Job Analysis Handbook for Business, Industry, and Government.* New York: Wiley.

Candidates available for selection are only as qualified as the people in the applicant pool. Currently, organizations are becoming extremely creative in broadening the diversity of the applicant pool, which is important in any competitive business environment.

THE RECRUITMENT PROCESS

The first step in staffing an organization, identifying a pool of qualified job applicants, is achieved by actively implementing an aggressive recruitment strategy.[4] Given the global competition facing many organizations today as well as the changing demographics of the work-force, it is becoming imperative from a survival perspective that companies actively recruit individuals workers from a variety of ethnic backgrounds and differing work experiences. This strategy requires all managers to do active HR-related planning and identify effective methods to reach potential employees.[5]

Internal Methods

Internal methods of recruitment aim to draw potential job candidates from those who already work for the organization and include:

- *Job posting*. Employers notify employees about new openings via newsletters, company bulletin boards, e-mail or the intranet.
- *Promotion from within*. This involves offering employees who have excelled in their current job (as evidenced by an accurate   performance appraisal) new positions with more responsibility and b e t t e r pay.
- *Referrals*. This involves current employees giving the company names of others qualified for possible hire.

The advantages to using current employees to fill job openings within the company include:

1. The organization knows more about the employee's skills, aptitudes, and interests, and the employee is already familiar with the culture of the organization, if not the actual position.

[4] Rynes, S. L., and A. E. Barber. 1990. "Applicant Attraction Strategies: An Organizational Perspective." *Academy of Management Review*, 15: 286-310.
[5] Breaugh, J. A. 1992. *Recruitment: Science and Practice*. Boston, MA: PWS-Kent.

2. Job applicants referred by an employee tend to have a more realistic understanding of the job and the organization as a whole than do walk-ins, so there is likely to be a better match between organization and employee needs.

3. Internal recruitment can be a motivator for employees to excel in their current job so that they will advance within the company.

The disadvantages to using current employees to fill job openings are:

1. The policy of promoting from within can create a homogeneous work-force. In this type of work-force, inbreeding of ideas may hinder organizational growth, innovation, and progress. Thus, creativity may be stifled.

2. Such practices may reinforce the demographic characteristics of the current work-force, to the disadvantage of women and minorities, which could well decrease the competitiveness of the organization in a global business market.

3. Subordinates may have a problem adjusting to a new supervisor who was once a peer or even a friend. The supervisor may have problems enforcing work rules and the subordinates may have problems respecting the supervisor's authority. Employees who are not chosen may be jealous and actually set out to make life miserable for the new supervisor.

External Methods

External methods of recruiting employees who as yet have no relationship, even indirect, with the organization include walk-ins, college recruiting, and advertising via newspapers, trade journals, professional conferences, radio, television, and the Internet. A factor to keep in mind in external recruiting is that sometimes people decide to leave the work-force to retire or spend more time at home; when they do, their knowledge and skills are generally lost. This knowledge and skill base is an untapped source of human capital for employers willing to be flexible by offering shorter work-weeks, telecommuting, and other flexible work schedules.[6]

---

[6] Wellner, A. S. 2002. "Tapping a Silver Mine: Older Workers Represent a Wealth of Talent—But May Require Increased Flexibility from HR." *HR Magazine*, 47: 26.

Using external sources means preparing a written advertisement. Exhibit 4.1 shows a typical advertisement. A good advertisement clearly identifies the company (name, location, contact name, phone number) and concise job responsibilities and specifications. A well-written advertisement should facilitate the process of matching the company with an applicant. Applicants should be motivated to apply only if their interests and KSAs correspond to what the company needs.

Exhibit 4.1: A Typical Recruiting Advertisement

Memorial Hospital
1000 University Avenue
Anywhere, USA

Employment Representative

Immediate opportunity for a dynamic human resources professional as full-time Health Care Recruiter. Responsibilities include all phases of recruitment, interviewing, and screening of nursing and other health care professionals; travel to conventions, college career events, and other recruitment activities; and planning, organizing, and hosting recruitment events, presentations, and hospital tours.

This fast-paced, highly visible position is an excellent opportunity for a recruiter with the right blend of organizational, marketing, and communication talents to play a key role in our continuing success. Requires B.S. in human resources or related field with minimum one year related experience.

Memorial Hospital is a 550+ bed teaching hospital and medical referral center for East Central Wherever, with over 2,300 employees. Excellent salary and benefit package.

To apply, send resume and salary history in complete confidence to Andrea Smith, Manager of Employment.

Companies of all sizes are increasingly using the Internet for external recruitment. The company's own Web site can help enlarge the pool of prospective employees as well as being an effective public relations tool. The Web's interactivity makes it possible to create highly personalized and responsive Web pages that deliver results for both the applicant and company. Some of the interactive tools used in the recruitment process are Web site search engines, interactive job application forms, and e-mail autoresponders.[7]

Getting new employees from outside the organization has several advantages:

- Such recruiting efforts are more likely to result in a heterogeneous work environment.

- External recruitment is more likely to bring in people with new and different ideas that may stimulate company growth and innovation.

Among the disadvantages of external recruitment:

- It may tend to lower the morale of current employees, which may decrease their motivation to do a better job.

- It is more difficult to assess the person-organization fit when the applicant comes from outside.

Realistic Job Preview

One way to ensure that a match will be appropriate when choosing an outside job applicant is to employ a realistic job preview (RJP). In an RJP, potential employees are informed about all aspects of the job, both positive and negative, so that they can better assess the match between their personal needs and the organization's needs. Making sure expectations are realistic has been associated with higher employee satisfaction and job involvement, lower turnover, and enhanced communication.[8] Information for the RJP should be taken directly from the job analysis.

Affirmative Action

In an attempt to make the organization more diverse, many organizations are voluntarily implementing affirmative action programs. These are based on the basic recruitment strategy of hiring the best possible candidate for a

---

[7] Dysart, J. 1999. "HR Recruiters Build Interactivity into Web Sites." HR Magazine, March, 106-110

[8] Bretz, R.D., and T. A. Judge. 1998. "Relisting Job Previews: A Test of Self-Selection Hypotheses." Journal of Applied Psychology, 83: 330-337; Wanous, J. P. 1989. "Installing a Realistic Job Preview: Ten Tough Choices." Personnel Psychology, 42: 117-133.

job, but broaden the recruitment effort by actively seeking out and recruiting minorities and women to fill open positions.

To respond effectively to equal opportunity requirements, the organization must first have a comprehensive recruitment plan that incorporates a good faith effort for recruiting employees from diverse backgrounds. Second, selection decisions must be made using methods that have proven validity. Affirmative action is not synonymous with quotas; nor does it mean hiring anyone who is incompetent. In fact, hiring someone who is incompetent is the worst solution to solving the problem of discrimination in the workplace because it works to perpetuate stereotypes.

Pre-employment Inquiries

Applicant information is collected in several ways during the recruitment phase. Often, the first information is collected from the application form. Today, the law limits the types of information an organization can obtain from a job applicant. Although application blanks may seem to be non-threatening, most application forms have traditionally required applicants to provide information that could be interpreted as illegal or discriminatory. Exhibit 4.2 lists important questions to be asked in examining the appropriateness of items on an application form.

Exhibit 4.2: Questions to Test Appropriateness of Application Blank Items

Yes   No

____ ____ 1. Will the answers to this question, if used in making a selection decision, have an adverse impact in screening out minorities or members of one sex?

____ ____ 2. Is this information really needed to judge an applicant's competence or qualifications for the job in question?

____ ____ 3. Does the question conflict with the EEOC guidelines or recent court decisions?

____ ____ 4. Does the question conflict with the spirit and intent of the Civil Rights Act or other federal and state statutes?

____ ____ 5. Is the question an invasion of privacy?

____ ____ 6. Is there information available that could be used to show that responses to a question are associated with success or failure on a specific job?

Adapted from Gatewood, R.D., H.S. Field, and T. Field. 2000. *Human Resource Selection*, 4th ed. Ft. Worth, TX: Dryden.

Because there are so many questions that may signal to a regulatory agency that the organization may be acting in a discriminatory way, it is important that the application form ask only for job-relevant information. Following are some guidelines for drafting an application form, with examples of potentially illegal questions.[9]

Gender

An application blank should not solicit information about the applicant's gender unless it can be proved that gender is a bona fide occupational qualification (BFOQ) for the position. Typically, gender is not a BFOQ except for certain entertainment positions (models or dancers) or for public morality reasons (female locker room attendant).

National Origin

It is not permissible to ask about the ancestry of applicants or their parents' or grandparents' unless there is a BFOQ (see section 703 of the 1964 Civil Rights Act).

U.S. Citizenship

Although it is not recommended that employers ask if applicants are U.S. citizens, it is strongly recommended that organizations ask if they have permission to work in the United States, though the actual form of this legal permission should not be taken into account when hiring an employee. After the selection decision, new employees have to provide evidence that they are allowed to work in the United States.

Age

It may be illegal to ask about someone's age or birth date because the ADEA prohibits organizations from discriminating against people who are 40 or older. It is permissible to inquire about an applicant's age only when age has been proven to be a legitimate BFOQ.

Based on the child labor provision of the Fair Labor Standards Act, however, it is permissible to ask if applicants are old enough to hold a given position. After a person is hired, it is acceptable to collect information about age because many jobs have age restrictions (e.g., pilot) or for administrative purposes.

---

[9] Arvey, R. D., and R. H. Faley. 1988. *Fairness in Selecting Employees*. New York: Addison-Wesley.

Race

An applicant's race should be asked only in collecting equal employment data. If this information is asked on an application blank, it should be set apart (often it is on a separate or perforated sheet) so that it can be separated before those who make hiring decisions see it.

Disabilities/Illnesses

Since the ADArequires reasonable accommodations, it is not acceptable to require that applicants list all the disabilities or illnesses they have had or that their relatives may have had in the past. After selection only, disability information may be used for making placement decisions.

Marital Status

It is not recommended that organizations ask about marital status because decision makers may use this information illegally, usually in the form of sex discrimination. A safe question to ask in the alternative is "Do you have any personal obligations that would in any way hinder your ability to perform this job?" It is important to remember that both males and females be asked this question if it is deemed absolutely necessary for the job.

Organizational Memberships

Only information about membership in professional organizations that relate to the job should be solicited on an application blank.

Height and Weight

Only in rare circumstances is height or weight a BFOQ. Even in those rare instances when a certain height or weight is necessary to a job, applicants should be asked not to provide specific numbers but to indicate whether their measurements fall within the required range.

SELECTION METHODS

After an appropriate applicant pool has been established, the actual selection process begins. Managers use many different methods to determine who is best qualified for the position and whose personal needs match those of the organization. Common selection techniques are interviews, personality tests, ability tests, honesty tests, and drug tests.

Interviews

Perhaps the most common method for selecting qualified employees today is the interview. In the 1970s companies often used paper-and-pencil tests, but after these fell under the scrutiny of courts and legal agencies, companies began to rely solely on the employment interview. However, as we shall see, courts view the interview as a test, so interviews must be just as reliable and valid as traditional paper-and-pencil tests.[10]

Interviews can be either structured or unstructured (free form), conducted individually or in groups, or administered by more than one interviewer. While it is generally recommended that organizations use the structured format described below, the use of group or board interviews may be appropriate, depending on the types of jobs being filled.

Problems

Although interviews can be a rich source of information about an applicant's motivation, interpersonal skills, and job enthusiasm, they have many problems.[11] A major one is that interviewers are often not knowledgeable about the position being filled, so the interview is spent discussing issues unrelated to the job. This means the interviewer gives the applicant no relevant information on which to make an informed selection decision, so that applicants may find themselves working for an organization that does not meet their own work needs. The resulting mismatch between applicant and organization needs carries a low validity coefficient.

Another problem with interviews is that interviewers tend to make decisions about the potential of interviewees within a few minutes after meeting them.[12] Such snap judgments can lead to serious errors in selection. Interviewers, like everyone else, tend to remember events that transpired either early (the primacy effect) or late (the recency effect) in the interview, forgetting what happened in the middle of the interview. Applicants who make an extremely good first impression may be evaluated too highly.

---

[10] Latham, G. P. 1988. "The Reliability, Validity, and Practicality of the Situational Interview," in Eder, R. W., and G. R. Ferris, eds. *The Employment Interview: Theory, Research and Practice.* Newbury Park, CA: Sage.

[11] Gatewood, R. D., H. S. Field, and T. Field. 2000. *Human Resource Selection*, 5 ed. Ft Worth, TX: Dryden Press.

[12] Bolster, B., and B. Springbett. 1961. "The Reaction of Interviewers to Favorable and Unfavorable Information." *Journal of Applied Psychology*, 45: 97-103.

The way to solve both problems is to train interviewers properly in both the job demands and interviewing techniques.

Interviewers in general often commit one of several judgment errors. A halo error occurs, for instance, when the interviewer bases a decision on only one positive or negative aspect of the interviewee. For example, the interviewer may falsely believe that the candidate is exceptional on all important characteristics required for the job because the candidate's style of dress was impressive.

Conversely, job applicants might be rejected solely based on their attire. This particular halo effect may result in the organization passing up a highly qualified individual who simply couldn't afford a new suit for interviewing purposes. It is extremely important for managers to base their hiring decisions only on job-related criteria.

The way to avoid most problems is to draft and conduct a structured interview. A structured interview is a set of job-related interview questions (based on the job analysis) that are asked consistently of each applicant for a specific job.[13] In addition, interviewers should have a predetermined set of criteria on which to base their judgments of each candidate's performance so that they are not comparing job applicants with each other but only with job specifications (the *contrast effect* judges candidates on the basis of prior candidates).

A final problem with interviews is that they represent what researchers call a *strong situation*. A strong situation is characterized by a set protocol of desired behaviors. We all know that we should make eye contact with the other party to the interview, greet the other with a strong handshake, and sit erect throughout. Since almost everyone is familiar with this etiquette, it is difficult for the interviewer to determine whether candidates are behaving in accordance with their true personality or according to what they know is correct interview behavior. For this reason, most organizations are reluctant to make a selection based solely on interview performance.

Recommendations

There are a number of ways to overcome problems associated with interviews, among them:

---

[13] Pursell, E. D., M. A. Campion, and S. R. Gaylord. 1980. "Structured Interviewing: Avoiding Selection Problems," *Personnel Journal*, 59: 908.

- Make sure the interviewer has a thorough understanding of important tasks associated with the job and is familiar with the current updated job description.

- Train interviewers to delay making any judgments about a candidate until after the interview.

- Insist that interviewers employ situational questions derived directly from a recent job analysis[14] and score them according to a predetermined procedure.[15] This procedure ensures that all interviewees, regardless of age, sex, nationality, or any other protected characteristic, are all treated similarly.

- Finally, for legal reasons, review the interview for any adverse impact.

Legal Questions

Several general job-related interview questions may be used to better understand the candidate (as long as each question is job-related). For example, the interviewer may start by asking, "What about this position and this company interests you?" Later the interviewer may ask, "Do you think you would accept the job if it was offered to you today? Why or why not?" Both these questions allow the interviewer to gauge the candidate's interest in and enthusiasm about the position, as well as how much homework about the company the candidate did before the interview. The interview should be a two-way communication process.

Other question that may be asked are, "Why do you think you are qualified for this position?" or "Is there anything else you can tell me about yourself that would help me make a decision about this position?" These give the candidate an opportunity to discuss past accomplishments and how those experiences may benefit the organization and gives the interviewer a better understanding of who the candidate is, including past experience and future goals.

---

[14] Field, H. S., and R. D. Gatewood. 1988. "Development of a Selection Interview a Job Content Strategy," In Eder, R. W., and G. R. Ferris, eds. *The Employment Interview: Theory, Research and Practice*. Newbury Park, CA; Sage.

[15] Campion, M. A., E. D. Pursell, and B. K. Brown. 1988. "Structured Interviewing: Raising the Psychometric Properties of the Employment Interview." *Personnel Psychology*, 41: 25-42.

Personality Assessment

Using personality measures to identify qualified job applicants has become quite common. These tests require job applicants to answer questions about their personal characteristics. Although personality measures can provide reliable and valid information, they do have two obvious limitations:

1. Off-the-shelf personality measures often are less useful than measures specifically designed for a particular position.[16]
2. Since the information is collected from candidates, the responses may be biased toward what applicants feel the employer wants them to say.[17] Although such responses do not benefit the individual or the organization, many job applicants do resort to it.

So when should personality measures be used for making selection decisions? For one thing, they should be used only when their validity for a particular situation has been established. And they may be more valuable as a selection tool in weak rather than strong situations.[18] In situations like interviews, an applicant's behavior is probably more a result of past learning than true personality because appropriate behaviors for these situations are well known.

Ability Tests

Since the 1992 ADA (see Chapter 2) requires organizations to accommodate people with disabilities, it has become extremely important for employers to identify the minimum ability requirements for a job and not discriminate against any applicants who meet them. Given the potential problems associated with personality measures, many organizations are now using ability tests to assess the relationship between the skills and qualifications necessary for the job and performance of the job. Common ability tests evaluate mental, mechanical, clerical, and such sensory abilities as hearing and vision acuity.

---

[16] Day, D. V., and S. B. Silverman. 1989. "Personality and Job Performance: Evidence of Incremental Validity." *Personnel Psychology*, 42: 25-36.

[17] Hough, L. M., N. K. Eaton, M. D. Dunnette, J. D. Kamp, and R. A. McCloy. 1990. "Criterion-Related Validities of Personality Constructs and the Effect of Response Distortion on Those Validities." *Journal of Applied Psychology*, 75: 581-595.

[18] Gatewood, Field, and Field, op. cit., n. 10.

Although the validity of these measures is quite well supported, it is strongly suggested that managers conduct their own reliability and validity studies because specific ability tests are more appropriate for some positions than others. Despite evidence indicating that adverse impact is minimal for ability tests, it is important that participants in any validity study represent the diversity present in the target employee population.

Honesty Testing

Because the Polygraph Act of 1988 prohibits most employers from using the polygraph as a selection device, many have turned to paper-and-pencil honesty tests. Honesty tests, whether oral or written, are usually administered in person or on the phone; their cost is minimal.[19]

Though it has been argued that honesty tests are essential for curbing employee theft, their validity has been highly criticized.[20] For example, many items on these tests inquire about personal habits that are unrelated to job performance. It is open to question whether the privacy of applicants is invaded by soliciting such information. Many items on these types of tests may have to be revised and additional research conducted on the psychometric acuity of honesty tests.

Physical Examinations

No matter what the circumstances, an employer cannot require a preemployment physical because of a perceived disability. A medical exam is permitted during the period between the job offer and the start of work, as long as this is the standard practice for all applicants for that particular job.[21] Physically challenged individuals cannot be singled out for physical exams.

Generally the employer pays for the entire costs of such an examination (which can be substantial), gives the applicant a copy of the results, and keep the results confidential. Depending on the results, accommodation for those with physical or other impairments may be required as long as it does not cause undue hardship to the employer.

---

[19] Arnold, D. W., and J. W. Jones. 2002. "Who the Devil's Applying Now? Companies Can Use Test to Screen out Dangerous Candidates." *Security Management*, 46: 85.

[20] Sackett, P. R., L. R. Burris, and C. Callahan. 1989. "Integrity Testing for Personnel Selection: An Update." *Personnel Psychology*, 42: 491-529.

[21] Hans, M. 1992. "Question of the Month." *Safety and Health*, February: 61-62.

Drug Tests

It has been estimated that employee alcohol and drug abuse costs employers at least $75 billion each year.[22] Given the high incidence of drug use in our society, many organizations are testing applicants as well as employees for drug use. Usually such a test requires the applicant or employee to give a medical specialist a urine, blood, or hair sample.

Among the potential problems associated with drug testing is the fact that many of the testing procedures are unreliable. There is also the possibility of adverse impact. Another problem is the potential violation of a person's right to privacy.

Several issues must be considered before implementing a legally defensible drug-testing program:

- Drug testing should be reserved for jobs that could endanger the lives of other employees, co-workers, or customers (e.g., bus or truck driver).

- It is more legally defensible to test job applicants than current employees, but in any case, employers should always obtain written consent before testing anyone for drugs.

- Given the low reliability of many screening procedures, any positive findings should be confirmed by a more comprehensive and elaborate test to ensure the validity of the results.

- Drug-testing procedures should be tested for possible adverse impact.

- Results from drug testing must be kept confidential.

Exhibit 4.3 lists some of the most common questions about drug testing in the workplace, for both applicants and current employees.

TEST RELIABILITY AND VALIDITY

Several concepts need to be considered in designing an effective and legally defensible selection system. Among them are reliability and validity,[23] which are both usually measured using a correlation coefficient. Establishing test reliability and validity is the strongest defense to any claim of illegal discrimination.

---

[22] Bell, A. H. 1992. *Extraviewing*. Illinois: Business One Irwin.
[23] Op. cit., n. 10.

Exhibit 4.3: Common Questions About Drug Testing

1. Do I have to test?

There is no legislation that makes drug testing mandatory in all organizations, but the federal government requires drug testing in three situations. Employers must use drug testing if:

- They have a contract with the federal government;
- They are in the transportation industry; or
- They construct or operate nuclear power plants.

2. If I have to test, what kind of testing should be used?

The options of when and whom to test include:

- Job Applicant Testing: Pre-employment drug screening is the most common substance abuse testing practice.
- Incident-driven Substance Abuse Testing: Specific incidents, such as a medical emergency, which appears to be drug-related, may warrant drug testing.
- Post-accident Investigation Testing: On-the-job accidents that may have involved human error may warrant drug testing.
- Retesting Employees After Drug Rehabilitation Programs: It is common to test employees who have participated in a drug rehabilitation program.
- Periodic Testing with Advanced Notice: Tests are scheduled in advance and usually made a part of a regular employee physical.
- Random, Unannounced Tests: Testing without prenotification is probably most likely to catch drug abusers. It is also most likely to cause morale problems and increase employee grievances.

3. Can I test even if I am not required to do it?

Yes. There is no federal law that prohibits drug screening. Also, drug testing is not a legal exception to at-will employment so it may be implemented.

4. What problems may arise when using a drug-testing program?

Among problem areas are the potential for:

- Violation of Title VII
- Compliance with the ADA
- Criminal and civil suits alleging defamation, false imprisonment, assault and battery, invasion of privacy, negligence, and intentional infliction of emotional distress.

5. Are there any special problems with alcohol testing?

Yes. The ADA considers alcohol tests to be medical examinations, so employers should treat them that way. Before alcohol testing for applicants, a conditional job offer must be made. The employer must show a business necessity to rescind the offer, proving that no reasonable accommodation can be made.

6. How are public employers affected?

The Fourth Amendment prohibits unlawful search and seizure by the government and the courts have found that drug testing may violate this amendment. A balancing test should be applied; specifically, it is all right to test if the interests of the government outweigh the interests of the employee or applicant.

7. What effect does a unionized environment have on implementing drug testing?

According to the National Labor Relations Board (NLRB), drug testing is a mandatory bargaining issue and the unilateral implementation of drug testing may be an unfair labor practice.

Source: Metzler, M. M., and William A. Lutz. "Questions and Answers Regarding Legal Issues in Employee Drug and Alcohol Testing," a presentation made to the East Central Indiana Chapter of the Society for Human Resource Management, November 1992.

Correlation Coefficient

A correlation coefficient is the linear relationship between two variables.[24] The relationship, which can be either positive or negative, ranges from -1 to +1. In the selection situation, a high positive correlation (r = +1) would mean that people who scored higher on the selection test also did job tasks better than those who scored lower. Such a relationship insures that the best-qualified individual will be hired.

Is there any situation where a manager might also be interested in a strong negative correlation (r = -0.9) between a selection test and job performance? Applicants for some jobs, such as police officer, are often given a battery of tests to assess their psychological stability. Here, a manager would hope to find a negative correlation between job performance and the selection test, because applicants who score low on tests assessing tendencies associated with psychological pathology, such as schizophrenia or depression, are more stable and perform better on the job.[25]

Is there any situation where a manager might be interested in a selection test that has no relationship (r = 0) with job performance? Probably not. Someone who scored high on a selection test could either perform extremely well or just as poorly, so the test would not be useful for making selection decisions and would only add unnecessary costs.

The relationship between two variables can be graphically depicted using a scattergram or scatter-plot (see Exhibit 4.4).[26] For example, the scattergram can show the relationship between a selection test and job performance; each dot on the scattergram would represent the intersection of the selection test score before hire and the applicant's on-the-job performance.

This linear relationship between two variables can best be explained by a straight-line equation:

$Y = ax + b$.

where:

Y = criterion variable
a = slope
x = predictor score
b = y-axis intercept

[24] Anastasi, A. 1982. *Psychological Testing.* New York: McGraw-Hill.
[25] Arvey and Faley, op. cit., n. 8.
[26] Gatewood, Field, and Field, op. cit., n. 10.

Exhibit 4.4: Typical Scattergram

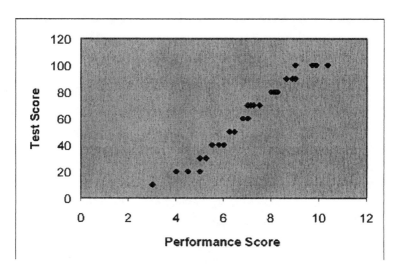

The straight-line equation can be very useful in selecting employees. For example, once the slope and intercept values are known, a manager can predict how well the job applicant will perform on the job by placing the selection test score in the equation. Although this equation cannot represent an exact relationship between a test score and job performance, it does represent a good estimate.

Reliability

Reliability refers to the consistency or stability of test scores over time. It also refers to the extent to which a measure is free from random error. Managers need a thorough understanding of at least four different types of reliability:

1. Test-retest

2. Parallel forms

3. Internal consistency

4. Inter-rater

Each method investigates reliability from a slightly different perspective.

Test-retest reliability refers to the consistency or stability of someone's test score over time. The procedure for determining test-retest reliability is to administer a test to a group of individuals and then administer the same test to the same group some time later. A test is thought to have high reliability to the extent that the test scores for each testing situation are highly correlated; the correlation coefficient for the two test scores is called the coefficient of stability.

A test-retest reliability study may have several problems. The main source of error is due to time sampling. For example, if the two tests are administered too close together in time, the scores for the second administration may be higher due to practice or memory effects (knowing the questions on the test). Conversely, if the tests are taken at times that are too far apart, the scores for the second administration may be higher due to other events that may have occurred (e.g., training or maturation). In evaluating a test-retest reliability study, it is important to pay special attention to the time interval.

Parallel forms reliability refers to the consistency of someone's test score across two equivalent tests that have similar content. The procedure is to find or create two different tests that cover the same domain of items, administer both tests to the same group, and determine the correlation coefficient between the two test scores. Again, the test is considered reliable to the extent that the two test scores are highly correlated. The correlation coefficient in this case is called the coefficient of equivalence.

The primary source of error for this type of test is sampling error. It is imperative that each test have not only the same type and number of items but also similar levels of difficulty. It is also important that both tests have similar mean and standard deviation scores.

Internal consistency (split-half reliability) refers to the extent to which items thought to measure the same thing actually correlate with each other. An advantage to this type of reliability is that it requires only one test administration. The manager splits a test in half and correlates the halves with each other to determine the reliability coefficient.

How should the manager split the test? For example, would it be wise to simply split it at the halfway mark and compare the first half with the second half? Probably not. First, people may not do as well on the second half due to fatigue. Second, many tests are designed according to item difficulty, with the most difficult items reserved for the latter part of the test, making it likely that many people may perform better on the first half of the test. It's therefore advisable to split the test in terms of odd-even items or to make sure the items in each half are equally difficult.

Inter-rater reliability is concerned with the agreement of ratings across several different managers who are raters of performance. For example, if several managers interview a job applicant together, you could expect their ratings to be highly consistent. If they were not, if there was a low correlation across managers' ratings, the implication is that the interview process was unreliable. In such a case, the managers would need to more clearly define the criteria on which to base evaluations of how well someone did in an interview.

Validity

Validity refers to how well a test measures what it purports to measure and how well it relates to other measures. Among the several types of validity that are important for all managers to understand,[27] the most important may be content and criterion-related validity.

Content validity refers to whether a test measures what it is supposed to measure. For example, does a selection test actually assess ability to perform the most important aspects of a given job? The best way to ensure content validity for selection measures is to incorporate into the measure information obtained in a thorough job analysis.

Determining content validity is a judgmental process in which several subject matter experts determine the relevance of test items to the performance desired.

Criterion-related validity is concerned with the relationship or correlation between a predictor (the selection test score) and a criterion (an aspect of job performance). Unlike content validity, criterion-related validity is objective—empirical. A criterion-related validity study would be studied by statistically assessing the relationship between a predictor and a criterion variable. There are two different types of criterion-related validation strategies: (1) concurrent and (2) predictive. The time perspective is the main difference between them. A concurrent validation study measures the relationship between predictor and criterion at the same time.

---

[27] Schneider, B., and N. Schmitt. 1992. *Staffing Organizations*. Prospect Heights, IL., Waveland Press.

Another unique characteristic of this validation strategy is that current employees are used in the study. For example, a manager might be interested in knowing whether age is a good predictor of job performance. To find out, the manager would first collect information about both employee age (predictor) and job performance (criterion). Next, the manager would perform a correlation analysis between the predictor and criterion. Of course, the study would have to control for such variables as job experience and type.

The major advantage to a concurrent validation strategy is the short time required to complete the study. The major disadvantage is that studying only current employees may create some bias if the test under investigation will be used for selection purposes. That is, current employees may perform differently on the test than job applicants because they are more knowledgeable about the job and culture of the organization and may be under less stress to perform well. In addition, the applicant pool may be more representative of minorities and females than the current work-force. It is recommended that, where feasible, a manager conduct a predictive rather than a concurrent validity study for selection purposes.

A predictive validity study uses job applicants and collects predictor and criterion information at two different times. The manager would administer the selection test to all job applicants and lock away the scores where no supervisor would have access to them. Next, the manager would identify the most qualified individuals to hire using selection methods with proven validity.

Once the selected applicants had an opportunity to perform the job tasks, criterion or job performance information would be collected and correlated with the earlier test score. If the correlation is high, the test may be used in making future selection decisions. Conversely, if the correlation is low or zero, it is clear that the selection test does not give any useful information for making selection decisions.

The major advantage to the predictive validity study is that it uses job applicants. Its major limitation is the length of time it takes to complete. In addition, it is imperative that supervisors not have access to the selection test scores before they do performance evaluations, or there will be criterion contamination, a problem that occurs when the manager responsible for providing criterion or job performance information is also familiar with the predictor information.

Relationship between Reliability and Validity

What is the relationship between reliability and validity?

The reliability coefficient is thought to set the upper limit for what may be expected from the validity coefficient. A reliability coefficient represents how a test score correlates with itself; a validity coefficient represents how a test score correlates with something else, usually job performance. It is unlikely that a test would correlate better with something else than with itself.

WRAP-UP

The first step in designing any selection procedure is a job analysis. In fact, this is the first piece of evidence courts investigate when an employee or applicant sues an organization.

There are two outcomes to any job analysis. The first is the job description, setting out all the tasks and duties associated with the job. This information is used as the basis for formulating criterion or job performance measures. It is important to conduct a content validity study of the performance appraisal measure to insure that it represents the important job responsibilities.

It is also important to establish the reliability of the performance measure. One method of establishing reliability would be to employ multiple raters: Someone's job performance evaluation should remain fairly consistent regardless of who is providing the rating. Finally, the performance measure should be assessed for potential adverse impact.

The second outcome of a job analysis is to identify employee specifications, the KSAs associated with a job. This information is then used to identify important predictors for a job. Examples of selection predictors are personality measures, honesty tests, and interviews. Here, too, the reliability and validity of predictors must be established. Predictors must also be investigated for potential adverse impact.

Once predictor and criterion measures have been identified, formulated, and evaluated, it's time to test the selection procedure. This can be done in a variety of ways. For example, the ideal selection evaluation program would conduct a predictive validity study to establish that there is indeed a relationship between the selection test or predictor and the job performance or criterion variables. Among the potential benefits of implementing a valid selection procedure are increased employee satisfaction, decreased turnover and absenteeism, and increased proficiency and therefore productivity.

It is important to consult *Uniform Guidelines for Selecting Employees* whenever any selection procedure is designed. This document, which was prepared by several different groups of selection experts, articulates the important social, ethical, empirical, and legal issues that must be taken into account in any selection program.

CHAPTER 5

Performance Management: Effective Evaluation and Development

In some firms, opinions about performance reviews have become a matter of conflict. While employees thirst for the positive motivation that comes with frequent encouraging performance appraisals, most managers instead treat reviews as tedious, unimportant, a hassle, or they simply do not give them proper thought. If performance review research has shown us anything, it is that many workers actually consider feedback more important than pay.

Lin Grensing-Pophal[1] lists many reasons why managers dislike performance evaluations, among them:

• The performance evaluation process is too complicated.

• Managers believe there is no evidence that evaluations affects the work quality of those whose performances are being reviewed.

• Some managers fear legal challenges if the employee ties a negative review to a missed promotion or a denied pay raise.

Regardless of the reason, Grensing-Pophal and hundreds of other HR researchers claim that the time saved by giving superficial reviews or avoiding reviews altogether will never make up for an employee's lost morale.

---

[1] Grensing-Pophal, Lin. 2001. "Motivate Managers to Review Performance." *HR Magazine*, March: 44-48.

To motivate employees, front-line managers must first motivate themselves to give proper evaluations; the short-term benefits alone will make up for the extra time this takes. Experts have suggested the following five steps:

1. *Make it meaningful.* Performance appraisals should be treated like a management process rather than a management task, and the past, present, and future of an employee's relationship with the company should be considered. Give an evaluation the significance that it deserves.

2. *Make everyone a player.* If you can get a couple of managers together and get them brainstorming, a tailored evaluation format can be achieved.

3. *Keep it simple.* "The more you can do to keep the process simple, the more likely you are to achieve compliance," Grensing-Pophal says.

4. *Train managers.* Managers need to understand how vital evaluations are in motivating employees. Though training alone will not be sufficient to make this clear, managers should be shown why the organization values performance appraisals, how individual performance benefits the organization, and how performance can be measured objectively.

5. *Make it a must.* Performance evaluations should not only be considered an important element in every manager's job, they should be regular and effective enough to keep the circle of inspiration turning.

THE MANAGER'S CHALLENGE

Performance management is probably the most difficult function for employers. Managers often find themselves with little or no time to systematically evaluate the behavior of employees. New managers who have been promoted up through the ranks may find it difficult to provide critical feedback to an employee who was once a co-worker and maybe even a friend. Finally, the need for consistency across managers makes performance appraisal hard to implement. Many managers want to do things their own way and in their own time, which makes getting managers to agree on a positive approach to performance appraisal a far from easy task.

For these and many other reasons, many firms fail to appraise employee performance, but the lack of assessment undermines quality, productivity, communication, and compliance with the law. Motivation research consistently emphasizes the importance of performance feedback. Setting performance standards is essential to high quality. Finally, documentation of performance deficiencies gives the organization support for a negative employment decision.

A systematic approach to performance appraisal is necessary for all types of organizations. Employee allegations of discrimination or wrongful discharge can be minimized or prevented altogether with a well-formulated performance appraisal system.

Such a system can also help the business prosper. Identification of key talent and early recognition of poor performers promotes the most efficient use of human resources. A strong performance appraisal system also helps identify future company training needs as the business grows, leading to increased company effectiveness. Finally, basing pay decisions on a systematic appraisal system can reduce turnover and increase employee satisfaction and morale.

Exhibit 5.1 (page 88) shows a systems model of performance appraisal. Its components include setting performance appraisal goals, assessing legal considerations, selecting or drafting an instrument, training evaluators, preparing to rate employees, performance appraisal interviews, and system evaluation. Adhering to such a model will result in a sense of procedural equity or fairness—something seldom realized in HR management. This model emphasizes *performance management*, with performance appraisal viewed as a continuous process where managers and subordinates manage performance year-round. Without such a systematic approach, managers make errors in judgment and allow personal biases to interfere, leading to the downfall of the performance appraisal process.[2]

A SYSTEMS PERSPECTIVE ON PERFORMANCE APPRAISAL

The following discussion describes the essential steps in building a useful performance appraisal program based on the systems model of performance appraisal.

---

[2] Gray, G. 2002. "Performance Appraisals Don't Work." *Industrial Management*, 44: 15.

Exhibit 5.1: Systems Model of Performance Appraisal

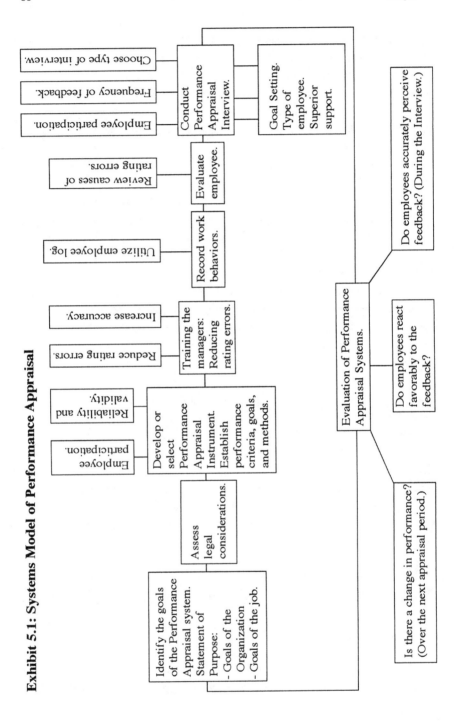

The Goals of the Performance Management System

A systematic model of performance appraisal begins with identifying goals. This requires drafting a statement of purpose, organizational goals, and job goals.

Statement of Purpose
The first step in designing a performance appraisal system (see Exhibit 5.1) is to construct a statement of purpose to ensure full participation, understanding, and support for the program. Many companies buy into or create appraisal systems that do not meet their specific needs; clear specification of the purpose of an employee appraisal system can prevent this. A clear statement of goals and objectives that is supported by upper management relieves the tension and ambiguity employees feel when any new program is implemented—especially in companies implementing HR management programs for the first time. Ambiguity and confusion about HR practices sets a tone that is hard to erase over time.

Performance appraisal systems suffer from many problems when their purpose is misdirected or not identified. Among them are poor definition, poor communication, inappropriateness, lack of support, and failure to monitor the system. A clear statement of purpose helps solve these problems.[3] The statement of purpose should answer the following questions:

- How does the appraisal system relate to corporate strategy?

- What are the reasons for and goals of the program?

- Who will be evaluated?

- Who will conduct the appraisal?

- When will the appraisal be conducted?

- How will the appraisal information be used?

Organizational Goals
The evaluation process gives the manager an opportunity to discuss with employees what they should be doing, answer their questions, recommend further training, and respond to complaints and problems. Employees can use the evaluation process to specify what their duties are and to both give

---

[3] Lee, C. 1989. "Poor Performance Appraisals Do more Harm than Good." *Personnel Journal*, September, 91-99.

and receive feedback. These considerations must be taken into account in deciding what the goals of the process should be for the organization. In order to identify organizational goals, the company must consider how performance appraisal information will be used. There are four general uses:[4]

1. The results of performance reviews allow the manager to make distinctions among individuals. They are the basis for:

   - *Pay raise recommendations:* It's clear that if pay is to be a motivator, employees must see a clear correlation or relationship with performance.[5]

   - *Promotion decisions:* A promotion-from-within policy helps decrease turnover, increase motivation, and attract good applicants.

   - *Placement decisions:* Appraisal results can be used to identify positions to which troubled or borderline employees can be transferred to better utilize their specific talents.

2. Performance appraisals help managers assess future HR needs. Many HR professionals[6] consider this to be the most productive aspect of performance appraisal. Specifically, they can help achieve the following objectives:

   - *Managerial feedback*: Employees find out where they stand with the manager. The absence of any systematic assessment of employee performance with formal feedback increases employee skepticism about their standing with the manager and in the com-

---

[4] Cleveland, J., K. R. Murphy, and R. W. Williams. 1989. "Multiple Uses of Performance Appraisal: Prevalence and Correlates." *Journal of Applied Psychology*, 74: 130-135.

[5] Schuster, J. R., and P. K. Zingheim. 1996. *The New Pay: Linking Pay and Organizational Performance.* San Francisco: Jossey Bass; Lawler, E. E. 1981. *Pay and Organizational Development.* Reading. MA: Addison-Wesley.

[6] Shaw, D., R. W. Beatty, L. S. Baird, and C. E. Schneier. 1997. *The Performance Measurement, Management, and Appraisal Sourcebook.* Amhurst, MA: Human Resource Development Press; Bernardin, H. J., and R.. W. Beatty. 1990. *Performance Appraisal: Assessing Human Behaviors at Work.* Boston, MA: Kent Publishing Co; Henderson, R. I. 1984. *Performance Appraisal,* 2nd ed. Reston, VA.: Reston Publishing Co.; Latham, G. P., and K. N. Wexley. 1993. *Increasing Productivity Through Performance Appraisal,* 2nd ed. Reading, MA: Addison-Wesley.

pany. An uninformed employee will be surprised or even shocked if passed over for promotion or pay raises.

- *Increased security*: Employees may not know what areas of their performance need improvement. The feedback provided through performance appraisal relieves employee fears and increases acceptance of management decisions.

- *Improved manager/employee relations*: The manager-subordinate relationship is strengthened because the process encourages mutual agreement on performance expectations. The key to an acceptable performance appraisal system is to encourage employee involvement at all stages of the program.

- *Identify training needs*: Performance appraisals reveal what knowledge and skills employees need to improve productivity on their present job and to be considered for promotion.

- *Improved communication*: The discussion phase of a performance review gives both manager and subordinate opportunities to express themselves on a variety of work-related issues. A key benefit of any successful performance appraisal system should be increased communication in all aspects of the working relationship. Because a fair system increases employee morale and trust, it often leads to effective communication.

3. Performance appraisal results can be used for validation. Title VII of the 1964 Civil Rights Act and its amendments require that selection procedures be job-related. The Uniform Guidelines define a selection procedure as anything used to make an employment decision. When performance appraisal results are used in test validation, the goal is to show a correlation or relationship between a selection procedure and job performance: The stronger the relationship, the more predictive the selection procedure is of job performance. The Uniform Guidelines consider this process (known as "criterion-related validity") to be the most accurate way to assess validity.

4. Performance appraisal information can be used to document any need for disciplinary actions against employees. Managers often claim that dealing with problem employees is one of the most trou-

blesome aspects of their jobs. Because they deal with job behaviors, data from performance appraisals can help relieve the stress of discipline as well as reduce the possibility of reprisals against management. A performance appraisal system that identifies employee problems through frequent observation and feedback provides both reasonable and legal justification for taking actions like denying a pay raise, demotion, or termination.

Top management support is essential to the performance appraisal program. Without it, the process may be administered haphazardly or simply ignored. Firm management commitment helps to ensure that the review results are both useful and used.

Top executives can show commitment to the appraisal process by budgeting resources of both money and time to design and implement the system, using appraisal results to make employment decisions, and setting a standard for effective performance management against which each manager is measured.

Job Goals

The *Albemarle* case[7] has made it clear that job expectations should be based on an accurate job analysis. More specifically, job analysis must objectively assess the critical job behaviors that will be evaluated in the performance appraisal process. Job analysis information ensures objective and valid performance criteria and reduces the likelihood of subjective appraisals by managers based on employee personality traits.

Legal Considerations

The next step in the performance appraisal model is to make sure performance appraisals are conducted in compliance with the law. The performance appraisal has legal implications whenever it is used as the basis for an employment decision,[8] such as promotions, pay raises, or selection for training programs. To be legal, evaluation of work behavior must be based on objective, job-related criteria so that the worker's employment situation is not unjustly affected by a manager's stereotypes or biases (see Chapter 2).

---

[7] *Albemarle Paper Company v. Moody.* U.S. Supreme Court. 10 F.E.P. Cases 1181, 1975. 422 U.S. 405 (1975).

[8] Bernardin and Beatty, op. cit. n. 5; Latham and Wexley, op. cit. n. 5.

The important court cases that directly influence the use of performance appraisals center on the issue of validity—on whether employee performance is evaluated in terms directly related to the job. The four court decisions that have directly influenced the use of performance appraisal are:

1. *Griggs v. Duke Power* (1971)[9] was the first Supreme Court decision related to Title VII of the 1964 Civil Rights Act. Duke Power Company employed blacks in only one department and whites in three higher-paying departments. To get a job in the departments where whites worked, applicants had to have a high school diploma or a satisfactory score on two standardized aptitude tests. According to the Supreme Court, this practice had an adverse impact on blacks, a protected group under Title VII of the 1964 Civil Rights Act. *Griggs* requires that employers demonstrate that all criteria used to make an employment decision are valid or job-related. Since performance appraisals are criteria used in many employment decisions, they too must be validated.

2. In *Brito v. Zia Company* (1973),[10] the Zia Company was found guilty of violating Title VII when it laid off a disproportionate number of Hispanics on the basis of low performance appraisal scores. The court ruled that this was illegal because the performance appraisal instrument used to make these decisions was not related to important elements of work behavior but was based only on "the best judgments and opinions of supervisors."

3. In *Wade v. Mississippi Cooperative Extension Service* (1974),[11] the Mississippi Cooperative Extension Service was found guilty of discriminating against blacks. The Extension Service used a performance appraisal instrument based on supervisory ratings of traits like leadership, public acceptance, attitude, grooming, resourcefulness, and outlook on life. The Court ruled that this method was not an objective appraisal of job performance and unfairly froze blacks in nonsupervisory positions.

---

[9] *Griggs v. Duke Power Company*, 401 U.S. 424, 1971. 3 E.P.D. 8137.
[10] *Brito v. Zia Company*, 478 F.2d. 1200. (1973).
[11] *Wade v. Mississippi Cooperative Extension Service,* 372 F. Supp. 126, 1974. 7 E.P.D. 9186

4. The court in *Albemarle Paper Company v. Moody* (1975),[12] ruled that the Albemarle Paper Company wrongly relied on subjective supervisory rankings as the criterion on which they validated their selection procedures. More specifically, the court stated that the company had failed to conduct a job analysis that could identify the critical requirements of the job. The implication of this case is that a job analysis must be the basis of a performance appraisal instrument that is used to validate selection procedures.

What Can Be Done

Congress and the Supreme Court have outlined the essential components of a legally defensible performance appraisal system. Characteristics of legally defensible performance appraisal systems[13] are shown in Exhibit 5.2, which might be used to train supervisors and managers before they conduct employee appraisals.

Exhibit 5.2: Characteristics of Legally Defensible Performance Appraisal Systems

1. Ensure that procedures for personnel decisions do not differ as a function of the race, sex, national origin, religion, or age of those affected by the decisions.
2. Use objective and unbiased data whenever available.
3. Provide a formal system of review or appeal to resolve disagreements about appraisals.
4. Use more than one independent evaluator of performance.
5. Use a formal standardized system for personnel decisions.
6. Ensure that evaluators have ample opportunity to observe employee performance before they rate subordinates.
7. Avoid rating on personality traits like drive, aptitude, or attitude.
8. Document performance counseling before performance-based termination decisions.
9. Communicate specific performance standards to employees.
10. Provide raters with written instructions on how to complete performance evaluations.
11. Evaluate employees on specific work dimensions, rather than on a single global measure.
12. Require documentation of specific behaviors (e.g., critical incidents) for extreme ratings.
13. Base the content of the appraisal form on a job analysis.
14. Give employees an opportunity to review their appraisals.
15. Educate personnel decision-makers on discrimination laws.

Adapted from: Bernardin, H. J., and W. F. Cascio. 1987. "Performance Appraisal and the Law," In Schuler, R. S., S. A. Youngblood, and V. Huber, eds. *Readings in Personnel and Human Resource Management*, 3rd ed. St. Paul, MN: West Publishing Co.

---

[12] *Albemarle Paper Company v. Moody*. U.S. Supreme Court. 10 F.E.P. Cases 1181, 1975. 422 U.S. 405 (1975)
[13] Bernardin, H. J., and W. F. Cascio. 1987. "Performance Appraisal and the Law," In Schuler, R. S., S. A. Youngblood, and V. Huber, eds. *Readings in Personnel and Human Resource Management*, 3rd ed. St. Paul, MN: West Publishing Co.

Essentially, a performance appraisal system that is based on a job analysis that identifies critical job duties is defensible in court. When developing a performance appraisal system, the legal considerations shown in Exhibit 5.2 should be kept in mind but should not be the driving force of the project. Instead, the main goal should be increasing company productivity and morale by identifying the most talented personnel and rewarding them with pay raises, promotions, and additional training. The only way to accomplish this objective is to base employment decisions on objective performance criteria.

The Performance Appraisal Instrument

After assessing the legal considerations, the next phase (see Exhibit 5.1) is drafting the performance appraisal instrument. This typically is accomplished by establishing criteria, selecting a method, and setting goals.

Performance Appraisal Criteria

As we have reiterated, a valid performance appraisal system must be job-related. The *Uniform Guidelines*[14] define validity as the evaluation of employee performance on criteria (job duties) identified in the job analysis and the achievement of pre-established performance goals. This process of establishing validity is what differentiates an objective appraisal (one based on an evaluation in terms of actual job duties) from a subjective one (general evaluations of personality, likability, etc.). Personality traits like disposition, sense of humor, and enthusiasm should not be evaluated unless they are directly related to job requirements.

Performance criteria should be multidimensional—a company should rely on more than just one general measure of job performance. Employees should be evaluated on each of their important job duties in order to achieve the most accurate assessment of job performance.

Finally, employee participation in setting the performance criteria adds to the accuracy and the acceptability of the performance appraisal results. It's normal to respond to criticism by feeling defensive and questioning the fairness of the criticism, but if employees have helped write the appraisal criteria, they are more likely to accept an objective statement when they have fallen short.

---

[14] "Uniform Guidelines on Employee Selection Procedures." 1978. *Federal Register*, 43: 39290-8315.

The Appraisal Method

Once the criteria for performance have been established, a method of appraisal is needed that differentiates good performers from bad: The two methods of appraisal are: (1) comparative methods and (2) absolute methods.

Comparative methods compare one employee to another. The most common comparative method is straight ranking, where the evaluator draws up a list of subordinates in order from best to worst. The criteria for the ranking are usually overall measures of job performance. The weakness is that the comparative method is subjective. Since the criterion is global (individual aspects of the job are ignored) and particular areas of job performance are ignored, this process is open to personal biases that may invite charges of illegal discrimination. Furthermore, subjective standards drastically reduce the usefulness of the performance appraisal information. For example, if pay cannot be tied directly to performance, the motivating potential of pay increases will drop.

In contrast, the use of an *absolute method* enables an evaluator to assess an employee's performance without reference to other employees. Also, employees can be evaluated on several dimensions of job performance instead of one global measure. Five of the most popular absolute methods are: (1) narrative essays, (2) critical incidents, (3) weighted checklists, (4) graphic rating scales, and (5) goal setting.

A *narrative essay* is the simplest form of absolute method. The supervisor is asked to describe in writing a subordinate's strengths, weaknesses, and potential, and to make suggestions for improvement. While narrative essays are useful for providing feedback to employees, comparisons across employees are virtually impossible, especially if different supervisors are doing the appraising. Because the information is qualitative only, no quantitative distinctions between employees can be made (i.e., pay and promotion).

The *critical incident* approach is based on manager observations of particularly effective or ineffective performance, what critical incidents that led to the good or bad performance, and the situation in which it occurred. This method gives employees specific feedback about performance. This approach is useful for smaller organizations that have few employees in the same or similar jobs, situations where objective measures of performance are unavailable, and those where budgetary limitations prohibit creating a system unique to the company.[15]

While critical incidents may be useful, three basic drawbacks reduce their viability as a sole means of measuring work performance:[16]

1. Because they are not quantitative, it is impossible to compare employees in making pay and promotion decisions.

2. Record-keeping is extremely time-consuming. Managers often grow weary of keeping track of incidents and keep fewer records as the appraisal period grows longer. Also, as the number of employees supervised increases, ability to observe and record critical incidents decreases.

3. The critical incidents are often not weighted in importance to their contributions to successful job performance and they assess performance on only a small percentage of the job.

Even though the critical incidents approach should not be the sole performance appraisal method, it is a good way to identify important job duties that should be incorporated into the appraisal system.

A *weighted checklist* uses both qualitative and quantitative data in doing appraisals. While the critical incidents technique is its foundation, this method eliminates some of the drawbacks of that technique by assigning weights or values to each incident. In the checklist, the evaluator simply checks the incidents or tasks that a job incumbent performs and then the values are totaled for a final performance score.

The major drawback of this approach is the difficulty of creating a checklist that is truly representative of a job, especially given the fact that by centering on critical incidents it leaves out the behaviors that are most frequently performed. Also, setting the weights is difficult for newer and smaller companies that do not have a large enough sample to calculate reliable critical incident values.

The *graphic rating scale* is the most widely used approach for assessing performance. It aims to identify important dimensions of job performance and then rate them on a continuum from excellent to poor, usually

[15] McEvoy, G. M. 1984. "Small Business Personnel Practices." October: 1-8.
[16] Jackson, S. E., and R. S. Schuler. 2003. *Managing Human Resources Through Strategic Partnerships*, 8th ed. Cincinnati: South-Western.

using a scale ranging from one to five or seven. Scales longer than seven points add little to rating accuracy while making the rating task much more confusing and difficult.[17]

Traditional graphic rating scales vary in the number of job dimensions measured, the specificity of these dimensions, and the extent to which each scale point is defined.[18] The indicators of performance vary from personality traits to specific job behaviors or duties, but to achieve the highest level of job-relatedness or validity, it is usually recommended that the performance dimensions be specific and as closely related to the job as possible. That would militate against measuring any personality traits. It is also recommended that the performance dimensions be taken from the important job duties identified in the job analysis. The simple scale shown in Exhibit 5.3 can be effective, easy to use, and more accurate than other absolute methods.

Exhibit 5.3: A Traditional Graphic Rating Scale

Please rate your subordinate on the following job duties. Use the following rating scale to make your ratings:

    1 = very poor
    2 = poor
    3 = average
    4 = above average
    5 = excellent
Job Duties (included are two examples)
    1. Defines instructions to subordinates.   1 2 3 4 5
    2. Completes paperwork by designated dates. 1 2 3 4 5

One graphic rating scale is the Behaviorally Anchored Rating Scale (BARS). BARS builds on the critical incident approach. It defines performance dimensions by creating anchors that correspond to different levels of performance.[19] Each performance dimension is described by a number of incidents associated with different levels of behavior.

[17] Lissitz, R. W., and S. B. Green. 1975. "Effects of the Number of Scale Points on Reliability: A Monte Carlo Approach." *Journal of Applied Psychology*, 60: 10-13.
[18] Cascio, W. F. 1997. *Applied Psychology in Human Resource Management*, 5th ed. Englewood Cliffs, NJ: Prentice-Hall.
[19] Smith, P., and L. Kendall. 1963. "Retranslation of Expectations: An Approach to the Construction of Unambiguous Anchors for Rating Scales." *Journal of Applied Psychology*, 47: 149-155.

The development of BARS includes the following three steps:

1. Critical incidents are collected.

2. Incidents are sorted into behavioral or performance dimensions.

3. For each performance dimension, incidents with high agreement are used as anchors for the rating scale.

While the BARS is easy to use, it is very time-consuming to develop, so that employers with many jobs or jobs that are rapidly changing may find BARS too cumbersome. Also, a BARS does not appear to add anything to traditional trait scales that are easier to put together.[20]

The main advantage of graphic rating scales is that they make it possible to calculate a quantitative score that accurately represents a job incumbent's performance. Furthermore, if all important job duties are rated using the same graphic rating scale, one employee's average score can be compared to that of others.

Although the graphic rating scale has the most advantages for appraising employee performance, it lacks the feedback potential of methods like critical incidents or narrative essays. That is why a well-constructed performance appraisal system usually incorporates more than one method. For example, the quantifiable score from the graphic rating scale makes pay and promotion decisions easier, while the narrative essay would help explain to the employee how the supervisor arrived at the ratings.

The final absolute method is *setting goals*. A performance appraisal program should not stop at simply evaluating past employee performance. In order to achieve goals like increased productivity or improved quality of work, the performance appraisal system must also deal with future job performance. This can be done during the formal performance appraisal interview, when manager and subordinate can together set goals that will guide the employee toward greater success on the job. The appraisal, if performed correctly, will identify areas of weakness; mutual goals can then be set that are reasonable, challenging, and that can correct the weaknesses in performance.

The most common method for incorporating mutual goal-setting into performance appraisal is Management by Objectives (MBO),[21] which has five basic steps:

---

[20] Wiersma, U., and G. Latham. 1986. "The Practicality of Behavioral Observation Scales, Behavior Expectation Scales, and Trait Scales." *Personnel Psychology*, 38: 619-628.

[21] Drucker, P. F. 1954. *The Practice of Management.* New York: Harper.

1. Goals are established for a new venture and its specific areas. These goals are performance-related and based on a one- to three-year time span.

2. Manager and subordinate agree on several objectives that are congruent with the goals identified in the first step. The time span for goal attainment is usually one year.

3. Performance requirements consisting of accomplishments, results, and timetables are established. These are the standards for measuring goal accomplishment.

4. Manager and subordinate hold interim progress reviews that allow corrective actions to be undertaken as necessary. For example, if changes occur that are out of the employee's control, the goals can be adjusted to make them more realistic.

5. At the end of the appraisal period, employee accomplishments are measured against performance objectives. Based on how well the goals were accomplished, objectives are set for the next appraisal period.

Two reasons help explain the popularity of an MBO.[22] First, it is based on the commonly held value that people should be rewarded for their accomplishments. Second, an MBO helps achieve greater "individual-organizational goal congruence." In other words, an MBO puts the manager and the employee on the same team with the same goals. an MBO is also attractive because, if constructed properly, the goals can be formulated very objectively.

However, like other appraisal systems, an MBO has some problems:

• If not done properly an MBO may not cover all the important dimensions of the job. As jobs increase in complexity, important dimensions of the jobs cannot always be measured.

• An MBO may cause a "results-at-all-costs" attitude among employees. For example, a salesperson may steal a client from a co-worker in order to reach a performance goal; this not only may cause dissension among the sales force, it may give the client a bad image of the company.

---

[22] Jackson and Schuler, op.cit., n. 15.

- Performance outcomes, in themselves, do not tell employees what they need to do to increase productivity. For example, a cable TV sales manager told that he failed to sign 500 new accounts in a year's time knows that he fell short of his goal but not what to do about it. What is needed is a clear explanation of what areas of job performance need improvement and the training that may make the improvement achievable.

- Lastly, many objective-based systems aim at reaching several objectives instead of dealing with only one or two meaningful objectives at a time.

For these reasons, MBOs should be combined with other performance appraisal methods to provide a fully detailed description and evaluation of an employee's job behavior.

In fact, there is no one best performance appraisal method. Appraisal systems serve a wide variety of purposes. To meet the many needs of the enterprise, a company may choose to rely on a variety of different performance appraisal methods. On the other hand, whoever is creating a performance appraisal system should never rely on methods such as ranking and trait-rating scales that are based on subjective criteria and allow personal biases to enter into the evaluation process. An employer who wishes to use nonquantitative techniques like narrative essays or critical incidents might also use graphic rating scales to measure job performance. Exhibit 5.4 outlines components critical to a performance appraisal program.

Training Managers

Once the appraisal criteria and methods are selected, managers should be trained in how to conduct effective appraisals in order to reduce rating errors and increase accuracy of evaluation. Ratings can easily become inflated due to leniency, halo error, and a failure to take the time to complete the appraisal properly. A supervisor can be too lenient, too strict, rate everyone as average, or be swayed by situational factors such as the order in which the evaluations are conducted. In the next section, the four most detrimental errors are described and ways to prevent or minimize them illustrated.

Exhibit 5.4: Critical Concepts for a Performance Review

1. Notify employees of the time and place of their review at least a week in advance to allow them time to prepare.
2. Conduct the review in a quiet place to minimize interruptions.
3. Allow employees a chance to rate themselves before the formal review. Give a copy of the performance appraisal form to each employee for completion before the review.
4. Set aside an adequate amount of time to evaluate each employee.
5. Explain to the employee the reason for the annual review and what the results will be used for. Try to clear up any misunderstandings about the review and your role in the process.
6. Be sure that the atmosphere is relaxed. The employee should feel free to make comments and ask questions. However, such a relationship cannot be developed overnight; the process of building a climate of trust and mutual respect should be an ongoing priority.
7. Listen to the employee carefully; be honest about your concerns about performance or lack of performance.
8. Be sure that all decisions about the employee's performance are based on the duties performed, not personal biases.
9. Explain opportunities the employee has to advance in the company.
10. Allow time for the employee to ask questions and make comments.
11. Set up a follow-up time to discuss any salary increase; discussion of salary will interfere with the developmental aspects of the performance appraisal review.
12. Sign the performance appraisal form and ask the employee to sign it. These signatures indicate that the manager has reviewed the performance ratings with the employee.

Central Tendency

Central tendency errors occur when managers consistently rate all their employees as average; they are identified by computing the mean and standard deviation of a supervisor's ratings. A mean rating close to the center of the scale and a low standard deviation warn of a central tendency error.

This error can be avoided in two ways. First, the rater should rank employees before rating them to make it easier to differentiate between good, average, and poor employees. Second, the manager should justify all ratings in writing.

Leniency and Severity

Leniency and severity errors occur when a manager consistently gives all employees favorable (leniency) or unfavorable (severity) ratings. These errors can be identified by computing the average of the ratings across all subordinates. If the average is close to either end of the rating scale, there may be a leniency or severity error. It can be avoided by reducing ambiguity by more clearly defining each of the points on the rating scale so managers can better assess the different levels of employee behavior. This error can also be avoided by enforcing a company policy that requires written justification of ratings.

Halo Errors

Halo errors occur when a rater generalizes a rating of good or bad performance on one dimension of job performance to other dimensions. This error is difficult to correct because it may not be made consistently across all subordinates. The best way to avoid the error is to consider each performance dimension independently and base each rating on specific examples of worker performance.

Contrast Effects

Contrast effects occur when a rater lets extremely bad or extremely good employee evaluations color evaluations of other employees. This is another difficult error to detect; it can best be controlled by not rating all subordinates in one sitting. An evaluator should put some time and distance between ratings so that the glow of the previous evaluation is forgotten and does not adversely affect the next evaluation.

In general, having written justification for all ratings can control the errors described. If the evaluator can provide specific examples of work behavior, and the manager reviews these comments before appraising them, performance appraisal will be more accurate. Extensive training to reduce rating errors is unnecessary.[23] Simply requiring raters to review the descriptions of the different types of possible errors and how to correct them before they rate each employee will give the same results at much less cost than training, in terms of both time and money. However, some training on decision-making and observation is necessary to increase rater accuracy.[24]

---

[23] Landy, F. J., and J. L. Farr. 1983. *The Measurement of Work Performance: Methods, Theory, and Applications.* New York: Academic Press Inc.
[24] Hedge, J. W., and M. J. Kavanagh. 1988. "Improving the Accuracy of Performance Evaluations: Comparison of Three Methods of Performance Appraiser Training." *Journal of Applied Psychology,* 73: 68-73.

Recording Work Behaviors

The next step in the performance appraisal process (see Exhibit 5.1) is to record work behaviors. It may help the supervisor to document employee behavior regularly (e.g., once a week), not just before a scheduled review. This will increase the accuracy of employee appraisals and make them more defensible in court. When recording both good and bad employee behaviors, the supervisor should include the time and date of each incident.

Evaluate Employees

Once work behaviors have been documented, the manager is now ready to begin the evaluation process. It is critical that the manager takes time to prepare for it properly. The four steps in appraisal preparation are:

1. Review each employee's job description, paying close attention to the duties the employee performs. If a particular job duty is no longer needed, the incumbent should be consulted and the necessary changes made.

2. Organize all notes about the employee's performance during the past appraisal period and review any previous performance appraisal report.

3. Meet with top executives to discuss company goals and objectives, as well as how employees will be rated, before conducting any formal review with employees.

4. Clear dates and times of reviews with HR or the manager who is coordinating this activity. Applying the appraisal process consistently across all departments is important.

Keeping good records and monitoring performance regularly is critical to making accurate ratings, especially as the number of employees directly supervised increases. The supervisor should take time out of the workweek to log important employee behaviors, critical or not. In addition to increasing the accuracy of the ratings given and ensuring compliance with the law, these notes are a good tool for feedback.

An effective appraisal system monitors performance year-round. Managers should keep daily records of employee behaviors. Information should be dated and reviewed for employee feedback. This documentation may also be useful when defending such employee actions as dismissal. Also, performance monitoring has a positive and independent effect on employee performance,[25] where it signals to employees the relative importance of the tasks they perform.

The Performance Appraisal Interview

The next element in the performance appraisal process is the feedback interview. This is a key link in the success of any performance appraisal system. In fact, all the work of selecting accurate performance appraisal criteria, goals, and methods can be wasted if the interview is not taken seriously. It connects evaluation of past employee performance with improvement in future performance.

The manager should be pointing out to employees whenever they perform well or poorly. It has been suggested that a formal performance review be conducted quarterly to coincide with required quarterly reports.[26] While quarterly review would allow for more frequent problem-solving and goal adjustment, it could also be too time-consuming and shorten the horizon for planning and goal-setting. It is usually recommended that managers conduct an annual formal performance review of every employee with informal feedback throughout the year. A special evaluation may be conducted at any point if employee work is unsatisfactory or if an employee is being recommended for a special pay raise or promotion that is based on previous work.

For the annual review, the immediate supervisor should conduct the appraisal interview as soon as the evaluation form is completed. Ratings should never be done during the interview because personal interactions and pressures during the interview can easily bias the evaluations.

The interview should also take place at a scheduled time and place. It should never be a spur-of-the-moment event because both parties need to prepare for it. More specifically, the interview should take place during regular working hours in a place that is nonthreatening, comfortable, and free from distractions.

---

[25] Larson, J. R., and C. Callahan. 1990. "Performance Monitoring: How it Affects Work Productivity." *Journal of Applied Psychology*, 75: 530-538.

[26] Odiorne, G. S. 1990. "The Trend Toward the Quarterly Performance Review." *Business Horizons*, July-August: 38-41.

The annual review or performance appraisal interview can be difficult for managers because they must act as judges. It is equally disturbing to employees because their work is being scrutinized. The research in the area of performance appraisal interviews also suggests the potential for other problems, including:[27]

- Employees may be more concerned about where they stand after the interview than before.

- Some subordinates never realize that a performance appraisal interview has taken place.

- Employees may rate their supervisors less favorably after the interview than before.

- Subordinates generally feel that supervisors act in an autocratic manner.

- Few cases of improvement were cited after the interview had taken place.

Evaluation of the Performance Appraisal System

A performance management program must be evaluated. A program that is not accomplishing its goals should be discontinued or changed or company resources will be wasted. On the other hand, even if the program is found to be successful, it may need fine-tuning for the long run. Therefore, no systematic model of performance appraisal should be without a component individual that evaluates its cognitive, affective, behavioral, and strategic elements. Here are some representative evaluation questions:

- Do employees accurately perceive feedback during the performance appraisal interview? (cognitive component)

- Do employees react favorably to the feedback immediately following the interview? (affective component)

- Is there a change in performance over the next performance appraisal period? (behavioral component)

- Are organizational goals fulfilled? (strategic component)

---

[27] Cederblom, D. 1982. "The Performance Appraisal Interview: Review, Implications, and Suggestions." *Academy of Management Review*, 7: 219-227.

Feedback about job performance is an essential component of any performance appraisal system that has employee development and change as a goal. Unfortunately, employees often report that no feedback was given in the interview or that the feedback was inaccurate.[28] These problems may result from a supervisor's authoritarian style,[29] inability to convey the feedback, the importance or unimportance of the feedback given, or the subordinate's lack of attention. Whatever the cause of a feedback problem, it must be corrected if the program is to succeed.

Five procedures can ease evaluation of the success of the performance appraisal program:

1. The manager should review all appraisals.

2. A formal grievance and review procedure for complaints about any part of the performance appraisal system should be implemented. The number and type of grievances received is a good indicator of employee acceptance of the program.

3. Employees should be surveyed about how they perceive the performance appraisal system. Specifically, the survey should attempt to measure rating accuracy and fairness, quality of feedback, and overall appraisal satisfaction. Suggestions provided by employees could help improve the system for the next appraisal period.

4. Overall employee performance changes should be assessed. If performance appraisal results are effectively linked to rewards, improvement should result. If not, there is a defect in the system.

5. Improvements in quality and quantity of output should be sought.

Performance appraisal is an ongoing process that needs fine-tuning yearly. A company that implements a performance appraisal program and does not evaluate its effectiveness runs the risk of alienating rather than motivating employees. Trust in the program is essential. Employee participation in all steps of the process helps build and sustain that trust and makes the enterprise more productive.

[28] French, J. R. P. Jr., E. Kay, and H. H. Meyer. 1966. "Participation and the Appraisal System." *Human Relations*, 19: 3-20.
[29] Maier, N. 1976. *The Appraisal Interview: Three Basic Approaches*. La Jolla, CA: University Associates.

WRAP-UP

Informal or formal, the primary goal of the performance appraisal is to provide feedback to employees about their job performance. The feedback should motivate each employee to continue doing a good job or to take corrective action to improve performance. However, regardless of the specific components of a system, employee perceptions of the appraisal system will affect its effectiveness.[30] The process described in this chapter should positively influence these perceptions.

Motivation and change are the central themes of the performance appraisal. The supervisor or rater seeks to motivate employees to perform at their highest level, and also to guide them toward this level. A performance appraisal is a continuous process, not an isolated occurrence. An informal performance appraisal occurs daily or weekly as the supervisor observes employee job behavior and performance. If the process is working effectively, informal evaluation, in the form of comments, constructive criticism, praise and suggestions, will provide the basis for a more formal evaluation.

All employees are accountable for performing their jobs in accordance with specific job duty standards and criteria. The desired level of performance must be clearly understood by both manager and employee before performance appraisals can be effective. It is critical to the success of any performance appraisal system that employees and supervisors understand what will be measured and evaluated, who will evaluate, when formal appraisal will occur, what assistance will be provided to improve performance, what the employee's role is, and what are the rewards for exceptional performance.

Finally, while formal appraisals are generally conducted yearly, weekly feedback to employees can go a long way in enhancing two-way communication and trust between manager and employee.[31] An example of an effective performance appraisal instrument can be found in Appendix A.

---

[30] Mohrman, A. M., and E. E. Lawler. 1981. "Improving the Contextual Fit of Appraisal Systems." Paper presented at the 89th Annual Convention of the American PsychologicalAssociation, Los Angeles, August.

[31] Keary, D. 2003. "Make Performance Appraisal Part of your Weekly Routine." *HR Tools*, Society for Human Resource Management.
www.shrm.org/managingsmart/articles/spring03/0403b.asp. Accessed 18, March 04.

CHAPTER 6

Employee Relations: Effective Development, Coaching, and Discipline

Without good manager-worker relations, employee motivation and productivity will decline along with satisfaction. While front-line managers may be the most directly involved in employee relations, they may find themselves without the needed experience, skills, or information

Skills a manager needs to keep employees happy include delegating responsibility, establishing strategic direction, making operational decisions promptly, building trust, and communicating effectively. They also need to know what their own supervisors expect of them as far as employee relations are concerned. Assuming they are aware of the specifics is a common mistake.

Managers should be trained in how to communicate effectively with staff—how to provide constructive feedback, respond to employee suggestions, deal with conflict, and especially share information with employees.[1]

THE MANAGER'S CHALLENGE

Whether the issue is improving employee skills or modifying employee behavior to conform to company policies, managers need systematic

---

[1] Much of the preceding material is drawn from Lin Grensing-Pophal, "7 Steps for Building Strong Manager/Employee Relations." *SHRM White Paper,* September 14, 2003. *www.shrm.org/hrresources/whitepapers_published/CMS_000392.asp.* Accessed 18 May 2004 (members only).

procedures to get the change needed. Training, discipline, and coaching are a true test of a manager's interpersonal skills. Managers are often called on to be a teacher or an enforcer without having the knowledge and tools they need to be effective.

Training is time-consuming and expensive. Employees are taken from their regular work, consultants/trainers may be hired to create and deliver training, and internal staff may have to administer and deliver the training effort. However, even if its direct and indirect costs are high, training is necessary for the viability of any growing organization. Managers should not chase the latest fad but assess their own needs, tailor programs to their employees, and evaluate training to be sure it is achieving its objectives. Training is an investment that will pay substantial dividends if it is done right.

Employee discipline has a negative connotation to most managers and supervisors. Where the pace is fast, employee discipline is especially problematic because there is little time to do it right. The situation is particularly awkward for newly promoted managers who must supervise former co-workers.

An unwritten rule in HR management is *document, document, docu - ment!* When a discipline decision adversely affects an employee, the company must have the necessary paper trail to prove that steps were taken in accordance with company policy and the employee handbook and that the measures taken were was consistent with those taken with others who committed similar policy violations. If the documentation is not complete, the company might find itself called to an unemployment hearings or sued for violation of employment-at-will doctrine or even employment discrimination. Poor supervision is often cited as a major cause of unionization efforts in the United States. Employers who take a positive and proactive approach to discipline generally report less turnover, improved management relations, and higher morale.

A DIAGNOSTIC APPROACH TO EMPLOYEE TRAINING AND DEVELOPMENT

Employee training and development activities can help corporations acquire a work force with the proper combination of skills and motivation a company needs to be competitive. Training affects an employer's ability to be flexible and to adapt quickly to changes in the environment. All in all, employee training is vital for ensuring organizational survival and growth. Unfortunately, many corporations are uncoordinated and inconsistent in their approach to training, even though U.S. companies spend close to $60 billion annually on such programs.[2] When, as often happens, training programs are not designed to fit the needs of individual employees, they are not geared to the strategic needs of the corporation.

The umbrella phrase "training and development" represents three different types of activities: (1) orienting new employees, (2) helping employees acquire new skills, and (3) helping them strengthen existing skills:

- *Orientation* refers to the training that introduces a new employee to the company and the job. It usually covers an overview of the organization and its policies and procedures, an outline of the compensation and benefits program, safety information, and a tour of the physical facilities.[3, 4]

- *Training* refers to a systematic effort by an organization to facilitate the learning of job-related knowledge, skills, and abilities.

- *Development* refers to the acquisition of knowledge, skills, and abilities that enhance an employee's performance.

The word *training* will be used in what follows to cover all three types of activities.

In 2001, U.S. employers spent some $57 billion dollars on all forms of training.[5] This amount underlines the importance companies place on training and development. However, very few organizations systematically analyze their training effort to use their training dollars more effectively. This chapter will discuss the major components of a systematic training and development program by presenting a diagnostic tool that helps organizations make their training more effective.

[2] "Industry Report 1998." *Training,* 35: 43-45.
[3] Premeaux, S. R., and R. W. Mondy. 1998. *Supervision,* 3rd ed. Eagan, MN: Thomson Custom Publishing; Premeaux, S. R. 1989. "The Need for Discipline." *Supervisory Management,* March: 39-41.
[4] Wexley, K. N., and G. P. Latham. 1997. *Developing and Training Human Resources in Organizations,* 2nd ed. Menlo Park, CA: Addison Wesley Longman Inc.
[5] Galvin, T. 2001. "The Money." *Training,* 38: 42-27.

The Goldstein Model is a well-known diagnostic approach for establishing a training program.[6] The model has three phases:

1. *Needs assessment* has two stages: (a) the needs assessment itself and (b) deriving training program objectives from it.

2. *Actual training* consists of (a) instructional design and (b) conducting the training.

3. *Evaluation* has five stages: (a) develop criteria; (b) pretest trainees; (c) monitor the actual training; (d) evaluate the training itself; and (e) evaluate how well the training transferred information.

All three phases of the Goldstein Model (see Exhibit 6.1) are discussed in detail below.

Needs Assessment

While the organization is responsible for providing an environment that encourages change, it is the employee's responsibility to take advantage of the learning opportunities that are provided. No matter how reliable selection and placement procedures are, there will be changes inside and outside of the organization that create a need for improvement. The needs assessment phase is the foundation of training. To conduct a needs assessment:

• Establish development objectives.

• Analyze the existing climate for change.

• Feed results back to management.

• Secure top management commitment to development objectives and to improving organizational practices that conflict with them.

• Secure top management participation in program design.

Especially where there is no formal training, it is necessary to discover what areas have deficiencies that call for training. Where there is a formal program, the first step is to analyze it to assess whether organizational goals are being met and how the program interacts with other organizational systems.

---

[6] Goldstein, I. L. 1993. *Training in Organizations,* 3rd ed. Pacific Grove, CA: Brooks/Cole Publishing Company; Goldstein, I. L. 1974. *Training: Program Development and Evaluation.* Thomson/Wadsworth Publishing Company, Inc.; Goldstein, I. L., and K. Ford. 2000. *Training in Organizations,* 4th ed. Thomson/Wadsworth Publishing Company, Inc., Course Technology, Inc.

Exhibit 6.1: Goldstein Systematic Training Model

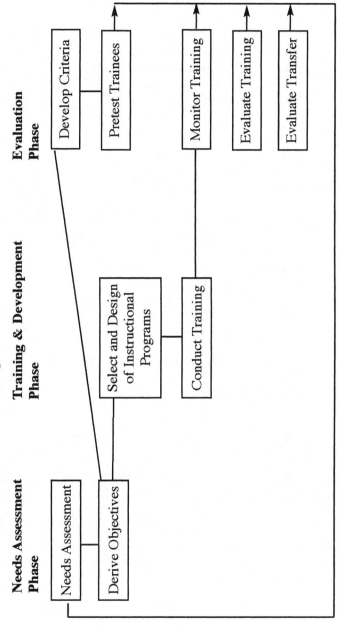

Adapted from Goldstein, I. L. 1974. *Training: Program Development and Evaluation.* Thomson/Wadsworth Publishing Company, Inc. and Golstein, I. L. 1993. *Training in Organizations*, 2nd ed. Pacific Grove, CA: Brooks/Cole Publishing Co.

After the analysis, training needs should be incorporated into clearly stated training objectives. The assessment of instructional need is the foundation for all aspects of training. Both actual training and evaluation depend on the results of the needs assessment, which builds on three types of analysis: (1) organization, (2) task, and (3) person.

An *organizational analysis* begins with looking at the short- and long-term goals of the organization. It moves on to consider the company's structure, strategy, and systems; the work to be done; and the norms and values that guide how individuals perform within the organization.[7] An organizational analysis that is incomplete or improperly completed will cause problems for the company down the road. Exhibit 6.2 lists basic questions that an organizational analysis should answer.

Exhibit 6.2: Questions to Ask in an Organizational Analysis

1. Are there unspecified organizational goals that should be translated into training objectives or criteria?
2. Are all levels in the organization committed to the training objectives?
3. Have all levels and interacting units in the organization participated in developing the program?
4. Are key personnel ready both to accept the behavior of the trainees and to serve as models of appropriate behaviors?
5. Will trainees be rewarded on the job for using the appropriate learned behavior?
6. Is training being used as a way to overcome other organizational problems or organizational conflicts that require other types of solutions?
7. Is top management willing to commit the necessary resources to keep work moving forward while individuals are being trained?

Source: Goldstein, I. L. 1993. *Training in Organizations,* 2nd ed. Pacific Grove, CA: Brooks/Cole Publishing Co.

The second step of the needs assessment is to conduct a *task analysis* to determine the requirements of the job for which training is needed. This begins with the job description incorporating the incumbent's duties and

---

[7] Mailick, S., S. J. Hoberman, and S. Wall. 1988. *The Practice of Management Development.* New York: Praeger Publishers.

conditions specific to the job,[8] as well as specifications for the tasks required to perform the job. For each task on the complete list, there must be information about what the worker does, how the worker does it, for whom or what, and why, plus information about the KSAs that are essential to the tasks. At this point it may be beneficial to interview job incumbents or their supervisors to gain insight into the full spectrum of tasks and KSAs for that particular job. (See Chapter 3 for a complete description of the job analysis process.) Exhibit 6.3 lists basic information a task analysis should address.

Exhibit 6.3: Task Analysis Information

1. Describe the characteristics of employees who perform this task well, and of those who perform it poorly.
2. Think of someone you know who is better than anyone else at this tasks and find out why.
3. What does a person need to know in order to do this task?
4. Ask a panel to recall concrete examples of effective or ineffective performance; then lead a discussion to explain causes or reasons.
5. If you are hiring a person to perform this tasks, what kind of knowledge, skills, and abilities (KSAs) would you look for?
6. What can persons learn in training that would make them effective at this tasks?[9]

Source: Mailick, S., S. J. Hoberman, and S. Wall. 1988. *The Practice of Management Development.* New York: Praeger Publishers.

All the information gathered is vital to ensure that training programs are job-specific and useful.

A *person analysis* can be conducted in two different ways: (1) comparing an evaluation of employee proficiency on each required skill dimension with the proficiency level required for each skill, or (2) comparing actual performance with the minimum acceptable standards of performance. The first method can be used to identify development needs for future jobs, the second method to determine training needs for current jobs because it is based on how an employee actually performs the job.

Other methods used to evaluate a person's training needs are *self-assessment* and an *attitude survey*. Self-assessment is based on the theory

---

[8] Ibid.
[9] Ibid.

that because employees are aware of their own weaknesses, they are best suited to decide whether they need training. Self-assessment can be as informal as simply posting a list of training activities for optional sign-up or as formal as completing a survey.

An attitude survey gives management information about services needed; it can also reveal employee deficiencies. The survey is usually completed by employees or customers. Attitude surveys help point out problems but they do not recommend solutions. The Supervisor Satisfaction Scale[10] shown in Exhibit 6.4 is typical; it assesses three necessary supervisory skills: (1) technical, (2) human relations, and (3) administrative.

Exhibit 6.4: Supervisor Satisfaction Scale

Please indicate how satisfied you are with your supervisor. Using the following scale, next to each item write the number that best represents your degree of satisfaction with that particular aspect of supervisory behavior.

Very Dissatisfied				Very Satisfied
1	2	3	4	5

1. The way supervisor listens when I have something important to say.
2. The way my supervisor sets clear work goals.
3. The way my supervisor treats me when I make a mistake.
4. My supervisor's fairness in appraising my job performance.
5. The way my supervisor is consistent in his or her behavior toward subordinates.
6. The way my supervisor helps me to get the job done.
7. The way my supervisor gives me credit for my ideas.
8. The way my supervisor gives me clear instructions.
9. The way my supervisor informs me about work changes ahead of time.
10. The way my supervisor follows through to get problems solved.
11. The way my supervisor understands the job problems I might run into.
12. The way my supervisor shows concern for my career progress.
13. The way my supervisor backs me up with other management.
14. The frequency with which I get a pat on the back for doing a good job.
15. The technical competence of my supervisor.

Source: Ledvinka, J., and V. Scarpello. 1991. *Federal Regulation of Personnel and Human Resource Management,* Boston, MA: PWS-Kent Publishing Co.

---

[10] Gulbinas-Scarpello, V. G., J. Ledvinka, and T. J. Bergmann. 1995. *Human Resource Management, Environments and Functions,* 2nd ed. Cincinnati: South-Western Publishing; Ledvinka, J., and V. G. Scarpello. 1991. *Federal Regulation of Personnel and Human Resource Management,* Boston, MA: PWS-Kent Publishing Co.

Trainers have noticed that often, though trainees are able to learn, they are not motivated to learn. One way to add motivation is for them to help assess the training process. Some adult learning theorists believe, though the evidence is scant, that people only learn what they want to learn, which is why they conclude that trainee involvement in selecting training programs can be a motivator to learn.[11]

Formulate Objectives

Once training needs are clear, specific objectives can be formulated. Training objectives can be stated in terms of *behaviors* or *operations:*

- Behavioral objectives are actions, movements, or behaviors that are observable and measurable.

- Operational objectives are expected results, such as lowering the cost of producing widgets by 5 percent by May 1, 2004.

These instructional objectives are based on the KSAs the trainee will have when training is completed. The more precise the objectives, the more likely the success of the organization.

Instruction and Training

The training phase consists of designing the instructional programs and conducting the training. Instructional design includes selecting learning principles and using appropriate training media.

Learning principles take into account behavioral modeling, the meaningfulness of the material, practice, feedback, individual differences, and transfer of training to the job. Selecting media depends on whether the training is on or off the job. It is important to conduct training in the environment best suited to the teaching techniques being used.

Instructional Design

The main objective of the training process is to promote efficient learning, long-term retention, and the ability to apply and transfer skills or factual information learned in training back to the job. To ensure that skills are learned, such traditional techniques as goal-setting, behavior modeling,

---

[11] Baldwin, T. T., R. J. Magjuka, and B. T. Loner. 1991. "The Perils of Participation: Effects of Choice Training on Trainee Motivation and Learning." *Personnel Psychology,* 44: 51-65.

practice, and feedback are useful. To ensure that facts are learned, it is necessary to use goal-setting, meaningful instructional material, practice, and feedback.

Motivation clearly plays a part in training,[12] and goal-setting is considered an important part of motivation, on the theory that conscious goals or intentions govern the behavior of individuals. To achieve a desired behavior, objectives must be set that are clear, concise, and within a specific time frame.[13] For example, "within two weeks, you will be able to assemble a widget to desired standards within two hours using correct step-by-step procedures, given the right machinery and electricity or other necessary equipment."

Goals should be challenging and difficult but obtainable if trainees are to achieve personal satisfaction. Difficult, yet obtainable, goals raise the level of performance. People will accept and work hard to attain difficult goals right up to the limits of their capabilities. If goals become too difficult, however, they may be rejected and performance will suffer.[14]

During training, informal check points, such as quizzes and evaluations, should be used to let employees feel successful or enable them to see areas that need improvement if the final goal is to be reached. Also, to increase trainee motivation, trainers must have and express their expectations and clearly want and encourage the employees to perform better.

Many employees learn by observing others through *behavior modeling* of specific successful behaviors. The trainer should also use a reward system to elicit the desired behavior. Training should move from simple to complex tasks, using repetition to encourage retention. The use of several models rather than just one helps trainees to learn because people learn in different ways. Trainees should always rehearse what has been demonstrated. There should always be a question-and-answer time for feedback and rewards.[15]

---

[12] Baron, R. A., and J. Greenberg. 1999. *Behavior in Organizations—Understanding and Managing the Human Side of Work,* 7th ed. Old Tappan, NJ: Prentice Hall.

[13] Mirabile, R. J. 1991. "Pinpointing Development Needs." *Training & Development,* 45(12): 19-25.

[14] Locke, E. A., and G. P. Latham. 1984. *Goal Setting for Individuals, Groups, and Organizations,* Chicago: Science Research Association.

[15] Baron and Greenberg, op. cit., n. 12.

Material that is meaningful to the trainee is more easily remembered. To maximize the learning process by making the material meaningful, the instructor must start with an overview of the content. Next, the material should be presented using down-to-earth examples, terms, and concepts. Key learning points should be reinforced. The training design itself should identify all essential components of a task if the desirable behavior is to be achieved.[16] It is also important to ensure that tasks are accomplished in their entirety and that connections from one component of the task to another are logical.

Practice is an essential component of any program designed to teach a new skill.[17] The training specialist should observe trainees practicing and give them recommendations to improve their skill. Because observed trainee behavior takes time, the instructor-trainee ratio should be low. If a task becomes second nature, it is said to be over-learned, which has several advantages:

- The training material is retained longer,
- The learned behavior becomes automatic even under stressful situations, and
- Transfer of the training to the job situations is facilitated.[18]

Practice is more effective if it is distributed over several periods rather than massed because continuous practice causes fatigue, which in turn leads to poorer performance.[19] Schedule breaks throughout the day, which should on no account last more than eight hours.

Feedback is essential; it increases trainee motivation. Feedback provides direct information so the trainee can make adjustments and reinforces correct behavior.[20] The trainer should always emphasize when and how the trainee performs correctly, immediately after the trainee's action. Success in achieving a desired behavior, reinforced by comments from the trainer,

---

[16] Ibid.

[17] Schendel, J. D., and J. D. Hagman. 1982. "On Sustaining Procedural Skills Over a Prolonged Retention Interval." *Journal of Applied Psychology,* 67: 605-610.

[18] Baron and Greenberg, op. cit., n. 12.

[19] Rothenberg, R. G., and T. R. Drye. 1991. "Train 700 People in Quality? No Problem." *Training & Development,* 45(12): 43-46.

[20] Mirabile, op. cit, n. 13.

increases the willingness of the trainee to learn. Specific goal-setting also helps maintain performance.[21]

The impact of training on job performance can be positive, negative, or neutral. Trainers must use long-term techniques and periodically retrain to reinforce information gained earlier. To *transfer training* in a positive manner, trainers should maximize the similarity between the training situation and job satisfaction; give trainees time to practice; give examples; ensure that principles are understood; design the training so that the trainee can easily see how it applies on the job; set goals together with the trainee; and, lastly, reward the trainee when the correct behavior has been transferred to the job. Supervisors and top management should aid in the reinforcement process.

Selecting Training Media

The choice of learning methods must take into account individual learning objectives, the education and experience of the audience, the personal style of the instructor, how the learning principles will be used to achieve the objectives of the organization, time, and cost.[22] A trainer should never choose—or refuse to choose—a method solely because it has been used in the past. Trainers may choose to combine methods based on well-founded learning theory and more advanced technology.

Employee training can take many forms, some very simple and others quite complex. The techniques may differ depending on whether the training takes place on the job or off. On-the-job methods give trainee hands-on experience; they are often more effective than more formal approaches because transfer of knowledge and experience to the job is immediate. Off-the-job methods may be best used to support on-the-job training. Exhibit 6.5 analyzes both types of training methods.

A needs analysis is useful in deciding to use specific on-the-job and off-the-job training methods because it is the basis for defining what needs to be taught. The methods chosen should accomplish the following:

- Motivate the trainee to improve or change to the desired performance.
- Clearly illustrate the desired skills.

---

[21] Rothenberg and Drye, op. cit., n. 19.

[22] Laird, D. 1990. *Approaches to Training and Development,* 2nd ed. Reading, MA: Addison-Wesley Publishing Company, Inc.

Exhibit 6.5: Training Methods

Training Method	Description
On-the-Job Methods	
Orientation	A clear understanding of the specific obligations of the company and employee is established. Employees are introduced to company policies and to the people they will work with.
Apprenticeship programs	An inexperienced trainee works alongside a senior co-worker for a certain number of years; often accompanied by formal classroom training; used to train skilled trade workers (e.g., carpenters, electricians).
Job instruction training	Trainees are told about the job, instructed on how to do it, allowed to try out the job, given feedback, and then permitted to work on their own (with someone nearby to help, if needed).
Coaching	The supervisor provides a periodic review of performance to improve communication and provides a framework for job improvement.
Mentoring	A senior employee teaches the new employee the "ropes" of the organization.
Job Aids	Instructional material is at the job site to help employees recall important information presented during training.
Off-the-Job Methods	
Lectures	Information is communicated in a one-way channel from the expert to the receiver. Problems can occur in transfer of training to the job.
Programmed instruction	A self-instructional method where the trainee gets evaluation of success at specific intervals; trainees are given feedback about the accuracy of responses and move through the information at their own pace.
Film/video presentations	Complex procedures not easily demonstrated in person may be shown on film or videotape. Because questions cannot be asked, presentations are often part of a live lecture by a knowledgeable trainer.
Teleconferencing	Learners participate in remote classrooms via satellite or telephone technology. Organizations no longer have to pay to develop in-house training programs.
Simulations	Simulations may range from the simplest procedures, such as cases and role-playing exercises used to train managers in interpersonal skills, to the complex computer-assisted simulations used to train astronauts for space flights.

- Give the trainee adequate participation and practice.
- Provide feedback and reinforce desired behaviors.
- Show how to adapt to change and handle problems as they arise.
- Be structured to go from simple to complex tasks or behaviors.
- Encourage the trainee so that positive training is transferred to the job situation.

Conducting the Training

The type of learning and the training materials selected will determine the environment in which the training will take place. Some organizations have designated training rooms; others must find the space (internal or external) themselves, which may take much planning. The trainer must ensure that the setting is similar enough to the work environment so that the trainee will transfer the skills learned to the job. A checklist a trainer should go through before training begins is shown in Exhibit 6.6.

Evaluation Phase

The first two phases of Goldstein's Model explain the actual steps in training, but to replicate them effectively, evaluation is necessary at every step. Evaluation can be defined as a process of appraising something carefully to determine its value.[23]

During the actual training phase, content, methods of training, instructional supplements, and environment are selected with a view to completion of company goals. Nevertheless, it does not matter how much consideration, planning, and attention goes into the process unless there is a way to evaluate whether training is, in practice, achieving its goals. Too, procedures and attitudes change as time passes, so to keep a training and development program viable, updating is imperative.

The four types of evaluation are: (1) reactions, (2) learning, (3) behavior, and (4) results:

1. Checking participant *reactions* is the easiest form of evaluation. This type usually consists of surveying trainees' feelings about important elements of the training program itself.

---

[23] Sredl, H. J., and W. J. Rothwell. 1987. *The ASTD Reference Guide to Professional Training Roles & Competencies,* Vols. I & II. Amherst, MA: HRD Press, Inc.

Exhibit 6.6: Instructor Preparation Checklist

Have you:
1. Followed appropriate steps to publicize your program?
2. Included the time, location, and subject matter on your announcement?
3. Arranged in advance the equipment to conduct your program?
    a. Seating arrangement
    b. Refreshments
    c. Podium
    d. Storage place for coats, purses, bags
    e. Appropriate temperature and lighting
    f. Laptops, cables, wires, Internet connections
    g. Dry-erase board or easel with paper, dry-erase markers, erasers
    h. Projection screen or empty wall
    i. Blank notepads and pens and pencils
    j. Adequate copies of handouts, books, visual aids
    k. Comfortable seating
4. Completed a dry run of the session to check that all equipment is in working order?
5. Written an agenda or course content handout?
    a. Include adequate breaks or meal times?
    b. Work in extra time for discussions to run over.
    c. Include student participation
    d. Leave time for a Q & A session.
6. Anticipated possible problems and ways to resolve the issues?
7. Minimize distractions while conducting the program

2. *Learning evaluations* assess whether or not the participant has learned the ideas, facts, or processes taught.

3. *Behavior evaluations* look at whether participants have incorporated learned facts and processes into their job—the first step in assessing how well training is transferred.

4. Finally, *results evaluations* measure bottom-line results, such as increased sales or decreased mistakes. Results evaluations are most effective for evaluating transfer of training to actual job behaviors.

A report to the American Society for Training and Development[24] criticized the lack of results-driven training evaluation. Managers are under increasing pressure to move away from simply measuring reactions (if they even do that) to tying training results to company performance. Given the costs of training programs, it simply is not enough to say that participants "liked" the training or "learned a lot." The real question is whether the information provided or skills learned are transferred to the job and cause the desired improvement in performance and ultimately productivity and profits.

Exhibit 6.7 lists important questions to be considered when evaluating training programs.

Exhibit 6.7: Evaluation Checklist

1. Was the needs assessment correctly accomplished?
2. Did the needs assessment correctly identify the training needs?
3. Are the objectives of the program correct?
4. Is the choice of trainees for the program on target?
5. Is the training content being delivered and received as intended?
6. Do the trainees actually apply the skills during the training?
7. Do the trainees transfer to the workplace the skills learned at the program?
8. Are the trainees achieving the performance goals they have established?

Source: Bienbrauer, H. 1987. "Trouble-Shooting Your Training Program." *Training and Development Journal,* September: 18-20.

There are six important steps to the entire training evaluation process, using the questions in Exhibit 6.7:

1. Draw up criteria.

2. Pretest trainees.

[24] Bassi, L. J., and M. E. VanBuren. 1999. "The 1999 ASTD State of the Industry Report." *Training and Development Journal,* Supplement: 1-26.

3. Monitor the training.

4. Do a preliminary evaluation of the training process.

5. Evaluate how well the information was transferred to the job.

6. Give trainers and instructional designers feedback.

Draw up Criteria

Instructional designers and instructors are involved throughout the first two phases of the Goldstein Model, and it is just as important for these same personnel to help identify the criteria for evaluation. This helps enable designers to look at the training from the point of view of what is important to the participants.

It is also important to identify potential problems with language, clarity, difficulty, design, and interest level, all in terms of the training objectives,[25] to make sure the training has credibility in the real world. If participants perceive no real application benefits from training, their interest, and therefore their retention, will be low.

Several factors weaken training results, among them the design and delivery of the training, the motivation and background of the trainees, and the environment within which trainees work.[26] If the previous phases have been accomplished competently, evaluation should be fairly easy, because specific criteria will track training program objectives.

Pretest Trainees

Pretesting enables designers and instructors to understand where a lack of training is causing employees to perform below par. The intention of pretesting is to evaluate the necessity for further training and how well employees accept new ideas and methods.

To better evaluate pretest results, objective testing is preferred to subjective. In determining content of the pretest, the program will benefit from more specific tasks and tests that measure KSAs. Competency tests before actual training are gaining acceptance because they seem to increase the motivation of participants, who perceive that a testing hurdle will also have to be passed at the end of training. Potential trainees might complete

---

[25] Connolly, S. M. 1988. "Integrating Evaluation, Design & Implementation." *Training and Development Journal,* February: 20-23.

[26] Ban, C., and S. R. Faerman. 1990. "Issues in the Evaluation of Management Training." *Public Productivity & Management Review,* Spring: 271-285.

questionnaires at their work stations some time before the actual training is implemented to reduce the anxiety of a test environment. This also enables trainees to become familiar with the types of training that will be offered and perceive their value before the actual training takes place.

A case study by Ban and Faerman for the New York State's Advanced Human Resources Development Program[27] shows that trainee variables like age, sex, education, years of service, years in current position, bargaining unit, grade level, previous training courses attended, and span of control had a significant relationship with the level of change. Respondents who scored lower on the pretest showed more improvement after training; those scoring higher lost retention of material much faster.

Supervisors should be consulted about employee participation. A pre-training questionnaire might also be completed by the supervisor to get a better idea of the needs of each participant. Participants should meet with supervisors to ascertain areas for further training and discuss what training might lead to advancement within the organization. Jointly, the participant and supervisor should be able to determine an appropriate area of training that responds to the participant's abilities, motivation, and determination to complete the training satisfactorily.

The difference between desired and actual performance will be the basis for identifying the employee's training needs. It is not advisable to train an employee who is already performing adequately and does not desire a change in position for which additional knowledge would be needed.

Monitor Training

It is important to monitor training to keep on top of changes or deficiencies within the training program. To continue to offer pertinent information, trainers should establish a systematic procedure for periodically collecting and documenting feedback from designers and subject matter experts (SMEs) for the duration of the program.

Trainers can also monitor participants to see whether they are acquiring the needed KSAs by periodically testing throughout the program. How often a test should be administered will depend on the length of the program. Areas to be addressed in monitoring training are:

- Trainees' perceived need for information on the subject

---

[27] Ibid.

- The trainer's ability to convey information
- How reasonable is the organization and sequence of subject material
- Time allocated for trainees to absorb information
- Quality of training materials, equipment, and strategies
- Facilities and logistics
- Ease of transportation to the training site
- Administration and management of the training program[28]

Midcourse evaluations help an instructor determine whether the class is meeting specified needs; if not, midcourse corrections can be made. Also, instructors will be able to elicit information about how well participants comprehend the material. If particular employees experience a problem, the instructor can place them back on track by meeting with them individually. This method also conveys the instructor's commitment to making the class work for the participant.

Evaluate the Training
Goal setting gives direction to the training program and clearly affects employee motivation to meet the expectations of the trainer. The higher the expectations, the more likely the participant will do well during the training course. Of course, the reason for attending a training course is to perform better on the job, so job expectations, and the goals set, must be reasonable and attainable. Participants and supervisors should work together to ascertain what goals to establish for the present and near future.

Many evaluators emphasize the necessity of objective behavioral measures of training, but many organizations do not have the resources to do this through direct observation. If they do, surveys using detailed and specific items that describe a wide range of actual job behaviors will allow the observer to draw more definite conclusions about behavior. Using both closed- and open-ended questionnaires on participants' reactions to the program, instructors should collect data from participants at the end of the course, including:

- Importance and relevance of content
- Value of exercises

---

[28] Connolly, op. cit., n. 26.

- Pace and length of the program
- Quality of materials
- Quality of instruction

Because multiple sources of data are critical, once the participant questionnaires are completed, in-depth interviews with trainees and supervisors should be used to verify the information.

Though end-of-course questionnaires may be subjective and are viewed as a weak evaluation tool, they can be a useful initial measurement of participant reactions to training. The rule of thumb is to keep them short and simple.[29]

Training must be evaluated by systematically, documenting outcomes in terms of how trainees actually behave back on their jobs and how relevant the trainees'behavior is to the objectives of the organization. The four basic questions for assessing the value of a training program are:

1. Did change occur?

2. Is the change due to training?

3. Is the change positively related to the achievement of organizational goals?

4. Will similar changes occur with new participants in the same training program?

Evaluating whether change is temporary or lasting is difficult. Although participants follow different patterns once training is over, it is quite common to see continual improvement over time, and a noticeable early improvement that is followed by a sharp drop-off almost to the pertaining level of performance.

Where participants do not acquire the KSAs, retraining may be a viable solution. Designers and instructors alike must also recognize that some employees are not trainable and further training efforts would be a waste of resources.

Evaluate How Well Training is Transferred
Three- to twelve-months after a training course, learning retention, application of training on the job, and organizational impact should be evaluated.

---

[29] Ibid.

A supervisor can observe on-the-job applications and express evaluations through reports and performance appraisals. If training was closely related to on-the-job expectations, performance appraisals should show an increase in ability. The instructor may occasionally visit the work site to ascertain how successful the transfer of information was and to clarify any questions the employee has, thereby reinforcing the learning process.

If the trainee fails to transfer training to the workplace, the trainer must ask whether the instruction was sound. If the failure is not within the program, the work environment should be examined to see whether circumstances beyond the employee's control are at play.

To successfully transfer training, employees must be motivated to apply their new knowledge and skills to the actual job and the environment must be flexible enough to accept the change. Employees returning to a hostile, nonreceptive atmosphere may institute the change initially but will not continue the practice, so post-training evaluation will show no real change in performance.

Employees are also motivated to continue to apply knowledge and skills learned when they know they will be asked to complete a questionnaire or submit to observation on the job at some point after training. This technique may be used effectively to encourage employees to take their training opportunities seriously.

TRENDS IN TRAINING

Almost 15 years ago in their article "Training System Issues in the Year 2000,"[30] Goldstein and Gilliam suggested that training must adapt to four major trends:

1. Changes in the demographic characteristics of persons entering the work force;

2. Increased technology in the world of work;

3. Shifts from manufacturing to service-oriented jobs; and

4. The increased influence of international markets.

---

[30] Goldstein, I. L., and P. Gilliam. 1990. "Training Issues in the Year 2000." *American Psychologist,* 45: 134-142.

All of these imply a need to continually readapt training to new situations. In addition, a survey of training experts identified many critical training issues. The top 10, in order, were:

1. Soft skills, such as leadership, supervisory skills, customer service, team-building, and ability to head off sexual harassment.

2. Technical skills related to computers and information technology.

3. Enhancing the quality of training through improved instructional design, better instructors, and improved needs analysis.

4. Business skills related to finance, marketing, and manufacturing.

5. Business alignment issues making it necessary to better relate training to company strategy and return on investment (ROI).

6. On-line learning using both ready-made and custom courses.

7. Sales training, including product training and sales process skills.

8. Safety compliance training to adhere to federal, state, and local rules.

9. Performance management for managers to effectively handle changing behaviors in the workplace.

10. HR-related training, including orientation, employee development and career planning.[31]

The trends cited by Goldstein and Gilliam continue apace. Advances in Internet training has increased the availability of training to many who otherwise would not be able to receive it. The use of teams has increased dramatically, bringing with it demand for team-based training in communication and joint problem-solving and decision-making.[32]

Front-line supervision is an area of great concern for training professionals. Too often, people are thrown into management positions and expected to learn on the job. The lack of formal preparation can cause employee morale problems, increased turnover, and legal problems like discrimination and harassment.[33]

---

[31] Hall, B. 2003. "The Top Training Priorities for 2003." *Training,* February: 36-39.

[32] Johnson, C. 1999. "Teams at Work: Getting the Best from Teams Requires Work on the Teams Themselves." *HR Magazine,* 44: 30-36.

[33] Segal, J. A. 1996. "Sexual Harassment: Where Are We Now?" *HR Magazine,* 41: 69-73.

Several other changes should be considered as we move deeper into the new century:

- Jobs will require complex cognitive and interpersonal skills but pay less than the average manufacturing job today. Advanced technology jobs will go unfilled because of a lack of qualified applicants.
- There will be more emphasis on increasing the skills of managers by making on-the-job training continuous and on integrating younger workers and workers from different cultures into the work force.
- Team-based and employee-empowered organizations will increase, causing additional pressures to attract a work force with strong interpersonal and decision-making skills. Managers will have to learn to adapt to new roles as their traditional function continues to fade.

All these issues are a major challenge to those involved in the training process. Perhaps a major implication is that those who manage training will themselves require more training so that they are prepared to design instructional programs that help their fellow workers address these issues.

EMPLOYEE DISCIPLINE, COUNSELING, AND COACHING

Discipline has been defined as that state of employee self-control and orderly conduct that supports the goals of the employer.[34] Employee discipline has become a greater problem in recent years, as managers see it as burdensome to enforce while employees see it as unfair and inconsistent in application. Poor disciplinary procedures may lead to high turnover, loss of morale, lower performance levels, legal problems, and a loss of employee respect for managers.

The rest of this chapter describes both a traditional progressive discipline procedure and some discipline procedures that take a more positive counseling approach. It also discusses how an employee assistance program (EAP) can be effective in dealing with some discipline problems. Finally, it deals with creating and administering a discipline program.

Progressive Discipline Procedures

Firms can use a number of procedures to discipline an employee whose performance is not up to company standards or whose behavior is inappropriate.

---

[34] Premeaux and Mondy, op. cit., n. 3; Premeaux, op. cit., n. 3.

All of them allow such employees time before termination is considered to improve their performance or behavior. But however a company approaches discipline, it must enforce disciplinary actions equally and fairly, without regard to a person's position in the company, sex, race, religion or any other nonjob-related factor.

Also, no matter what type of discipline is being implemented or at what stage, documentation is critical[35] in case the employee should attempt to challenge the decision in court. Written and dated reports should state the events that led up to the discipline; the outcome of the discipline; and a description of what will occur if the behavior is repeated.

In certain cases, the employer might want to bypass progressive discipline and immediately terminate an employee who has violated a company policy. The employee handbook should spell out which types of offenses merit immediate termination. Typically, these would include committing a felony on company grounds (i.e., selling drugs, theft, assault, sexual harassment). Performance problems, such as low productivity and lack of respect for the supervisor, and psychological problems, such as drug and alcohol addiction, usually merit progressive discipline.

A copy of a discipline action report form can be found in Appendix A.

Progressive discipline is the most common company discipline system today. Exhibit 6.8 shows four typical procedures: (1) oral warning, (2) written warning, (3) suspension, transfer or demotion, and (4) termination. The following discussion analyzes the components of this process.

Oral Warning

An *oral warning* is the first step management takes to improve an employee's performance. This is a formal conversation between supervisor and subordinate about a performance or behavior problem. In this conversation, the supervisor should remind the employee of, first, the performance standards or the behavioral expectations the company has for its employees, and, second, the employee's responsibility for meeting the standards and expectations. The supervisor must then inform the employee of the changes expected and make it clear that the supervisor has confidence that the employee can solve the problem.

---

[35] Goemaat, J. 2003. "Documentation Makes the Difference." *Security Management,* 47: 94-100.

Exhibit 6.8: Typical Progressive Discipline Procedure

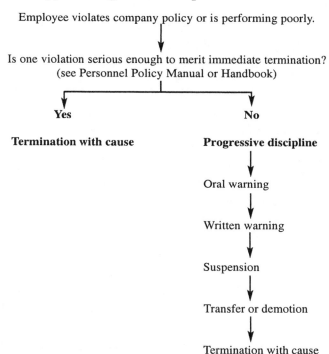

Employee violates company policy or is performing poorly.

Is one violation serious enough to merit immediate termination?
(see Personnel Policy Manual or Handbook)

Yes **No**

Termination with cause **Progressive discipline**

Oral warning

Written warning

Suspension

Transfer or demotion

Termination with cause

A copy of the report documenting the conversation should be kept in the supervisor's file; it may or may not be put in the employee's personnel file. The document should state the time, place, date, and nature of the warning. It should summarize what was said and state the consequences if the problem recurs.

A Written Warning

A written warning is the second step in the progressive system. At a second meeting the supervisor, making no threats about termination, gives the employee a written statement about why and how the employee needs to improve performance or behavior. To correct the situation, both parties should agree upon specified steps to be taken, and actions that will follow up future violations should be written down. In this case, in addition to the supervisor's copy, a copy should be put in the employee's personnel file in case there are ultimately legal questions.

Depending on the company's discipline policies, if neither the oral or written warning is successful in improving performance or changing behavior, an employee may be *suspended* or put on *probation.* Probation usually involves a one- to three-month period during which the employee must avoid any more infractions or there will be serious repercussions, up to and including discharge. The employee should view this probation period as a last chance to improve behavior.

Either as an alternative to probation or as a follow-on step, the supervisor may suspend the employee for as little as part of a day or as long as several months, with or without pay, depending on how serious the discipline problem is. Although supervisors may have some discretion to determine the length and conditions of the suspension, they should be given written guidelines in advance. Suspensions with pay are usually short; they are used to help employees assess their situation or give the employer time to collect evidence before a more definitive job action is taken. Documentation should describe the policy violation and detail the terms of the probation or suspension. The employee should be asked to sign the paperwork to acknowledge receipt and express understanding of the seriousness of the situation.

Sometimes after a probationary period, the employer may decide to *demote* or *transfer* the employee to take the pressure off the situation and all the people involved. Disciplinary transfers are common where an employee has a personality conflict with another employee or supervisor.

Another reason for a disciplinary transfer or demotion is failure to adapt to technological changes. Sometimes employees do not have the skill to operate new equipment and need to be transferred to a position that matches their skill level.

A manager should be careful not to simply pass along a problem employee to another department or work unit. This is especially true with sexual harassment situations. If an employee is sexually harassing a co-worker and is transferred to another department rather than being subjected to the appropriate level of discipline, the employer risks greater liability if the employee should repeat the sexual harassment in the new work unit.

The final step that can be taken to discipline an employee is *termination.* A manager has the right to terminate an employee without going through all the steps if the violation is serious.

Supervisors should conduct termination interviews in the employee's office or elsewhere, but not in their own offices where they will not be able to get away if the employee should become emotional. Any such termination interview should be very brief. Statements should be limited to the reasons for termination and proof that problems have occurred. The firing supervisor should utilize the following six rules for termination:

1. Present the situation in a clear, concise, and definitive manner.

2. Avoid debates or a rehash of the past.

3. Never talk down to anyone being fired.

4. Be empathetic, but not compromising.

5. Offer severance pay or job outplacement services when appropriate.[36]

6. Recognize that many employees do not hear anything after they realize that they have been terminated.

It's recommended that another manager or an HR professional witness terminations to ensure that all company policies were correctly administered.

Appeals and Grievances

Once a disciplinary step has been taken, employees should be allowed organizational due process through a right to appeal the disciplinary decision. Typically, when an employee challenges such a decision, an appeal or grievance committee of both peers and managers is used to conduct an investigation. This committee hears from all parties, collects supporting evidence, and renders a decision (usually subject to approval of a senior manager). All committee decisions must be consistent with company policies as stated in the employee handbook.

Alternative Discipline Approaches

While many employers use the traditional approach to employee discipline as is, some HR experts recommend modifying the process to include more

---

[36] Cascio, W. F. 2002. *Managing Human Resource,* 6th ed. Boston: McGraw-Hill/Irwin.

proactive employee counseling. Two examples of a counseling approach to discipline are described next.

Mark Tavernier and Brian Kleiner[37] believe that employees are disaffected by traditional methods of discipline (warnings, probations, firings) because they have not been involved in selecting them. Also, the traditional approach does not encourage identifying the root causes of the behavior. They recommend a "different way," using the following ideas to promote the rules of an organization and at the same time maintain the performance and morale of the employees:

- Invite employee input when rules, policies, and procedures are formulated. When their input is used, they are more likely to follow the rules.

- Give every employee a written statement of the rules and penalties so that all know what the rules are and the penalties for violating them.

- Observe employee actions directly or ask other employees to provide feedback about the employee who is having problems.

- Identify problems as quickly as possible so that employees can improve and avoid future problems. A manager must prove beyond doubt the validity of a rule violation.

- Tell employees what they are doing wrong and make suggestions on how to correct it. Before doing this, the manager must make sure that a rule has actually been violated and must say so orally and in writing.

- When there is a problem, set aside at least fifteen minutes to discuss it without interruption. Make sure employees understand the rules they have broken and recognize a problem and give time to explain their version of what happened.

- Set up a time to meet with the employee again to follow up on progress towards satisfactory performance. Once manager and employee agree on a disciplinary action, it should be carried out according to company guidelines.

---

[37] Tavernier, M. R., and B. H. Kleiner. 1988. "ADifferent Way to Discipline." *Management World,* July/August: 24-25.

- Make sure that all conversations about unsatisfactory behavior are documented in case termination is the final option.
- At the follow-up review, compliment the employee on improvement; if there has been none, explain the company's right to take stronger disciplinary action, such as probation or suspension.
- Evaluate the company rules to make sure that they are fair to employees.

The result of following these steps should be improved employee conduct and performance, and a smoother manager-employee relationship.

Another positive approach to discipline is FRACT,[38] an acronym for Facts, Reasons, Audit, Consequences, and Type of Infraction. This approach to discipline gives managers an outline to follow to determine the most appropriate form of discipline for a given situation. The outline identifies questions for the manager to ask to fully understand the situation. The answers then direct the manager to the appropriate type of discipline. In the five FRACT steps, the manager takes on a different role.

Step 1: Facts
The manager gathers all the facts to get a full picture of what happened—the who, what, when, where, and how of the incident. The manager, as the investigator, interviews all the parties and reviews all pertinent documentation.

Step 2: Reasons
In this step, the manager must be a counselor, listening to the employee's reasons for the incident or policy violation. At this time, the employee should be allowed to confront any accusers.

A manager does not have to accept the employee's reasoning if there is sound proof that something did actually happen, but employees need a chance to give their side of the story, if only to prevent harm to employee morale in general.

Step 3: Audit
The manager becomes an auditor, reviewing the personnel files of employees involved in the incident. If the problem is with performance, a previous performance appraisal and the disciplinary record may contradict each

---

[38] Markowich, M. M. 1989. "The Positive Approach to Discipline." *Personnel,* August: 60-63.

another. This does not mean that disciplinary action should not be taken.

Step 4: Consequences
The manager highlights all possible consequences of the employee's actions. In other words, the manager becomes an analyst, quantifying the impact of an infraction.

Step 5: Type of Infraction
The last role a manager performs is that of a specialist who defines the policy or procedure that has been violated. Some offenses are worse than others and therefore deserve more severe punishment.

Once the FRACT process is completed, the manager does one more review of the situation to make sure that the right decision is being made and that the disciplinary action taken is demonstrably reasonable. Most employers may consider this method too time-consuming, but it is well worth the effort in case of future litigation.

Both the FRACT approach and Tavernier and Kleiner's different way to discipline, add an employee-counseling dimension to progressive discipline. Counseling may be a viable alternative to punishment, especially for employees who are experiencing personal problems. Employees may sometimes bring to work their difficulty in coping with personal issues, such as marital or other family problems, substance abuse, and low self-esteem. They may also be suffering work-related problems, such as low motivation or a high level of work stress. Counseling is an effective option that offers assistance to employees through diagnostic counseling sessions and rehabilitation programs so that employees have to solve their problems rather than just be subjected to punishment. Organizations that emphasize counseling often use employee assistance programs (EAPs).

EMPLOYEE ASSISTANCE PROGRAMS (EAPs)

An EAP is a workplace-centered effort to provide counseling services for employees. EAPs are designed to help employees with personal problems like drug addiction, emotional disturbance, or financial or family problems that may hinder job performance. For an EAPto be effective, there must be a set of company or union policies or procedures in place for identifying or responding to personal or emotional problems.[39]

EAPs have become common because of changes in modern society and industry's response to those changes. An increasing number of employees are not highly productive because of personal problems. Organizations are realizing that it is not only humanitarian but also cost-effective to take more responsibility for helping employees solve these problems.

The intentionally broad title of EPAs achieves two major purposes:

1. It conveys that the program exists to help employees regardless of the type of problem they are facing.

2. It avoids the negative connotation that may be attached to a narrower program, such as one specifically identified as directed at alcohol and drug problems.

Troubled employees are referred to EAPs for whatever counseling and care is appropriate and available.[40] Supervisors are not required to diagnose the problem but only to recognize problem behavior. Often, an employee is given the option of disciplinary action or successfully completing the EAP protocol. EAPs can be in-house or outsourced to professional service providers. It is generally recommended that the services be offered offsite to protect the confidentiality of those receiving treatment or services.

Essential Ingredients of an EAP

Once a company decides to start an EAPand has selected the type of model it would like to follow, it needs to ensure the following twelve ingredients:

1. Program support

2. A program plan

3. A policy statement

4. An information assessment and referral service

5. Appropriate staffing

6. A confidential record-keeping system

---

[39] Ramanathan, C. 1990. "Employee Assistance Programs: Past, Present, and Future." *Human Resource Management Perspectives and Issues,* 2nd ed. Boston, MA: Allyn and Bacon, 411-417.

[40] Ibid.; Brammer, L. M., and F. E. Humberger. 1984. *Outplacement and Inplacement Counseling.* Englewood Cliffs, NJ: Prentice-Hall.

7. A community referral network

8. An appropriate location

9. Adequate funding

10. Resolution of any legal questions

11. Training of personnel

12. Program evaluation

Even if outside services are used, the program must still have top-management support, adequate funding (usually through health insurance), security to maintain confidentiality, and trained and licensed personnel. Employees who use EAP services should be surveyed to assess their satisfaction and support decisions about future service providers.

HOW TO RECOGNIZE THE TROUBLED EMPLOYEE

Front-line managers need to be trained to recognize employees that may need help or possible referral to an EAP. They do not necessarily need to be able, say, to pick out drug users simply on physical appearance, but they do need to be aware of factors that can reveal a troubled employee. Often, the first sign that an employee is having problems is chronic absenteeism, which is particularly a possible symptom of addiction. When addiction takes top priority, work suddenly takes a back seat. It is vital that the managers also keep a watchful eye on those who are present but come to work late or leave early.

The next element to look for is the employee's productivity. It may be necessary to chart an employee's output to see if there have been any drastic changes.

It should be stressed here that high absenteeism and low productivity do not necessarily mean a drug or alcohol problem. Assessing absenteeism effectively depends on the unique characteristics of the particular work environment. In the manufacturing industry, for instance, the work force tends to be highly supervised, which means that any substance abuse will most likely occur off the job. This is where the manager should be aware of those employees that are either late for work or leaving early.

The problems of white-collar workers are often harder to identify. Because these workers have more independence, they can hide problems from management. It is recommended that the manager watch for employees who often miss meetings or perhaps take extended lunch periods. A sharp downturn in performance may also be a sign of a possible problem.

It is very important for the supervisor to document repeated poor performance. We may all be tardy a few times or have slow days at work, but the troubled employee shows a pattern of repeated unacceptable behavior. One-on-one contact with an employee suspected of having the problem can give the manager some vital information. The one thing that cannot be stressed enough is the need to approach such employees in a positive way, letting them know that you're on their side. The goal is to break down any barriers to open and honest communication.[41] It is, however, true that where employees have previously been disciplined for their problems, other measures may need to be taken.

HOW TO SET UP A DISCIPLINE PROGRAM

"Implementing a fair and consistent system of discipline is management's best method of reinforcing corporate philosophy and directing employee performance toward the achievement of company objectives."[42] Many companies, especially smaller and growing ones, lack a formal employee discipline program. The result is that some employees are allowed to continue certain behaviors that others are punished for. This results in employee resentment and loss of employee respect for both the manager and the company's policies and rules.

There are at least four steps in developing a discipline policy. The first step is to establish rules. Management should make rules not to restrict employee rights but to protect the rights of both employees and management. Rules should be communicated to every employee so that ignorance of rules does not become an excuse. Each rule should be tested by examining the reason for the rule, what is accomplished by enforcing it, and what might happen without the rule. As more rules and policies are necessary, an employee handbook is a helpful way to communicate information.

The second step is to take action. Managers are often reluctant to invoke disciplinary actions because they fear that it will harm their

---

[41] Ibid.
[42] 1987. "Employee Discipline: Written Guidelines Protect Employees and Management." *Small Business Report,* October: 37-42.

relationship with their employees. However, failure to take necessary action actually condones the violation. Weak discipline can also lead to more violations.

The third step is confronting the employee. When they perceive a violation, managers need to investigate. To do this, they should:

- Clarify the problem
- Discuss other perspectives
- Respond to the employee
- Establish authority
- Follow up

The fourth and final step is the discipline checklist. It is very important for employees to believe that they are being treated fairly. Instruct managers to consider the nature of the violation and seek answers to these questions:

- Did the employee know what was expected?
- Was the employee capable of following company policy?
- Were there extenuating circumstances?
- Was the violation deliberate?

Exhibit 6.9 is an example of a well-worded discipline policy that has proven to be effective.

Exhibit 6.9: Example of a Discipline Policy

It is the policy of the company that when disciplinary action must be taken against employees, such action will be:

1. Undertaken only in cases where good reasons and clear evidence exist.
2. Appropriate to the severity of the offense.
3. Demonstrably fair and consistent with previous action in similar circumstances.
4. Administered only after employees are aware of the standards expected of them and the rules to which they must conform.
5. Designed to allow employees the right to be represented by a manager or co-worker during any formal proceedings.

Source: "Employee Discipline: Written Guidelines Protect Employees and Management." 1987. *Small Business Report,* October: 37-42.

DISCIPLINE AND THE EMPLOYMENT-AT-WILL DOCTRINE

The notion behind employment-at-will means that employment is "at the will of" the employer or the employee. In other words, unless there is a contract, either party can end the work relationship at any time.

There are four major exceptions to employment-at-will that could allow an employee to file a wrongful discharge suit. An employee could charge that:

- The firing violated a law (e.g., discrimination).
- It violated public policy (e.g., the employee was discharged after refusing to do something illegal or unsafe).
- It violated an implied contract between the employer and the employee.
- The termination came just before the employee was due to receive a financial benefit (know as the *implied covenant of good faith and fair dealing*), such as a bonus or vesting in a pension fund.

In recent years, the courts have become more willing to hear wrongful discharge suits, and have been finding for the plaintiff over 70 percent of the time, with the average award being about $500,000 dollars.[43] With these high costs on the line, employers should supervise company discipline procedures closely to make sure they are followed and that all discipline interactions are consistent. Supervisors should be trained to avoid making implied commitments of any kind without senior management support.

Handled properly, progressive discipline does not negate employment-at-will. Even though discipline steps are outlined, termination at any time is possible as long as the right to do so has been reserved: An employer must expressly assert the right to exercise the at-will employment option at any time by writing it into the discipline policy.[44]

---

[43] Copeland, J. B., Wright, W. T., and D. Shapiro 1987. "The Revenge of the Fired." *Newsweek,* February 16: 46-47.

[44] Falcone, P. A. 1999. "Legal Dichotomy? Employment-at-Will Doesn't Mean You Should Ignore Progressive Discipline." *HR Magazine,* May: 110-115; Premeaux and Mondy, op. cit., n. 3; Premeaux, op. cit., n. 3.

However, since the latitude of the at-will doctrine varies from state to state, it's a good idea to maintain detailed documentation as prescribed in the progressive discipline steps. Many states have narrowed the employer's right to fire at will so that evidence that an employee was terminated for just cause may be necessary.

WRAP-UP

Training is vital to organizational survival and growth. Federal and state governments have established guidelines to protect employees that extend to training and development programs. The three-phase Goldstein Model is a well-known approach to establishing a training program. The needs assessment phase consists of determining the instructional need of employees and formulating objectives. The training and development phase focuses on instructional design and conducting training. The environment plays a major part in how trainees absorb information during a training program. The evaluation phase, though often left out of training programs, is actually the most important aspect of the program because it elicits constant input from participants. The ability to continually update and define training programs contributes to an innovative and aggressive organizational strategy. Finally, over the next decade, training specialists face many challenges due to the changing complexity of the work force and the jobs performed.

Dealing effectively with employee problems consists of both employee discipline and assistance to employees. However, too many organizations either ignore these types of programs or give them too little attention. Managers do not like to confront subordinates and discuss work-related problems. It is the responsibility of management to put in place progressive discipline procedures that allow for due process and help employees correct their problems. The key components of any discipline and assistance programs should include:

- A promise of confidentiality
- Documentation
- Professional behavior
- Progressive steps
- Top management support

- Mutual trust between managers and subordinates

A formal program that incorporates these components will allow managers to take the actions needed to improve work performance and deal directly with work-related problems.

CHAPTER 7

Performance Rewards: Effective Compensation and Benefits

A dollar buys very little these days, not only in a shopping sense but from an HR perspective as well. Numerous studies are sending shock waves to managers by finding that *pay is not the number one attraction of a job from the average employee's point of view.* Employees want more feedback and encouragement. Firms that equated increased pay with increased motivation have been surprised to find themselves still losing good employees. What is the real "pay challenge" and how do we keep our best people?

Today, more and more managers are shifting from the simplistic pay-motivation mantra and are looking at much broader compensation and benefits plans based on *total rewards.* The power of this approach is that it recognizes that every employee has a multiplicity of needs, and that, while compensation satisfies financial needs and benefits generally satisfy needs for protection, other aspects of the work itself must satisfy intangible yet critical needs for personal fulfillment and development, status, and achieving other life goals.

World at Work (formerly the American Compensation Association), an organization that certifies professionals who specialize in compensation and benefits, has been the major player in the total rewards movement. To keep employees attentive and motivated, World at Work's latest model suggests emphasizing these elements:

- *Acknowledgement and recognition*—being valued and respected
- *Balance of work and life*—including family and friends in the mix of everyday life
- *Culture*—associating with an organization whose values are similar
- *Development*—growing in comprehension and skills
- *Environment*—safety, resources, aesthetics, etc.

Pay is only a fraction of the "acknowledgement and recognition" slice of this model. Now that so many managers realize that pay is truly not everything, using the total rewards approach to keeping workers motivated will forever be more than just signing a check.[1]

THE MANAGER'S CHALLENGE

Designing and implementing a compensation plan that offers employees internally and externally equitable pay rates is a critical task for any organization in a competitive environment. The survival and prosperity of an organization depends on its ability to attract and retain qualified workers, to whom its manager must offer a competitive compensation package to motivate them to leave their current positions. Selecting an appropriate mix of base pay, incentives, and benefits is critical to successful staffing. Companies must assess their ability to pay, study wage rates in the current market, and understand both financial and nonfinancial needs of employees.

While many frontline managers may not need to conduct some of the compensation analysis described here, their understanding and ability to explain pay determination procedures is crucial to employee acceptance.

Making equitable recommendations for employee pay adjustments often requires reliance on performance appraisals, so a successful compensation plan depends on assessing job worth, determining market value, and equitably distributing the rewards for work. Doing this is often a particular challenge for managers in the emerging firm, but it is necessary to formalize HR functions for effective growth.

Compensation has been defined as "all forms of financial returns and tangible services and benefits employees receive as part of an employment

---

[1] *See* Richter, A. S. 2003. "Total Rewards: Meeting the Pay Challenge." *Strategic HR Review,* 3 November - December: 16-19.

relationship."[2] While this definition is accurate, its simplicity might be seen to imply that compensation is a relatively simple concept. It is not. How does an organization determine how much each employee is worth? Moreover, what about indirect compensation? Direct compensation consists of straightforward monetary payments, such as a base wage or a bonus; indirect compensation includes benefits such as health insurance, paid time off for sick leave and vacations, retirement benefits, workers compensation, and any other benefits a company chooses to offer its employees. This chapter analyzes both types of compensation in detail and discusses how they are administered.

THE FUNCTIONS OF COMPENSATION

Among the many reasons why companies need to pay attention to the compensation function, the three most critical are the following:

1. **Attracting employees:** Firms must compete against other employers to get enough people with the skills they need to achieve their goals.
2. **Retaining employees:** Employees must perceive the company's compensation system as fair and competitive in the market or they will not stay.
3. **Motivating employees:** Compensation is used to reward and encourage good performance.

The compensation system must also fulfill legal requirements like the Equal Pay Act, follow guidelines set by union agreements, and facilitate the achievement of the company's strategic goals.

Equity is clearly the central notion. The relationships between compensation and employee behaviors, such as productivity, turnover, or filing a lawsuit, depend heavily on employees' perceptions of how equitable their compensation is.

Types of Equity

Employees usually compare their wages, including bonuses and raises, to those of others in similar positions. Edward Lawler sees the compensation system as a feedback mechanism that allows employees to adjust their

---

[2] Milkovich, G. T., and J. M. Newman. 2004. *Compensation.* 8th ed. Boston, MA: McGraw-Hill/Irwin.

behavior based on the equity (or lack of it) they perceive.[3] When people perceive an inequity, especially if they feel underpaid, seeing themselves as receiving fewer rewards for the amount of inputs, they will strive to behave in a way that will bring about equity. Typical behaviors are decreasing productivity, slowing down, being absent more often, asking for a transfer, or quitting. Given how much employers invest in recruiting, selecting, and training employees, an equitable compensation system will pay off by helping employers keep and motivate their best personnel.

Three different types of equity affect an employee's perception of pay fairness: (1) internal equity, (2) external equity, and (3) individual equity.

Internal Equity

Internal equity requires that all jobs be evaluated in terms of the value of that job to the organization in terms of the KSAs it requires. That means the company must first conduct a job analysis for each position within the firm (see Chapter 3). Only after job descriptions are available can the various positions be valued. This is the process of job evaluation.

External Equity

How an employee's compensation compares to others performing the same job in other companies is an especially important issue for employees who hold jobs for which there is strong demand in the labor force. Employees who perceive their pay as being below market will be motivated to find employment elsewhere, and the company not only loses all the money, time, and other resources it has spent on selecting and training that person, but it has to invest even more in hiring and training a new employee. The instrument used to determine market pay rates is the market survey.

Individual Equity

Individual equity relates to how an employee's merit pay compares to others in the organization. Employees compare their inputs (effort, skill, etc.) to their co-workers' as well as the rewards they receive based on those inputs. An employee whose individual equity comparison leads to the perception of being under-rewarded may be motivated to reduce effort, change jobs, or engage in other behaviors to bring about equity. The performance appraisal system is usually employed to determine individual equity. The

[3] Lawler, E. E. 1981. *Pay and Organizational Development.* Reading, MA: Addison-Wesley.

remainder of this chapter will expand on the concepts of internal and external equity.

HOW TO ESTABLISH INTERNAL EQUITY

The process of job evaluation helps establish the relative worth of a job to an employer. The ultimate goal of job evaluation is a pay structure that is equitable to employees and consistent with the goals of the company. In the United States, approximately two-thirds of the jobs have been evaluated; the following are the most common reasons why:[4]

- To establish a systematic and formal structure of jobs based on their worth to the organization
- To justify the existing pay structure or replace it with one that is internally equitable
- To provide bargaining information when negotiating pay rates with a union
- To identify to employees a hierarchy of pay progression
- To comply with compensation legislation
- To develop a basis for merit and incentive pay programs
- To see if pay rates are comparable to those for similar positions in other organizations

Organizations can use one evaluation system or many. Some use different systems to evaluate labor, sales, management, technical and professional, and clerical jobs. Proponents of multiple plans believe that the work content of different types of jobs is too diverse to be adequately represented in a single system. However, a number of problems arise from the use of multiple plans, among them:

- Multiple plans can build discrimination into the pay system. For example, if clerical workers are evaluated on a completely different scale than laborers, the entire group of clerical workers may be undercompensated compared to laborers. Because a high percent-

[4] Mount, M. K., and R. A. Ellis. 1987. "Investigations of Bias In Job Evaluation Ratings of Comparable Worth Study Participants." *Personnel Psychology,* 40(1): 85-96; Henderson, R. I. 1993. *Compensation Management: Rewarding Performance.* 5th ed. Englewood Cliffs, NJ: Prentice Hall.

age of clerical workers are women, there is therefore an increased likelihood of a possible problem with sex discrimination.

• Because multiple plans prohibit the comparison of jobs in different pay plans, there may be difficulty with promotions, transfers, and other employment decisions.

• There is a problem with comparable worth: How can you compare the value of a manager versus an engineer if the value of their jobs was determined using different evaluation systems? There have been as yet no successful lawsuits concerning comparable worth, but it continues to be an issue that should be of concern to managers.

Job evaluation methods raise three different questions:

1. Are evaluations based on the whole job, or are only specific factors of the job evaluated?

2. Is the method relative or absolute? Does it compare one job to another, or does it compare each job to a standard?

3. Are evaluations quantitative or qualitative?

These questions apply in all four of the basic methods of evaluating jobs: (1) job ranking, (2) job classification, (3) factor comparison, and (4) the point-factor system.

Job Ranking

Job ranking is relative—it uses the whole job for making evaluations, rating one job against another—and it is qualitative. In general, jobs are ranked in order of worth from most to least valuable.

Ranking is the simplest method. This method is generally used in smaller organizations that have a limited number of positions to evaluate. A committee will review the descriptions for all jobs in the organization and rank them in order of their relative worth to the company. This is a fast, straight-forward method that is easily understood.

The disadvantages are that job ranking lacks any quantitative support and is based on the subjective opinions of committee members. Jobs are compared to one another but there is no set of compensable factors against which they are compared to determine their worth. Moreover, with no quantitative measures determining the value of each job, it is virtually impossible to identify real differences in the worth of jobs. It may be determined that an office manager is more important than a secretary, but how much more important?

A final drawback of this method is that unless the firm is very small, it is unlikely that any one person will be familiar enough with all of the positions it needs to be able to adequately compare and rank them.

Job Classification

Job classification is a whole-job evaluation method. Jobs are evaluated against a standard based on qualitative factors. Concepts of worth are divided into classes or categories and jobs are slotted into the categories.

There are at least three steps to job classification systems:

1. The job evaluator decides on the number of classes the system will have—usually five to 15. It is important that there be enough grades to fully represent the range of jobs being evaluated.

2. Each class is defined in general terms, such as the amount of supervision required or given, the experience needed, or the working conditions.

3. Job descriptions are matched to class definitions to determine a class for each job.

A job classification system is relatively easy to administer, can be used throughout an organization, and can reduce the need to reevaluate jobs when there are minor changes in content. Job classification is used extensively in public organizations.[5] The federal government system has a total of 18 grades. Most jobs fit within the first 15; the upper three "super grades" (SES1, SES2, and SES3) cover senior executives.

This system is relatively easy to organize but it, too, is qualitative. Problems can arise when grades are set up with one particular function in mind, such as sales, and then generalized to incorporate other functions.

Factor Comparison

The process used in the factor comparison approach has at least seven steps:

1. Appoint an evaluation committee of about five employees to make the evaluation decisions.

2. Select compensable factors that reflect the different components of

---

[5] Wallace, M. C., and C. H. Fay. 1988. *Compensation Theory and Practice.* Boston, MA: PWS-Kent.

work that the organization values; these are usually based on the 1963 Equal Pay Act. The factors usually chosen are:
- Responsibilities   • Skill
- Physical effort   • Mental effort
- Working conditions

These factors could differ based on the types of jobs being evaluated.

3. Choose 10 to 20 benchmark jobs to be used as a basis of comparison. Benchmark jobs are jobs that are common in the local labor market and represent the range of job levels being evaluated.

4. Rank the benchmark jobs on each of the factors. Jobs that contain more of a factor are ranked higher.

5. Determine the wage or salary for these benchmark jobs, usually based on a market survey, and allocate a portion of the wage to each factor depending on the importance of the factor to the job.

6. Compare the two sets of rankings (4 and 5) to check on evaluation accuracy.

7. Construct a rate structure that displays the benchmark jobs and the money values each job received for each factor. This rate structure becomes the evaluation instrument for nonbenchmark jobs. Money values are assigned to jobs based on how they compare to the benchmark anchors.

Point Factor System

The point factor system is the most common evaluation system.[6] This is a quantitative method that uses specific factors. The approach has at least six steps:

1. After a job analysis, a job description is written for each job.

2. An evaluation committee with about five members is chosen to conduct the evaluation.

3. As in the factor comparison method, factors (usually four to nine) are chosen to represent the job requirements to be used as a basis for paying employees.

4. Factor scales are drawn up to reflect the different degrees or levels

[6] Schwab, D. P. 1980. "Job Evaluation and Pay-Setting: Concepts and Practices," in Livernash, E. R., ed. *Comparable Worth: Issues and Alternatives.* Washington, D.C.: Equal Employment Advisory Council.

within each factor (see Exhibit 7.1).

5. Points are assigned to each factor based on its value. To estimate the number of points, a typical rule of thumb is to take the highest current salary for the jobs being evaluated, divide it by the lowest current salary, and multiply the result by 100. For example:

Highest salary = $50,000
Lowest salary = $10,000
Points   =   500

6. Points are assigned to each level within each factor; first to the highest level and then proportionately fewer to each lower level.[7]

Exhibit 7.1: Illustration of Factor Scaling

Knowledge
This factor measures the knowledge or equivalent training required to perform the position duties.

1st Degree
Use of reading and writing, adding and subtracting of whole numbers; following of instructions; use of fixed gauges, direct reading instruments and similar devices; where interpretation is not required.

2nd Degree
Use of addition, subtraction, multiplication, and division of numbers, including decimals and fractions; simple use of formulas, charts, tables, drawings, specifications, schedules, wiring diagrams; use of adjustable measuring instruments; checking of reports, forms, records and comparable data; where interpretation is required.

3rd Degree
Use of mathematics together with the use of complicated drawings, specifications, charts, and tables; various types of precision measuring instruments. Equivalent to one to three years applied trades training in a particular or specialized occupation.

4th Degree
Use of advanced trades mathematics, together with the use of complicated drawings, specifications, charts, tables handbook formulas; all varieties of precision-measuring instruments. Equivalent to complete accredited apprenticeship in a recognized trade, craft or occupation; or equivalent to a two-year technical college education.

5th Degree
Use of higher mathematics involved in the application of engineering principles and the performance of related practical operations, together with a comprehensive knowledge of the theories and practices of mechanical, electrical, chemical, civil or like engineering field. Equivalent to complete four years of technical college or university education.

Source: Milkovich, G. T., and J. M. Newman. 2004. *Compensation.* 8th ed. Boston, MA: McGraw-Hill/Irwin.

---

[7] Fisher, D. C., L. F. Schoenfeldt, and J. B. Shaw. 2002. *Human Resource Management.* 5th ed. Boston, MA: Houghton Mifflin Co.

7. Once points have been allocated to factors and to the scales within each factor, the committee evaluates each job against the job description, assigning points based on how much each factor is represented in the job.

There are several commercial point factor evaluation systems available, such as the Hay Plan,[8] the committee can use if there is no in-house expertise.

HOW TO ESTABLISH EXTERNAL EQUITY

A pay system that is equitable externally as well as internally should be a major goal of any compensation strategy because each firm competes against all the others in its market for the workers it needs to accomplish its goals. Employees who perceive that a firm pays them less than the market rate will leave to find employment elsewhere.

The Market Survey

To see how equitable pay might be perceived to be, a firm needs to find out the going rate for various jobs in the market place. A market survey is a systematic process of collecting data about the compensation practices of other employers.

There are various sources for market survey information. Market surveys can be conducted by third parties, such as the federal government, which conducts surveys based on area and industry through the Bureau of Labor Statistics that are available free of charge. The surveys break down the data by type of occupation, such as professional, administrative, technical, and clerical. Professional associations like the Society for Human Resource Management, the American Compensation Association, the Administrative Management Society, and the Chamber of Commerce also conduct market surveys.

Commercial firms like consultants Arthur Young, Hay Associates, and Robert Half International do market surveys, as do academics from time to time.

The advantage of third-party surveys is that data in summary form based on a large sample of jobs across many employers can be obtained cheaply and quickly. The disadvantages are that the relevance of the data to

[8] Hay, E. N., and D. Purves. 1951. "The Profile Method of High Level Job Evaluation." *Personnel*, September: 162-170.

the given company may be limited. It can be difficult to determine from data presented in summary form just how relevant it is to the company, and the data—especially from government sources—may be out of date.[9]

A survey custom-designed for the company allows for maximum control over the data collected. The drawback is that it can be expensive, particularly for small firms with limited resources.

There are a number of steps to consider should a firm decide to conduct its own survey.

The first task is to define the relevant labor market. There are three factors to consider in defining the market to survey:

1. **Geography:** One rule of thumb is to survey the area from which the firm draws 95 percent of its employees.

2. **Occupational level:** Different occupational groups have different markets. Information about compensation for secretaries might be derived locally, while information about pay for CEOs might have to be derived nationally or even internationally. Generally, the more skills the job requires, the larger the geographic area that will have to be surveyed.

3. **Firms to be surveyed:** It is necessary to first identify all employers in the relevant labor market and to draw from them a random sample to survey. It is best to focus on where the company's products are marketed and what firms compete with it in those markets. The cost of labor affects how competitive a company can be in its product market.

Second, which jobs to include in the survey must be determined. Not every job in an organization translates to other firms, and the cost of doing a survey for every position would be prohibitive. Benchmark positions are usually used for market surveys. A benchmark job is one that is common to all employers and that is relatively stable—it does not change significantly from year to year.

Next, a method of carrying out the survey must be chosen. Telephone surveys are quick and fairly inexpensive, but the amount of data that can be gathered is limited. However, if pay for a few jobs is the objective, it may be possible to collect the information over the phone instead of using a

---

[9] Milkovich and Newman, op. cit., n. 2.

mailed survey. Written surveys will elicit more information, but they cost more and the response rate is likely to be lower.

Finally, whether the survey is by phone or mail, questionnaires must be drawn up. Ask only for the specific information needed. Keep the survey as short as possible; response rate correlates negatively with the length of the survey. A typical compensation survey has as many as four parts:

1. *An organizational policy section* seeking information on number of employees, normal work week, time allotted for breaks, shift work questions, overtime policies, and pay adjustments made in the last year.

2. *An employee benefits section* (if desired) seeking information on paid vacations, paid holidays, sick leave, other leaves, insurance benefits, pension plans, and anything else not specifically mentioned.

3. *A merit pay plan section* asking whether or not the company pays for performance and if so, how (e.g., bonuses, commissions, etc.).

4. *A job salary data section* that gives summary job descriptions of the positions for which information is being sought and guidelines to help respondents match their positions with those described.

For a written survey, be sure to include a letter of transmittal that gives the purpose of the survey; the desired response date; an overview of survey content; an assurance of anonymity; a commitment to share the information gathered with respondents; the name, address, and phone number of a contact person; and an expression of appreciation. The survey should be sent to a specific person who has already been identified to ensure a higher response rate. It may be helpful to conduct telephone follow-ups to those who fail to respond.

How to Analyze Market Data

The first step in analyzing survey data is to check the accuracy of the data. Data that is unusually high or low should be examined and, if possible, compared with a job description provided by the respondent firm. Only after data has been checked for accuracy and relatedness can it be analyzed.

The simplest form of analysis is to compute the mean of the salaries reported for each job. To get a simple mean, the average wages of the respondents are summed and then divided by the number of respondents.

Probably a more representative measure is to use a weighted average to figure the mean. A simple mean may not accurately reflect the true average of the labor market surveyed. A weighted average takes into account the number of incumbents in the jobs surveyed. To calculate a weighted mean, multiply the wage data reported by the number of job incumbents, then divide the answer by the total number of incumbents from all companies reporting wage information for that job (see Exhibit 7.2 for the calculation).

Exhibit 7.2: How to Calculate a Weighted Mean

Company	No. of Incumbents	Average Hourly Salary
A	10	$8.
B	1	$12
C	20	$5
D	5	$6

Step 1: Multiply incumbents by average salary
Company A:　　$80
Company B:　　$12
Company C:　　$100
Company D:　　$30

Step 2: Tally total cost from Step 1 and total number of incumbents in all jobs
Total cost　　=　$222
Total incumbents =　36

Step 3: Divide total cost by total incumbents
　　$222/36　=　$6.17 (weighted mean)

The simple mean equals $7.75.

HOW TO LINK INTERNAL AND EXTERNAL EQUITY

The point factor system is an excellent mechanism for linking job requirements to market conditions.[10] The job evaluation process establishes a hierarchy of jobs based on their point value. Once this hierarchy is established,

---

[10] Schwab, op. cit., n. 6.

market salaries can be used to craft a formal wage structure. Before doing so, two important questions must be answered:

1. Does the company want to set a specific pay rate for each job or group jobs together into pay grades? The purpose of establishing grades is to make it more convenient and equitable to administer the pay system,[11] and to ensure that jobs of similar importance or value to the company are compensated equally. Point factor systems make it possible to arrange jobs along a continuum of points, but that requires evaluating the pay for each individual job, which would not be efficient.

2. How does the organization want to compete in the labor market? The three basic options are to (1) lead, (2) match, or (3) lag behind it.[12] The option chosen should be based on such things as the supply of quality labor in the community, the type of industry, the company's ability to pay, and the benefits and other forms of compensation offered.

Establishing Pay Grades

There are some basic guidelines to follow in determining the number of pay grades needed. There should be enough grades to achieve perceived internal pay equity; if one job is considered a promotion from another, both jobs cannot fall within the same pay grade.

The number of grades can be determined either quantitatively or qualitatively. Establishing grades quantitatively uses a mathematical procedure that follows these steps:

1. Using information gathered from the wage survey, determine the midpoint wage rate for the lowest- and highest-paid jobs.

2. Set a percentage increase in pay from one grade midpoint to the next.

3. Determine how many times the lowest midpoint pay rate must be compounded to reach the highest midpoint rate given the desired percent raise for each grade.

[11] Bergman, T. J., and V. G. Scarpello. 2000. *Compensation Decision Making*. 4th ed. Ft. Worth, TX: Harcourt College Publishers.
[12] Fisher, Schoenfeldt, and Shaw, op. cit., n. 5.

Exhibit 7.3 shows an example of this calculation.

Exhibit 7.3: Qualitative Determination of the Number of Pay Grades

Low salary midpoint: $10,000

High salary midpoint: $20,000

Desired percent increase: 5%

Solving for the number of grades:

a. Divide the high midpoint by the low midpoint to find the ratio:

$$20,000/10,000 = 2$$

b. Add the desired increase to 1:

$$1 + 0.05 = 1.05$$

c. Determine to what power the number determined in step 2 must be raised in order to reach the ratio determined in a:

$$1.05_n = 2.0$$

When the equation is solved for n, n will be the desired number of grades—in this case, 15.

The qualitative approach to determining the number of pay grades involves looking for rational point breaks in the job rankings. When a point factor method has been used, there may be natural breaks in the distribution of jobs that would be appropriate separations between grades.

Setting Pay Ranges

Once grades have been established, it is necessary to set pay ranges for each grade. Wage ranges serve a number of purposes: they allow a firm, for instance, to differentiate pay based on performance or on seniority or to offer different pay for probationary periods. In effect, ranges give the firm latitude in deciding what to pay individual workers, while setting guidelines for categories of work.

The midpoint set for each pay grade should be based on the information acquired in the market survey for jobs in the pay grade. Then a range around that will set guidelines for pay for each job within that range.

How wide should the pay ranges be for each grade? In answering the question, the following three factors need to be taken into consideration: (1) length of service, (2) merit, and (3) the importance of meaningful pay increases. Usually ranges vary around the midpoint by 25 to 30 percent.

Ranges must be wide enough to insure that employee salaries will not top out too early. Being unable to increase wages comparable to others in the grade could lead to turnover problems.

There must also be some range overlap. This is not a threat to internal equity because it provides a mechanism for employees in lower grades to make more than employees in higher grades based on seniority and performance.

Implementing the Pay Structure

What is most important to successful implementation of a new pay structure is communicating with the employees. Managers play a crucial role in the communication of how base pay, raises, bonuses, and other pay issues are determined. Their understanding of the process can help employees understand better.

Employees are naturally anxious when compensation decisions are being made. They need to be kept informed through every step of the process. They need to be told that a system is going to be set up, when it starts, and what its goals are, and they need to be assured that no one's pay will be reduced as a result of the process. Once a new structure is constructed, employees need to be shown where they fit into the str'' re and how it will affect them in the future.

When the pay structure is finally complete, it is inevitable that some current wages will fall above and some below the ranges appropriate for the given position. Those that fall below, called green *circle rates,* should be adjusted upward to the minimum pay level for the grade. Where jobs are being paid more than their grade would justify (called *red circle rates*), the current employees should not have their pay reduced. The pay scale for the job will eventually be brought into line as new people move into these positions and are paid appropriately for the grade. The only other adjustment which may be made to bring red circled jobs into line is to give these employees smaller pay raises or one-time bonus payments instead of raises to bring them more in line with the pay structure.

Administering the Pay Structure

Once the pay structure has been established, it will should be periodically updated. Jobs and wage rates change. A system that is not updated can become obsolete fairly quickly, which would require going through the entire development process all over again.

The following general guidelines should be followed to keep the pay structure current:

- Jobs should be resurveyed every two to three years to keep the structure current with the marketplace.

- Jobs should be re-evaluated every three years to keep job descriptions current and to make sure that they are still appropriately placed within the structure.

- Jobs must be re-evaluated whenever their content changes. Most jobs change gradually over time, which is why all jobs need evaluating every three years, but some jobs are restructured suddenly.

- Rather than re-evaluating all jobs every third year, a rotation system should be established so that one-third are done each year to spread the work out evenly.

INDIVIDUAL EQUITY

External equity deals with keeping the firm's compensation system competitive with other firms who are competing for the same employees. Internal equity is concerned with compensating particular jobs according to the value of that job to the organization. However, there is also a need for individual equity—compensating individuals according to their worth to the organization. Individual equity is what explains differences in pay among people who hold the same job.

The most important element in individual equity is performance-based pay, meaning that compensation is in some way tied to how well each individual performs for the organization. Performance-based pay is founded on at least three strategic concepts:

1. Employees have needs, and the desire to satisfy these needs will motivate good performance.

2. Employee behavior should be shaped to achieve company objectives.

3. Employers should link achievement of organizational objectives with satisfaction of individual needs.

Performance-based pay is generally administered through incentive plans that set a standard against which employee performance can be measured. How these standards are set is what differentiates incentive systems, which can be based on group or on individual performance.

Performance-Based Pay Methods

There are many forms of individualized performance-based pay systems. Some of the most common are merit pay, individual incentive plans like piece rates, standard hour and bonuses, skill/knowledge based pay, and spot awards.

Merit Pay

Merit pay systems have been defined as "programs in which increases in base pay for specific individuals are geared to the performance assessment of those individuals for a specific time period."[13] Merit pay does not include across-the-board increases, like cost of living or seniority increases, or any one-time payments that do not permanently increase an employee's base pay. Most U.S. organizations use some form of merit pay program.[14]

Generally, merit raises are given once a year based on the performance appraisal for the past 12 months. If these systems are to serve a true motivational function, the performance appraisal system must be set up in a way that accurately recognizes the differences in performance that are necessary to do a job successfully. They must be quantitative and based on job analysis information. Exhibit 7.4 shows guidelines for how pay can be linked to a performance evaluation system that ranks employee performance on a scale of one to five.

Usually, managers play an important role in making decisions about merit raises. Sometimes it is the manager's sole decision; sometimes there is a tool like that in Exhibit 7.4 to guide a company's managers.

It is important that raises sincerely differentiate good performers from average and poor performers, especially when the merit increase budget is tight. Minor differences in pay raises across employees at different levels of performance raise equity issues that may cause employees to withdraw or even quit.[15]

---

[13] Hills, F. S., R. M. Madigan, K. D. Scott, and S. E. Markam. 1987. "Tracking the Merit of Merit Pay." *Personnel Administrator,* 32: 50-57.
[14] Ibid.
[15] Bates, S. 2003. "Top Pay for Best Performance." *HR Magazine,* January: 31-38.

Exhibit 7.4: How Merit Increases Can Be Linked to Performance Appraisal Ratings.

		RATING			
	Outstanding *5*	Above Average *4*	Satisfactory *3*	Below Average *2*	Unsatisfactory *1*
Merit increase	5%-7%	3%-5%	2%-3%	1%-2%	0%

Individual Incentives

Individual incentives are pay methods in which take-home pay is calculated based on actual performance criteria for that pay period. For our purposes, four methods will be discussed: (1) piece rates, (2) standard hour plans, (3) commission systems, and (4) bonus plans.

In *piece rate systems,* employees are paid by the number of units they produce. To determine the rate per unit, it is first necessary to determine what is standard performance based on job analysis and time and motion studies. The standard is set at the average production per hour for all employees on the job. Once the standard is calculated, the desired average pay rate must be determined. This desired average pay is then divided by the average number of units produced to determine the pay per unit.

Piece rate systems need good administrative systems to keep track of each employee's performance. They also need to be tied to measures of quality as well quantity; if they are not, quality will be sacrificed to greater production. Monitoring true production levels is necessary to insure that labor costs do not get out of line. Additionally, the standard must be reassessed after any event that creates a change in the level of production, such as the introduction of new technology. Exhibit 7.5 illustrates how a piece-rate is calculated.

Exhibit 7.5: Piece Rate and Worker Pay Calculations

Piece rate calculation:
Average production of widgets per hour per employee: 57 units
Target average wage per hour: $7.50
Piece rate per unit: $7.50/57 = $0.13/unit (rounded)

Worker pay calculation:
Number of units produced, January 1 - January 5: 3,000
Piece rate: x 0.13/unit
Employee wage for week ended January 5: $390.00

Standard hour plans are similar to piece rate plans except that instead of determining a standard number of units produced per hour, these systems establish a standard length of time for accomplishing a given task. Standard hours are common in the auto repair industry. For example, job analysis and time and motion studies determine that the average employee requires 15 minutes to change the oil in a car. This means that the number of standard hours for an oil change is 0.25 hours. An employee who changes the oil in six cars in one hour, will be paid for 1.5 hours of work based on a standard hour system. As in piece rate systems, these methods require good administrative systems and ties to quality measures if they are to work efficiently.

Commission pay systems are common for salespeople. Commission plans tie compensation directly to performance by paying employees a percentage of the sales they make.

There are several kinds of commission plans. Straight commission systems are based solely on percentage of sales. The salary plus commission method guarantees a base salary with commissions paid on top of the base, though the commission rate is generally lower than for straight commissions. The draw plus commission method—really a variant of straight commissions—allows the employee to draw (take a loan) against future sales commissions. This method is often used for individuals new to sales. Since initial sales may be low, the employee can borrow against future commissions for living expenses. The draw aspect of the plan is often temporary, discontinued usually six months to a year after the employee starts with the company.

The problems associated with commission pay are similar to those associated with the piece rate and standard hour. Strong administration systems are necessary and attention to quality must be constant. Without monitoring quality in commission pay systems, sales representatives may fail to give good customer service, oversell to customers, or sell them unneeded items—all practices that can result in loss of customers. Equity between salespeople, and morale, can suffer if districts or areas assigned provide unequal opportunities for sales. When revising a sales compensation plan, move slowly, consider what makes salespeople effective, and tie compensation to sales, minimizing or eliminating base pay.[16]

---

[16] Fiedler, D. 2002. "Should You Adjust Your Sales Compensation?" *HR Magazine,* February: 79-80.

A *bonus plan* gives lump sum payments as a reward for achieving performance levels over a given period of time (usually a year). The required levels of performance may be measured at the department, division, or even corporate level. Sales bonuses are usually determined by success at achieving preset figures. Bonuses for management personnel are usually calculated on a pre-set formula based on a percentage of base pay that will be paid out. A decade ago, one survey found that bonus plans were used by almost 85 percent of the organizations surveyed.[17] Bonuses are subject to the same problems as other incentive programs. In addition, it may be very difficult to determine the extent to which an individual manager is actually contributing to the success of the firm or department, which limits the effectiveness of bonuses as a motivator for better performance.

Another problem associated with bonus systems, and indeed all incentive systems, is that they are short-term in nature. Because they are focused on performance during the current bonus period, they do not consider the best interests of the company over time. To alleviate this problem, firms may tie bonuses to the achievement of longer-range performance goals. Another option is to give bonuses in the form of stock so that the future performance of the company will affect the value of the bonus, encouraging the recipient to work toward the company's best long-range interests.

Skill- and Knowledge-Based Pay

Skill- and knowledge-based pay systems seek to reward employees for acquiring additional skills. The reasoning behind them is that employees are more valuable to the employer when they can perform more than one function because it gives the company more flexibility to adjust to changes in the environment. Most plans do limit the amount of additional pay that can be attained and the types of positions allowed addtional training. Zitaner ranks this method of compensation along with gain-sharing as the most effective way to link pay with performance and to reward participation and empowerment in organizational culture.[18] Lawler, Ledford, and Chang found that 51 percent of Fortune 500 companies used some form of skill-based pay.[19]

---

[17] Zitaner, E. D. 1992. "Variable Pay Programs: Tracking Their Direction." *Compensation and Benefits Review*, 24: 8.

[18] Ibid.

[19] Lawler, E. E., G. E. Ledford, and L. Chang. 1993. "Who Uses Skill-based Pay, and Why." *Compensation and Benefits Review*, March-April: 22-26.

Spot Awards or One-Time Bonuses

Spot awards are lump-sum payments that recognize individual or group achievements. They are generally associated with a particular task or project and result from nominations by supervisors. These rewards are normally derived from a pool the firm has set aside for this purpose. This type of compensation tends to be more popular with firms that pay at the upper end of the market; it allows them to reward outstanding performance without raising their labor costs significantly.

Group Incentives

In some cases, individual incentive plans may not be feasible. For one thing, as the use of technology increases, it becomes more difficult to assess the contributions of individuals. Also, piece rates may increase waste or encourage hoarding of materials. Individual incentives may pit workers against one another and discourage the cooperation that leads to production increases for everyone.[20] For these reasons, where cooperation is essential, group incentives may be more appropriate.

Group incentives can take the form of small-group or plant-wide incentives. Each member of the group is rewarded based on the performance of the group as a whole. Group and plant-wide incentive plans are based on the theory that an organization can only be successful if all its employees work together. The two basic forms of group incentives are: (1) gainsharing/cost-reduction plans and (2) profit-sharing plans. Gainsharing plans are administered based on the performance of distinguishable groups, such as a production unit, department, or division, or the performance of the entire company. Company-wide gainsharing plans are more common in smaller firms. Profit-sharing plans are generally based on the performance of the firm as a whole.

Gainsharing Plans

The purpose of gainsharing plans is to share financial gains from productivity improvements with employees who are responsible for the improvements.[21] They may be tied to improvements in either performance

---

[20] Kaufman, R. T. 1992. "The Effects of IMPROSHARE on Productivity." *Industrial and Labor Relations Review,* 45: 311-322.

[21] Ewing, J. C. 1989. "Gainsharing Plans: Two Key Factors." *Compensation and Benefits Review,* 21: 49-53.

or efficiency. Target goals and the rewards associated with their attainment are set for the unit at the start of a set period, typically a year. When the target goals are achieved, the employees earn the specified rewards.

If gainsharing plans are to be successful, there must be high levels of trust, cooperation, and communication between employees and management. Moreover, employees must be involved in the process from the start, helping to set goals and planning how they can be accomplished. Finally, accurate cost-accounting procedures must be in place to properly measure productivity changes.

Scanlon plans are the oldest and best-known gainsharing plans. Union leader Joseph Scanlon created the concept in the 1930s. The steel plant at which Scanlon worked was failing. Recognizing that only cooperation between workers and management could save the plant, he recommended that profits resulting from increases in labor productivity would be shared with the workers who created the savings.

That first plan was based primarily on labor cost savings. Since then, the concept has been modified to incorporate such factors as quality improvements and scrap reduction. To put a Scanlon plan in place, a firm must gather production and cost information for a base period that will be used in calculating gains in future periods. Base periods must be chosen with care, because a period of low productivity would set standards too low, so that too much would be paid out in bonuses. Contrarily, periods of extremely high productivity would result in goals that are too difficult to achieve. Standards must be updated periodically to reflect changes in technology or products that affect productivity. A basic Scanlon plan is illustrated in Exhibit 7.6.

Profit-sharing

Profit-sharing plans simply distribute some percentage of the company's profits in a given period (usually a year) to the employees. Generally these funds are deposited in a trust fund until the employee's retirement or departure from the firm. Their usefulness as a motivator is limited because an individual employee may have little or no control over the means to produce profits; profitability can be a function of, among other things, the economy, fads and fashions, and technological advances. They may have more motivating value if profit shares are paid in stock.

Exhibit 7.6: Application of the Scanlon Plan

Step 1: Calculate the Scanlon ratio.

Sales value of production (SVOP), base year: $23,000,000
Total wage bill: $ 9,890,000

Scanlon ratio: $ 9,890,000
                                    $23,000,000 = 0.43*

*This means that 43 percent of the sales value of the goods produced goes to pay labor costs in the base period. Suppose that in the current period the sales value of goods produced increases to $25,000,000 and the total wage bill is $10,000,000. The gains available for distribution would be calculated as follows:

Step 2: Calculate the sales and wage bill for the current year.
SVOP current period: $25,000,000

Allowable wage bill: $25,000,000 x 0.43 = $10,750,000
Actual wage bill: $10,000,000
Savings (allowable less actual wages): $ 750,000 *

*Savings achieved through reduced labor costs are usually split between workers and the company. A typical split would give 75 percent of the savings to the workers and 25 percent to the firm. Most plans also retain some percentage of the gains in case of reduced production in future periods. Any net holdings at the end of the year are distributed to the workers. The amount to be paid out in the current period for this example would be calculated as follows:

Step 3: Calculate bonuses for employee distribution.
Savings available for distribution: $750,000
Less company share (25%):   (187,500)
Total available for distribution to employees: $562,500
Less retained savings (25%):   (140,625)
Available for distribution this period: $421,875

Regardless of the incentive system used, it is essential that the employee have some control over output and quality levels. Someone working on an assembly line that often breaks down, someone whose production is limited by the amount the company can sell, and someone who tries to add value to a product that is already defective when it arrives at that work station has no control over production amount and quality.

EMPLOYEE BENEFITS

Benefits are the noncash aspects of compensation that further provide for the welfare of the employee. Typical components of a benefit package, not including such legally required benefits as worker's compensation, are health insurance, retirement, and paid time off. Benefit packages vary greatly from employer to employer. McCaffery says, "While a company can define benefits for internal purposes in any way it chooses, external comparisons are more difficult because of the lack of a uniform standard."[22] In general, employee benefits attempt to reinforce the loyalty of employees to their employer and to attract strong employees to the organization. Other common reasons for offering benefits are improved employee morale, increased job satisfaction, reduced turnover, reduced unionization activity, and enhanced employee security. Estimates indicate that the total cost of benefits is approximately 41 percent of total payroll.

Insurance

The continuous rise in health care costs in recent years has made employee health care a very controversial issue in compensation, but health care benefits are usually at the top of an employee's list of the most important benefits. A complete health benefit package might cover health care, dental care, vision care, and prescription drugs. These benefits can be financed and provided to employees through private insurance companies, self-funding plans, health maintenance organizations (HMOs), and preferred provider organizations (PPOs).

Private Insurance Companies
An organization can contract with a private insurance company to pay the medical bills of its employees. As with any other type of insurance, employers pay a premium to the insurance company for the health care protection. The amount of the premium is based on such variables as company size, type of industry, incidence rates, pre-existing condition clauses, and deductible amounts. Since the 1990s, it has become common to shop around for better premium rates because of high premium increases. Insurance companies often offer teaser rates that are lower than the rates of

[22] McCaffery, R. M. 1992. *Employee Benefit Programs: A Total Compensation Perspective.* 1st and 2nd eds. Boston, MA: PWS-Kent Publishing.

other companies to attract the business, but then they increase the premium after the first year or so to a more profitable amount.

Self-funded Plans

Given the rising costs of health insurance, many organizations see self-insurance as a viable alternative. These programs vary from company to company. Some firms self-fund their entire insurance plan; others by supplemental insurance from a private insurance company for major medical claims that could cause substantial financial loss. Such a plan might pay claims for up to $10,000 per person per year and use a commercial insurance company for claims over that amount. Self-insured companies often use a third-party administrator to process claims.

Health Maintenance Organizations (HMOs)

HMOs evolved after the passage of the 1973 Health Maintenance Act. An HMO offers prepaid medical services for a per-employee charge at a specific site (often a hospital). HMOs need a large number of subscribers if they are to provide adequate services to their clients.[23] Many employees complain about the quality of care because HMOs are motivated to reduce covered procedures to maximize their profits.

Preferred Provider Organizations (PPOs)

PPOs are an alternative to HMOs. A PPO is a contractual relationship between employers, health care providers, and sometimes an insurance company. Health care providers in a PPO contract to offer discounts to an employer if their services are used; the employees are given a list of providers from which to choose. Workers in the United States are willing to pay more for their employee benefits, it has been found, if they have a greater say in deciding which health care benefits they receive. A survey by Pulse Surveys of America for Colonial Life and Accident Insurance Company found 63.1 percent of employees surveyed would pay more to have more say in benefit allocations, 28.5 percent would not pay more, and 8.1 percent were uncertain. These results suggest that health care programs should focus more on flexibility and choice than on who pays.[24]

---

[23] Henderson. R. I. 2002. *Compensation Management in a Knowledge-Based World.* 9th ed. Englewood Cliffs, NJ: Prentice-Hall.

[24] Hoffman, M. A. 1992. "Workers Want Say in Benefits, New Study Says Over 60% Would Pay More for Choice." *Business Insurance,* 20: 3.

HMOs and PPOs are considered *managed care plans.* One study found that 75 percent of employers surveyed offered some kind of managed care plan and 45 percent of the workers were covered by an HMO.[25]

Pay for Time Not Worked

Paid time off is one of the many benefits employees look for in choosing an employer. According to the United States Chamber of Commerce, payments for time not worked in United States accounted for just over 10 percent of payroll.[26] Holidays, vacations, sick leave, personal absences, and paid rest periods are all part of this calculation.

Holidays

Six holidays are usually recognized and paid for by virtually all U.S. employers—New Year's Day, Memorial Day, Independence Day, Labor Day, Thanksgiving Day, and Christmas Day—and most employers offer four to six other holidays, though the specific number and the dates vary with employer and employee preference, affordability, and industry practices. Common paid holidays are New Year's Eve, Christmas Eve, the day after Thanksgiving, Martin Luther King Day, and other personal days, such as the employee's birthday.

Vacation

Companies grant vacation time to their employees, first, in the belief that employees should be rewarded for their commitment to the organization, and, second, to give employees time away from the mental and physical demands of their job. Time allotted for vacation ranges from one to five weeks; usually employees start with one or two weeks and earn additional time with seniority. Hourly or nonexempt employees generally earn less vacation time than salaried or exempt employees.

Sick Leave

Sick leave gives employees some income protection when they have a personal illness or accident. Most employers allow between five and 12 sick days a year. Employees can usually accumulate sick days from year to year

---

[25] "Managed-care Health Plans Gain More Popularity, but Slowly." 1992. *Wall Street Journal,* April 7.

[26] U.S. Chamber of Commerce. *Employee Benefits.* 1997 edition. Washington, D.C.

to provide for a more serious illness or injury. Also, some employers allow employees to use sick leave to take care of close relatives who are ill.

A common problem for organizations today is sick leave abuse—employees using sick days for vacation or personal days. If this becomes too widespread, a firm can tighten its sick leave policies by requiring health care provider certification, not paying for the first day of illness, reducing the days allotted, or simply combining sick leave and vacation leave into a category called employee leave or paid time off (PTO). For instance, a company that offered 10 days of vacation and 10 sick days might offer a total of 20 days of employee leave instead. Employees could use their leave for vacation, personal days, or illness.

Personal Absences

Most employees at one time or another will have to miss work for a reason that is beyond their control. The most common types of personal absences are jury duty, witness duty, family death, and military duty. The number of days allotted for each type of personal absence varies greatly from company to company. The personnel handbook should state the company's policies on these matters.

Paid Rest Periods

Paid rest periods include lunch, coffee breaks, travel time, and clothes-change or get-ready time. Paid rest periods are always subject to time limits, but a combination of employee trust and supervision is necessary to be sure people observe the stated limits. Though the cost of paid rest periods is not usually included in benefits statements and employees are not inclined to recognize the costs as meaningful, it can be high in terms of work not completed or extra employees required to absorb lost work time.

For some occupations, rest periods are legally mandated for safety reasons.

Retirement Benefits

The normal retirement age has decreased in recent years from age 65 to ages 60 to 62. In many retirement plans, benefits for those retiring at 60 are similar to those for employees retiring at 65.[27]

---

[27] Mamorsky, J. D. 2001. *Employee Benefits Handbook.* Boston, MA: Warren, Gorham & Lamont Inc.

Many employers set up a pension plan to help employees accumulate retirement benefits during their active working years. In order to be *quali - fied,* a pension plan must conform to stringent requirements contained in the Internal Revenue Code (IRC). The Tax Reform Act of 1986 states that qualified plans should focus on retirement income and retirement savings and not lump-sum distributions and early withdrawals. The Employee Retirement Income Security Act (ERISA) sets out specific procedures for eligibility, vesting, and financial standards.

The major types of retirement plans are defined benefit and defined contribution. Many large firms offer a combination of the two. A *defined benefit* plan lets employees know how much they will receive in retirement income and gives them the security of a guaranteed benefit based on years of service to the company. For example, an employee might receive 2 percent of base salary for every year of service, so that employees with 30 years of service would receive 60 percent of their base salary (usually an average of the last three- to five-years of employment) for their retirement.

The two types of *defined contribution* plans are: (1) the money purchase plan and (2) the profit-sharing plan. The money purchase plan requires the employer to make fixed and regular contributions for participants. Typically, 4 to 7 percent of pay is allocated annually. Profit-sharing plans give employees a share of the company's profits.

Profit-sharing plans used with 401(k) savings and investment plans have expanded rapidly in recent years. The 401(k) plan is a savings plan where employees can elect to contribute up to 6 percent of their salary to an account and the employer will match some proportion of that amount. Most plans permit employees to make additional unmatched contributions. A 401(k) is usually attractive to higher-paid employee because it defers payment of taxes until the person retires, at which time they are likely to have a lower tax rate.

Qualified Plans

The term *qualified* relates to a variety of employer-offered benefits. In IRC §401(a), qualified, as it relates to pension, profit-sharing, and stock bonus plans, permits the employer to deduct all contributions to such plans in the year the contribution is made, and none of the contribution is treated as taxable earnings to the employee until it is distributed (as a pension payment) to the employee. If a plan is to be qualified, it must meet all the following qualifications:

- The plan must be in writing.
- The rights of employees under the plan must be legally enforceable.
- The employer must intend to maintain the plan indefinitely.
- The employer must provide for reasonable notification to employees of benefits under the plan.
- The plan must be maintained for the exclusive benefit of employees (and in some cases, their spouses and dependents).
- Benefits must be funded.
- Eligibility must not discriminate in favor of shareholders, officers, or highly compensated employees.
- Contributions and benefits covered by the plan must not become forfeitable and must not discriminate in favor of shareholders, officers, or highly compensated employees, though it can discriminate in favor of lower-paid employees.
- The plan must be for the benefit of employees and be nondiscriminatory.
- It must cover all employees in the covered group who are at least 21 years old and have completed one year of service.

Disability Benefits

It is almost certain that everyone will miss at least one day of work a year due to illness or injury, but sometimes sickness and accident cause an extended absence. Disability plans are one way to help cover the costs of such absence. These plans are insured arrangements that replace a portion of pay, usually 50 to 60 percent, after an employee has been absent for a specified period of time. Premiums for disability vary depending on the waiting period allowed before insurance is paid; the longer the waiting period, the lower the premium.

Long-term disability (LTD), defined as three to six-months of absence, and pension benefits are similar in that they both give continuous income to an employee who cannot work for an extended time. Most large employers provide LTD benefits until a person reaches 65, at which time pension benefits take over. The Equal Employment Opportunity Commission (EEOC) says that benefits depend on the age of the employee at the onset of the disability. The EEOC authorizes termination of disability benefits on the following schedule:

- For disabilities that begin at or before age 60, benefits may cease at 65.

- For disabilities that begin after 60, benefits may cease five years after disablement.

Rules for coordinating LTD and pension benefits are stated in the Supreme Court decision and the passage by Congress of the Older Workers Benefit Protection Act of 1990. The amount and duration of benefits provided to older workers cannot be reduced on account of age unless the reduction can be justified on the basis of cost.

FLEXIBLE BENEFITS

Given all the different needs of employees in today's diverse work force, it may help in recruitment and retention to offer employees a choice in their benefits package. That is the idea behind flexible benefit plans. *Flexible benefits, flexible compensation, cafeteria plans,* and *flexible plans* are interchangeable terms for plans that give employees a choice of benefits. Flexible benefit programs are growing in popularity. Many employers stress the importance of increasing employee understanding of the options in a flexible benefit program; others cite the ability of these plans to meet the wide range of individual worker needs.

There are two main reasons why employers look to flexible benefit plans:

1. Employers want more credit and appreciation from employees for their benefits package.

2. Employers can save money and maximize the buying power of their benefit dollars.[28]

---

[28] Commerce Clearing House, Inc. 1988. *Flexible Benefits: Will They Work for You?* Chicago, IL.

On the other hand, flexible benefit plans do have some disadvantages:

* Employees may not choose the appropriate mix of benefits.
* Employees may forfeit unused portions of their benefit plans.
* Employees are not assured a net gain.[29]

Other possible negatives of such plans are their administrative complexity, the difficulty and cost of communicating benefit options, possible union opposition, and tax and legal uncertainties.

Types of Flexible Benefit Plans

The five basic types of flexible benefit plans are:

1. The reimbursement or flexible spending account
2. The additional allowance or add-on approach
3. Mix-and-match options
4. Core carve-out or core plus options
5. Modular plans

Most employers will choose a plan or a combination of plans based on the variety of benefits they wish to offer and the amount of discretion in choosing benefits they want their employees to have.

Reimbursement or Flexible Spending Account

The reimbursement account, or flexible spending account, which became popular in 1983, is the simplest type of plan. It allows employees to pay for certain services—among them health care premiums, medical expenses not covered by the employer's tax-deductible plan, dependent care, and qualified group legal services—with pre-tax dollars.

Additional Allowance or Add-On

The additional allowance or add-on approach supplements standard benefits with optional ones. Based on seniority, each employee is given a certain number of flexible credits to buy the additional benefits. If the amount spent exceeds the amount of credits received, the difference is taken from

---

[29] Guest, D. K. 1991. "Flexible Benefits Plans Are Studied and Praised." *Pension World,* 52.

the employee's salary. If all the credits are not spent, the difference is transferred into a 401(k) plan. This approach ensures that employees are adequately protected by giving everyone the essential benefits and then offering employees the opportunity to select a benefit that meets an individual need.

Mix-and-Match Options

The mix-and-match option also works with a standard package, but the employee has the opportunity to select different levels of coverage. Choosing lower coverage in one area allows the employee to select higher coverage in another. The employee may also choose mainly high coverage in all areas and help pay some of the costs through salary reduction. This option gives the employee flexibility without affecting employer costs.

Core Carve-Out or Core-Plus Options

The core carve-out plan, or the core-plus options plan, is like the additional allowance plan except that, instead of maintaining current benefits, it reduces the current package to create a two-part plan consisting of fixed-core coverage and flexible coverage. The core is usually a skeleton providing basic benefits, such as a comprehensive medical plan, group term life insurance, partial income replacement during extended disability, a pension plan, and standard paid time off. The residual amount after the core has been carved out is flexible credits that can be used to increase the coverage supplied by the core or buy additional benefits or be converted into cash.

Modular Plans

The modular plan is a prepackaged plan that has a number of modules, each with the same range of benefits but with varying levels of coverage. Each module is designed with the needs of a particular employee segment in mind. The number of modules offered depends on the perceived difference in variation between employee segments in comparison to the price of administering two or more benefit packages. Sometimes, all the modules are of equal value; in other plans, the employee who chooses a more expensive module must pay the difference. In a survey conducted by Hewitt Associates, it was found that 67 percent of flexible benefit plans allowed choices in benefits and flexible spending accounts, 22 percent offered spending accounts only, and 11 percent allowed choice-making only.[30]

OTHER ISSUES

In determining pay decisions, it is necessary to keep in mind other issues such as the company culture, corporate life cycle, compensation laws, employee needs and unions. The impact of these factors on compensation decision making is discussed below.

Corporate Life Cycles

Companies that are in different parts of their life cycles will need to consider pay decisions differently. The amount of money that they have available for compensation varies greatly. A firm just starting out lacks the financial resources to pay high wages and benefits. Instead, it may pay lower wages, but offer greater incentives based on the future performance of the firm such as stock options. This promise of future return can be enough of an incentive to be able to attract talented individuals despite the lower base pay. A firm that has already reached its full growth and is stable can afford high salaries and benefits, but may have little to gain by offering large incentives to employees.

Organizational Culture

Each firm has an individual outlook on how employees should be treated. A firm may view employees paternalistically; thinking of its employees as children of sorts which the firm must look after. Employees can be viewed as members of one cooperative team which must work together to achieve success. Companies can be very competitive in nature within their structure and admire individual accomplishment. Or companies may even view employees as just another input of production that can be easily substituted by another worker or a machine.

The view held by the organization toward its employees should influence the type of compensation that it offers. A paternalistic firm may offer full benefits to all of its employees. A team-based view may result in pay systems dependent on the overall performance of the firm or department. Internally competitive firms will reward individual performance. And the

---

[30] *www.was4.hewitt.com* (based on subscription).

firm that views employees as another cog in the production machine will offer little more than what is necessary to get enough employees to carry out its functions.

Employee Needs

Employees within a firm are not homogeneous. As such, they will have different needs that may affect the means of compensation that a firm offers in order to keep employees satisfied. Two specific ways in which employees'needs can vary are their age and whether or not their spouse works.

The age of workers can influence the type of pay desired. Younger employees need larger base pay to pay for housing, cars, etc. Older employees current expenses may not be as great, and they may prefer tax deferred forms of payment such as 401K plans that defer both the income and tax until retirement.

Dual career couples may seek to eliminate duplication of benefits between their two jobs and opt for more cash in hand instead. If a firm is ignorant of its employees' needs, even a well-designed compensation system may fail due to its inability to meet employee needs.

Unions

The existence of unions operating within a firm will effect its compensation system. In terms of corporate strategy, it may be very important that a firm avoid a strike at all cost. Perhaps it is in a highly competitive business where clients would be quickly lost if the firm were unable to live up to its commitments. Under such circumstances, the influences on the compensation systems will be much more affected by unions.

Union negotiations can affect every area of a compensation plan. They generally seek to reward seniority, and most plans have a higher percentage of their total compensation in the form of indirect pay/benefits than do non-union pay systems. In addition, unions tend to be less enthusiastic about individual incentives and pay based on performance.

The existence of unions can affect compensation systems even if they are not present in a given firm. It may be the goal of an organization to prevent a union from getting established. As such, it will make decisions regarding pay to prevent this occurrence. It will offer as much, or even more, than union firms in order to prevent unionization.

The Legal Environment

There were legal constraints on pay as early as the Middle Ages when the church imposed the "Just Wage Doctrine". Following the black plague, there was a shortage of labor causing pay rates to rise. The church set up this doctrine to control pay rates and to establish relative pay between certain occupational groups.

The church no longer has the power to affect pay, but the government certainly does, and it has imposed much legislation to protect workers. Besides the Equal Employment Opportunity legislation discussed in Chapter 2, several other pieces of legislation directly impact the practice of compensation administration.

1938 Fair Labor Standards Act
The FLSA applies to all employers with two or more employees, who are engaged in commerce and/or retail operations, with gross sales of $500,000. Also included in the act are federal, state, and local governments, and labor unions.

The FLSA divides employees into exempt and non-exempt categories. Exempt employees are those who are exempted from the overtime provisions of the act. There are five classes of employees who fall into the exempt category.

- Executives
- Administrators
- Computer Professionals
- Professionals/Creative
- Outside Sales People

The title of a job alone is not enough for it to be an exempt job. It must meet FLSA duties and salary test guidelines. Specifically, an employee must earn 455 dollars per week or $23,600 annually and have a majority of their duties fall in one of the five categories listed above.

Overtime Pay
This is the most significant provision of the act. It states that if a non-exempt employee works more than forty hours in any one week, the company must pay the employee one and one half times the normal rate of pay

for each hour over forty.

While this is the minimum legal requirement, some union contracts sate that overtime must be paid if more than eight hours are worded in a day regardless of how many hours may be worked in the week. One variation in the forty-hour work week rule applies to hospitals and nursing homes. It allows up to eighty hours in a two week pay period before overtime pay is required. This allows for flexibility in scheduling workers who have to work rotating and swing shifts.

Minimum Wage
Under the act, covered employers are currently required to pay employees a wage that is at least $5.15 per hour. In addition, employees of certain individually owned service or retail establishments, employees of seasonal amusement or recreational establishments, employees on certain small newspapers, small telephone company switchboard operations, sea workers on foreign vessels, and employees engaging in fishing operations, babysitters, certain farm workers, and elderly companions are covered along with non-exempt workers.

Child Labor
The child labor provision was set up with two main goals in mind. It was intended to protect the educational opportunities for children, and to protect them in jobs that may be detrimental to their health. The major limitations of the FLSA on children working outside the agriculture are:

- There are no restrictions concerning anyone over the age of eighteen.
- Ages sixteen and seventeen can work in any non-hazardous job with unlimited hours.
- Ages fourteen and fifteen can work in non-hazardous jobs outside of school hours subject to the following conditions.
    - no more than three hours on a school day
    - no more than eighteen hours in a school week
    - no more than eight hours on a non-school day or forty hours in an non-school week
    - work cannot begin until seven A.M. and must end at seven P.M. except between June 1 and Labor Day, when work can end at nine P.M.

Enforcement of the FLSA

The act is to be enforced by the Wage and Hour Division of the U.S. Department of Labor. Its enforcement includes the right to the following:

- The right to investigate any complaints filed under the act, which includes the right to obtain any or all records.
- An investigator may order an employer to change its pay practices or pay back wages. The statute of limitations on back pay is two years, unless the violation was intentional, in which case it is three years. Intentional fines carry a possible $10,000 fine and jail sentence.

Wage Legislation for Government Contractors

Government contractors are held to a somewhat higher standard than other businesses. There are three acts commonly referred to as "prevailing wage laws." A prevailing wage is the minimum wage allowed for work on government related projects. The prevailing wage must accurately reflect the labor market in which the project is conducted and is usually assessed by using a market survey of some kind. Three important prevailing wage laws are described below.

- **Davis-Bacon Act of 1931** – Covers mechanics and laborers on public construction projects if the contract is over $2,0000
- **Walsh-Healy Act of 1936** – Extends the Davis-Bacon Act to manufacturers and suppliers of goods for government contracts if the amount exceeds $10,000.
- **The Service Contract Act of 1965** – Extends prevailing wage requirements to all suppliers of services to the federal government if the services exceed $2,500.

Workman's Compensation Laws

Workman's compensation laws came into existence on the state level as a response to growing industrialization and increasing numbers of accidents on the job. They vary from state to state, but have these basic functions:

- To guarantee benefits to victims of industrial accidents on a no-fault basis.
- To provide an efficient method by which claims are filed.

- To assure income protection.
- To encourage employer interest in safety by setting compensation insurance premiums on an actuarial basis.
- To encourage investigation of work accidents so that they are avoided in the future.

Most states require state approved insurance, but others allow companies to self-insure if they comply with state safety and financial standards. Payments for workman's compensation can be temporary disability, permanent partial disability, or total disability.

Social Security Act of 1935
The Social Security Act of 1935 was part of Roosevelt's New Deal legislation of the Great Depression. Its main function is to provide retirement, disability, and health insurance for retired persons and those unable to work. Social Security is funded through payroll deductions and matching contributions by employers. As of January 1, 1992, the payment was 7.62% on the first $55,500 of wages earned each year. Companies are required by law to make these payments to social security quarterly.

Consumer Credit Protection Act of 1968
The Consumer Credit Protection Act deals with garnishments. Garnishments are court orders requiring an employer to deduct money from an employee's paycheck to repay a bad debt. Until 1968, state laws covered garnishments and allowed entire paychecks to be garnished.

The Consumer Credit Protection Act applies to all employer and state and local governments. Federal employees are exempt from garnishments. Under the act:

- The amount that can be garnished is related to take home pay. If take home pay is less than $100.50 per week, it cannot be garnished. That is the amount that an employee is guaranteed to be able to take home. Beyond that, their earnings can be garnished up to 25% of their wages.
- In order to garnish wages, a court order must be obtained.
- An employer cannot fire an employee for garnishments that result from a bad debt.
- The act is to be enforced by the Wage and Hour division of the Department of Labor.

Employee Retirement Income Security Act (ERISA) of 1974
ERISA was designed to protect the rights of employees to funds in private pension plans managed by their employers. Until this act, an employee's right to these funds was only assured by the company's promise to pay. Companies usually paid pensions out of current revenues rather than having funds set up in trust. Employees could get out of their obligations by retiring employees early, or forcing them to quit.

ERISA regulates private pension plans and establishes standards that must be met. The four provisions of the act are fiduciary standards, funding, vesting, and portability.

Fiduciary Standards

Prior to ERISA, companies had pension fund managers who invested the funds. This provided for a conflict of interest because funds could be invested according to the best interests of the company rather than the best interests of the employees. To eliminate this conflict of interest, plans must now be managed by outside companies.

Funding

Before ERISA, most plans were not fully funded. When companies lost money, they could not make pension payments. ERISA requires firms to fund pensions in the same year that the obligation occurred. Employers with existing plans were given 20 years in which to become fully funded.

Vesting

Formerly, an employer was always entitled to monies plus interest paid into pension plans. ERISA insures the employees' rights to funds invested on their behalf. ERISA provides two vesting formulas, and requires that all employees must be fully vested after 15 years of participation in the pension plan.

Portability

Portability refers to whether or not pension money can be transferred from one plan to another. ERISA allows for transference of funds without incurring tax liability if both plans are ERISAapproved. Under ERISA, pension reporting must be provided to both the Department of Labor's Pension and

Welfare Benefits Programs unit and the IRS. The Department of Labor oversees the administration of qualified pension plans. It requires the filing of a summary plan description that outlines all the plan's benefits. The IRS determines if the plan is tax exempt.

WRAP-UP

The purpose of this chapter was to outline a process for designing a fair and equitable compensation plan. Activities inherent in doing so include job analysis, job evaluation, and market surveys.

There are many types of benefits that can be incorporated into the compensation plan, including time off, insurance, disability, executive benefits, and retirement programs. Flexible benefit programs can be used to meet the needs of different employees, giving them all a choice and an opportunity to design a unique package of benefits.

There are no hard and fast rules in the area of compensation and benefits decision making. The manager must only establish the strategic direction and follow the legal requirements in making compensation decisions.

CHAPTER 8

Company Policies: Writing an Effective HR Handbook

In any company, the employee handbook summarizes the HR policies that every employee needs to know. All the important functional areas of HR management have already been described (selection procedures, compensation, benefits, performance appraisal, and discipline). The goal of a handbook is to illustrate these functions in order to help orient both new and existing employees to company practices.

As many business executives who have survived a lawsuit will tell attest, a properly constructed employee handbook is extremely vital to a company's well-being—as is having front-line managers who consistently follow the handbook.[1] Even when a manager has the best of intentions, if company policies are not applied uniformly, the company has a serious problem. Unfortunately, most of the trouble starts at the beginning—choosing the wrong phrasing for the handbook can mean that management is making false promises, overextending the company, or, even worse, treating the employees unfairly. By avoiding these handbook pitfalls, a company has a better chance of developing a sound document.

When beginning to prepare a handbook, make sure it cannot be interpreted as a contract that could be enforced in court. State plainly and

---

[1] This opening section draws heavily on Bolden-Barrett, V. 1999. "What your Employee Handbook Says about You." *HR Briefing,* December 15: 2-3.

prominently up front that the handbook does not represent a contact, can be changed by management as needed, and is simply for the general guidance of the employee.

Because that language alone will not eliminate all possibilities of grievance, carefully read through the document to make sure that none of the language gives away any rights that were not intended. For instance, avoid statements and phrases like the following:

- *"Employees will be terminated for the following reasons."* This wording protects employees from punishment for any activities not listed, no matter how heinous. If you wish to list reasons, make it clear that the list consists only of examples and is not to be considered comprehensive.

- *"Termination may occur after the following four-step disciplinary process has begun."* Some events are so extreme that the manager's good judgment would skip any or all of the steps, but this wording makes all four steps mandatory.

- *"We promise to always treat employees fairly."* Though this sounds appropriate, it's not a good idea to make promises, especially ones that are vague and open to personal interpretation. Employees have the right to sue the company if they do not feel this promise is being met. Starting sentences with "we will or do" is also a problem; use "we try" instead.

- *"Just cause"* and *"employment at will"* are the kinds of expressions that conventionally are nothing but trouble.

Employee relations depend heavily on the quality of the employee handbook. At a time when lawsuits seem almost ordinary, the phrasing of a company policy could bury the strongest corporations. Managers should try to be as connected as possible with the drafting of a handbook because they will never be unconnected from it once it is written.

THE MANAGER'S CHALLENGE

As a company grows, communications between employees and front-line managers seems to become less effective. Employees lose the feedback they received when the firm was small and supervisors had more time for hands-on management.

Setting up rules and policies is commonly one of the first steps to formalizing HR management. As the company grows and adds more managers, consistency in enforcing policy becomes problematic, making employees frustrated and disgruntled over apparent favoritism. Yet many laws (see Chapter 2) require formal communication of an employee's rights (e.g., family leave, sexual harassment, and dealing with disabilities). Also, documenting that employees have received and understand the company's policies makes it easier to take disciplinary actions.

Essentially, the handbook is a guidebook to the policies of the company. It is an effective and relatively inexpensive way to communicate to workers important information about company rules, procedures, and goals, as well as abstract things like the company's expectations and philosophy. Employee handbooks save valuable time in explaining to new employees how the organization functions. A good employee handbook is a reliable source to which employees can turn when questions arise.

In addition to helping to train new employees, handbooks also open lines of communication with employees. When workers know the company's philosophy, goals, and motivations, they are likely to feel they are part of the organization. Also, since employee handbooks usually cover disciplinary procedures, they can be an effective management tool for dealing with problem employees. (An example of a complete employee handbook can be found in Appendix B.) It's important to begin writing the handbook by examining its goals and objectives.

HANDBOOK GOALS AND OBJECTIVES

The first step in creating a viable handbook is to determine who will be responsible for drafting it. A single individual is the best choice to write and produce the manual, but it is advisable that a committee of employees from all affected organizational levels review and approve the contents before publication.

The person chosen to write the handbook should be familiar with all aspects of the organization and its personnel policies. This suggests it should be someone from the HR department, if there is one, or whoever is, in practice, in charge of the HR function.

Once someone has been selected to head the process, the company must decide what the objectives of the handbook are to be. Writing without direction is one of the greatest pitfalls in creating an employee manual.[2] Handbooks can serve several purposes; those that are successful narrow these purposes down to a realistic goal. In its book *How to Prepare an Employee Handbook,*[3] the Management Information Center identified five basic objectives in writing an employee handbook, based on responses it obtained from 65 companies who had done so:

1. To build understanding between employer and employee

2. To accurately communicate the company philosophy

3. To make the new employee comfortable

4. To improve employee and community relations

5. To keep management aware of its responsibilities and those of the employees

A company's goals for its handbook might include none of these or all of them, but no matter what the goals are, it is vital to set them early so as to give direction to the person writing the manual.

One researcher suggests that every handbook have at least two elements:

1. A section that preserves employment-at-will status, stating in so many words, as we have already mentioned, that nothing in the handbook should be taken to effect a contract that negates the employer's rights under the at-will doctrine.

2. A discrimination and harassment section that describes the types of behaviors prohibited and the consequences of violating the policies.

Other important areas that might be given prominence are policies about privacy, drug use, and drug testing.[4]

One way to determine the handbook's objectives is to assess the attitudes and feelings of the employees, perhaps raising questions from the following list:

---

[2] Management Information Center. 1968. *How to Prepare an Employee Handbook,* Albuquerque, NM: MIS Inc.

[3] Ibid.

[4] Flynn, G. 2000. "Take Another Look at the Employee Handbook." *Workforce,* 79: 132-134.

- What areas have new employees had the most trouble with?
- Does everyone know what is expected of employees in this company?
- How many people do not know how to do something because they are afraid of asking dumb questions?
- How good are employee/employer relations?
- How complete is the training process?
- How many seasoned employees still do not know the company philosophy?

In finding out where weaknesses lie in the current system, the objectives of the handbook fall into place. The manual should fill any voids left after all areas of the company are examined.

COMPONENTS OF THE HANDBOOK

Once goals are in place, it's time to get down to the business of writing. The handbook coordinator should not just sit down and crank out the written document. Every section of the book should be carefully researched so that employees are given the most accurate information available. The coordinator should determine who in the company is most qualified to provide which information and seek out those people.

Though the content will of course depend upon the objectives, a good handbook should cover certain basic concepts. Fourteen areas have been identified that should be given attention.[5]

The Welcome

The welcome section should make the reader feel comfortable with the company, giving employees positive reinforcement for their decision to join the company and extending good wishes for their future with the company. It should also welcome the new employee to the handbook, which represents the first real contact for newcomers. This section should explain the purpose of the handbook and emphasize its value as a resource to help the employee succeed in the company.

---

[5] Harris, J. 1986. *Create Your Employee Handbook Fast and Professionally.* New York: Asher-Gallant Press.

As a first impression, the welcome can make or break the handbook. It sets the tone for the rest of the book. If it is very formal and strict, readers may not want to continue, while a lighter, though not frivolous, tone may make them want to read on. Getting all employees to read the book should be a primary consideration.

Description of the Company

This section is the backbone of a good employee handbook. It should reveal the focus of the company and how individual employees fit into the picture. It can be broken down into three areas: (1) what the company does, (2) its history, and (3) its philosophy.

In covering the first area, the handbook should be very specific. Explain every facet of the company's operations, from the underlying concept to the actual everyday functions. All products and services should be listed because it is important that each employee understands how they are interwoven into the whole operation. The founder and CEO of Whole Food Markets, John Mackey, stresses the importance of keeping these explanations as short as possible. "If it's too long, they'll blow it off," he says.[6] Give a clear, concise summary but make sure it includes all the most important information and explains where employees can get more information if they want it.

Another important part of the company section is a brief summary of company history. By addressing this, the handbook gives new employees an idea of both where the company is coming from and where they can hope to go with it in the future.

Explicating the company's philosophy is also crucial. "Employees are much more sympathetic to what the company is trying to accomplish if they understand the overall context in which they are operating. The handbook is a great vehicle for passing along your goals," Mackay says.[7] The philosophy statement not only gives the company a chance to share its goals with employees, it also gives employees the opportunity to see how important they really are and how they fit in.[8] Employees who realize their importance to the company are very likely to be motivated to do their best work.

---

[6] Posner, B. 1989. "Best Little Handbook in Texas." *INC.*, February: 84-88.
[7] Ibid.
[8] Harris, J., op. cit., n. 4.

Company Organization

An organizational chart is useful for giving new employees an overview of the company. Show how each position from management on down relates to the others and tell who the people are who hold each position. Photos of higher management are useful, giving employees an opportunity to "meet" everyone before they run into them in the elevator or the break room.

Part of explaining the company's organization is outlining each department and its functions. While all the departments should be on the chart, space limitation usually allows for only a minimally detailed explanation. After the chart, list each department and give a brief description of its functions, as well as a general idea of its structure.

Hiring Procedures

This section should explain everything the new employee would want to know about the company's hiring practices. An equal opportunity statement is an important part of it because it ensures that employees are hired and promoted because of their qualifications and nothing else.

A good manual should also have an explanation of the qualifications the company looks for in its actual hiring procedures, including the reasons for each requirement. Hiring procedures should be listed specifically with each step in the correct order, so the process is clear.

The hiring procedures section should also explain what employees should do if they know others who want to work at the company. Company policies differ in regard to employees referring job candidates. Explain your company's policy and why it exists. If recommendations are accepted, be sure to outline the process. Can relatives be hired or is there a nepotism policy? Are incentives offered for finding good job candidates?

Promotion Policies

This section should have a detailed description of how employees can apply for open positions and an explanation of any role of seniority in the promotion process, as well as how seniority is determined and what difference it makes in the employee's duties, salary, or job security.

The process of transferring to another part of the company is also covered in this section. While some companies encourage movement within, others discourage it. Make your company's position known, with a full explanation.

Explain why employees might want to transfer, how they should go about requesting to do so, and how a transfer would affect seniority or salary.

Discipline and Termination Procedures

Being disciplined or leaving the company is not what most employees are thinking about when they read their employee handbook, but these topics do have to be addressed. The handbook should describe the types of offenses that may lead to immediate discharge, those that lead to suspension or probation, and those that lead to progressive discipline. Reaffirm that as an employer you have the right to terminate an employee at any time for a specific disciplinary infraction.

Do not be afraid to talk about things that seem negative. Employees need and want to know what *not* to do as much as what to do. Simply explaining the causes for discipline can eliminate confusion.

The handbook should also explain what employees should do when they decide to leave the company voluntarily. To whom should they give notice? How much notice? Does it have to be in writing? By making the procedure clear, an employee is likely to manage the process the way the company would want, thereby eliminating such problems as a hurried search for a replacement.

Performance Evaluations

Use this section to explain when and how often employees are evaluated, by whom, and how the appraisal relates to seniority or salary. Are evaluations announced or are they surprises? When do employees get to see written appraisals? Can they appeal an unsatisfactory one? How? Outline what evaluations are based upon and what they are designed to measure. Many employees are uncomfortable thinking someone is looking over their shoulders; letting them know how the procedure works will set them at ease.

Company Communication Channels

Very few companies are structured in such a way that employees and managers have no contact, but employees don't always know who they can tell what. Explain the role of an employee's supervisor and how the employee can communicate with him or her. This is an excellent opportunity to stress the importance of open lines of communication, both between manager and worker and between employees on the same level.

Another issue to be addressed here is communication between departments. Explain to employees whether they are expected to have direct contact with other departments or when it is necessary for a supervisor to approve contact.

Salary Procedures

The salary procedures section will probably receive the most attention from new employees. Employees want to know how to get a paycheck, where to pick it up, when they might expect a raise, if they can receive bonuses, when they can expect promotions, the basic pay scales, who has an expense account, and the rules for expense accounts.

If the company uses time cards, this section should explain where to get them, what information goes on them, when to turn them in, what happens if they're turned in late, how far ahead of payday they must be turned in, and when paydays fall. Will checks be hand-delivered or put in mailboxes? What happens if payday falls on a holiday? What can be done if an employee loses a check? How can an employee who is not at work on payday get the check? Explain what deductions will be taken from paychecks and what number employees can call if they have questions.

It is very important to discuss how and when raises are decided, as well as the company's policy on bonuses. Employees wants to know how hard work will be rewarded and how often they can hope for a pay increase.

Days and Hours of Work

In this section the handbook should specify what constitutes normal work hours, work days, and work weeks. Explain the policy on lunch and coffee breaks. If the company works in shifts, give the shift starting and stopping times. Be so specific that there is no confusion.

Here is where overtime and attendance policies should be discussed, as well as how absences should be reported, what to do about jury duty, bad weather closings, and tardiness procedures. Be sure to explain any exceptions to the rules.

Time Off

Here the manual would outline sick leave and personal day policies. Explain when employees are eligible for sick days, how many they earn, and when they can use them. Detail how the Family and Medical Leave Act applies, if it does. If personal days are awarded, explain their purpose and use.

This is also the place for information about holiday, vacation, family leave, and emergency leave policies. List the holidays observed and the policy on payment for these days. Explain what happens if a holiday falls on a weekend. Religious holiday policies vary, so be specific. Go over the rules for using the various types of time off: when employees are eligible, how long they get, how they should schedule days off, and what happens to unused vacation time. Also cover what happens in the case of emergencies such as a death or accident in the family. Specify which relatives qualify for bereavement leave, sick leave, etc. Finally, explain what happens if employees accumulate leave days, especially if a use-or-lose policy exists. Include the following:

- Make clear the rules on how many, if any, days can be carried over into the following year.
- Explain how much leave may be taken at any one time.
- Specify any procedures for cashing in days.

Allowing employees to accumulate days is often seen as a positive benefit since employees can take longer vacations or build up time to cover major illnesses.

Company Policies and Procedures

Though this may seem like a grab-bag category, it is very important. It can cover everything from stationery and filing systems to handling a complaint. Explain day-to-day operations like what forms to use for what, how to order supplies, how to use the phone system, how to make suggestions, or how to use company mail. Nowadays it is particularly important to spell out policies related to electronic communications, such as e-mail.

List the company's expectations for employee conduct. A code of conduct is common; it outlines, in general terms, the ideal behavior expected of employees.

The rules section usually addresses policies on matters like smoking, personal calls, mail, safety, visitors, and dress. This section may also state specific policies on sexual harassment.

Sexual Harassment Policy

A company can reduce the likelihood of and its liability for sexual harassment by having a clearly written policy, a specified investigative procedure, and training to explain the policy and procedures to all employees. To meet the standards set forth by the EEOC, a sexual harassment policy should meet the following requirements:[9]

- Be in writing;
- Define what constitutes harassment;
- Declare that it will not be tolerated;
- Use training and education to sensitize supervisors and employees to harassment issues;
- Require prompt and thorough investigation of every complaint;
- Provide for an investigation that results in prompt corrective action, including disciplinary action if it is determined that unlawful harassment occurred; and
- If the investigation reveals that harassment did occur, employers must take immediate corrective action.

Benefits

Give a complete statement of all the benefits the company offers, but don't delve too deeply into their intricacies. Keep the listing simple, and for each item provide a phone number where more information can be obtained. Simplicity is important; companies often change benefits and such a change need not be accompanied by expensive and time-consuming revisions of the handbook.

Special Services

This section tells the new employee what else your company has to offer, perks like a cafeteria or food service, service awards, lost and found, free parking, sports team sponsorships, credit unions, and social events.

Special Policies

Any specific policies not covered elsewhere in the handbook should be in this section. In essence, most organizations have distinctive cultures and

---

[9] Equal Employment Opportunity Center. 1990 March 19. *Policy Guidance on Current Issues of Sexual Harassment,* Sec. 4. E. 2. *www.eeoc.gov.* Accessed 18 May 2004.

the handbook should include all the policies that help form or that reflect the culture.

Employee Sign Off

In addition to the handbook components covered, the employee sign-off is also a necessary component. At the end of the handbook, there should be a detachable page that allows for employees to sign-off that they have read and understood the stated policies and procedures. This does not mean they have to agree with them, it means only that they understood and intend to abide by them.

Employment-at-Will Statement

The employment-at-will doctrine states that employment is at the will of both the employer or the employee. Either can terminate the employment relationship at any time unless the termination is in violation of a contract (either written or implied), law, or public policy.

The handbook should not be construed in any way as an employee contract. Therefore, at-will statements should be made in at least three sections of the employee handbook: (1) the employment, (2) discipline, and (3) employee sign-off sections.

These statements should not be the focus of the handbook. Certainly the orientation of new employees should not center on the fact that they can be fired at any time. Exhibit 8.1 shows a typical employment-at-will statement that is part of the employee sign off.

Exhibit 8.1: An Employment-at-Will Statement for the Employee Sign-off

Date: _____

I, _____, have read and understand the policies described in this handbook. I understand that this handbook does not construe an employment contract and that employment can be terminated by either employee or employer at any time.

_____   _____
Employee Signature   Witness

Employee handbooks will vary from company to company, and not all the components described may be necessary for a particular organization. Some HR experts believe the manual should be short, so that employees do not interpret the contents to be a form of contract. Other experts believe that certain pieces of information are essential because they protect the organization from legal claims by employees. Exhibit 8.2 illustrates many possible topics that can be incorporated into an effective employee handbook.

Exhibit 8.2: Possible Topics for an Employee Handbook

Section 1: Introduction
Welcome from the President
Equal Employment Opportunity Statement
Harassment Policy
Company History
Statement of Union or Non-Union Status
How to Use this Handbook

Section 2: Employee Relations
Open Door Policy
Group Meetings
Employee Suggestions
Recognition/Award Programs
Company Newsletter
Policy on Solicitation or Distributions of Literature
Bulletin Boards
Complaint Resolution Procedure

Section 3: Employment
Employment Classifications
Physical Examinations
Work Assignments
Working Hours
Performance Appraisal
Progressive Discipline
Career Planning and Development
Training Programs
Job Openings
Layoff and Recall
Military Duty
Terminations of Employment
Exit Interviews
Access to Personnel Files
Requests for References

Section 4: Compensation and Benefits
Reporting Change of Status
Wages
Pay/Paychecks
Time Card/Time Clock Policies
Overtime
Premium Pay Policies
Social Security
Wage Garnishments
Unemployment Compensation

Section 4: Compensation and Benefits, *Cont'd*
Benefits Eligibility
Health and Dental Insurance
Life Insurance
Retirement Plan
Vacations
Holidays
Death in Family
Jury Duty
Family and Medical Leave
Return from Authorized Leave
Credit Union
Direct Deposit
Cafeteria
Employee Discounts
Parking
Travel Reimbursement
Tuition Reimbursement
Child Care
Employee Savings Plans
Disability

Section 5: Employee Responsibilities
Conflict of Interest
Disclosure of Confidential Information
Attendance
Weather Emergencies
Company Rules
Drug and Alcohol Usage and Screening
Personal Phone Calls
Personal Visits
Nepotism

Section 6: Health and Safety
Housekeeping
Dress
Smoking
Life-Threatening Illnesses
In Case of Injury
Building Security
Employee Searches

Index

REVIEW OF THE HANDBOOK DRAFT

Once the handbook is drafted, it should be reviewed carefully for completeness and accuracy, style, syntax, and legality. This should be accomplished in four separate steps, as it is very difficult to evaluate a handbook on all levels at the same time.

Completeness and Accuracy

The entire book should be examined first to make sure nothing has been omitted. Several members of the management team, especially senior managers, should read the book in its entirety to make sure all pertinent topics have been covered. Each reader should receive an unmarked copy on which to note suggestions for improvement. The readers should also be given a written survey that notes specific areas of concern.

Exhibit 8.3 suggests a method for conducting employee focus groups on the handbook draft.

Exhibit 8.3: Steps for Conducting an Employee Focus Group

Step 1: Select no more than 10 employees representative of a variety of the job levels covered by the handbook. If more employees need to be involved, conduct additional focus groups.

Step 2: At least one week before the meeting give the members of the focus group a draft copy of the handbook. Since the policies do not yet have formal approval, advise each member that they must be kept confidential.

Step 3: Convene the meeting with a facilitator to explain the purpose of the meeting and answer any questions from the group.

Step 4: During the meeting, have the facilitator move the group through each section of the handbook. Each policy should be reviewed and all employee comments recorded.

Step 5: Summarize the comments of the group for the handbook committee or the HR department, which should discuss and respond to the comments by taking appropriate action, either by making the suggested changes or by explaining to the focus group members in writing why they disagree.

These steps should not only lead to improved policies but should also increase employee acceptance of the policies.

Style

When it has been ascertained that the book is complete in its coverage of employee concerns, it should be read for style. The tone of the book should be positive, to encourage employees to read it in its entirety. The writing should be clear and simple, with no jargon. Adding graphics may make the handbook more appealing. It should be packed with information, yet not in such detail that it hampers or overwhelms the reader. It should also be written at the reading level appropriate for the intended employee groups. The whole point is for employees to understand the handbook's content.

Syntax

It is important to make sure the grammar and spelling are correct and the handbook is organized into logical paragraphs. Repetitious phrases should be avoided. Proofreading may be an arduous process, but it is necessary. Employees will not be impressed by a handbook talking about the need for accuracy and pride in work if the handbook is rife with spelling errors.

Legality

When all company reviews have been completed, a lawyer should examine the handbook to ensure that everything in it meets all legal requirements and that all the policy wordings are clear. This is a vital step in protecting a company from future legal problems; several lawsuits in recent years have resulted from the way employee handbooks have been worded.[10]

Once it has passed all these examinations, the employee handbook is ready for publication. It should first be distributed to current employees to enhance communication. Veteran employees need to be kept up-to-date on company policies and procedures, especially if any policy changes have been made. Managers should hold formal employee meetings to explain the policies in detail, especially those policies that are new or that have been substantially rephrased.

---

[10] Johnson, P., and S. Gardner. 1989. "Legal Pitfalls of Employee Handbooks." *SAM Advanced Management Journal,* Spring: 42-46.

LIMITATIONS OF AN EMPLOYEE HANDBOOK

There are, unfortunately, numerous possible limitations to an employee handbook, but only the four most common will be discussed here:

1. Many companies put time, effort, and resources into publishing a handbook but fail to use it as a guide for managing the work force. The result is inconsistent treatment of employees and the likelihood of problems in defending unemployment claims and other employment-related cases.

2. Many firms go into over-kill when they describe their policies and procedures. An effective employee manual should be no more than 30 pages long. It is impossible to outline every possible procedure; the manual should describe only the most critical policies necessary to the smooth operation of the enterprise.

3. Many employers feel that a handbook limits managerial discretion in dealing with employee issues and problems. In fact, that may well be the point. When policies provide step-by-step procedures on how to handle work issues, management should not differentiate treatment according to years of service, type of employee, or type of position held. When management does not insist that the policies in the handbook be followed consistently, they have no defense against accusations of bias.

4. Finally, the employee manual is not a replacement for formal employee orientation. The employer should not simply hand the employee the manual with instructions to read it and go to work. Orientation is much more than understanding the company policies. It should familiarize new employees with company culture, enroll them into the benefit plan (if there is one), highlight certain policies, and offer a forum for questions.

WHERE TO GO FOR HELP

Publications by Commerce Clearing House (CCH) and the Bureau of National Affairs offer step-by-step guidelines on writing employee handbooks. Labor lawyers often give their clients skeleton handbooks on which to base their own. Professional publications like *Personnel, HR Magazine,* and *Supervision* regularly run articles by practitioners who discuss their experiences with writing handbooks and HR policies. Finally, there are computer software packages where policies can be plugged into an existing format.

Caution: Never adopt a prepackaged handbook. The writing style, cultural and philosophical statements, and rules for each company are unique and the handbook should reflect that. In addition to accurately stating policies, the handbook must also reflect compliance with federal and local law.

WRAP-UP

A quality employee handbook is an excellent training tool that costs far less time and money than other training methods, a tool that does not end its usefulness when the orientation session is completed. A handbook is a resource employees can turn to when they have questions about organizational policies. It helps new employees feel part of the team and keeps older employees informed of important changes. It helps create a productive atmosphere, because workers know what is expected of them, know why specific policies exist, and know they are appreciated for their hard work. Because it is usually the manager's responsibility to help employees interpret the handbook, it is particularly important that they understand the policies it contains and administer them consistently.

CHAPTER 9

Company Safety: Effective Management of Workplace Safety and Health

As the current safety management literature illustrates, there are far too many approaches to keeping employees out of harm's way. Some are based on the average worker's behavior, some on the actions of management, and some are simply ergonomic. Often, all the approaches combined will not work, leaving some companies totally bewildered about how to deal with the safety issue.

Instead of focusing on metrics and prescriptions, many experts now take a strategic, long-term approach to safety, though even here, the sheer quantity of suggestions can be overwhelming. By taking the most highly regarded strategic viewpoints and transforming them into company-specific standards, however, safety can be dealt with effectively. These are ten basic suggestions that underlie a strong safety program:[1]

1. *Recognize the difference between managing and leading.* Leading means that managers show employees why safety matters and why they should be motivated to support it and want to do it. Leading is the way to go.

2. *Integrate all approaches in the safety **program** into a single compre - hensive management **system**.* The more complete and clear, the better.

---

[1] *Adapted from* Smith, S. 2003. "The Top 10 Ways to Improve Safety Management." *Occupational Hazards,* 65 (12): 33-35.

3. *POLICE the safety system:* Plan, Organize, Lead, Inspect, Correct, and Evaluate the potential of a safety design.

4. *Integrate safety into all the processes of the business.* Don't use the word *safety* separately. If it's isolated and treated separately, it could easily be subordinated to something that in the long run proves less important.

5. *Identify clients and internal customers who see value in safety and make them boss.* This is especially important if not supported enough by peers and supervisors.

6. *Don't make safety a "priority."* Instead, make safety a *central part* of your entire strategy.

7. *A safety system depends on management commitment and leader - ship and on employee participation.* Meaningful employee involvement in the safety system requires that front-line managers genuinely lead.

8. *Take a rational, disciplined approach to safety.* Nothing else in a successful business depends on emotion, why should safety?

9. Make everyone accountable for safety. Successful business leaders should be graded not only on a financial scorecard but also on their ability to integrate safety into the business process.

10. *Get results or get fired.*

Because front-line managers must take responsibility for every one of their employees, safety will always be one of the elements that must be considered. Taking a more strategic approach to safety systems will help the entire organization to "think safety."

THE MANAGER'S CHALLENGE

Old equipment, old buildings, an inexperienced workforce, and a need to increase productivity are some of the reasons why workplace safety and health demand attention. Also, managers who find federal regulations designed to protect employee safety overly restrictive sometimes ignore safety concerns until an accident happens or an inspector arrives from the Occupational Safety and Health Administration (OSHA) due to an employee complaint. Without strong leadership, there is little effort to conduct safety audits and to employ safety professionals to help maintain a safe workplace.

Nevertheless, businesses of all sizes have a social as well as legal responsibility to protect their workforce and visitors, not to mention a financial responsibility to the company to keep OSHAfines to a minimum. Front-line managers must constantly model safe behavior to get their employees to comply with the safety rules.

Occupational safety and health is an area concerned with conditions in the work environment and their effects on employees and visitors. Working conditions apply not only to the physiological but also to the psychological welfare of people in the workplace. Among other topics, this chapter will discuss the Occupational Safety and Health Act and related legal considerations; the effects of drugs and alcohol on workplace safety; training for OSHA compliance; and future trends in workplace safety.

THE OCCUPATIONAL SAFETY AND HEALTH ACT

Congress passed the Occupational Safety and Health Act of 1970 (the act) in response to rising concern about workplace safety and health. It regulates safety and health standards in companies of all sizes. The act prescribes investigation of organizations for safety and health hazards; record keeping and reporting by employers; investigations of accidents and allegations of hazards; communication of hazards to employees; and establishment of safety standards.

The act established three organizations, the most notable being OSHA. The other two are the National Institute of Occupational Safety and Health (NIOSH) and the Occupational Safety and Health Review Commission (OSHRC). OSHA is responsible for setting and enforcing occupational safety and health standards, inspecting work sites, and issuing citations to organizations that violate these standards. While OSHA may request an inspection at any time, employers do not have to let OSHA inspectors on company property unless they have a search warrant.[2] After OSHAissues a citation, the OSHRC is responsible for handling any appeals the accused company makes. NIOSH conducts research and distributes information about occupational health.

---

[2] *Marshall v. Barlow's, Inc.* 1978. Supreme Court of the U.S. No. 76-1143 (1978).

The OSHA General Duty Clause and Safety Standards

OSHA does not concern itself with minimal or superficial violations.[3] Under the act, employers have a "general duty" to provide a workplace free of recognizable hazards. This general duty clause gives OSHA a mechanism to address the most basic problems in the workplace, whether or not the agency has set any specific standards. OSHAthus has the right to investigate every hazard or safety deficiency it becomes aware of, whether or not an accident has occurred.

OSHAhas also instituted many specific safety standards, especially for high-risk work processes and environments; some of the best known deal with blood-borne pathogens, hazardous chemicals, and lockout/tagout rules. Exhibit 9.1 describes several of the key safety standards. These standards and the general duty clause have at least three dimensions: (1) recording safety incidents, (2) investigating and enforcing safety standards, and (3) implementing programs to inform employees of standards and safe practices and to improve workplace safety.

Recording Safety Incidents

Businesses must keep safety and health records so that OSHA can compile statistics on work-related injuries and illnesses. Essentially, if death, illness, or injury to an employee results from a work-related accident or an adverse work environment, it must be recorded in the OSHA 300 log and kept on file. Recordings in the log must include the time and date of the injury, the extent of the injury, and the amount of work time lost due to the injury.

The employer must also complete OSHA Form 301, which gives detailed information about each incident: where the employee was when the accident occurred, what the employee was doing, how the accident occurred, a detailed description of the resulting injury or illness, and what was the agent of the injury or illness. The OSHA Web site (*www.osha.gov*) gives examples of Form 301. This information must be kept for at least five years and summarized yearly for OSHA. Employers with 10 or fewer employees are exempt from most requirements.

---

[3] O'Brien, R. F., and V. A. Gallagher. 1990. "OSHAand the General Duty Clause." *Professional Safety,* December: 31-34.

Exhibit 9.1: Major OSHA Safety Standards

- *Bloodborne Pathogens.* Employers must protect workers from exposure. The employer must have in place exposure control plans, cleaning procedures, protective equipment requirements, information and training procedures, and a system for keeping records. This standard limits exposure to diseases like hepatitis, HIV/AIDS, and tuberculosis.

- *Emergency Exit Procedures.* There must be an unobstructed means of egress (exit) from any point in the building. Emergency action plans for evacuating each building are also required.

- *Noise Exposure.* Employers must reduce noise levels in the workplace that exceed 85 decibels for an eight-hour average. This standard requires monitoring noise, conducting annual audiograms of those exposed to noise, and informing employees about the results.

- *Machine Guarding.* Employers must protect operators of machinery from the hazards of operation. Common guarding requirements are shielding and ergonomic designs that prevent any parts of the body from getting caught in the equipment.

- *Hazard Communication.* Employers must inventory all hazardous chemicals, communicate hazards of handling the chemicals to employees, and train them on proper handling procedures.

- *Lockout/Tagout.* Employers must install lockout and tagout devices to prevent unexpected start-up of equipment or release of energy. All employees who work with or maintain the equipment must be trained in lockout/tagout procedures.

- *Confined Space Entry.* Workers in and visitors to confined spaces must be protected from hazardous atmospheres, including toxic substances, small airborne particles, and poor ventilation. Confined spaces must be labeled and permits required for entry.

- *Personal Protective Equipment.* Employers must mandate the use of personal protective equipment whenever employees face safety hazards. Protection for the eyes, face, head, and extremities is usually required, in the form of equipment like goggles, hardhats, ear plugs, protective clothing, and steel-toed shoes.

Inspection Process

OSHA has a priority system for conducting inspections:

- **Priority 1:** Situations of *imminent danger*—any situation where there is a very high risk of severe illness or injury.

- **Priority 2:** *Catastrophes and fatal accidents* resulting in the hospitalization of three or more individuals.
- **Priority 3:** Follow-ups to *employee complaints* of alleged violation of OSHA standards or the general duty clause.
- **Priority 4:** *High-hazard industries*—those like construction and mining where there is an abnormally high incidence of illness, injury, or death.
- **Priority 5:** *Followup inspections* to ensure the correction of previous violations.

The actual OSHAinspection incorporates an opening conference, a physical inspection of the facility, and a closing conference.[4] In the opening conference, the inspector describes to the employer why the business was selected, the purpose of the visit, the scope of the inspection, and the applicable OSHA standards. The employer may require the inspector to have a search warrant, but most experts advise letting the inspector conduct the investigation rather than possibly provoking expansion of the scope of the investigation.

If there is a search warrant, it should identify the specific areas to be inspected. However, the "plain view doctrine" allows inspectors to investigate beyond the warrant any problems they see in plain view in the course of their investigation. Inspectors may also expand investigations on their own, but the employer may always ask for an additional search warrant if the new issue raised is not covered by the plain view doctrine.

During the actual physical inspection, the inspector will review the OSHA 300 log, inspect the facility for compliance with OSHA standards, review safety procedures and the training conducted, and note any hazards. It is advisable that the employer assign the safety director or another experienced employee to accompany the inspector on the tour. That person can note the hazards identified by the inspector and take immediate steps to correct problems. OSHA inspectors are held to strict confidentiality; they cannot divulge any trade secrets they learn of while on company premises.

Once the inspection is completed, a closing conference is conducted with the employer and other employees, such as the safety director, in which the inspector discusses all hazards found during the inspection. The

[4] Atkinson, W. 1999. "When OSHAComes Knocking." *HR Magazine,* October: 34-38.

employer has a chance to ask questions and describe steps being taken to correct the hazards.

OSHA Enforcement

After the closing conference, the OSHA inspector issues a report describing the violations and assesses penalties based on the nature of the offense. Possible violations and corresponding fines include:

- Willful Violation, up to $70,000
- Serious Violation, up to $7,000
- Other-than-Serious Violation, up to $7,000
- Repeat Violation, up to $70,000
- Failure-to-Abate, up to $7,000

These fines are for each separate violation identified. The employer can have 95 percent of the fines levied for Other-than-Serious violations waived if proof is provided that the problem has been corrected.

While the 1980s saw an increase in workplace accidents and complaints, the 1990s saw the incidence rate (incidents per 100 workers) slow. The rate dropped from just over 8 per 100 to just over 6.[5]

Programs to Improve Workplace Safety

There are three approaches to safety management:[6]

1. The *organizational* approach is to redesign jobs, implement safety policies, establish safety committees, and coordinate safety investigations.

2. The *engineering* approach is to redesign the work environment, review equipment, and conduct an ergonomic assessment.

3. The *individual* approach is to reinforce safety attitudes, conduct safety training, and give employees incentives for safe behavior.

---

[5] Occupational Safety and Health Administration. 2002. "Occupational Injury & Illness Incidence Rates per 100-Full Time Workers, 1973-1998." *www.osha.gov/oshstats/bltable.html,* February 19. Accessed 18 May 2004.
[6] Mathis, W., and J. H. Jackson. 2001. *Human Resource Management: Essential Perspectives,* 2nd ed. Cincinnati: South-Western.

For all three approaches the employer must make an active commitment to manage safety. Questions managers need to answer include:

- How much information do employees need about the safety of their work environment?

- What role should the employer play in preventing accidents and promoting a safe workplace?

Essential ways to answer these questions are to create hazard communication programs, appoint a safety director who is an expert, write a safety manual, and train employees on safe work habits. Training employees and then reinforcing correct safety behavior is a particular responsibility of front-line managers.

Hazard Communication

The act that created OSHA called for worker participation in handling workplace health and safety problems. The Hazard Communication Standard specifies what employers must convey to employees about the safety of the work environment. The federally approved hazard communication program has five major elements. Employers must:

1. Inventory all chemicals used in the workplace, other than consumer products.

2. Obtain material safety and data sheets (MSDSs) from all manufacturers or suppliers of chemical products on the inventory list.

3. Set up a system to ensure that all chemical products are properly labeled and that necessary warnings to employees are posted.

4. Train all employees to recognize label warnings and instructions, to handle all chemicals properly, to interpret the material safety data sheets, and to protect themselves in case of exposure.

5. Create a written hazard communication program, specific to the business, that lists chemicals on hand, usage procedures, and safety precautions. Employees should sign a statement indicating that the employer has trained them and that they understand the safety procedures.

The company "safety director" is in charge of setting up a program to ensure that operations comply with current laws and regulations and with corporate policies. The safety director is often transferred internally and usually has several years of production experience.

The safety director should conduct safety audits in such areas as industrial hygiene, air pollution, water pollution, spill prevention, hazardous waste disposal, safety and loss prevention, and product safety.

In an occupational health audit related to industrial hygiene, for instance, the safety director staff needs to make sure that all chemicals and dust hazards have been identified and exposures assessed. It is important for a safety director to periodically review the results of past audits to identify trends and correct them before someone is adversely affected—or before an OSHA inspector is notified.

Another function of the safety staff is to effectively communicate safety policies and increase employee training and awareness.[7] Areas in which training is important include engineering controls, noise control and hearing conservation, respiratory protection, hazardous chemical exposures, emergency planning, and employee access to exposure records.

The "safety manual," while similar to an employee manual, focuses solely on maintaining a safe and healthy workplace for employees and visitors. Major components of a safety manual are:

- Statement of company safety philosophy

- Overview of OSHArequirements

- Explanation of general safe working practices, including hand safety, lifting guidelines, and use of hand tools, ladders, fork lifts, and similar devices

- General housekeeping requirements: nothing to block aisles and hallways, no clutter in the workspace, no wiring under carpets, proper storage of tools, and speed limits in parking lots

- Requirements for safety concerns specific to the facility, such as protective equipment, hazardous chemicals, confined space, noise, and air quality

- Emergency procedures for when an accident happens

- Accident reporting procedures

- Safety motivation programs and incentives

---

[7] Minter, S. G. 2003. "Have You Heard About Safety?" *Occupational Hazards,* 65: 44-46.

Step-by-step procedures should be listed in each section of the manual. Safety should be part of the orientation of every new employee. An example of a safety manual developed for a large organization, BorgWarner, is provided in Appendix C.

Training on OSHA Compliance
Safety training is the most important component of any successful safety program. Teaching employees the causes of accidents, their results, and how to prevent them cuts deeply into the accident toll and improves organizational efficiency. Most effective training programs have at least the following four components:

1. *Recognition:* Instructing workers about proper safety procedures and possible job hazards is not enough. Employers must make sure their employees can recognize hazards and understand why protection is needed.

2. *Review:* An exchange of ideas, opinions, and suggestions between management and workers helps increase the safety awareness of both groups. Employee-management safety committees are often used to ensure continuous review.

3. *Response:* Besides providing controls and safety equipment, management must respond quickly to concerns and complaints about workplace safety or working conditions.

4. *Results:* The result of any safety program should be reduced number of injuries. All safety incidents should be investigated and their root causes determined so that their recurrence can be prevented.

DRUGS AND ALCOHOL IN THE WORKPLACE

The health and safety of the organization can be affected by its own employees. No matter how good a company's safety policies are, if employees choose not to follow proper procedures, safety problems and violations of OSHA are likely.

In particular, when employees use drugs and alcohol on the job, they can compromise not only their own safety but also that of their fellow employees. In an early study, the American Management Association and

Arizona State University learned that one in ten workers use illegal drugs in the workplace although the effects of illegal drug use can be as slight as a loss of short-term memory, they can also go so far as to cause the death of a fellow worker.[8]

The U.S. Department of Labor estimates the annual cost of drug use in the workplace to be from $75 billion to $100 billion in lost workdays, accidents, and worker's compensation and health care expenses. Some other important statistics:

- Marijuana use was the cause of about 59 percent of positive drug tests.

- Twenty-five to 30 percent of workplace drug abuse now involves prescription drugs.

- Though small- to mid-size firms employ most of the workers in the U.S., few of them test employees for drugs, even though it is estimated that 60 percent of drug abusers work for such firms.

- There has been a marked increase in worksite arrests for drug sales.[9]

Some specific areas of drug/substance abuse are described below.

Alcohol

Alcohol is the most common drug. It's popular because it is not only readily available, it is legal.

Alcohol mainly inhibits judgment and motor skills. The employee who uses alcohol on the job is a real threat to the organization. The U.S. Department of Transportation commissioned a study of alcohol use by railroad employees and found that:

- 75 percent of the employees drink alcoholic beverages.

- 25 percent drink on the job.

- 66 percent became drunk on a regular basis, some once a year, some once a week.

- 5 percent admittedly had been very drunk on duty.

- 15 percent admitted to being somewhat drunk.[10]

---

[8] Walsh, J. M., and S. C. Yohay. 1987. "Drug Abuse in the Workplace," Employment Policy Foundation. New York: American Management Association. *www.amenet.org.*
[9] Bahls, J. E. 1998. "Drugs in the Workplace," *HR Magazine,* February.

Marijuana

Marijuana is the most common illegal drug. Its effects are the subject of debate, but impairment of judgment and the sensory-motor functions can occur. Memory can so be affected that an employee may forget an important message taken only 15 minutes before. A survey done in the mid-eighties in Silicon Valley in California found that over the previous year at least a third of the work force had at some point worked under the influence of the drug.[11]

Cocaine

Cocaine is a very serious drug, the use of which can cause death. Cocaine causes serious psychological, physiological, and physical effects. Employees who use cocaine usually believe that they are performing well when actually they are performing poorly and dangerously. In a poll of 227 workers, the Cocaine National Help line in New Jersey found that:

- 75 percent admitted to using illegal drugs on the job.
- 64 percent stated that drugs interfered with their work.
- 44 percent sold drugs to their co-workers.
- 18 percent admitted to having had a drug-related accident.
- 18 percent admitted to stealing from their employer in order to buy more drugs.[12]

Searching for Drugs and Alcohol

If an employee's behavior or appearance changes, it's reasonable to suspect drug use. The best way to handle drug use is to catch it before it becomes uncontrollable, so it's important to pay attention to the signs of drug use, though these are sometimes well-hidden. Signs associated with certain drugs are listed in Exhibit 9.2.

---

[11] Ibid.
[12] Ibid.

Exhibit 9.2: Signs of Drug Abuse

Alcohol

- Changes in appearance, whether gradual or sudden, such as bruises, flushed skin, and an odor of alcohol.
- Attitude changes, such as irritability, argumentative behavior, or uncharacteristically passive behavior.
- Changes in job behavior, whether gradual or abrupt, with increased absenteeism.
- Extreme behavior in general, such as withdrawal or bouts of loudness.
- Loss of memory.

Marijuana

- Apparent sleepiness or even stupor.
- Inflamed or irritated eyes.
- Attitude changes, from unprovoked laughter to a distorted sense of time or place.
- Forgetfulness, such as losing a train of thought mid-sentence.
- Changes in job behavior, such as increased tardiness and absenteeism without explanation.

Cocaine

- Changes in appearance: dilated pupils, dry mouth and nose, and frequent lip-licking.
- Irregular attitude with unpredictable symptoms, especially increased nervousness.
- Changes in job behavior, especially in how the employee seems to think and work.
- Decreased productivity and uneven production.

Source: Miller-Browne, A. 1991. *Working Dazed: Why Drugs Pervade the Workplace and What Can Be Done About It.* New York: Perseus Publishing.

Drug Screening

Drug screening or drug testing is becoming a must for most employers, but how to approach it can be difficult, given some lack of clarity about the legal rights of employees with regard to drug testing and the resultant fear of employer liability. Exhibit 9.3 contains a list of possible employee objections to the legality of drug testing in the workplace.

Exhibit 9.3: Legal Issues Raised by Drug Testing

- *Invasion of privacy:* An employer can be liable if the employee feels that a drug test has infringed on his or her right to privacy.
- *Infliction of emotional stress:* An employer who does not give ample notification before administering a test risks liability if the lack of notice causes anguish for some employees.
- *Assault and battery:* An employer may not use force to exact employee compliance with mandatory testing.
- *False arrest or imprisonment:* An employer should not hold an employee after hours for a drug test.

Source: Adapted from Ice, Miller, Donadio & Ryan Law Firm. 1988.

Protection for the Employer

It is possible to take precautions to avoid problems with a drug testing policy. If your company decides to implement a mandatory drug testing policy, for its own protection it can follow guidelines created by an Indianapolis law firm:

- Publish a clear "no-alcohol, no drugs" policy, making changes in the employee manual if necessary.
- Incorporate into every employee contract a statement that the employer has the right to conduct medical drug testing.
- Draw up a consent form for all current employees and applicants to sign, defining the reasoning for drug testing and stating that if results are positive, disciplinary action will be taken.
- Use only scientifically valid tests.
- Limit drug testing to hiring, any general medical examinations that may be required, and situations where there is reasonable cause to test.
- Establish a strict chain of procedures for testing and the retention of testing samples.
- Ensure that testing is done in private and that the results are kept confidential.

- Require that adverse results be confirmed by a second analyst.
- Publicize the availability of rehabilitation and employee assistance programs.
- Apply procedures and disciplinary actions consistently.
- Train managers and supervisors in the symptoms of drug abusers and in how to document their findings so as to justify any disciplinary action that might be needed.[13]

Essentially, all employers who decide to use drug testing must respect the privacy of whoever is being tested. Be careful to avoid any defamation of character, such as characterizing someone falsely as a drug user; protect American's with Disabilities rights; and negotiate with any unions represented in the company if it is decided to institute drug testing for current employees.[14]

TRENDS IN OCCUPATION HEALTH AND SAFETY

Besides the ever-continuing substance abuse issues, regulatory efforts in the near future are likely to deal with ergonomics, workplace violence, and air quality.

Ergonomics

Ergonomic problems, especially such repetitive motion injuries as carpal tunnel syndrome, result from the deterioration of muscles, tendons, and ligaments as a result of repeating the same job activity. Specific initiatives by Congress and the Executive Branch have been directed at implementing an ergonomics standard; the issue will not simply disappear, given the high cost of injuries in this area. Currently, under the general duty clause of the act, firms are required to abate situations that produce high rates of repetitive motion injuries. It is inevitable that a more specific ergonomic standard will eventually be implemented.

---

[13] *Implementing Workplace Medical Testing.* 1998. Presentation by Ice, Miller, Donadio & Ryan Law Firm, Indianapolis, IN.,American Management Association, *www.amanet.org*
[14] Bahls, J. E. 1998. "Dealing with Drugs: Keep it Legal." *HR Magazine,* March: 104-110.

Workplace Violence

The events of September 11, 2001, forced many employers to pay more attention to security issues. Also, incidents of disgruntled employees or former employees injuring or even murdering others at the workplace seem to be on the rise. Firms that employ retail clerks and service workers who engage with the public are also vulnerable.[15] OSHA has issued guidelines for retail workers in late-night industries with very specific precautions about areas like traffic monitoring equipment, emergency response procedures, and employee training. Firms with employees who engage with the public are advised to implement OSHAprocedures. Experts have also recommended other measures to prevent workplace violence:

* Refine hiring procedures to avoid hiring violent workers in the first place.
* Have clear, fair, and strong policies against workplace violence.
* Use constructive discipline policies to defuse possible violent situations.
* Terminate employment in a professional and sensitive way.
* Seek outside counsel if you are unsure of what to do.[16]

Indoor Air Quality

A few years ago, OSHAestimated that about 1.34 million U.S. office buildings suffer from poor air quality and that at least 20 million workers face health care problems due to poor air quality at work.[17] While OSHA has a specific standard for confined spaces, the statistics suggest a far more pervasive problem. Poor air quality and ventilation is a problem in both manufacturing and office environments; steps to improve air quality should be taken if higher levels of related illnesses are reported. It is important to document illnesses, periodically test air quality in all work areas, and take immediate action to correct problems.

---

[15] Tyler, K. 1999. "Targets Behind the Counter." *HR Magazine,* August: 106-110.
[16] Miller, L. 2002. "How Safe Is your Job? The Threat of Workplace Violence." *USA Today Magazine,* March: 52-55.
[17] Grossman, K. 2000. "Out With the Bad Air." *HR Magazine,* October: 36-45.

WRAP-UP

In the past, employers had the attitude that meeting minimal safety standards was enough; there was no need to be proactive, but in the 1990s, workplace safety problems, particularly those related to handling toxic chemicals and dealing with unsafe machinery, led to increased OSHA enforcement and a tightening of OSHA requirements. It is advisable now to appoint a person to be safety director whose main responsibility is staying current with OSHA requirements and making changes in workplace procedures to comply with these requirements.

Moreover, continual training of managers and employees in safety procedures is essential to maintaining a safe workplace.

CHAPTER 10

Forecasting Company Needs: Effective HR Strategic Planning

As with many other important elements of a business, with HR, decision-makers often ask the question, "Why plan?" It often takes a while for some managers to turn to HR for help and it can be almost impossible to talk the boss into planning for HR needs. Yet HR depends heavily on in-depth planning. As the saying goes, "Failing to plan is planning to fail." Or should we say, "Failing to plan is planning to get fired"?

A panel of experts made the following observations about the basics of HR planning:[1]

- An HR plan should be strategy-based.

- HR should always be treated as "a credible strategic partner."

- The HR role should be more tactical than technical.

- Any HR department should consist of "professionals who have strategic competencies."

- Those who manage HR should see themselves as important to a firm's long-term success.

- HR should design and operate "a measurement system to display its influence in achieving the business strategy."

---

[1] *Adapted from* Macaleer, B., and S. Jones. 2003. "Does HR Planning Improve Business Performance?" *Industrial Management,* 45(1): 15-20.

Defining the purposes of an HR department, or of HR management responsibilities if the company isn't large enough to warrant an entire department, is the first step in many of the tactical suggestions that have been discussed throughout this book. A strategic HR plan is no exception. Even front-line managers will find that connecting the people component to forecasting increases the likelihood of success; by treating HR as an important component in planning, company success may be only one important decision away.

THE MANAGER'S CHALLENGE

"Fail to plan, plan to fail!" HR planning is the process of forecasting an organization's HR needs and crafting effective action plans to fulfill those needs. HR planning is considered a process because it is ongoing and must consider the success or failure of previous planning attempts. Moreover, HR planning is not an isolated activity; it is tied closely to the overarching strategic business planning of a given organization.

As organizations grow and prosper or as the environment changes, perhaps because of economic shifts or new technology, a systematic process for assessing staffing needs is essential. Moreover, as a firm grows, the record keeping required by federal, state, and local laws is almost overwhelming. An HR information system can relieve some of the pressure and serve as a strategic tool for planning future employee directions.

The U.S. work force has changed dramatically in recent years:

- Employment is expected to increase to approximately 151 million by 2006.
- Hispanic and Asian Americans represent the fastest-growing segment of the work force.
- About one-third of the work force is part-time or temporary.
- The average worker will be approximately 40 in 2006.[2]

All these factors must be considered in HR planning.

---

[2] Bohlander, G., S. Snell, and A. Sherman. 2003. *Managing Human Resources,* 13th ed. Cincinnati: South-Western Publishing Co.

Good HR planning has three fundamental rationales:

1. It allows for a more effective and efficient utilization of company personnel. Accurate forecasting will help alleviate chronic problems of overstaffing in some areas and understaffing in others.
2. HR planning enhances worker satisfaction and employee development. Keeping an up-to-date employee inventory enables companies to better match employee abilities and interests to job requirements.
3. Planning makes EEO compliance easier. Thorough planning will ease the burden of completing the utilization reports required by a variety of government agencies.[3]

As shown in Exhibit 10.1, HR planning does not exist in a vacuum. The strategic HR decisions a firm makes are tied directly to other strategic decisions being made for the organization.

A company pursuing the growth strategy of horizontal integration has made a decision to acquire a competing firm in the same line of business. From the HR perspective, there must be careful consideration of such critical factors as staffing levels needed after the acquisition, integration of two different sets of HR policies and procedures, pay equity issues, and the need for new performance standards.

However, it is important to realize that an HR strategy is not implemented automatically when a single corporate strategy plays out. Ideally, it will follow a more fully integrated strategic plan that is an interactive process between corporate business and HR needs.[4] The ideal HR strategic plan is one that can be a key component in the overall corporate strategy.

This chapter looks at five specific steps in HR planning:

1. Environmental analysis
2. Forecasting the company's demand for workers
3. Forecasting the supply of workers
4. Drafting and implementation of HR objectives and strategies
5. Control and evaluation

---

[3] Ivancevich, G. 2003. *Human Resource Management,* 9th ed. Boston: McGraw Hill/Irwin.
[4] Butler, J. F., R. F. Gerald, and N. K. Napier. 1991. *Strategy and Human Resource Management.* Cincinnati: South-Western Publishing Co., p. 18.

Exhibit 10.1: The Human Resource Planning Process

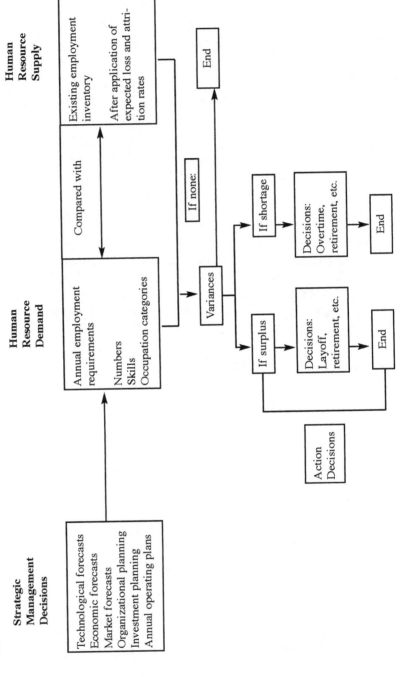

ENVIRONMENTAL ANALYSIS

Like the humans that run them, organizations are systems that consume energy from their environment. We, as humans, must eat food and drink water to maintain life-sustaining energy; moreover, we are adaptable, altering our behavior as the environment changes. Organizations must also react quickly to changes in the environment if they are to compete effectively and survive. They must be able to detect changes as they are occurring and promptly initiate adaptive responses.[5]

It is important to conduct regular environmental analyses to be aware of and respond to significant changes as they happen. These analyses typically are three-tiered:

1. A scan of the general environment should include all the economic, legal, and political factors that affect all organizations equally. For example, the Americans with Disabilities Act of 1990 was a significant piece of legislation that directly affected the HR function. Firms that gain early knowledge of the scope and effect of such legal changes are better prepared to implement early policies to ease the financial impact of strictures like "reasonable accommodation."

2. An assessment of the company's operating environment. This assessment includes factors unique to a particular firm's mission, like labor availability, customers, suppliers, and competitors. To maintain a competitive advantage, a firm must make accurate predictions and secure scarce resources before competitors can do so, because companies with similar missions will be vying for the same human resources in the local market. Growing firms that can predict demand for and availability of workers are likely to be better at recruiting than their less well-informed competitors.

3. A survey of the internal environment, which consists of the company's organizational strategy and corporate culture. The opinions and attitudes of key executives, or even middle managers, are likely to affect the way the HR function is accomplished. For example, bigotry in an organizational unit may affect the productivity of that unit,

---

[5] Schuler, R. S. 1989. "Scanning the Environment: Planning for Human Resource and Organizational Change." *Human Resource Planning,* 12(4): 257-276.

as well as alienating talented applicants from protected groups. Indicators that may be symptoms of internal environmental problems are falling productivity, increased absenteeism and turnover, increased number and gravity of grievances, increased number and gravity of disciplinary actions, and accident rates. Certain survey techniques may be particularly helpful in pinpointing or even predicting internal environmental problems.

Once data has been collected from the environmental analysis, environmental trends and their implications for human resource planning can be considered. Exhibit 10.2 lists possible environmental analysis outcomes and their implications for HR planning. It is important to note that an environmental analysis is never finished, because the continuously changing environment must be continually scanned.

Exhibit 10.2: Environmental Scanning Results and Implications

Trend	HRM Implications
Increasing age of current work force	• Increased emphasis on career planning. • More attention to succession planning. • Greater awareness of potential age discrimination issues.
Influx of women into the work force	• Flextime and job-sharing options added to benefits packages. • Greater awareness of sex discrimination issues. • Greater awareness of pay equity issues.
Availability of lower-priced personal computers	• Potential for greater automation of Human Resource Information Systems (HRIS).
Fewer engineering college graduates entering job market	• Improved recruitment. • Greater emphasis on internal transfer. • Training and development programs.
Rising gasoline prices	• Possible temporary layoffs in shipping department.
EEOC adjudications of disability discrimination	• Greater awareness of disability discrimination. • Disability education/awareness programs.
Recent problems with absenteeism and turnover	• Emphasis on organizational development.
Recent complaints of favoritism in promotion decisions	• Critical review of existing performance appraisal instrument.

FORECASTING COMPANY DEMAND FOR WORKERS

One of the most important considerations facing a growing firm is predicting how many and what kinds of employees it will need in the coming years. Threats to organizational profitability arise when a firm employs either too few or too many employees relative to demand for its products or services.[6] To diminish this threat, many organizations try to forecast their HR needs ahead of time. The many forecasting techniques available vary widely in their sophistication, and some are more popular than others.

Employee Replacement Charts

Employee replacement charts are graphical diagrams containing data like employee name, years with the company, positions to which each can be promoted, and names of probable replacements (see Exhibit 10.3). By comparing likely retirements and promotion readiness, the HR specialist can discern a pattern of HR needs in the future. Replacement charts help with both replacement and succession planning.

Exhibit 10.3: Employee Replacement Chart

Organizational Unit   Date_____   Page __ of __

Position		
Incumbent	Age Yrs.	Empl. Yrs.
Promotable to:	When	Yrs./mos.
Replacement 1	Age Yrs.	Empl. Yrs.
Present position	When	Yrs./mos.
Replacement 2	Age Yrs.	Empl. Yrs.
Present position	When	Yrs./mos.

Source: Milkovich, G. T., and T. A. Mahoney. 1976. "Human Resource Planning and PAIR Policy." In Yoder, D., and H. G. Heneman, Jr., eds. *Planning and Auditing PAIR.* Washington, D.C.: Bureau of National Affairs.

---

[6] Sullivan, J. 2002. "Workforce Planning: Why Start Now?" *Workforce,* November: 46-50.

Zero-based Forecasting

This technique uses current employment levels as a starting point for predicting future HR resource needs. If an employee quits or is promoted, transferred, or terminated, it is not automatically assumed that the position will be filled. Instead, whether each position should be filled must be justified by a cost-benefit analysis. This process of having to justify new hires and staffing changes forces the company to avoid "business-as-usual" HR practices. This requires the company to consciously consider the need for a given worker in relation to the larger environmental demands.

Zero-based budgeting, a bottoms-up approach to forecasting, is typically accomplished in two phases:

1. Several staffing options are formulated, each representing a different HR alternative. Each option is accompanied by a complete description of why the alternative is necessary and what consequences arise by not implementing it.

2. Each option is ranked from "essential" to "would be nice to have." The choice of a particular option is based on both the cost of the alternative and its congruence with current organizational objectives.

Unit Demand

Taking the unit demand approach, each work unit within the organization predicts what its HR needs will be for the coming year. Total HR demand is then estimated by summing the demand for all units. This technique assumes that supervisors at the unit level are most affected by critical shortages in staffing. This technique is not as sensitive to overstaffing as the zero-based technique.

Expert Estimate

HR professionals, both inside and outside the organization, are often excellent sources of data on future demand for human resources. The Delphi technique, is one way of combining data from several experts. In this technique a questionnaire representing the problem is sent to the experts. After they return the questionnaire, the results are compiled and the questionnaire is revised to be more specific. The experts then complete the second questionnaire and the results are compiled into a report, which the experts again review. The process continues until consensus is reached.

A similar method, the nominal group technique, requires the experts to meet in a group, where each presents solutions to the problem; the other experts refrain from criticism. After all the solutions are presented, the group votes on them to reach consensus.

Delphi and nominal group techniques seem to be superior to other forecasting techniques that use groups as a means of decision making. For example, brainstorming uses experts to generate unique decision alternatives, but the technique may be biased toward those with more organizational power who use their influence to sway the input of others into the decision. Nominal group and Delphi techniques introduce anonymity into the decision process and may decrease political influence.

Regression Analysis

A more sophisticated approach to forecasting HR needs is through statistical methods like simple and multiple linear regression. Simple linear regression predicts present staffing needs by establishing a relationship between current employment at the company and a predictor variable, such as sales. For many firms, however, predicting employment levels from one variable is too simplistic. They get better results from multiple linear regression, which incorporates additional variables, such as work efficiency or worker attrition, into the prediction equation.

Time Series Analysis

Time series analysis is a variation of regression analysis in which the independent variable is time, rather than sales or efficiency. The dependent variable is demand for a product or service. The resulting analysis predicts product demand over a specified period of time. For companies whose HR staffing levels are closely related to product demand, this estimation may be very useful.

Markov Matrix

Like linear regression and time series analysis, the Markov matrix is a statistical technique. The analysis begins with construction of a transition matrix that presents average rates of historical movements between job categories. For example, the historical movements shown in section A of Exhibit 10.4 reveal that 10 percent of middle managers moved to top management, 80 percent stayed at the present level, and 5 percent were demoted to lower management. With this historical data at hand, a growing firm can make projections about staff movements (section B) and anticipate shortages and surpluses. For example, in the M2 column of section B, it can be seen that 160 middle managers are likely to stay in their present positions and 30 lower-level managers will move up to middle management, so 10 middle-level manager positions are expected to be open in the coming period.

Exhibit 10.4: Markov Transition Matrix

Human Resource Classification

A: Historical Movements		M1	M2	M3	Exit
Top management (M1)		0.80			0.20
Middle management (M2)		0.10	0.80	0.05	0.05
Lower management (M3)			0.05	0.80	0.15
B: Projections	Beginning Personnel Levels	M1	M2	M3	Exit
Top management (M1)	100	80			20
Middle management (M2)	200	20	160	10	10
Lower management (M3)	600		30	480	90
Forecasted Availabilities		*100*	*190*	*490*	

Source: Ferris, Rowland, and Buckley. 1990. *Human Resource Management: Perspectives and Issues.* 2nd ed. Boston, MA: Allyn and Bacon.

Simulation

As HR information systems (HRIS) become more sophisticated, computers can be used to simulate a real HR system. Essentially, these simulations model the activities of a company in the real world; variables that are assumed important to predicting employment levels are represented through mathematical logic. This software helps the HR specialist to answer many "what if" questions about future staffing, such as:

- What if we add one more paid holiday?
- What if we increase production by adding another shift and pay a shift differential?
- What if we lay off 15 employees for three months?

Answers to these and countless other HR questions make it possible to understand the total consequences of planned actions *before* they are implemented.

Regardless of which technique is actually used, a well-implemented forecast of HR demand is invaluable to the total success of a company. For example, a company that is expanding quickly or diversifying into new areas will need adequate staff to meet new demand. Indeed, if a company cannot predict its own growth and thus *underestimates* staffing levels, potential profits will be lost because it will be unable to make potential sales. Loss of profit could also result from *overestimating* staffing levels. Having too many employees wastes salary and benefit costs, and may result in inefficiency through redundancy in assigned responsibilities. Thus, organizational efficiency hinges in part on the ability of firms to gather accurate, relevant information about their HR needs.

FORECASTING THE SUPPLY OF WORKERS

Being able to predict internal HR demand is only part of the HR planning picture. In a competitive environment, the growing firm must also be able to target prime sources of quality job candidates. Therefore, forecasting HR supply is an essential complement to demand forecasting.

Internal Sources

Many organizations have a policy of first considering current employees for future positions before looking outside the organization. Most companies have invested a great deal of time and money in selecting and developing current employees, who already understand the corporate culture and have acquired important KSAs that are specific to the company. It makes sense that present employees present less risk than those hired from external sources.

In assessing the job-related potential of current employees, companies use a number of tools to evaluate their strengths and weaknesses. For example, management inventories are useful in identifying employees who are prepared for movement into higher-level positions. Such inventories detail an employee's work history, job-related strengths and weaknesses, promotion potential, developmental needs, and career goals. For nonmanagerial positions, a firm must consider slightly different variables;

for these, skills inventories are helpful. Skills inventories identify an employee's KSAs, work experience, biographical data, supervisory ratings, and career goals.

External Sources

Although internal sources often yield organizationally trained, skilled employees, they are only part of the analysis needed to forecast HR supply. At some point, the external labor market becomes important to attaining qualified personnel.

The best external sources vary by industry and geographic location. Some firms may rely heavily on college recruitment, others on vocational schools, still others on walk-ins, or unsolicited applications. Determining the best sources of external supply may take time. It is a good idea to maintain detailed statistics on where employees were recruited—and to correlate employee performance data with recruitment source so that future recruitment efforts can be concentrated in areas that consistently yield superior-performing employees in a given job class. Such a database needs to be built up and maintained over time and integrated with other aspects of the HR information system to augment future prediction of external sources of supply.

HR OBJECTIVES AND STRATEGIES

The next step in the HR planning process is to identify any resource gap between demand and supply. For example, high turnover in the present year and a lack of qualified applicants would suggest that demand exceeds supply, presaging an unsuccessful recruitment year. Low demand in the current year and a high external supply of applicants suggest that the firm can be selective in maintaining present staffing levels. In both instances, a discrepancy between the supply of and demand for labor necessitates action.

To narrow the gap between supply and demand, objectives need to be written that specify what needs to be accomplished in the coming planning period. The objectives need to be articulated clearly so that they may be evaluated at the end of the planning period.

Typically, there are three guidelines for writing objectives:

1. Write specific objectives for separate functional areas within human resources. For example, separate objectives would be

written for such subareas as staffing levels, productivity, labor costs, and recruitment.

2. Put numbers on the objectives, quantitative units that can be measured and recorded. Examples are *percentage* increase in productivity or the hiring of a set *number* of employees.

3. Set deadlines for achieving objectives. This can be expressed in a wide range of units—from days to years.

Objectives that are not specific, quantitative, and deadline-oriented are of little use in the planning process because they mean the success or failure of the planning program cannot be evaluated. If there is no method of assessing whether objectives have been accomplished, it will be impossible to make improvements in future planning cycles. Exhibit 10.5 shows a few examples of HR planning objectives for separate functional areas.

Exhibit 10.5: Human Resource Planning Objectives

1. Area: *Productivity*
Poor: Increase productivity among plant workers.
Better: Increase output per employee among lathe operators by 10 percent by January 1.

2. Area: *Staffing*
Poor: Reduce present staffing levels.
Better: Reduce middle management staffing by 50 employees by June 12.

3. Area: *Training*
Poor: Train employees in the use of the new performance appraisal instrument.
Better: Train all supervisors at Plant #1 in the use of the new performance appraisal instrument by January 1.

4. Area: *Compensation*
Poor: Conduct a wage and salary market survey.
Better: Conduct a wage and salary market survey of company clerical positions within skill levels 3 and 4 by May 5.

5. Area: *Job Analysis*
Poor: Reanalyze company jobs.
Better: Reanalyze 50 percent of professional classification jobs by January 1.

6. Area: *Affirmative Action*
Poor: Increase minority representation among company jobs.
Better: Increase the number of minorities represented in middle- and upper-level management by 15 percent within two years (state actual data).

Once objectives are identified, it is time to write specific HR planning strategies (plans of action) to facilitate accomplishment of goals. In doing this, knowledge, experience, and even creativity are essential for an effective plan. Although there are no cookbook recipes for the perfect plan, there are guidelines that can reduce some of the uncertainty, among them generating multiple alternatives, identifying criteria for choosing among alternatives, and choosing which action to take.

Multiple Alternatives

The methods used for generating strategies for HR planning should help people overcome the mental barriers that limit creative problem-solving. One common method is brainstorming, where ideas are generated according to rules that encourage free thinking. In brainstorming groups:

- Freethinking is welcome: Participants are encouraged to tell the group whatever comes to mind.

- Criticism is prohibited: To encourage free thinking, no participant may be made to feel that an idea is "stupid" or "ignorant."

- Quantity is encouraged: As the number of suggestions increase, so does the likelihood that one or more will be workable.

- Combination and improvement is sought: Participants are asked to take suggestions and improve on them, or to generate new ideas by combining the thoughts of others with their own.[7]

Brainstorming sessions are usually 30 to 45 minutes long, but the group may be reconvened to reconsider ideas or generate further alternatives.

The Delphi and nominal group techniques discussed early under forecasting techniques may also be adapted to the task of generating strategies. Regardless of the technique employed, the goal of this first step is to generate an extensive number of HR strategic alternatives.

Criteria Generation

Once strategic alternatives have been generated, it's necessary to decide what criteria will be used to select the best of them. Every strategic alternative carries with it certain pros and cons for implementation. For example,

---

[7]Wagner, J. A., and J. R. Hollenbeck. 1992. *Management of Organizational Behavior.* Englewood Cliffs, NJ: Prentice Hall, Inc., p. 393.

while a decision to lay off workers may decrease some HR costs, other costs will be incurred in retraining and reorganizing the work of the remaining employees. Again, though the decision to train supervisors in a new performance appraisal technique may have heavy initial costs, the long-term attractiveness of the new program may increase profits.

Without selection criteria that are relevant to the present strategic situation, the best plans of action are doomed to failure. Common criteria may be the cost/benefit of the alternative, time constraints for implementing it, budgetary constraints, or ease of implementation.

Choosing an Action Plan

The final step in a strategic plan is actually choosing among the alternatives already formulated. In this step, the strengths and weaknesses of each strategic alternative are considered, and the best alternatives chosen. Typically, a single strategy plan is chosen for each objective. Exhibit 10.6 lists examples of alternatives firms might typically choose from. It presents two scenarios: employee surplus and employee shortage. For each, multiple alternatives are presented, none of which may be the best plan of action for a given situation. The list is by no means exhaustive; additional company-specific alternatives might be generated during further brainstorming sessions. The example considers only the relatively limited problem of staffing. Multiple alternatives also exist for productivity, labor costs, compensation, training, and a host of other HR areas.

Exhibit 10.6: Human Resource Planning Strategy

Employee Shortage	**Employee Surplus**
Long-term options	*Long-term options*
• Recalls	• Retirement incentives
• Hires	• Freeze hires and use attrition to reduce staff
• Permanent in-transfers	• Layoffs
• Retrain	• Permanent out-transfers
• Transfer work out	• Retrain
Short-term options	• Transfer work in
• Increase overtime or part-time work	*Short-term options*
• Increase subcontracts	• Freeze hires and use attrition to reduce staff
• Increase productivity	• Reduce overtime or part-time work
• Buy back vacation or holidays	• Transfer work in
• Temporary assignments	• Reduce the work week
• Temporary hires	• Temporary shutdown or layoff
• Transfer work out	• Excused absences
	• Temporary assignments
	• Retrain or train
	• Accumulate surplus inventory

Source: Heneman, Schwab, Fossum, & Dyer. 1986. *Personnel/Human Resource Management.* 3rd ed. Homewood, IL: Irwin.

HR PLANNING AND CAREER DEVELOPMENT

Career planning has become an integral part of the HR planning effort. Milkovich and Anderson[8] cite four reasons to account for its rising importance:

1. Rising concern over quality of work life in the United States
2. The critical need for skilled personnel, especially in technical and managerial fields
3. Pressures from EEO agencies to promote protected groups
4. Rising expectations of younger workers coupled with diminished advancement opportunities

The process of career planning has two basic approaches: (1) organizational assistance at various career stages and (2) self-management. Self-management of individual careers essentially implies a process to match individual needs for achievement with organizational needs as expressed in HR planning efforts (e.g., plans for growth or replacement).[9] An individual can engage in at least six activities to help find a match with a desired organization:

1. Conduct a self-analysis: Inventory KSAs and strengths and weaknesses.
2. Set occupational goals: Decide which job and career path is desired.
3. Get information about the occupation and relevant companies: Use the resources of current employer and local college and community libraries to learn more about whether and where there may be a match between personal strengths and the needs of the organization.
4. Write a personal action plan: After all the background research is completed, work out the steps needed to get there, such as, if specific training, a different degree, or a transfer to a different position for experience. The personal action plan should have a timetable for accomplishing goals.

---

[8] Milkovich, G. T., and J. C. Anderson. 1990. "Career Planning and Management," in Ferris, G. R., K. M. Rowland, and M. R. Buckley, eds. *Human Resource Management: Perspectives and Issues.* Boston, MA: Allyn and Bacon.
[9] Shein, E. H. 1982. *Career Dynamics: Matching Individual and Organizational Needs.* Reading, MA: Addison-Wesley.

5. Find a mentor: Find someone who can help in the job search. This might be someone in a company with experience and contacts who can help arrange job interviews.
6. Continuously evaluate progress toward goals: Every year, evaluate the progress against established goals and timetables.

A personal career action plan may need to be adjusted depending on changes in objectives or in company plans.

The other approach to career planning, organizational assistance, implies a formal effort by the company to plan a career path for each employee. Depending on individual skills and company needs, the company can play an important role in seeing that all employees receive the training and experience they need to stay on their prescribed career path. Fandt[10] describes three tools that firms can use for formal career planning: (1) the assessment center, (2) employee counseling, and (3) establishing mentor-protégé relationships.

Assessment centers offer an array of tests to help employees demonstrate individual skills and abilities. Assessment centers are often used to identify candidates for managerial positions.

Career counseling services, usually housed in an HR department, can help employees in at least three ways:

1. They give information on training and development opportunities.
2. They offer a sounding board for employees concerned about career progression.
3. In a time of reorganization, restructuring and downsizing, they inform employees about transfers, layoffs, and other types of job changes to help them make educated decisions about their future role in the company.

Formalized career planning is often overlooked, yet employees are one of the most expensive resources for any organization. As with any other expensive resource, there should be an accurate accounting of the "inven-

---

[10] Fandt, P. M. 1992. "Linking Business Strategy and Career Management: An Integrative Framework," in Ferris, Rowland, and Buckley, op. cit., n. 7.

tory," the inventory must be maintained, and new methods for improving the quality of the inventory must be devised.

THE ROLE OF THE HUMAN RESOURCE INFORMATION SYSTEM (HRIS)

An HRIS may be a prepackaged computerized system or an internally developed, comprehensive HR management information system. It may be an elaborate mainframe payroll/personnel system, a network of personal computers, or several stand-alone PCs that serve specific functions. It could also be a subunit of an enterprise resource planning (ERP) system like PeopleSoft, SAP, or Oracle.

HRISs are known for their ability to produce more accurate and timelier information for operating, controlling, and planning purposes than the old manual or payroll-based systems. Many of the reports generated by an HRIS take only minutes to produce, though they would take many hours or days to do manually. HRISs do have their disadvantages, the major one being the expense of the initial financial outlay and the labor necessary to implement the system. Also, an HRIS can be intimidating to certain employees who have a basic fear of computers.

Anyone considering the feasibility of an HRIS should always remember that its overriding purpose should be to assist, not overwhelm, managers in making sound decisions. Front-line managers, especially, should be well-versed in how to use the HRIS as a tool for decision making. Quick access to information about employees is invaluable when a manager is faced with decisions about staffing, promotions, pay increases, and discipline.

An HRIS usually supports at least five distinct HR functions:

1. Planning and forecasting

2. Staffing (recruitment, screening, and hiring)

3. Training and development

4. Compensation and benefits

5. Performance management

How an HRIS can be applied to these functions is discussed further below.

The *HR planning process* consists of four major components: (1) environmental scanning, (2) business plan analysis, (3) personnel planning, and (4) program and policy review. *Environmental scanning* refers to reviewing external conditions to identify opportunities and threats related to a company's human resources. *Business plan analysis* refers to examining the company's business plans to identify company direction and areas of potential HR intervention. *Personnel planning* attempts to forecast future supply and demand and reconcile any imbalance between them. *Program and policy review* is a detailed examination of HR programs and policies to ensure that they are addressing organizational needs. All four of these components are designed to identify critical HR issues that should be addressed in supporting the strategic direction of a company.

The *staffing function* includes identifying, attracting, and selecting prospective employees within budgetary and legal guidelines, as well as maintaining employee data over time. Computer applications designed to support the employment/staffing function are applicant tracking, recruiting analysis, basic employee information, equal employment opportunity, position control, scheduling, selection aids, and affirmative action.

An *applicant tracking* system helps maintain information to provide faster, more accurate information on applicants and help identify appropriate applicants for specific positions. It may also monitor costs and provide data for subsequent EEO/AA analysis.

A *recruiting analysis* application evaluates the effectiveness of recruiting efforts to better target subsequent recruiting.

Basic employee information is the first module in most HRISs. An EEO application maintains data on employee demographics, evaluates legal compliance, helps assess the effectiveness of special programs, and generates the reports required by the federal government.

Position control applications are used to control labor costs by monitoring head count.

Scheduling applications perform analyses designed to facilitate the scheduling of personnel.

An HRIS can help with *employee selection* as well. It can scan resumes to identify candidates who meet specific criteria. It can also be used to assess the validity or success of the selection process.

The HRIS can also help with *affirmative action* reporting by analyzing whether women and minorities are appropriately employed within the organization.

Even though *training and career development* might be seen as part of the same process, they are treated as two separate factors in HRIS applications. The *training factors* consist of training administration, training needs, formal education needs, training evaluation, and computer-based training. Training administration is a system used to determine who needs training, who has already had training, and how much that training costs. The training needs application should be able to generate lists of employees who need specific training programs.

The *career development* function consists of maintaining a career profile for each employee. The profile would list all previous work experience for both the employer and previous employers, all in-service and formal education, and specific skills linked to the company's master list of specific skills.

Managing *compensation and benefits* is always important, no matter what the size of the firm. Some of the applications in this area are compensation planning, job evaluation and wage surveys, executive compensation, compensation management, benefits communication, COBRA compliance, and benefits management. *Compensation planning* models the costs associated with various combinations of compensation and benefits.

The *performance management* applications deal with performance, discipline, and grievances. *Performance appraisal* evaluates an employee's job performance against the standards in the job description. In *unit pro - ductivity,* criteria of unit performance are used to determine whether the unit is performing as expected. *Project management* transforms project management technologies into interactive software. *Time and attendance* applications record the time and the attendance data for all employees. The *discipline* application not only ensures that any discipline action is recorded but also guides the line manager through the steps in the discipline process. The last application, *grievances,* explains the grievance procedures to employees in interactive mode; it can be used in both union and nonunion environments.

Quality of work life (QWL) is a term that has come to refer to any program that leads to an improvement in working conditions. QWL applications include health and safety, employee assistance programs, survey processing, and organization development. The *health and safety* application can provide reports to individual employees on the history of their exposure to toxic materials as well as unit and total company reports for hazards for both government and management use. The *employee assistance* application should maintain confidential information and records on employees who are involved with EAP programs.

CONTROL AND EVALUATION OF HR PLANNING

Selection of viable HR strategies is not the end of the HR planning process. HR planning is ongoing and must be supported by the effort needed to ensure its success.[12] It is inappropriate to call control and evaluation the last step in the HR resource planning process because at every step, data is being gathered and monitored that will help determine the success of a planning program. For example, at the beginning of a planning period, firms set new objectives, but to do this, they must assess the success or failure of previous planning initiatives. If previous objectives were not specific, quantitative, and time oriented, then the time and effort that went into drafting plans was wasted.

The control and evaluation of a successful HR planning program hinges on a firm's HRIS facilities. HRISs collect and analyze HR-related data. For example, a well-maintained HR database is continuously updated with new information about job analysis, recruitment, compensation, worker performance, worker histories, accident and safety data, union memberships, and even employee attitudes. Such information may be used to document important trends in the HR function. Careful monitoring of trends gives an up-to-the-moment report on the success of current HR programs. This is important feedback for controlling strategic plans as they unfold.

Besides constant monitoring and control of the HR function, HRIS reports are also useful in evaluating HR strategic plans. Stated goals are compared to quantitative outcomes in the HRIS database. Planning initiatives that are falling short of their stated objectives can be reformulated in the next planning period. Objectives that are achieved provide a yardstick for measuring the success of HR planning, as well as laying a foundation for specific goals in the future.

---

[12] Macaleer, B., and J. Shannon. 2003. "Does HR Planning Improve Business Performance?" *Industrial Management,* January/February: 15-20.

WRAP-UP

Human resource planning is an essential part of every company's strategic planning process. As the external environment evolves, growing firms must continuously scan it to stay abreast of changes that may affect the HR function. Effective human resource planning relies on accurate predictions of HR demand and supply using a variety of forecasting techniques. The balance of HR supply and demand dictates the types of objectives and strategies that growing firms pursue in the future.

However, HR planning does not stop when a strategic plan is written. Rather, HR plans are monitored and updated throughout implementation. An HRIS is an effective tool to help manage the planning function.

APPENDIX A

HR TOOLS

GUIDELINES-ORIENTED JOB ANALYSIS QUESTIONNAIRE (GOJA)

Part I. Identification

Name: _____ Date: _____

Job Title: _____Department: _____

Supervisor's Name: _____ Supervisor's Title: _____

Employed in this classification since: _____

Part II. Domain

Please list below the domains (major areas of responsibility) normally associated with your job. Blank spaces are provided for you to identify and describe each domain. Please indicate the percentage of your job that is accounted for by each domain.

Domain: _____ Pct: _____

Domain: _____ Pct: _____

Domain: _____ Pct: _____

Domain: _____ Pct: _____

Domain: _____ Pct: _____

TOTAL   100%

Part III. Job Duties

At the top of the forms in this section, write the domains that you identified in Section II, with the domain accounting for the highest percentage of your job listed first as Domain A.

Under each domain, list the duties you perform. These will be identified as 1, 2, 3, etc. Indicate the importance of each duty on a scale of 1 to 5, with 1 = not at all important and 5 = extremely important. Also, indicate how often the duty is performed on a scale of 1 to 5, with 1 = very seldom and 5 = frequently.

Domain A:

List the duties you perform as part of this domain:	How important?	How often?
1. _____	_____	_____
2. _____	_____	_____
3. _____	_____	_____
4. _____	_____	_____
5. _____	_____	_____
6. _____	_____	_____
7. _____	_____	_____
8. _____	_____	_____
9. _____	_____	_____
10. _____	_____	_____

Domain B:

List the duties you perform as part of this domain:	How important?	How often?
1.		
2.		
3.		
4.		
5.		
6.		
7.		
8.		
9.		
10.		

Domain C:

List the duties you perform as part of this domain:	How important?	How often?
1.		
2.		
3.		
4.		
5.		
6.		
7.		
8.		
9.		
10.		

Domain D:

List the duties you perform as part of this domain:	How important?	How often?
1.		
2.		
3.		
4.		
5.		
6.		
7.		
8.		
9.		
10.		

Domain E:

List the duties you perform as part of this domain:	How important?	How often?
1.		
2.		
3.		
4.		
5.		
6.		
7.		
8.		
9.		
10.		

Part IV. Job Qualifications

In the forms in this section list the qualifications needed to perform your job. Be as specific as possible. Where possible, relate qualifications to one or more domain letters and numbers (A.5, B.6, etc.)

Knowledge, skill, or ability needed for successful job performance:	Needed for?	Learn in 8 hours or less?
Knowledge of: _____	_____	_____
Knowledge of: _____	_____	_____
Knowledge of: _____	_____	_____
Verbal communication skills to: _____	_____	_____
Writing skills to: _____	_____	_____
Math skills to: _____	_____	_____
Reading skills to: _____	_____	_____
Ability to: _____	_____	_____
Ability to: _____	_____	_____

Physical characteristics needed for successful job performance:	Needed for?
See well enough to: _____	_____
Hear well enough to:_____	_____
Speak well enough to:_____	_____
Have strength to: _____	_____
Have use of hands and fingers to: _____	_____
Have mobility to: _____	_____

Please identify the kind of education needed on your job.

Formal education (check one only)

___ Less than high school

___ High school or equivalency

___ Technical school _____ years; course: _____

___ College training _____ years; course: _____

___ College degree; major: _____

___ Graduate training; field: _____

Other (check all that apply)

___ Specialized course in: _____

___ Apprenticeship in: _____

___ Other: _____

Please identify the types of licensure and certification needed on your job.

___ Valid driver's license

___ Operator's license for_____

___ Certification in _____

___ Other: _____

___ Other: _____

How much previous job-related experience is necessary for a person starting this job?

___ None	___ 1 to 3 years	___ Other:
___ Less than 3 months	___ 3 to 5 years	
___ 3 months to 1 year	___ 5 to 10 years	

Please give examples of experience needed:

_____

_____

_____

How long should it take an employee with the qualifications shown above to become proficient in this job?

___ 1 week or less	___ 6 months
___ 1 month or less	___ 1 year
___ 3 months	___ Other: _____

Please identify and explain any special requirements of your job.

___ Work non-standard hours	___ Furnish tools or equipment
___ Work more than 40 hours per week	___ Other: _____
___ Drive a vehicle	___ Other: _____
___ Travel overnight	___ Other: _____

Part V. Supervision Received

Read each statement carefully and check the box opposite the one that best describes how your work is supervised.

___ **Under immediate direction:** Normally perform duty assignments after receiving detailed instructions as to methods, procedures, and desired end results. The immediate supervisor provides close and constant review.

___ **Under general direction:** Normally perform duty assignments after receiving general instructions as to methods, procedures, and desired end results. The assignment is reviewed upon completion.

___ **Under direction:** Normally perform duty assignments according to my own judgment, requesting supervisory assistance only when necessary. The assignment is reviewed upon completion.

___ **Under administrative direction:** Normally perform duty assignments within broad parameters defined by general organizational regulations and procedures. Results determine effectiveness of job performance.

___ **Under guidelines set by policy:** Normally perform duty assignments using methods and procedures at my own discretion, limited only by policies set by administrative or legislative authority. Results determine effectiveness.

Part VI. Supervision Given

List your supervisory responsibilities.

Job Title	How many persons?	How many do they supervise?
1. _____	_____	_____
2. _____	_____	_____
3-6. _____	_____	_____

Total supervised directly: _____

If your position involves functional (staff) supervision over programs or functions other than those of your immediate subordinates, please indicate the programs or functions over which you exercise such supervision and the nature of it.

Program or Function   Nature of Supervision

1. _____   _____

2. _____   _____

3-6. _____   _____

Part VII. Contacts

Describe the contacts you make as part of your job. Indicate frequency using the same code used in Part III.

Contacts	Example and Purpose	How often?
Other departments		
Other company locations		
Other companies or organizations		
Government agencies		
General public		
Other		

Part VIII. Responsibility

Please describe the types of decisions you make on the job.

_____

_____

_____

_____

Are your decisions usually reviewed by a higher authority before coming effective? If so, by whom?

_____

_____

_____

_____

Part IX. Consequences of Error

Please describe typical kinds of errors that could occur on your job and identify their possible effect, using the following scale:

1 = would likely cause loss of own time to correct error
2 = would likely cause loss of own time and other's time to correct the error
3 = would likely cause loss of production, excess waste, or damage to equipment, usually confined to department
4 = would likely cause loss of production, excess waste, or damage to equipment, affecting other departments
5 = would likely cause substantial loss of funds, serious delays in schedules, diminished public confidence, legal action, or adverse political reaction

Type of Error   Effect

_____   _____

_____   _____

_____   _____

Part X. Working Conditions

Check appropriate boxes and list any unusual conditions.
%
Time   Type
_____ Office conditions: _____

_____ Shop conditions: _____
_____ Outdoor conditions: _____
_____ Other (give example): _____

Part XI. Additional Remarks

Provide other information or make comments that you feel would be helpful to further explain the nature of your job.

_____

_____

_____

_____

Comments:

_____

_____

_____

_____

PERFORMANCE APPRAISAL INSTRUMENT

An effective formal performance appraisal program includes completion of an evaluation form before the performance appraisal meeting; completion of the form in the presence of the employee may bias the appraisal. Critical elements of the performance appraisal form:

Part I: Identification

Fill in this section completely. It is particularly important to be accurate on the number of months the rater has directly observed job performance.

Part II: Rating Scales

In this section, appraise how well the person carried out the duties and responsibilites of the job. Read carefully and understand the description of each job duty identified in the job analysis. Disregard the general impression of the person being rated and concentrate on one job duty at a time. Then rate the person on typical performance during the entire rating period, using the scale below:

1 - 2   Is not reasonable and consistent with normal expectations of job proficiency.

3 - 4 - 5   Is reasonable and consistent with normal expectations of job proficiency.

6 - 7   Exceeds normal expectations of job proficiency.

When rating each standard it is important to observe the following rules:

1. Rating must be based on facts.
2. Previous ratings should carry no weight.
3. Although several duties might be related, each duty must be rated independently.
4. Remember that the best employee has weaknesses, while the poorest employee has strong points.
5. Raters can appraise performance *only* on those duties they have regularly and directly observed.

Make comments in the blank space provided at the right of each set of duties. For duties rated 3- 4- 5 comments are optional, but explain any rating below 3 or above 5.

Part III: Goal Accomplishment

In this section, appraise achievement of specified goals during the rating period. Both supervisor and employee should have agreed upon the goals. The blank space entitled "Goal" should indicate the goal from the last appraisal review. The space entitled "Measure" indicates how the goal was measured. Use the same 1 to 7 rating scale to assess how well goals were achieved over the past appraisal period. Space is provided for four organizational goals and two personal goals.

As part of the appraisal process, supervisor and subordinate must hold periodic conferences to review progress, overcome obstacles, and possibly modify goals in light of changed conditions. The final appraisal must also specify factors beyond the control of the subordinate that influenced performance.

Part IV: Development Appraisal Summary

Review the analysis of the employee in attaining acceptable levels of performance. Consider the employee's strengths and weaknesses in terms of job requirements. Determine whether the employee's knowledge, skills, and abilities are adequate, less than adequate, or more than adequate for the job. In the comments include:
1. A statement of job performance as a whole
2. Employee strengths and weaknesses
3. Areas that need improvement
4. Specific actions needed for growth and development

Part V: Goals for the Next Review Period

These work sheets are designed to help manager and subordinate reach mutual agreement on goals to be accomplished during the next rating period and to provide a basis for appraising results achieved. Space is provided for four organizational goals and two personal goals.

Goals should be specific, stated in measurable terms. Use such indicators as staff-hours, dollars, dates, and percentages wherever possible. The goals must support the mission of the department. They may fall within one major work area of the job, such as planning, or they may cut across several areas. They may be related to innovation or to improvement of normal work output. Identify only goals that can be reasonably accomplished during the rating period without causing normal work output to suffer as a consequence of the attention they receive. Do not set standards unrealistically high or unrealistically low.

Part VI: Career Path Goals (Optional)

The supervisor, especially in a growing company, should ask the employee being appraised what goals he or she has for his or her career with the company. This information will help the company in its human resource planning and training and development efforts. This discussion should include the following:

1. Whether or not employees are satisfied with their current position.
2. Whether or not there are other jobs in the company they would like.
3. A projected time schedule for attaining a desired job.

The manager should then comment on the employee's career goals by making suggestions and outlining steps for the employee to take to obtain the desired position.

Part VII: Job Description Review

During the performance appraisal review, the manager and employee should discuss the accuracy of the job description. It is essential that this document be kept up-to-date to ensure the validity of the performance appraisal. Enter any changes or corrections in the space allotted. These changes will become part of the updated performance appraisal instrument to be used during the next appraisal period.

Part VIII: Signatures

Both employee and manager should sign the completed appraisal form. The employee's signature does not necessarily indicate agreement with the rating but is evidence that the employee has seen and reviewed the ratings. (This should be made explicit to the employee.) The employee should carefully study the ratings given and may ask the rater for more information. The employee should then sign the appraisal form.

PART I. IDENTIFICATION

Name _____

Position _____

Rating Period From _____ To _____

Rater Name_____

Title_____

Number of months rater has directly observed job performance _____

PART II. RATING SCALES

Job Duties	Rating	Comments
1. _____	1 2 3 4 5 6 7	_____
2. _____	1 2 3 4 5 6 7	_____
3. _____	1 2 3 4 5 6 7	_____
4. _____	1 2 3 4 5 6 7	_____
5. _____	1 2 3 4 5 6 7	_____
6. _____	1 2 3 4 5 6 7	_____
7. _____	1 2 3 4 5 6 7	_____
8. _____	1 2 3 4 5 6 7	_____
9. _____	1 2 3 4 5 6 7	_____
10. _____	1 2 3 4 5 6 7	_____

PART III. GOAL ACCOMPLISHMENT

Organizational Goals

Goal #1:   Measure:

_____   _____

Performance Assessment   1 2 3 4 5 6 7

Goal #2:   Measure:

_____   _____

Performance Assessment   1 2 3 4 5 6 7

Goal #3:   Measure:

_____   _____

Performance Assessment   1 2 3 4 5 6 7

Goal #4:   Measure:

_____   _____

Performance Assessment   1 2 3 4 5 6 7

Personal Goals
Goal #5   Measure:

_____   _____

Performance Assessment   1 2 3 4 5 6 7

Goal #6   Measure:

_____   _____

Performance Assessment   1 2 3 4 5 6 7

PART IV. DEVELOPMENTAL APPRAISAL SUMMARY

_____

_____

_____

_____

_____

_____

_____

_____

_____

_____

_____

PART V. GOAL SETTING

(for the next review period)

Organizational Goals

Goal #1:   Measure:

_____   _____

_____   _____

Performance Assessment   1 2 3 4 5 6 7

Goal #2:   Measure:

_____   _____

_____   _____

Performance Assessment   1 2 3 4 5 6 7

Goal #3:   Measure:

_____   _____

_____   _____

Performance Assessment   1 2 3 4 5 6 7

Goal #4:   Measure:

_____   _____

_____   _____

Performance Assessment   1 2 3 4 5 6 7

Personal Goals

Goal #5   Measure:

_____   _____

_____   _____

Performance Assessment   1 2 3 4 5 6 7

Goal #6   Measure:

_____   _____

_____   _____

Performance Assessment   1 2 3 4 5 6 7

PART VI. EMPLOYEE CAREER GOALS

Are you satisfied with your current position?

_____

_____

_____

Is there another job in this company that you would like to have?

_____

_____

_____

What are your ultimate career goals with this company?

_____

_____

_____

Supervisor comments and recommendations for career goals:

_____

_____

_____

_____

_____

_____

_____

_____

_____

_____

PART VII. JOB DESCRIPTION REVIEW

List any changes or corrections to be made for the next review period.

_____

_____

_____

_____

_____

_____

_____

_____

_____

_____

_____

PART VIII. SIGNATURES

This report is based on my observation and knowledge. My signature indicates that I have reviewed this appraisal of both employee and job. It does not mean that I agree with the results.

_____   _____
Employee   Date

_____   _____
Supervisor   Date

The above performance appraisal appears to be accurate and complete.

_____   _____
Human Resources Representative   Date

PROGRESSIVE DISCIPLINE GUIDELINES AND FORMS

Progressive Discipline Guidelines

- Have a progressive system that starts with warnings and progresses through increasingly severe further actions.
- Document every disciplinary action, including warnings.
- Make sure that all employees are aware of employment policies and procedures.
- Be consistent in applying the discipline procedures. Handle similar circumstances in the same way.
- Do not administer discipline in a public setting or when an employee is in an extremely emotional state.
- Set a time to meet and discuss the issue in private but in a timely manner.
- Take a third party, such as a human resources or other manager, into the meeting as a witness in more serious situations and terminations.
- At the meeting:
  - Explain to the employee the offense, the action to be taken, and the consequences if the incident happens again.
  - Discuss details of the behavior in question.
  - Review the steps in the discipline process with the employee.
  - Give the employee a chance to explain the incident.
  - Connect the discipline to the behavior exhibited personally to the employee.
  - Encourage the employee to work on improving or eliminating the behavior.
  - Secure the signatures of the employee, the supervisor, and any witness on any documentation presented.

PROGRESSIVE DISCIPLINE FORMS
First Warning

Employee Name: _____ Date: _____

Summary of Incident (Please relate to company handbook/policies where possible):

_____

_____

_____

Action to Be Taken:

_____

_____

_____

Action to Be Taken if Incident Occurs Again:

_____

_____

_____

Comments:

_____

_____

_____

_____   _____
Employee Signature   Date

_____   _____
Supervisor Signature   Date

_____   _____
Witness (If employee refuses to sign)   Date

Second Warning

Employee Name: _____ Date: _____

Summary of Incident (Please relate to company handbook/policies where possible):

_____

_____

_____

Action to Be Taken:

_____

_____

_____

Action to Be Taken if Incident Occurs Again:

_____

_____

_____

Comments:

_____

_____

_____

_____   _____
Employee Signature   Date

_____   _____
Supervisor Signature   Date

_____   _____
Witness (If employee refuses to sign)   Date

Suspension/Probation Notice

Employee Name: _____ Date: _____

Summary of Incident (Please relate to company handbook/policies where possible):

_____

_____

_____

Action To Be Taken:

Suspension with pay _____ without pay _____ # of days _____

Action To Be Taken if Incident Occurs Again:

_____

_____

_____

Comments:

_____

_____

_____

_____   _____
Employee Signature   Date

_____   _____
Supervisor Signature   Date

_____   _____
Witness (HR professional or another manager)   Date

Termination Notice

Please make sure that all guidelines for termination have been followed before meeting with the employee.

Employee Name: _____ Date: _____

Summary of Incident (Please relate to company handbook/policies where possible):

_____

_____

_____

_____

_____

_____

Termination Effective Date: _____

Comments:

_____

_____

_____

_____   _____

Employee Signature   Date

_____   _____

Supervisor Signature   Date

_____   _____

Witness (HR professional or another manager)   Date

APPENDIX B

Sample Employee Handbook*

XYZ COMPANY
EMPLOYEE MANUAL

---

*This handbook is meant to serve only as an example. It is an actual company handbook, with the customary flaws found in most manuals.

TABLE OF CONTENTS

DEFINITIONS

BENEFIT ACCRUAL

Benefits begin accruing on the first day after three (3) full months of employment for all full-time employees. For those employees with prior full-time employment with XYZ COMPANY, benefit accrual will begin on the employee's most recent date of hire into a full-time position

FULL-TIME EMPLOYMENT DATE

The date on which the employee began working full-time for XYZ COMPANY.

YEAR

The operating year that relates to personnel policies begins on January 1 and ends on the following December 31. However, changes may be made during this period if approved by the President.

CATEGORIES OF EMPLOYMENT

FULL-TIME STAFF

Examples of full-time staff/staff services are employees working as store managers and operations coordinator. This precludes all individuals who are paid on an hourly, per diem, or activity basis. In certain instances employees who work less than 36 hours could be considered full-time. The President will make this determination.

PART-TIME STAFF

Part-time staff are those paid on an hourly basis and working less than 35 hours a week. They are not considered full-time staff and are not eligible for any full-time benefits.

EXEMPT EMPLOYEES

Exempt employees are those personnel who are paid on a salary basis and employed in executive, administrative, professional, or sales capacities. Included would be positions such as President and Operations Coordinator. These employees are exempt from overtime pay.

NON-EXEMPT EMPLOYEES

Personnel who are employed in capacities that are not classified as exempt from overtime pay are considered non-exempt employees. Although job title is not a perfect indicator of how an employee should be classified, the positions of store manager, secretary, receptionist, accounts receivable/payable, maintenance, and clerk would typically be included in this category. Overtime for these individuals will be calculated on a salary basis.

2

GENERAL INFORMATION

ANTI-NEPOTISM POLICY

This anti-nepotism policy is intended to enforce XYZ COMPANY's commitment to employment practices that create and maintain constructive working relationships. XYZ COMPANY is committed to management practices that are fairly and evenly applied to XYZ COMPANY employees and applicants for employment without actual or apparent bias or favoritism.

1. It is the general policy of XYZ COMPANY not to employ, or continue to employ, relatives on a full-time or part-time basis within the same administrative office or department, or to have a relative under the direct supervision of another relative.

   a) A relative, for the purposes of this policy, is defined as a parent, child, brother, sister, spouse, aunt, uncle, niece, nephew, grandparent, grandchild, and all in-laws and step relationships within these categories, and any individual for whom an employee has been assigned legal responsibility in a guardianship capacity.

   b) Direct supervision, for the purposes of this policy, means the lowest level of supervision responsible for assigning work, supervisory activities related to that work, appraising performance, determining salaries or wage increases, and/or making decisions in regard to hiring, firing, and disciplining of an employee.

2. If any relationships defined in paragraph 1 are created after the employment of the affected employee, one of the persons affected must relinquish his or her position no later than six (6) months from the date the relationship was established. Within thirty (30) days after the relationship has been established, the affected persons must inform the President in writing that such a relationship has been established and must state which affected person will relinquish his or her position; it will be assumed that the affected employee with the least seniority will do so. The person giving up a position may be re-employed by XYZ COMPANY, subject to the needs of the organization. The President may make exceptions to this policy when necessary.

3. If the President is made aware of possible violations of this policy, the matter will be investigated. If the allegations are found to be correct and establish a violation of this policy, the President may terminate the employees violating this policy.

3

ATTENDANCE

Promptness and regularity in attendance reflect your commitment to your work and your concern for the efficient operation of your store. If you are unable to report to work, you must notify your manager by 6:30 a.m. This will allow time to arrange for a substitute employee. You should give the reason and the expected duration of your absence.

CHANGING PERSONAL INFORMATION

Up-to-date personnel records are necessary for proper administration of payroll, end-of-the-year tax withholding forms, and benefits. If an employee has a change of name, address, home telephone, emergency telephone, or other status, the President must be notified. Disclosure of personal information to authorized individuals and government agencies will be made when appropriate.

DEATH WHILE ACTIVELY EMPLOYED

In the event of the death of an actively employed full or part-time individual, the final payment of salary or wages will be paid to the designated beneficiary.

DRUG-FREE COMPANY AND WORK PLACE STATEMENT

Employees are prohibited from the unlawful manufacture, distribution, dispensing, possession, or use of a controlled substance or alcohol anywhere on property used by XYZ COMPANY. Employees who violate this policy will be subject to disciplinary action up to and including termination of employment.

Once hired, an employee may be subject to a drug test. Failure of the drug test could result in termination. Employees may also be subject to random drug testing during employment at the discretion of XYZ COMPANY.

As a condition of employment, employees must abide by the terms of this policy or XYZ COMPANY will take one or more of the following actions within 30 days:

1. Report the violation to law enforcement officials.

2. Take disciplinary action against such employee, up to and including termination of employment.

3. Require the employee to participate in a substance abuse rehabilitation program approved for such purposes by a federal, state, local health, law enforcement, or other appropriate agency.

GRIEVANCE PROCEDURE

Since management believes that open discussion is the only way conditions that create dissatisfaction will become known, all employees are encouraged to discuss all work-related problems with their immediate managers. The following procedures should be followed when addressing work-related problems:

- FIRST STEP: The employee should discuss the problem with the manager as soon as possible after the problem arises but no later than five (5) days after the incident.

- SECOND STEP: If the problem is not settled at the first step, the matter will be referred to the President. The President's decision will be final and binding on all parties.

During the course of a grievance proceeding, the employee will be treated fairly and with dignity. All the facts presented will be reviewed in accordance with company policies. Corrective action will be taken promptly if the company is in error; an employee who has made a mistake will receive an explanation and clarification of company policy.

HOLIDAYS

All full-time employees are eligible for the following paid holidays:

New Year's Day	Memorial Day
Labor Day	Fourth of July
Thanksgiving Day	Christmas Day

In order to receive holiday pay, the employee must work the day before and the day after the holiday. If the holiday falls on Saturday, one-half day pay will be provided.

HOURS OF EMPLOYMENT

Staff (Full-time): The specific work hour designation will depend upon the demands of each location.

All nonexempt staff employees must submit weekly time sheets to comply with federal regulations. All nonexempt employees must get prior approval from the President or the appropriate manager to work more than 40 hours in any given work week.

Any exceptions from the above must be approved by the manager. Where hours of employment are significantly different from the above, those hours will be outlined by the manager.

JURY DUTY

If a full or part-time employee is called upon to report for jury duty, the employee shall notify the manager immediately and keep the manager informed of the probable length of service.

Full-time employees will continue to be salaried during time away and receive the regular base pay *reduced* by any jury pay received. The employee must submit a Juror Service Certificate stating the days of service and the compensation received. The employee should report to work if there is any free time during this period.

LEAVE PROGRAMS

XYZ COMPANY offers full-time employees the opportunity to earn two hours per week up to 96 hours per year of paid leave. Employees will be eligible to accrue leave after completing three (3) full calendar months of employment. Leave accrual will begin on the first day of the month after the qualification period is completed. This paid time off (PTO) can be used for vacation, sickness, or personal reasons. Whenever possible, PTO must be used in full one-day increments, except on Saturdays, when it can be used in four-hour increments.

PTO must be approved by the immediate manager. Notice of leave should be given as soon as possible.

When PTO is used for sick leave, employees should notify the immediate manager at least *three hours* before their shift is to begin to allow for arranging store coverage in your absence.

PTO for personal days should be requested at least *one week* in advance to allow for arranging store coverage.

PTO for vacations should be requested *one month* in advance to allow for arranging store coverage.

Except for sick leave purposes, PTO is subject to approval by the President. Leave will be limited during busy seasons.

Benefit accrual such as PTO or holiday benefits will be suspended during the time an employee is on approved leave.

6

An employee may carry over twenty-four (24) hours of PTO into the next year. All other PTO must be used in the current year or will be lost.

In the event of resignation or termination, an employee will be paid for any unused PTO.

FAMILY LEAVE

The Family and Medical Leave Act (FMLA) provides eligible employees with up to 12 workweeks of unpaid leave for certain family and medical reasons during a 12-month period. During this leave, an eligible employee is entitled to continue group health plan coverage as if the employee had continued to work. At the conclusion of the leave, with some exceptions, an employee generally has a right to return to the same or an equivalent position.

Employee Eligibility Criteria

To be eligible for FMLA leave, an employee must have been employed by XYZ COMPANY:

- for at least 12 months (which need not be consecutive);
- for at least 1,250 hours during the 12-month period immediately preceding the commencement of the leave; and
- at a worksite (a) with 50 or more employees, or (b) where 50 or more employees are located within 75 miles of the worksite.

Events that May Entitle an Employee to FMLA Leave

FMLA leave may be taken for any one or a combination of the following reasons:

- the birth of the employee's child or to care for the newborn child;
- the placement of a child with the employee for adoption or foster care or to care for the newly placed child;
- to care for the employee's spouse, child, or parent (but not in-law) with a serious health condition; or
- a serious health condition of the employee that makes the employee unable to perform one or more of the essential functions of the job.

A "serious health condition" is an injury, illness, impairment, or physical or mental condition that involves inpatient care or continuing treatment by a health care provider.

7

How Much FMLA Leave May Be Taken?

An eligible employee is entitled to up to 12 workweeks of unpaid leave during a 12-month period for any FMLA qualifying reason(s). The 12-month period is a rolling 12-month period measured backward from the date an employee uses any FMLA leave.

Limitations on FMLA Leave

When both spouses are employed by XYZ COMPANY, they are together entitled to a combined total of 12 workweeks of FMLA leave within the designated 12-month period for the birth, adoption, or foster care placement of a child with the employees, for aftercare of the newborn or newly placed child, and to care for a parent (but not in-law) with a serious health condition. Each spouse may be entitled to additional FMLA leave for other FMLA qualifying reasons (i.e., the difference between the leave taken individually for any of the above reasons and 12 workweeks, but not more than a total of 12 workweeks per person).

For example, if each spouse took six (6) weeks of leave to care for a newborn child, each could later use an additional six weeks if he or she had a serious health condition or to care for a child with a serious health condition.

Intermittent or Reduced Work Schedule Leave

Intermittent leave is leave taken in separate blocks of time. A reduced work schedule leave is a leave schedule that reduces an employee's usual number of hours per workweek or hours per workday.

Leave to care for a newborn or for a newly placed child may not be taken intermittently or on a reduced work schedule unless XYZ COMPANY agrees to an individual leave request.

Leave because of an employee's own serious health condition, or to care for an employee's spouse, child, or parent with a serious health condition, may be taken all at once or, where medically necessary, intermittently or on a reduced work schedule.

If an employee takes leave intermittently or on a reduced work schedule basis, the employee must, when requested, attempt to schedule the leave so as not to unduly disrupt the XYZ COMPANY's operations. When an employee takes intermittent or reduced work schedule leave for foreseeable planned medical treatment, XYZ COMPANY may temporarily transfer the employee to an alternative position with equivalent pay and benefits for which the employee is qualified and which better accommodates recurring periods of leave.

8

Requests for FMLA Leave

An employee should request FMLA leave by completing the Employer's Request for Leave form and submitting it to the Human Resources Representative.

When leave is foreseeable for childbirth, placement of a child, or planned medical treatment for the employee's or family member's serious health condition, the employee must provide XYZ COMPANY with at least 30 days advance notice, or such shorter notice as is practicable (i.e., within 1 or 2 business days of learning of the need for the leave). When the timing of the leave is not foreseeable, the employee must provide XYZ COMPANY with notice of the need for leave as soon as practicable (i.e., within 1 or 2 business days of learning of the need for the leave).

Required Documentation

When leave is taken to care for a family member, XYZ COMPANY may require the employee to provide documentation or a statement of family relationship (e.g., birth certificate or court document).

An employee may be required to submit medical certification from a health care provider to support a request for FMLA leave for the employee's or a family member's serious health condition. Medical certification forms are available from the Human Resources Representative.

During FMLA leave, XYZ COMPANY may request that the employee provide recertification of a serious health condition at intervals in accordance with the FMLA. In addition, during FMLA leave, the employee must provide XYZ COMPANY with periodic reports regarding the employee's status and intent to return to work. If the employee's anticipated return to work date changes and it becomes necessary for the employee to take more or less leave than originally anticipated, the employee must provide XYZ COMPANY with reasonable notice (i.e., within 2 business days) of the employee's changed circumstances and new return to work date. If the employee gives XYZ COMPANY notice of the employee's intent not to return to work, the employee will be considered to have voluntarily resigned.

Before the employee returns to work from FMLA leave for the employee's own serious health condition, the employee may be required to submit a fitness for duty certification from the health care provider with respect to the condition for which the leave was taken, stating that the employee is able to resume work.

9

FMLA leave or return to work may be delayed or denied if documentation is not provided in a timely manner. Also, a failure to provide requested documentation of the reason for an absence from work may lead to termination of employment.

Use of Paid and Unpaid Leave

FMLA provides eligible employees with up to 12 workweeks of unpaid leave. If an employee has accrued paid leave (e.g., vacation, sick leave, personal leave), however, the employee must use any qualifying paid leave first. "Qualifying paid leave" is leave that would otherwise be available to the employee for the purpose for which the FMLA leave is taken. The remainder of the 12 workweeks of leave, if any, will be unpaid FMLA leave. Any paid leave used for an FMLA qualifying reason will be charged against an employee's entitlement to FMLA leave. This includes leave for disability or workers' compensation injury/illness, provided that the leave meets FMLA requirements. The substitution of paid leave for unpaid leave does not extend the 12-workweek leave period.

Designation of Leave

XYZ COMPANY will notify the employee that leave has been designated as FMLA leave. XYZ COMPANY may provisionally designate the employee's leave as FMLA leave if XYZ COMPANY has not received medical certification or has not otherwise been able to confirm that the employee's leave qualifies as FMLA leave. If the employee has not notified XYZ COMPANY of the reason for the leave, and the employee desires that leave be counted as FMLA leave, the employee must notify the Human Resources Representative within two (2) business days of the employee's return to work that the leave was for an FMLA reason.

Maintenance of Health Benefits

During FMLA leave an employee is entitled to continued group health plan coverage under the same conditions as if the employee had continued to work.

Pregnancy Leave for Full-time Employees

XYZ COMPANY provides pregnancy leave, with or without pay, to eligible employees who are temporarily unable to work due to a disability related to pregnancy, childbirth, or related medical conditions. Compensation during a pregnancy leave will be provided if the employee has unused PTO. When all PTO has been used, the employee may continue on unpaid leave at the discretion of the President. No other benefits will be accrued while the employee is on unpaid leave.

Employees may request pregnancy leave only after three (3) months of service.

10

If an employee fails to report to work promptly at the end of the pregnancy leave, XYZ Company will assume that the employee has resigned.

Funeral Leave
In the event of the death of an immediate family member, full-time employees will be allowed an absence with pay for up to three (3) calendar days following death. For purposes of this policy, "immediate family" is defined as spouse, child, parent, brother, sister, mother-in-law, father-in-law, grandparent, or legal guardian. If the deceased is not an immediate relative, the employee may take time off to attend the funeral and time off will be charged against PTO.

Leave of Absence (Full-time Employees)
A written request for unpaid leave of absence for the purpose of improving the educational or practical qualifications of the employee or for extreme personal circumstances will be considered by the President. If the request is granted, every attempt will be made on return to place the individual in a position equal to the one vacated. The request should state when the employee plans to return to work. Failure to report to work following the completion of the leave will be viewed as a resignation.

Benefit accrual, such as PTO and holiday benefits will be suspended during the leave of absence and will resume upon return to active employment.

Military Leave (Reserve Duty)
All employees who are called for National Guard or Military Reserve during the two-week summer training program will receive their regular salary less the amount paid by the Armed Forces, not to exceed two weeks. Pay slips should be submitted to the Corporate Business Office for payroll adjustment. Before or after completing the two-week summer training obligation, you may take your regular PTO with pay subject to approval from your manager. However, your PTO and military summer training cannot run consecutively; they must be separated by at least one week's time.

Any military reservist called to active duty should request a Leave of Absence (refer to the Leave of Absence section of this manual).

LETTERS OF RECOMMENDATION

No letter recommending or evaluating an employee for future employment will be issued without the consent of the President.

MISREPRESENTATION

Any employee whose actions, by omission or commission, are contrary to the stated goals, objectives, and policies of the company or who jeopardizes its integrity will be subject to immediate termination of employment. Such acts include, but are not limited to, the following:

1. Misrepresentation of material facts to customers or to XYZ COMPANY.

2. Use of bribery, coercion, or other methods to influence people.

3. Acceptance of compensation, gifts, or favors from individuals or organizations with whom XYZ COMPANY has, or may have, a relationship. (Normal business entertainment is excluded.)

4. Misuse of inside information, such as confidential policies, etc.

5. Disparagement of the company, its name, or its employees.

OCCUPATIONAL INJURIES AND ILLNESSES

Any employee who experiences an occupational injury or illness is required to file a report with the President or his representative. Worker's compensation insurance is in force to cover all employees.

OCCUPATIONAL SAFETY AND HEALTH ACT AND OSHA

The Act is a federal law established to assure every working man and woman in the nation safe and healthful working conditions and to preserve our human resources—in short: to keep employees safe and comfortable while working. Any problems to which the Act may apply should be reported to your manager.

OUTSIDE EMPLOYMENT

Employees may hold outside jobs as long as they meet the performance standards of their job with XYZ COMPANY. All employees will be judged by the same performance standards and will be held to XYZ COMPANY's scheduling demands, regardless of any outside work requirements.

If XYZ COMPANY determines that an employee's outside work interferes with his or her performance or ability to meet the requirements of XYZ COMPANY as they are modified from time to time, the employee may be asked to terminate the outside employment if he or she wishes to remain with XYZ COMPANY.

12

Outside employment that constitutes a conflict of interest is prohibited. Employees may not receive any income or material gain from individuals outside XYZ COMPANY for materials produced or services rendered while performing their jobs.

Employees may not work at another loan or financial office.

OVERTIME PAY (NON-EXEMPT EMPLOYEES)

All nonexempt employees must submit a weekly time report to comply with federal regulations. **All nonexempt employees must obtain prior approval from their manager to work more than 40 hours in any workweek.**

Overtime compensation will be paid to individuals on salary for hours they work in excess of 40 per week at a rate of 1.5 times the hourly rate. For example:

If an employee who has a salary of $400.00 per week works 44 hours in the week, overtime would be based on an hourly rate of 9.09 (400/44). The weekly pay calculation would be 44 X 9.09 plus 0.5 X 9.09 for each of the four hours over forty. The total compensation would be 418.18.

The workweek is defined as Sunday to Saturday. Overtime will be paid only for time worked in excess of 40 hours within that seven-day period.

PAYDAYS

XYZ COMPANY pays its employees biweekly.

PERFORMANCE EVALUATIONS

All employees will have their performance reviewed on an ongoing basis by their manager. Individual performance will be measured against objective standards established by the company. XYZ COMPANY will attempt to conduct formal evaluations annually and copies of these evaluations, signed by both parties, will be placed in the employee's personnel file.

Salary increases will be based upon the results of the performance evaluation and on management discretion.

PERSONAL APPEARANCE

All employees are expected to use discretion and good judgment in dressing for work; at all times your attire should reflect the nature of our business.

PERSONAL DAYS

A full-time employee who must tend to personal business that cannot be attended to outside the normal workday or observe a religious day not listed on the holiday schedule may request PTO, following the steps outlined in the description of personal days. An employee who fails to obtain a manager's approval to take a personal day will be considered to be taking a leave day without pay. In an emergency when there is no time to obtain the manager's approval, the situation should be discussed with the manager and PTO may be taken if it is available.

QUALIFICATION PERIOD

All full-time employees are required to complete a qualification period of three (3) continuous months. Once employees complete the qualification period, they will receive a performance appraisal for developmental purposes.

Satisfactory completion of the qualification period does not affect the fact that all employees are employed at will. Employment at all times is at the mutual consent of XYZ COMPANY and the employee. Either XYZ COMPANY or the employee may terminate the employment relationship at any time without notice and without further compensation.

PROGRESSIVE DISCIPLINARY PROCEDURE

This procedure applies to all persons employed by XYZ COMPANY. The seriousness of the offense is considered when determining the action to be taken; however, XYZ COMPANY reserves the right to implement discipline at any step it considers appropriate, to bypass progressive discipline as necessary, and to take any disciplinary action it considers appropriate for the misconduct.

1. Verbal Counseling. Used as the first step regarding a performance problem or for minor offenses, counseling informs employees of performance deficiencies or behavior problems. If the situation does not improve within a reasonable period of time (depending on the seriousness of the situation), step two of this procedure is followed. Documentation of this meeting should include date, time, and reason for the discipline as well as the consequences if the behavior continues.

2. Written Warning. For repeated performance problems or minor offenses, or for a more serious offense, the supervisor will prepare a written warning notice. The warning must be reviewed with the employee and the employee is asked to sign it. (If an employee refuses to sign, this will be noted and the

14

form will be signed by the operations coordinator or the President. Documentation of this meeting should include date, time, and reason for the discipline as well as the consequences if the behavior continues. A copy of the written warning must be forwarded to the President. The length of the warning period is normally 90 days but can vary according to the circumstances.

3. Probation. If performance does not improve, or if another offense is committed, or for a major offense, the employee can be placed on probation. The supervisor must complete the probation form and review it with the employee. The employee should sign the form, which must be forwarded to the President. If an employee refuses to sign, this will be noted and the form will be signed by the operations coordinator or President. The probation period should not exceed six (6) months. At the end of the probation period, the supervisor must complete a Probation Disposition form, which indicates the action taken, either dismissal or removal from probation.

4. Dismissal. If the employee does not meet the terms of probation or commits another offense during probation, or for the most serious violations of the company rules, an employee may be dismissed. Complete and thorough documentation and the involvement of the President are required in such cases.

Other Forms of Disciplinary Action:
Suspension. For serious infractions, the employee may be suspended for a specified period of time. This action must be approved by the President. Pay will also be suspended. During the suspension, an investigation will be conducted to determine the action to be taken, which can include dismissal.

Recurring Disciplinary Problems. When an employee has had previous disciplinary problems and has been warned or placed on probation, managers may take appropriate action without being obligated to follow the steps outlined above. However, they must obtain the concurrence of the President whenever this is done.

REDUCTION IN FORCE
Reductions in the XYZ COMPANY work force that may be necessary will be accomplished through normal attrition whenever possible, but the work force may be reduced due to budget constraints, lack of work, or reorganization of work as deemed necessary by XYZ COMPANY.

15

RESIGNATION

Employees should submit a written notice of resignation to their manager two (2) weeks before the last day of employment. The company reserves the right to release the employee from normal obligations with pay any time during the notice period.

When an employee resigns, final payment will include the amount of salary due to the last day of employment plus accrued PTO, if any. Final compensation is restricted to base salary and unused PTO.

RULES AND REGULATIONS

Responsible conduct is necessary in order to provide a safe, pleasant, and efficient environment for employees of XYZ COMPANY. To achieve this, all employees are expected to comply with all company rules, as well as specific rules in their own department.

The following are examples of violations of rules that will result in disciplinary action, possibly including dismissal. The severity of the disciplinary action will depend on the nature of the violation.

1. Violation of the stated XYZ COMPANY Employee Rules provided to all employees at the start of their employment.
2. Failure to carry out written or oral instructions given by a management representative, including insubordination or refusal to work on jobs assigned.
3. Destruction of company property, assets, equipment, or materials.
4. Gambling, fighting, disorderly conduct, or conduct that violates common decency or morality, including abusive language.
5. Promotion, sale, possession of, or working under the influence of alcohol, dangerous drugs, or other controlled substances while on company premises.
6. Gross neglect of duty, including any breach of duty in connection with work that is reasonable and owed to the employer.
7. Incarceration or conviction for a felony or other crime involving dishonesty or breach of trust, violence, or predatory sex acts.
8. Bringing or attempting to bring onto company premises any firearm, explosive, flammable liquid, or combustible mixture without proper authority, or furnishing false information related to such items.

16

9. Falsification of XYZ COMPANY records (e.g., company documents, employment application, or required reports).

10. Unauthorized solicitation on company premises during working hours, or where work is being performed; unauthorized distribution of literature or other matter in working areas or during work time; posting literature or other matter on company premises without proper authority.

11. Sleeping or loitering during scheduled work hours.

12. Failure to report to work from a leave of absence upon its expiration or unreported absences of three (3) days or more.

13. Excessive absenteeism or tardiness, as set by departmental standards.

14. Causing disturbances among fellow employees, spreading rumors, failing to cooperate with others, or showing a lack of respect for fellow employees.

SALARY CHANGES

Salary changes are normally associated with employee performance evaluations. Salary changes generally reflect individual employee performance.

SEXUAL HARASSMENT

As defined in Section 702 of Title VII of the Civil Rights Act of 1964, sexual harassment is "unwelcome sexual advances, requests for sexual favors and other verbal or physical conduct of a sexual nature when: (1) submission of such conduct is made, explicitly or implicitly, a term or condition of an individual's employment, (2) submission to or rejection of such conduct by an individual is used as the basis for an employment decision affecting the individual, or (3) such conduct has the purpose or effect of unreasonably interfering with an individual's work performance or creating an intimidating, hostile, or offensive work environment."

Any deliberate or repeated unsolicited verbal comment, gesture, or physical contact of a sexual nature that is unwelcome shall be considered sexual harassment. This may include, but is not limited to:

1. Sex-oriented verbal "kidding" or abuse.

2. Subtle pressure for sexual activity.

3. Physical contact such as patting, pinching, or constant brushing against another's body.

4. Demands for sexual favors accompanied by implied or overt promises of preferential treatment or threats concerning an individual's employment status.

17

Sexual harassment does not refer to occasional compliments. It refers to behavior that is personally offensive and disables morale, and that therefore interferes with the work effectiveness of its victims and their coworkers.

Sexual harassment as defined above is forbidden and will not be tolerated on the part of an employee in a position of authority over another employee or by coworkers when such conduct has the effect of unreasonably interfering with an individual's work performance (including promotion of employees who submit to sexual advances or refusal to promote employees who resist or protest sexual overtures).

XYZ COMPANY also desires to protect its employees from sexual harassment by non-employees, such as vendors or customers. All employees who believe themselves to be the objects of actions prohibited by this policy are strongly urged to bring these violations to the immediate attention of XYZ COMPANY through the lowest level of noninvolved management.

Sexual harassment falls into two broad categories:

1. That in which the employee suffers a tangible job detriment in retaliation for refusing to submit to sexual demands.
2. That in which there is no tangible job loss but the harassment creates an offensive or hostile environment.

Procedure

1. Managers are responsible for maintaining work environments free from sexual harassment. This includes but is not limited to affirmatively raising the subject when necessary and expressing strong disapproval, and informing employees of their right to report any incident they believe constitutes sexual harassment.
2. An employee who believes he or she has been a victim of sexual harassment should file a complaint with the supervisor or the Human Resources Director.
3. In determining whether alleged conduct constitutes sexual harassment, the supervisor and the President will look at the record as a whole and at the totality of the circumstances, such as the nature of the sexual advance and the context in which the alleged incidents occurred.
4. Sexual harassment of another employee may subject the offender to disciplinary action up to and including involuntary termination.

5. Complaints will be treated confidentially and will be analyzed and investigated promptly upon receipt and the investigative report will filed with the President.

SMOKE-FREE ENVIRONMENT

XYZ Company buildings are smoke-free. No smoking is permitted within any location.

SNOW DAYS

Company closing announcements due to snow are made by the President or his representative.

TIME SHEETS

All nonexempt employees who work overtime or who are employed on a part-time basis must submit a time sheet at the end of each week.

RECEIPT OF EMPLOYEE MANUAL

I hereby acknowledge that I have received a copy of the XYZ COMPANY Employee Manual and XYZ COMPANY Employee Rules. I have been given a chance to ask questions regarding the requirements and work rules described. I also acknowledge that this manual does not constitute an employment contract. I understand that all employees are employed at will; employment at all times is at the mutual consent of XYZ COMPANY and the employee. Either XYZ COMPANY or the employee may terminate the employment relationship at any time without notice and without further compensation.

_____   _____

Employee Signature   Date

My signature indicates that I have been provided a copy of the XYZ COMPANY Employee Manual and have been given a chance to ask questions for clarification.

19

APPENDIX C

Sample Safety Handbook

SAFETY PHILOSOPHY OF XYZ COMPANY

It is the philosophy of XYZ COMPANY that to provide a quality product at a competitive price, a safe work place is a necessity. Accidents not only affect the lifestyle and livelihood of the employee, they add additional costs and delays to the delivery of our product to the customer. In line with our goal of an accident-free environment, we further believe that:

- Accidents are *not* a necessary part of doing business.
- No task is to be performed without proper training and awareness of the hazards involved.
- Your involvement is necessary for a successful safety program and is crucial for good communications.
- Safety is everyone's job. While management is responsible for providing a safe work environment, you are responsible for your own actions.
- Housekeeping practices affect the safety, quality, and productivity of our company.

A real measure of success for a safety program is how you leave at the end of a day. We intend for you to leave the same way you came to work.

PLANT SAFE WORKING PRACTICES

GENERAL SAFETY TIPS

- Never run in the plant.

- Horseplay eventually results in personal injury or property damage. Don't do it.

- Wear required personal protective equipment at all times. It is there to protect you from injury.

- Maintain your hair so that it will not become entangled in the machinery or obstruct your vision.

- All clothing should cover your midriff and have hemmed, not frayed, edges. Clothing must be suitable and appropriate for the hazard involved, the weather, and the duties performed. When you are working around moving machinery, loose-fitting clothing and ties are not permitted.

- The wearing of jewelry on the job is not recommended, particularly if you are working around moving or rotating parts.

- If you are not sure, ask. If you don't know how, don't do it.

HAND SAFETY

Hand injuries are the most common type of injury. Whether it is a simple scratch, a minor burn, a deep laceration, or an amputation, it is preventable by concentrating on the job and the risk involved, and using the safety devices provided. The following are guidelines to help prevent injury to your hands:

- First and foremost, *think.* You may not get another chance to use your head.

- Never put your hands where you can't see them.

- Make sure your hand tools are in good shape.

- Always pull wrenches towards you.

- Never use your hands as hammers.

- Use push sticks, not your fingers, to move materials near the point of operation of a machine.

- Use gloves wisely. A chuck or bit can grab a gloved hand.

- Never wipe off machinery while it is still running.

- Read and obey all warning labels and signs.

- Never run machinery with a missing guard or safety device.

- If you suffer an injury, get medical care promptly.

LIFTING GUIDELINES

- Always test the load before you lift. Know what to expect.
- Do not attempt to lift or push objects that may be too heavy for one person. Ask for assistance.
- If two or more people are involved in lifting, communicate the action about to be taken.
- Use a mechanical device, such as a hoist, when it is available or the job requires it.
- Plan your move. Where are you going? Is the path clear?
- Use a wide stance, with one foot ahead of the other.
- Keep your lower back in its natural curved position.
- Bring the load close to your body.
- Keep your head back and your shoulders up.
- Tighten your stomach muscles as the lift begins.
- Lift with your legs. They have the strongest muscles in your body.
- Take a deep breath before lifting an object. Inflated lungs will help support your back.
- Move your feet, not your hips.
- Lift and lower in smooth motions using your arms and legs.
- Never twist your body. Keep your shoulders and hips moving together.

EQUIPMENT AND MACHINERY

- Always operate machines with safeguards in place. Do not bypass, alter, damage, or remove safeguards. Safety guards and devices serve one purpose: to prevent injury to you. Report missing or damaged safeguards to your supervisor.
- Do not operate, repair, or test any equipment unless it is part of your assigned duties.
- Never adjust, repair, clean, or oil machinery or equipment while any of its parts are in motion.
- Regularly inspect equipment and machinery for cracks, stretching, etc., on cables, chains, clamps, hooks, and other equipment that is often under stress. Spreading, crimps, or cracks are warning signs of danger.

- Report any defective equipment to your supervisor immediately.

- Before opening valves, turning on switches, or starting machinery, check the locations and safety of others in the area.

HAND TOOLS

- Always know how to use hand and power tools properly before starting the job; follow operating instructions and use the proper accessories. If you are unfamiliar with how a tool operates or is to be used, get advice and instruction from your supervisor.

- Do not use any tool for anything except its intended use.

- Keep all cutting tools sharp and in a safe condition, without broken or damaged parts.

- Do not use defective tools. Report them to your supervisor and return the equipment to the Tool Room or appropriate department for repair.

- Never leave hand tools lying on the floor or workbench or where they may fall on someone.

- Always use the right tool for the job.

LADDER GUIDELINES

Please refer to Safety Policy—SAFE-21, Ladder Safety:

- Ladders must be used only for their intended purpose.

- Ladders must be inspected before being put into service.

- Keep ladders in good condition at all times.

- Unsafe ladders should be removed from the site immediately and marked "Dangerous, DO NOT USE."

- Store ladders in such a way as to provide ease of access or inspection and to prevent the danger of an accident.

- Keep rungs and steps free of grease, oil, mud, or other slippery substances that may cause falls.

- Ladders shall not be used by more than one person at a time.

- Do not place ladders in front of a door unless the door is blocked open, locked, or guarded.

- Do not place ladders on boxes, barrels, or other unstable structures to obtain additional height. Set ladder only on firm level surface with secure footing.

- Do not allow any type of ladder to come in contact with electrical wires or equipment. Metal ladders are never to be used near electrical equipment.

- All straight ladders must extend three rungs over the touch point.
- Face the ladder and use both hands when ascending or descending.
- Do not stand on the top or second rung of a step ladder.
- Do not use a ladder if you tire easily, are subject to fainting spells, are using medicines or alcohol, or are physically unable.

COMPRESSED AIR AND GASES

- Do not use compressed air and gases for cleaning clothing or body areas.
- Exercise care when using compressed air and gases.
- Compressed air or gases should not be connected to new installations or serviced without prior approval.
- All compressed air nozzles must include pressure relief capability. Pressure is *not to exceed 30 PSI.*

HOUSEKEEPING

Housekeeping is a measure of safety awareness as well as a basic part of all job procedures. Good housekeeping combined with the use of proper working procedures promotes job safety. Proper housekeeping procedures include the following:

- Do NOT block aisles, walkways, exits, or doorways at any time.
- Keep all break areas clean.
- Keep desks and tables clean and orderly. They should not be used for storage.
- Dispose of your tobacco refuse properly.
- No electrical or telephone cords are to be run under rugs or through windows.
- Electrical outlets are not to be overloaded.
- Emergency showers, eye wash stations, fire extinguishers, fire alarms, and switch poles must be properly marked and easily accessible.
- All extinguishers must at all times be unobstructed.
- Throw trash and scrap in proper waste containers.
- Return tools and other equipment to the proper storage place after use.

- You are responsible for keeping your own work area clean and in good housekeeping condition.
- If it does not belong there, do not put it there.

GROUNDS AND PARKING LOTS

- Speeding endangers lives and property. Use your head, not your foot, when driving in parking lots.
- The speed limit throughout the plant and grounds is 10 mph.
- Reserved, Handicapped, and Visitor parking spaces are restricted areas. Unauthorized use of these spaces can result in towing of the vehicle *at the owner's expense.*
- Vehicles cannot be left on a lot more than 24 hours without permission of Plant Security unless the employee is away on company business. Abandoned vehicles are subject to towing *at the owner's expense.*
- Do not block exits, lanes, gates, or any area posted as a No Parking Area. Parking next to the building is not allowed due to fire lane needs.
- Any vehicle or its contents that pose a threat to the safety and security of our employees or facilities will not be allowed on the premises.
- Firearms, explosives, alcoholic beverages, or any illegal substances are not allowed on the premises.
- Any vehicle that creates a possible security, safety, or traffic concern will be removed *at the owner's expense.*

PERSONAL PROTECTIVE EQUIPMENT (PPE)

It is the policy of XYZ COMPANY to comply with the Personal Protective Equipment (PPE) OSHA Standard. The objective of this standard is to ensure that hazards that require PPE be assessed so that proper PPE can be used to protect you. The standard ensures that you will be trained on how, when, and where to use the PPE.

GENERAL PPE TIPS

- Wear only approved PPE.
- Use your PPE according to the manufacturer's instructions.
- Be sure all your PPE fits correctly and comfortably.
- Inspect your PPE before each use, and keep it clean and in good condition.
- Report damaged PPE to your supervisor so it can be replaced.

EMPLOYEE FOOTWEAR

One potential cause of industrial injury is wearing improper footwear. Proper footwear will protect your feet from falling objects, protruding nails, chemical splashes, or contact with oily or wet conditions.

The following footwear are *prohibited* in the plant:

- Canvas shoes, shoes with open toes or heels, and other similar lightweight footwear.
- High heels above two (2) inches.

SAFETY GLASSES

Eye protection is to be worn throughout the plant at all times. Under NO circumstances will you be allowed near operating machinery without wearing approved eye protection. Safety glasses protect your eyes from flying chips, sparks, dust, and chemical splashes. If you do not have your safety glasses, you may obtain a loaner pair from the First Aid Department or Plant Security. Refer to Safety Policy— SAFE-06, Personal Protective Equipment Policy.

Areas Where Safety Glasses Are NOT Required:

- Cafeteria
- Office areas
- First Aid Department
- Restrooms
- Designated break areas during breaks or lunch periods

Safety glasses must meet the requirements for industrial eye protection established by OSHA. This standard requires that the frame and each lens be marked with "Z87" logo The Safety Department must approve all glasses not provided by the company *before* they are used.

For information on prescription safety glasses, see the nurse in First Aid.

GLOVES

Gloves protect your hands against burns, cold, cuts, electric shock, or chemicals. Gloves are issued from the dispensing cribs to employees on any of the following jobs:

- Handlers of hot, rough, burred, or sharp-edged material
- Polishing operations

- Sorting of some materials from finishing operations
- Heat-treating operations
- Broaching operations where the broaching tool is handled by hand
- Burring operations on rubber wheels
- Certain blanking operations
- Certain gear-cutting operations where hands are exposed to sharp edges, burrs, etc.
- Outside labor during cold weather

Gloves are *never* approved for drilling or milling operations or on any operation where there is a possibility of a glove being caught in revolving equipment.

OTHER PROTECTIVE EQUIPMENT
Rubber aprons, dust masks, finger guards, ear plugs, protective creams, etc., are available for your use from First Aid or E30 Crib. Full face shields, visor goggles, and welding goggles are provided by the company; they are available from First Aid and E30 Crib. Disposable respirators such as dust masks are available for employees who choose to use them. Other types of respirators are available to those employees whose jobs requires them and who have completed all testing and training on their use.

RESPIRATORY PROTECTION PROGRAM

The primary objective is to protect employees from exposure to harmful dusts, fogs, fumes, mists, gases, and vapors.

MEDICAL EXAMS
Using a respirator may place a physiological burden on employees that varies with the type of respirator worn, the job and workplace conditions in which the respirator is used, and the medical status of the employee. The company provides a medical evaluation to determine an employee's ability to use a respirator before the employee is fit-tested or required to use the respirator in the workplace.

TRAINING
- For safe and proper use of any respirator, employees will be trained properly in respiratory use, limitations, and maintenance.
- Training will give the user an opportunity to handle the respirator, have it fitted properly, test its facepiece-to-face seal, and wear it in normal air.

EMPLOYEES' RESPONSIBILITIES INCLUDE

- Using the respirator provided in accordance with the instructions and training received;
- Inspecting all respiratory protection equipment before each use;
- Cleaning and disinfecting respirators daily;
- Properly storing respirators to protect against dust, excessive moisture, or damaging chemicals;
- Maintaining a clean shave to ensure a tight seal; and
- Reporting any malfunction of the respirator to the supervisor.
- If a respirator is mistreated or lost, the employee will be charged for replacing it.

See Safety Policy—SAFE-07, Respiratory Protection Policy.

HEARING CONSERVATION PROGRAM

To prevent hearing loss due to noise exposure and to comply with OSHA regulations, XYZ COMPANY will administer a hearing conservation program for all employees whose noise exposures equal or exceed an eight-hour time-weighted average (TWA) sound level of 85 decibels (dB). Please refer to Safety Policy—SAFE-08, Hearing Conservation Policy.

Plant engineering personnel will conduct periodic plant noise surveys to comply with the program's purpose. From the survey, the areas identified as part of the hearing conservation program will have signs posted where hearing protection is recommended or required.

XYZ COMPANY has facilities on site for audiometric testing of employees. All employees in the hearing conservation program will receive a baseline test and annual tests to detect any significant threshold shift in hearing. In addition, all new employees shall be tested for future referral within six months of first exposure. Any employee who shows a significant threshold shift shall be referred to appropriate medical evaluation.

HEARING PROTECTION EQUIPMENT

- Employees exposed to noise levels equal to or exceeding 85 dB TWA but *not* equal to or exceeding 90 dB TWA shall have protection made available to them.

- Any employee exposed to noise levels equal to or exceeding 90 dB TWA is required to wear hearing protection.
- Employees will be given the opportunity to select their hearing protectors from a variety of suitable types at no cost to them.
- Employees will be held accountable for the equipment furnished.

TRAINING PROGRAM

- A training program on hearing conservation is conducted annually for all employees exposed to an 8-hour TWA equal to or exceeding 85 dB.
- All affected employees are required to participate in the hearing conservation training program.

USE OF PERSONAL RADIOS

The following corrective actions have been implemented to help reduce the noise levels so that XYZ COMPANY does not have to require all employees to use earplugs:

- Radios are not permitted on the plant floor.
- You are allowed to listen to your music through personal Walkman-type radios. Keep the volume at a level in which you can hear your surroundings.
- Management will review jobs to determine if the use of a Walkman-type radio would present a safety hazard or a job performance issue. Radios will not be allowed in those areas (e.g., Trucking, Test Stand).

HEAT CONCERNS

Heat Stress is a condition where an individual sweats profusely and fails to replace the bodily nutrients lost through the skin. Heat stress cases differ in severity starting with heat cramps (the most common case) through heat exhaustion and ending with the most dangerous case, heat stroke.

WAYS TO PREVENT HEAT STRESS

- Replace water lost through perspiration. Do not wait until you are thirsty.
- Drink extra water if you sweat heavily. If urine output decreases, increase your water intake.
- Replace potassium, phosphate, magnesium, and calcium lost through sweating. These electrolytes may be found in fruit juices, Gatorade, etc.
- Replace salt through normal diet.

- Wear light, loose-fitting clothing in hot weather.

- If you become overheated, improve the ventilation: Open a window or use a fan. This promotes sweat evaporation, which cools the skin.

REPORTING ACCIDENTS AND MEDICAL EMERGENCIES

The First Aid Department at XYZ COMPANY is staffed with a nurse every weekday from 7:30 a.m. to 3:30 p.m.

The company doctor's office is in the First Aid Department. The doctor is available Monday and Thursday mornings, 8 a.m. to 11 a.m.

First Aid/Medical Services: extension 6458.

REPORTING OF INJURIES

You must report all injuries to First Aid within 24 hours of their occurrence or at the start of business on Monday morning if the injury occurred over the weekend. Inform your supervisor of the injury immediately so that he or she can administer first aid and make the proper entries on the reports.

It is the responsibility of XYZ COMPANY to see that proper medical care is provided when an injury occurs as a result of your job. Any unauthorized visits to a doctor of your own choice will be your financial responsibility. If you neglect or refuse to accept these services immediately upon an injury incurred in the plant, you may be deprived of future rights for medical aid or compensation. Failure to report injuries or illnesses may result in disciplinary action.

In the event of an emergency, contact Plant Security at extension 6555. Plant Security will contact a First Responder on duty and will then call an outside ambulance if necessary.

MEDICAL EMERGENCIES

Emergency medical situations include, but may not be limited to:

a. *Potential loss of life or limb.* Examples: Condition is causing difficulty in breathing, chest pains, numbness in limbs, shock.

b. *Entrapment or confinement.* Example: Employee is caught in machinery.

c. *Unconsciousness or incoherent behavior.* Example: Lack of response or incoherent response.

d. *Traumatic injury to the body.* Examples: Broken bones, amputations, blunt trauma, bleeding from ear.

e. *Falls.* Examples: Fall from a height of 10 feet or more.

f. *Head injury.* Example: Struck on head by a falling object.

g. *Severe bleeding.* Example: Laceration of a main blood vessel causing large loss of blood.

WORKERS' COMPENSATION

The following information is presented to clarify your responsibility in making a claim for a work-related injury or illness. Abiding by these guidelines will reduce complications that can affect your maximum medical recovery and the processing of your claim.

1. A work-related illness or injury must be reported to First Aid immediately unless there is an emergency. The injured employee must first make the supervisor aware of the need to visit First Aid. First Aid staff will help the employee file a First Report of Injury at the appropriate time.

2. If First Aid is not open, the supervisor will determine the medical care necessary. The employee must notify the First Aid Department, at the earliest opportunity, of the injury and treatment authorized by the supervisor.

3. After initial treatment the employee is required to follow up with the company physician at the earliest possible time. ***Contact First Aid to schedule an appointment 555-5555.***

4. The company physician will examine the employee to help determine whether the injury or illness is work-related. For an illness or injury to qualify for Workers' Compensation coverage, it must have arisen out of the course of employment.

5. Except in special circumstances, employees who do not properly report a work- related illness or injury or seek medical care on their own, will be responsible for all unauthorized medical bills. Once an injury or illness has been accepted as a Workers' Comp claim, benefits can begin.

6. If the illness or injury is determined to be work related, Workers' Compensation benefits will be available. These include, but are not limited to, 100 percent coverage of all authorized medical treatment and temporary total disability coverage. Our medical staff will manage a course of treatment for you to attain maximum medical recovery.

7. Workers' Compensation benefits can and will be suspended if the employee fails to comply with the course of treatment. Failure to comply with the course of treatment includes the following:

   a. Failure to attend scheduled medical appointments, both in plant and with authorized medical referrals outside the plant.

   b. Failure to comply with prescribed and essential testing procedures.

   c. Failure to participate in prescribed physical therapy, both in plant and with outside sources such as Work Hardening programs.

   d. Inability or unavailability to work for reasons unrelated to the injury.

   e. Return to any employment.

Questions regarding your injury, claim, or course of treatment can be directed to our medical staff at 555-0000.

If you have any workers' compensation concerns, please feel free to contact the Workers' Compensation Board at (100) 555-1111.

INCIDENT REVIEW-PLAN OF ACTION PROGRAM

XYZ COMPANY investigates accidents that result in, or could have resulted in, serious injury, to help prevent recurrence and to improve safety management. The Incident Review-Plan of Action Program (IRP) is a process conducted by the Health and Safety Taskforce to investigate work-related injuries and accidents.

After an incident occurs, a meeting is held to obtain a description of the incident, the causes, and possible corrective actions to be taken to address the immediate problem.

The team members involved in conducting the IRP are the employee involved in the incident, his or her manager, the supervisor, the steward or committeeperson, an engineer, and a member of the Health and Safety Taskforce.

FIRST RESPONDER PROGRAM

First Responder Team members are selected by XYZ COMPANY to provide emergency medical care to injured or ill employees in order to stabilize them for transport and further care. Members of the First Responder Team are certified by the State of _____.

If there is an emergency, ***contact Plant Security at extension 6555.*** Plant Security will contact the First Responder on duty and will then call an outside ambulance.

HEALTH AND SAFETY TASKFORCE

The XYZ COMPANY Health and Safety Taskforce provides input into the design and execution of plant-wide safety programs. Specific area or department hazards will be addressed if they have the potential to become a plant-wide concern. This taskforce is not a policy making body but is rather a source of information and ideas for policies and programs. The cross-section of membership provides a variety of backgrounds and expertise from which the Taskforce can draw ideas and support.

FIRE OR CHEMICAL SPILLS

To report fire or the release of hazardous material, contact Plant Security at extension 6555. Security will alert the Fire Department or the proper authorities.

FIRE PREVENTION GUIDELINES

- Know where the fire exits, alarms, extinguishers, etc. are located at all times.
- Know the uses and limitations of fire extinguishers. Note: Only employees who have been trained in the use of fire extinguishers are permitted to use them.
- Smoke only in areas approved for smoking. Dispose of smoke refuse in the proper receptacles.
- Combustible scrap materials, such as oily rags, must be stored in approved containers.
- Damaged or poor wiring conditions can cause an industrial fire.
- Be aware of possible electrical hazards in your department.
- Do not block fire exits, aisles, stairways, doors, extinguishers, hoses, alarms, or other emergency equipment.
- Good housekeeping reduces the chances of fire and accidents.
- Never use a chemical for reasons other than its intended purpose.
- Flammable liquids must be stored or disposed of properly.

FIRE CONTROL

The standard method of extinguishing a fire is with the proper extinguishers. Any fire that requires the use of an extinguisher must be reported to the supervisor. If the fire cannot be contained with a single extinguisher or could threaten personnel or equipment, contact Plant Security at extension 6555. Note: Only employees who have been *trained* in the use of fire extinguishers are *permitted to use them.*

MAGNESIUM FIRE FIGHTING

The only fire fighting agent to be used is METAL X or a special powder for Class D fires. The following CANNOT be used on a Magnesium Fire:

- Water from the fire truck or drop hoses
- Carbon dioxide and ABC dry powder
- Halon extinguishers.

EMERGENCY ALARMS

This system is tested every month for maintenance and employee education purposes. Shelter and Evacuation layouts are posted throughout the facility.

- **Fire/Evacuation:** There will be a long tone on the plant public announcement (PA) system followed by an *announcement.* You should exit the building.
- **Severe Weather:** There will be a *long* tone on the plant PA system followed by an *announcement.* You should seek shelter.

FORKLIFT PROGRAM

The purpose of the forklift training program is to assure that all individuals operating a forklift have been trained in proper forklift procedures. This program has been designed to satisfy specifications set forth by OSHA.

TRAINING

You must be trained before operating an industrial forklift. Training will consist of either a CD-ROM program or a classroom discussion during which you will be administered an exam. After successfully completing the test, you must pass a skills test.

REQUIREMENTS

Any employee who is assigned to operate a forklift must meet the following minimum requirements:

- Be tall enough to operate the controls and have an unobstructed view over controls and dashboard.
- Have coordination between eyes, hands, and feet.

- Be able to understand signs, labels, and instructions.
- Have received training on forklift rules and operations within the past two years and passed the written exam and skills test.
- Must read, sign, and date a statement that assures that a copy of the rules for powered industrial truck operations has been received.
- Obey the Forklift Operator Rules at all times.

PLANT TRAFFIC RULES

- Maintain the plant speed limit of 10 mph.
- Obey in-plant stop signs.
- Honor No Parking signs.
- Never block an exit, electrical panel, walkway, or fire extinguisher.
- Slow down and proceed with caution at flashing yellow lights, which designate high traffic areas.
- Stop at red flashing lights, then proceed with caution.
- Give traffic moving east/west the right of way.

Please refer to Safety Policy—SAFE-22, Forklift Safety Program for additional information.

LOCKOUT/TAGOUT PROGRAM

DEFINITIONS

- **Lockout** is a method that prevents the energizing of machinery or equipment.
- **Tagout** is a warning device that indicates that the machine or equipment to which it is attached is not to be operated until the tagout device is removed.

USE LOCKOUT/TAGOUT WHEN

- Performing service or maintenance around a machine where there is a danger of unexpected start up.
- Removing or bypassing a guard or other safety device.
- Placing a body part into a point of operation or a danger zone during an operating cycle. This includes activities such as adjustments, setup, or maintenance.

IMPORTANT GUIDELINES

- Only authorized employees can perform lockout/tagout procedures.
- Only the employee who locks and tags out machinery, equipment, or processes may remove that lock or tag.
- All authorized employees will be trained on lockout/tagout procedures.
- All affected employees will be notified that the machinery, equipment, or process will be out of service.
- Never try to start equipment that is locked or tagged.
- Never try to bypass or remove a lock or tag if you are not authorized to do so.
- Disciplinary action will be taken if you do not follow the lockout/tagout procedures.

Please refer to Safety Policy—SAFE-23, Lockout/Tagout Policy for additional information.

CONFINED SPACE ENTRY PROGRAM

The hazards encountered and associated with entering and working in confined spaces are capable of causing bodily injury, illness, and death to the worker. However, if all rules and guidelines for confined space entry are followed without exception, the risk can be significantly reduced. Please refer to Safety Policy—SAFE-24, Confined Space Entry Policy.

Accidents occur when workers fail to recognize that a confined space is a potential hazard. Therefore, it is best to act as if the most unfavorable situation exists in every case and that there is a danger of explosion, poisoning, and asphyxiation at the onset of entry.

All entrants, attendants, and individuals in charge of entry or responsible for authorizing permits must be trained.

DEFINITIONS

- **Confined space:** A work environment above or below ground level, which may be stationary, mobile, or afloat, that has limited or restricted means for entry and exit and is not intended to be occupied by human beings on a regular basis. Enclosed structural configurations may contain an accumulation of toxic, poisonous, or explosive gases, particles, or vapors.

- **Hazardous atmosphere:** An atmosphere that exposes employees to possible death, incapacitation, injury, or acute illness.

COMMON REASONS TO ENTER CONFINED SPACES

- To clean and remove sludge and other waste material
- To inspect the physical integrity and process equipment
- For maintenance purposes, such as abrasive blasting, application of surface coatings, and repairs
- To rescue workers who are injured or overcome inside the space

DO'S AND DON'TS OF CONFINED SPACE ENTRY
Do:

- Obtain an entry permit from your supervisor or the area supervisor before attempting initial entry.
- Wait to enter until the supervisor tests the confined space for the presence of toxic, flammable gases or vapors, and oxygen deficiency and record the information on the permit.
- Isolate the vessel or confined space from all other operations (lockout/tagout).
- Properly ventilate the workspace by opening all clean-out openings, hatches, doors, and manhole covers and moving the air within the space with mechanical ventilating equipment.
- Remove any liquid, sludge, residue, or gas from the confined space before entry.
- Enter only in the presence of an attendant, who must call 6555 immediately if a confined space rescue is required.

Don't:

- Do not enter a confined space unless you have been trained and authorized to do so.
- Do not enter a confined space without a trained attendant.
- Do not enter a confined space without wearing the proper respiratory equipment and a safety harness with an attached lifeline when appropriate.
- Do not attempt to rescue a worker in a confined space unless you have had the proper training, have made a call for help, and have additional attendants on the lifelines.

HAZARD COMMUNICATION PROGRAM

This program provides you with information and training in the hazardous substances used in your work area in order to prevent injury or illness due to handling and contact with these hazardous substances. This program has been established to comply with the OSHA Hazard Communication Standard. Please refer to Safety Policy—SAFE-26, Hazard Communication Program.

DEFINITIONS

- **Hazardous chemical:** Any chemical that is a physical hazard or health hazard.
- **Material Safety Data Sheet (MSDS).** A document that gives information on each hazardous material used in the workplace.

DO'S AND DON'TS ON HANDLING HAZARDOUS MATERIALS

Do:

- When transferred to a new area, ask your supervisor about any hazardous materials used in the area.
- Read the container label and the MSDS before starting a job.
- Keep your work area clean.
- Use protective clothing and equipment.
- Follow safety rules.
- Use approved and labeled containers for storing and transporting hazardous materials.
- Keep chemicals that may react with each other separate. Check the MSDS.
- Follow company instructions when removing hazardous materials from containers.
- Make sure there is enough ventilation, especially in a confined space.
- Keep compressed gas, flammables, and explosive materials away from heat.
- Check that containers and hoses are in good working condition.
- Take safety training seriously.

Don't:

- Do not leave containers open when not in use.
- Do not siphon by mouth.

- Do not depend on a "funny smell" to detect hazardous gases in the air; some are odorless.
- Do not mix a chemical with another substance—even water—unless you are instructed to. Even then, follow the instructions exactly.
- Do not breathe gases produced from chemical reactions.
- Do not pour water into acid.
- Do not smoke, eat, or drink around hazardous substances.
- Do not store hazardous chemicals next to each other without checking their MSDS sheets for possible reactions.
- Do not wear contact lenses around toxic vapors.
- Do not cut corners on handling procedures.

MATERIAL SAFETY DATA SHEETS (MSDS)

This hazard communication tool gives details on chemical and physical dangers, safety procedures, and emergency response procedures. XYZ COMPANY has an MSDS for every chemical and hazardous product in the workplace. It provides additional information that cannot easily be put on the label. The MSDS covers the following:

1. *Identity of hazardous material:* Manufacturer's name and address or supplier information, emergency phone numbers, and date prepared

2. *Hazardous ingredients* as determined by government agencies

3. *Physical and chemical characteristics:* Boiling point, appearance, odor, density, etc.

4. *Physical hazards,* such as fire or explosion

5. *Reactivity:* substances or situations to keep the material away from to prevent reaction

6. *Precautions* for safe handling and use

7. *Control measures* to reduce harmful exposure.

EMPLOYEE INFORMATION AND TRAINING

- You have the right to review any MSDS for any material used in our facility.
- Our MSDS are computerized and are available in the following locations:
  —Safety Manager's Office   —Environmental Engineer's Office
  —First Aid Department   —Employment Manager's Office
  —Committee Room   —Labor Supervisor's Office
  —Shift Superintendent's Office   —Cafeteria

- No chemical is allowed in this facility without approval from the Chemical Review Committee.
- You will receive information and training on the hazardous substances used in your work area from the area supervisor.
  —At the time of your initial assignment, and
  —Whenever a new hazard is introduced to the work area.

LABELS

- Each container of hazardous substances used in the workplace will be labeled, tagged, or marked with the following information:

  —Identity of the hazardous chemicals contained therein

  —Appropriate hazard warnings.

- Do not stop with reading the label just once. Read the label every time you handle the can, barrel, drum, or pipe that contains a chemical that you use. At least look at the hazard warning to remind yourself whether the chemical is flammable or combustible and what the health hazards might be.
- DO NOT remove or deface labels on incoming containers of hazardous chemicals unless the container is immediately marked with the required information.

DRUGS AND ALCOHOL POLICY

XYZ COMPANY is committed to providing you with a workplace that is drug-free. The use of illegal drugs and alcohol subjects all employees to unacceptable safety risks and prevents our company from working effectively and efficiently.

The following activities are *prohibited:*

1. Reporting to work under the influence of intoxicants or a controlled substance
2. Reporting for work impaired or becoming impaired at work due to legal drugs
3. Reporting for work impaired or becoming impaired at work by being under the influence of intoxicants or a controlled substance
4. Possessing or using intoxicants or a controlled substance on Company property

SMOKING POLICY

This policy has been implemented with the intent of providing a clean and healthy environment throughout the plant.

Smoking is permitted in specific designated areas only. Bulletins are posted in each department identifying the designated areas and you are expected to limit any smoking to these areas.

Posted NO SMOKING areas are to be strictly observed. You should be aware of these areas and the hazards they contain. There will be NO smoking in the office areas of the plant or in the lobby. All conference rooms, restrooms, and the First Aid Department are designated NO SMOKING areas. Smokers are to properly dispose of their smoking refuse; please place all extinguished tobacco products into the proper receptacles.

SECURITY PROCEDURES

To restrict access to the office or plant to strangers, and for your safety, we ask you to follow basic security procedures:

1. When an unaccompanied stranger enters your work area, ask for identification. Please report any loiterers or persons acting suspiciously to your supervisor or to Security.

2. Company property cannot be removed from the premises without authorization. Security personnel will require a pass or release before allowing removal.

3. You are advised to store all personal property in a secure place. Personal property includes wallets, purses, credit cards, money, and jewelry. The company will not accept responsibility for lost personal property.

4. Security checks on employees include:
   - An I.D. card that you must have available at all times.
   - When leaving the plant at any time other than shift change, you must have a proper pass signed by your supervisor. A material pass is necessary when you take out personal property, such as a toolbox, that need not be returned.
   - When leaving the plant with packages, tools, or other XYZ COMPANY property that must be returned or that may have been purchased by or given to you, you must have the proper material pass signed by an authorized person.

- When material is removed from the plant, the material or package is subject to inspection.
- When entering the plant for any reason other than reporting for regular employment, you should have an employee pass issued by Plant Security.

OSHA

We strive to maintain an open, honest relationship with the Occupational Health and Safety Administration. The XYZ COMPANY safety program will not knowingly violate any federal safety regulation. If you would like to contact OSHA for any reason, the phone number is:

Department of Labor, State of _____: (000) 555-1111.

ATTITUDE FOR SAFETY

A BAD ATTITUDE FOR SAFETY IS BEING

- **Complacent**—on "automatic pilot" because a job has been done so often
- **Emotional**—angry or upset by something that has happened at home or at work
- **Tired**—worn out from too little sleep or too many hours on the job
- **Risk-taking**—does a job without enough training, doesn't pay enough attention to training, or takes shortcuts
- **Reckless**—thinks that safety rules aren't important or don't apply to ME
- **Selfish**—thinks that no one else is affected by MY actions
- **Careless**—eats or smokes in work areas where there are hazardous materials or combustibles.

A bad attitude sets you up for a painful accident. Don't take a time-out for safety. Take it seriously ALL the time.

A GOOD ATTITUDE FOR SAFETY MEANS BEING

- **Attentive** to safety training and safety talks
- **Eager** to understand workplace procedures, asking questions about anything not understood
- **Alert** for anything that doesn't "feel" right and anything that could go wrong, before a job is started

- **Careful,** taking precautions and wearing protective clothing and equipment
- **Focused** on the job
- **Team-oriented,** using the buddy system for hazardous tasks
- **Serious** about safety—never fooling around on the job

SAFETY ON OUR "STREETS"

It is human nature to adapt to our surroundings, but at work in a factory we must continue to remind ourselves that our aisles are *not* like the hallways in our homes. They are the streets we travel, and must be treated as such. To conduct our business, we must have motorized (and human-powered) vehicles driving on our streets. Some of these vehicles weigh five tons and more—not something human flesh and bones can go up against and survive. The following are safety tips on driving, cycling, and walking on our streets:

1. First and foremost, continuously remind yourself that the aisle is actually a street (or even a highway if that makes a more significant impression in your mind).

2. Pedestrians have the RIGHT OF WAY, but vehicles need enough reaction time to stop or slow down. You are responsible for your own safety.

3. ALWAYS: LOOK BOTH WAYS BEFORE CROSSING THE STREET! This is important for everyone—pedestrians, truckers, forklift drivers—everyone!

4. Use the mirrors at intersections; they have been placed there to assist you.

5. Obey all signs and lights. A STOP sign means you must stop and a FLASH-ING RED LIGHT also means you are to stop—every time.

6. Truckers must always be aware that some folks don't pay as close of attention to their surroundings as they should and could step in front of you. In other words, truckers need to be on their toes and always *drive defensively.*

7. All vehicles on our streets need to maintain a safe distance from the vehicle in front of them.

8. Our streets are for traveling from one point to another; they are not parking lots or offices where we hold conversations. If you need to discuss something with someone as you travel down our streets, *pull off the road* and out of the way of traffic.

9. Headphones and walkman-type radios are *not* allowed on our streets. The best practice is to wear these devices only during your break in a designated break area.

ELECTRICAL SAFETY/PERSONAL HEATERS

GROUND RULES FOR ELECTRICAL SAFETY

Do:

- Make sure the work area is safe: no standing water, plenty of light, ladders with non-metal side rails, and signs or barriers to manage traffic.
- Stay away from exposed electrical parts unless you are a qualified worker.
- Check that wire insulation is in good condition and electrical equipment is properly grounded.
- Keep machines and tools properly lubricated.
- Use extension cords only when necessary and only if they are rated high enough for the job.
- Unplug cords at the plug, not by pulling at the cord.
- Use waterproof cords outdoors.
- Use only approved extension lamps.
- Leave at least 3 feet of workspace around electrical equipment for instant access.
- Keep the work area clean. Be especially careful with oily rags, paper, sawdust, or anything that could burn.
- Use the appropriate protective equipment, such as rubber mats and electrical rated gloves.
- Follow the manufacturer's instructions for all electrical equipment.
- Leave electrical repairs to qualified personnel.

Don't:

- Don't overload outlets or motors.
- Don't let grease, dust, or dirt build up on machinery.
- Don't place cords near heat or water.
- Don't run cords along the floor where they can be damaged.
- Don't touch anything electric with wet hands.
- Don't put anything but an electric plug into an electric outlet.
- Don't use temporary wiring in place of permanent wiring.

PERSONAL HEATERS

The use of personal heaters can be a fire hazard if they are not operated properly. Please note the following guidelines:

- All personal heaters must either be grounded, with a three-prong plug, or be made of plastic or ceramic. If your heater does not meet these criteria, turn it in to Office Services and if necessary order a proper replacement heater.

- If you are using an extension cord with your heater (or with any other electrical product), it must also be grounded (thicker cord with a three prong plug).

- Most heaters come with a warning *not to place them* within three (3) feet of any furniture or any type of potential fuel source (trash can, paper shredder, stack of books, etc.). Please note your heater's warnings and operate accordingly.

- Do not overload a single electrical outlet. The best practice is to have your heater on its own outlet.

- DO NOT LEAVE YOUR HEATER RUNNING WHEN YOU ARE NOT PRESENT. DOUBLE CHECK THAT YOU HAVE TURNED THE HEATER OFF AT THE END OF THE DAY.

A fire, power outage, electrocution, and/or property damage are all possibilities when we don't operate equipment (especially heaters) properly.

PREVENTING SLIPS AND TRIPS

DON'T BE IN A HURRY

Trips and falls often occur while we are in a hurry, when we often take short cuts and don't pay attention to what we are doing. We have all tried to jump across an obstacle instead of walking the long way around. These types of acts are unsafe. Learn to slow down and avoid potentially hazardous short cuts.

CLEAN UP THE SPILL

Slippery surfaces don't appear dangerous until you step on them, and then it's too late. Clean up the leak or spill as soon as you notice it. You will be helping to prevent a potential injury, yours or co-workers'.

PRACTICE WALKING SAFELY

If you cannot avoid walking on a slippery or wet surface, take slow, short steps with your toes pointed slightly outward. Never run, jump or slide across the wet surface. For additional balance, keep your hands at your side (not in your pockets) to support you if you begin to fall. Remember that a freshly polished floor can also be very slick, even though it doesn't appear hazardous.

USE NONSKID SHOES AND SURFACES

If you work in an area that has slippery surfaces, check with your supervisor about the use of nonskid mats. Always wear shoes with slip-resistant soles. Keep your shoes and floors as clean as possible.

MAINTAIN PROPER LIGHTING

Inadequate lighting can camouflage what is in your way, so have your supervisor immediately replace light fixtures or bulbs that don't work. When you enter a darkened room, always turn on the light first, even if you only plan to stay a moment. Keep walkways clean and clear of obstructions. Request additional lighting where needed.

STAIR SAFETY

Always look for potential hazards on or around stairs, such as broken or worn steps, wet surfaces, loose carpet, materials on the steps, and improper lighting. Never run up or down stairs, or skip steps. Take it slow and hold on to the railing.

INSPECT YOUR LADDER

Check your ladder to ensure that it's the correct height, is in good condition, and is stable.

PINCH POINTS

DEFINITION

A pinch point can be described as any point where two firm surfaces can come together with the potential of doing bodily harm.

COMMON LOCATIONS FOR PINCH POINTS

Belts and pulleys	Doors	Rollers
Chains and sprockets	Loading parts	Table slides
Conveyors	Presses	Tooling

HOW TO PROTECT YOURSELF

- **Machine guards:** Keep you from getting in the way. DON'T operate machines or equipment without guards in place.
- **Light shields:** Interrupt the process of creating a pinch point.
- **Two-hand controls:** Keep your hands busy and away from the pinch point.
- **Hand tools:** Let you go near but not into the pinch point area.

- **Your own eyes and judgment:** Your mind must be on the job 100% of the time.
- **Don't take chances:** Use guards, light shields, and two hand controls.

Safety is something we sometimes assume happens automatically. Unfortunately it does not. Safety is every employee's job. Please,

THINK SAFETY FIRST!

Index

SHY GIRL & SHY GUY

SHY GIRL & SHY GUY

Kiersi Burkhart and
Amber J. Keyser

darbycreek
MINNEAPOLIS

Darby Creek
A division of Lerner Publishing Group, Inc.
241 First Avenue North
Minneapolis, MN 55401 USA

For reading levels and more information, look up this title at www.lernerbooks.com.

The images in this book are used with the permission of: © iStockphoto.com/Piotr Krześlak (wood background).

Front cover: © Barbara O'Brien Photography.
Back cover: © iStockphoto.com/ImagineGolf

Main body text set in Bembo Std regular 12.5/17.
Typeface provided by Monotype Typography.

Library of Congress Cataloging-in-Publication Data

Names: Burkhart, Kiersi, author. | Keyser, Amber, author.
Title: Shy Girl & Shy Guy / by Kiersi Burkhart & Amber J. Keyser.
Other titles: Shy Girl and Shy Guy
Description: Minneapolis : Darby Creek, [2017] | Series: Quartz Creek Ranch |
    Summary: "The beautiful gray gelding Shy Guy is just as afraid of people as Hanna
    is of horses, but when a greedy local couple steal him, only Hanna and her friend
    can get him back"— Provided by publisher.
Identifiers: LCCN 2015034005| ISBN 9781467792530 (lb : alk. paper) |
    ISBN 9781467795685 (pb : alk. paper) | ISBN 9781467795692 (eb pdf)
Subjects: | CYAC: Human-animal relationships—Fiction. | Horses—Fiction. |
    Bashfulness—Fiction.
Classification: LCC PZ7.1.B88 Sh 2017 | DDC [Fic]—dc23

LC record available at https://lccn.loc.gov/2015034005

Manufactured in the United States of America
1-38281-20006-8/1/2016

For Mom and Dad: thank you for taking a chance on me, and for all the sacrifices you made so I could ride horses.

—**K.B.**

For my amazing cousins, Timshel and Theodora: you were the heart of my childhood and I am so grateful.

—**A.K.**

CHAPTER ONE

Hanna pressed her cheek to the cool window as the clunky old Econoline van trundled off the highway. Hills carpeted in evergreens and wildflower meadows gave way to a cute, old-fashioned mountain town. It looked like it had been pulled right out of a painting hanging in her grandma's house, one of those perfectly picturesque country villages. A quaint diner sat between a candy store and a rock shop. Couples walked hand in hand down Main Street. And every store had a horse painted on the sign.

Horses. It was always horses.

At least Quartz Creek Ranch was beautiful— or it had looked that way in the brochures Hanna's mom showed her. *As part of the ranch experience,* the brochure had read, *youth will be paired up with a therapy horse and given thorough riding instruction.* Just the thought of the horses sent shivers prickling up and down Hanna's arms. She retied her long, sandy-blonde ponytail for the tenth time and pulled her long legs up to her chest on the seat.

"Everyone!" The brunette who had introduced herself as Madison back at the airport waved at them from the front of the van. "We're almost to the ranch. If you look out the window on the left side, you can see our very own Quartz Creek!" She was one of the two head trainers at the ranch. The other was driving—a black guy who'd been the one waiting at the airport for her with a sign reading *Hanna.* He'd introduced himself as "Fletch," spoke with a thick New York accent, and wore a big cowboy hat. Both trainers looked like they were in college.

The two girls sitting up in the middle seat shuffled over to the left side so they could look out the window, crowding the skinny kid who'd sat down there first. Hanna had claimed the far back seat, thinking that was the best way to avoid attention—and to get enough room for her long, gangly legs.

But that plan had backfired.

"What's her deal?" asked the Latina girl with bushy hair, glancing back over the seats at Hanna—and not appearing to care that anyone else could hear her. "She hasn't said a word since we left the airport."

The redhead with the upturned nose shrugged. "She's probably messed up." *As if everyone here wasn't messed up in some way*, thought Hanna. Parents didn't send their kids to Quartz Creek Ranch for fun. It was rehab for "struggling youth," as the brochure had put it. Without using the word *rehab*, of course.

But Hanna wasn't a "struggling youth." Okay, so she'd made some bad judgment calls. She certainly didn't deserve being banished like this. Six weeks in the dead heat of summer in the middle of nowhere, Colorado.

You've always liked horses, Hanna, her mom had said as she filled out Hanna's application for rehab camp—even attaching a pristine school photo in the top corner. *Horses! You should be happy.*

Learning to ride will be great for your posture.

They'll teach you discipline and manners. You could use some of those.

The van took a sharp right turn, and Hanna grabbed the ripped seat back for balance. At least

3

there was one rule about this place she liked: parents couldn't call or write letters. Kids couldn't even bring phones or computers with them. Quartz Creek Ranch was a no-contact zone for a whole six weeks.

Like going to Antarctica.

"This is Bridlemile Road," said Madison, gesturing out the front window to the gravel road that ran between a row of trees and a glittering creek. "Named for Will Bridle's great-grandpa. Mr. Bridle's family has ranched on this land for generations." Fletch followed up with a few jolly honks of the van's horn. Hanna closed her eyes and leaned back in the seat.

Maybe this whole thing could be all right, she thought. Maybe her mother sending her off to this remote place could be cool, as long as she was left alone to enjoy its natural beauty.

By herself.

Alone.

Maybe the horses were optional.

Soon the van stopped, and Madison bounded off to open the gate for them. Through the windshield, Hanna could make out a sign erected above it: QUARTZ CREEK RANCH. The letters were smoky and blackened around the edges, like a cattle brand.

Once the van had passed through the gate, Madison closed it behind them and hopped back in. "You may think Disneyland is the most fun place on Earth," she said conspiratorially, "but it doesn't hold a candle to Quartz Creek."

The girls at the front rolled their eyes and laughed to each other.

As the van drove by, horses trotted up to the fence on the other side of the creek, snorting and swinging their heads. Hanna's chest tightened at the sight of them.

"Ooooh," said Frizzy-Hair Girl. "I hope I get to ride that pretty black one."

Right—they'd expect Hanna to ride here. The tightness in her chest dropped into her stomach. Those weren't six-inch-tall plastic critters with painted-on manes, like the hundreds of toy horses she'd amassed on her bedroom shelves as a little girl—the ones that had made her mom think the ranch was a good idea.

No. Out in the field stood real, living, breathing horses, a thousand pounds each and all of it hooves and muscle. Even if Hanna could get *on* a horse, she'd never be any good at riding. She'd end up thrown and trampled, and her mom's long list of ways Hanna hadn't lived up to her expectations would grow longer.

Soon the van pulled into a driveway and parked in a lot in front of a big ranch house. Hanna waited until she was the last one in the van before departing with her backpack. Fletch was waiting for her as she came out the sliding door.

"You okay?" he asked when he saw her face.

Of course she wasn't okay. She could be hanging out with her friends back home—swimming in the neighborhood pool, going camping with her dad, and getting ready for track season. Instead, she was stuck here for six weeks.

"Fine," Hanna said. "I'm fine."

Fletch tilted his head, his hat almost slipping off his short hair.

"All right, well, head on inside the house, Hanna."

He said her name like he knew her, like they were friends already. It made her happy and sad, all at the same time, because she knew she'd disappoint him, as she always disappointed everyone else.

CHAPTER TWO

The ranch house had a towering, sloped roof that blocked the blazing sun as it set to the west. Madison led the five kids around the side of the house, past the main doors, and onto a screened back porch. She opened a smaller door there into the house. "First, the mudroom," she explained. "For your dirty shoes. Come on in."

Inside the house, the walls were painted rust red and it smelled like cinnamon buns. Hanna's mouth watered as she followed the others down the hall and into the main room, where a wood fire crackled invitingly.

"There they are!" An old woman with a wild

mane of curly hair shot up from her chair. "Welcome, welcome! Come on in. Dinner's almost ready."

"What are you cooking in there, Ma Etty?" asked Madison. "I smell cinnamon."

The old woman laughed. "Just wait. That's dessert." She ushered the kids inside, and Hanna took a seat on the end of the couch with Fletch and one of the boys from the van—the tall, dark-haired one who'd slept most of the trip.

"Hey," he said to her, holding out a hand. "I'm Josh."

Hanna was so surprised by Josh introducing himself first that she took a lot longer to reply than was probably normal.

"Hey," she managed to say. His blue eyes glittered as she accepted his firm handshake. "I'm Hanna."

"Cool."

"All right, all right," the older woman said, raising her voice a smidgen, but it was enough to get everyone's attention. "You'll all quickly find out we believe in action, not talk, around here—except this once. We're gonna talk a little, lay some ground rules. I'm Henrietta, but you can call me Etty."

"We all call her Ma Etty," said Fletch.

"You're welcome to call me that, if you like,"

Etty agreed. "I've worked this ranch for twenty years and raised three kids, so I've certainly earned a 'Ma' somewhere in there." Her smile was big and real, and unconsciously, Hanna unclenched her hands in her lap. "This here is my husband, Will Bridle."

A man emerged from nowhere, tall as a tree. His black hair was shot through with gray, and deep lines grooved his face. He reminded Hanna of an Indian chief dressed in settlers' clothing in some old photograph.

Mr. Bridle took off his hat, pressed it to his chest, and dipped his head politely. "Hey there. Name's Willard, but you can call me Will."

"We still call him Mr. Bridle," Madison stage-whispered to them.

"My overly polite horse trainers aside," said Mr. Bridle, raising an eyebrow at her, "I'm pleased to welcome you all to Quartz Creek Ranch." His voice was so deep it sounded like a bear growling. "I'm not going to lecture. You all know what you're doing here, as do Ma Etty and I. We picked each of you from our pool of applicants because we felt you'd make a good fit for our program and for each other. So our time together doesn't have to be punishment. Great things happen to people on this ranch—if they keep their minds open to it. Just be respectful. That's all I ask. Treat everyone and everything here with respect, and we'll all get along great."

Etty grinned widely. "And I welcome y'all too. Our home is your home. While you're here, don't hesitate to ask for help if anything is troubling you." She gestured to the two trainers, who stood up. "Madison and Fletch? Will you tell us a little bit about yourselves?"

Madison was the first to speak. "I'm Madison Clark. I just finished my freshman year at the University of Colorado, on a swimming scholarship." She jokingly flexed one arm. "On summer break, I come home, here, to the ranch." She looked pleased to say that word—*home*. "My only advice is to have fun. And steer clear of my horse, Snow White. I love her, but she can be a real brat."

Mr. Bridle nodded sagely. Madison plopped down on the couch, and Fletch went next.

"The name's Samuel Harris," he said, lifting his hat, "but everyone here calls me 'Fletch.' You know, after George Fletcher?" The kids all returned blank expressions. "Well, anyway. George was a famous bronc rider, like I hope to be someday."

"You will be," called out Madison.

"Thanks," said Fletch, dipping his head so his hat slipped over his sheepish grin, and he returned to his seat.

"At one time," said Ma Etty, "Fletch and Madison here were just like all of you. But I'll let them tell you their stories when they feel up to it. Know that you can trust them with anything—they've both seen a lot."

Hanna could tell that much from Fletch's eyes. Even when he smiled, they looked somehow sad.

"All right," Ma Etty went on, holding up a sheet of paper and scanning it. "It's time for you kids to introduce yourselves." She looked right at Hanna then, and a jolt of fear shot through her. Hanna sat up as straight as she could, as if her mother were right behind her saying, *Stop slouching all the time! Look at you, you look like a cavewoman.*

Ma Etty read the panic on her face and turned to someone else instead.

"Cade?" she asked the thin, pale, freckly boy sitting across the room. "Will you go first? Tell us a little bit about yourself."

Cade swallowed, and then a torrent of words tumbled out of him: "I'm Cade William Benison and I just flew in from California and you wouldn't guess by how pale I am, right? Everyone says that, but it's because I really like video games and spend all my time inside or that's what my mom told me when she signed me up for this."

A long moment of silence passed. Then Ma Etty cleared her throat. "Wonderful. Thank you, Cade. The ranch is a fantastic place to rediscover nature and the outdoors." When Cade stayed standing, Ma Etty said, "You can sit. Who's next?"

No one raised a hand. Eventually she said, "How about you, Rae Ann?"

The redheaded girl with the upturned nose jumped at the sound of her name. "Oh, well, okay. Hi, everyone." She waved, as if the group was a pageant audience. "I'm Rae Ann Willis. Um, I'm from Vermont and my favorite color is blue and, um, I have a cat named Sadie. Who I miss. Already."

She quickly sat down.

"Thank you, Rae Ann. Who's ne—"

"I'll go." The short girl with the big, frizzy hair stood up, interrupting Ma Etty mid-sentence. "My name's Isabel, but you can call me Izzy. If I like you. Which I might not. But at least I'll be honest about it. I'm from Arizona, and I've always wanted to ride fast horses, which is why I'm here."

Hanna didn't think that was likely to be true. You didn't end up at Quartz Creek Ranch just because you wanted to ride horses.

"Thank you, Izzy," said Ma Etty.

"I'm not done," she replied, which made the old woman's face look, to Hanna, like a cat's when its tail gets stepped on. "Everyone should know I plan to be the best. The best cow milker, the best horse brusher, the best egg finder, the best—"

"Quite," interrupted Mr. Bridle. "Thank you, Izzy. Please take a seat."

Izzy's face turned bright red. Then she dropped back down to the couch with a loud *hmph*.

"Josh?" asked Ma Etty.

The quiet guy sitting next to Hanna shrugged and then stood up. "Name's Josh Chiu. I'm Chinese. Well, my dad's Chinese. But don't ask me to say anything in Chinese—I don't know it. I, uh . . . I live in Tennessee." He shrugged again and offered nothing else.

Ma Etty's hair looked even more frazzled than it had a few minutes ago. "Well, then," she said, taking a deep breath. "Thank you, Josh." He nodded and sat down.

Dread slithered up Hanna's spine. She knew what was coming.

"Hanna?" asked Ma Etty. "Can you tell us a little about yourself?"

Hanna crossed her arms over her lap but didn't move.

"Stand up," urged Fletch in a whisper, and Hanna felt her legs rising to the occasion without her permission. Every face in the room turned to her. She probably looked like a praying mantis, all long, gangly limbs, her hands uncomfortably crossed. And she was even taller than Ma Etty now that she was standing.

"Hanna?" the old lady asked her again.

"Um," sputtered Hanna. "My name's Hanna. Hanna Abbott. That's *A-B-B-O-T-T* . . . with two *T*s. And I, um, well, I grew up in . . . Michigan. And I . . ." She looked around the room, trying to think of anything else she could say, anything that wouldn't sound stupid and forced, but her mind was a blank, white sheet. She heard her mom saying, *Stand up straight! I can't believe I raised such a slouch. And that stuttering! You've never stuttered before, Hanna. Use complete sentences!*

"I like the color green and I steal."

She didn't mean for it to come out, but it was the most complete thought in her head—that nonsense responsible for this whole stupid trip to Quartz Creek in the first place. Hanna abruptly sat down and stared at the floor, unwilling to look at the faces around her after that impromptu confession.

The room was quiet for a second before Ma Etty said, in a low, sincere voice, "Thank you for that, Hanna. That was very brave of you. I'm sure everyone here has a thing or two they're not proud of, and it's important to remember our mistakes as well as our successes—so we can learn from them." Hanna's face burned like it were filled with lava. But Ma Etty clapped her hands together and moved on. "Well, I have one last thing to say before we sit down for dinner."

She paused for a long moment, surveying the five kids sitting around the room.

"Please know that no matter what, we're here for you. My husband and I started the Quartz Creek Ranch program as a place to learn and grow. We're all here to get better, and we can help each other do that. Do your best at each thing you do, and the rewards will return to you twofold. We give you free time on the ranch so you can pursue your own interests—please be responsible with the freedom you are given. When privileges are abused, they can be revoked. So if you have any concerns at all, any of us are more than happy to help, to care, or just to listen.

"Now let's get eating!"

\\

After a huge dinner of roll-it-yourself burritos, Fletch and Madison led them back to the van for their luggage. Fletch took the boys, the three of them laughing over some inside joke they'd already come up with, leaving Hanna with Izzy and Rae Ann.

"Come on, girls," said Madison. "Grab your stuff and head that way." She pointed after the boys, where two little bunkhouses stood kitty-corner to the chicken coop and a huge, old barn with tractor parts piled up outside it like chopped wood.

They had to pick their way past chickens pecking in the yard to get to the girls' bunkhouse. "Honey!" Madison shouted up ahead, startling a hen. "Stay out from under foot or you'll end up McNuggets!"

The bunkhouse looked like something from an old western movie. The front porch creaked as Madison led them up the steps and through the equally squeaky front door. She pointed out the bathroom and then tapped a closed door. "This is my room. The rest is all you."

Two bunks occupied the main room, with a single bed relegated to the corner—enough to sleep five. Izzy and Rae Ann quickly took the bunk closest to the door and bounced up and down on the mattresses. Hanna wasn't about to sleep in a bunk alone, top or bottom, so she dragged her duffel bag to the opposite end of the bunkhouse and deposited it on the lonely bed.

"All the way over there, Hanna?" asked Madison, concern creeping into her voice. Hanna shrugged. "Okay, well . . . if the bunks are picked, we have a little tradition around here. Each new group gets to pick a name for the bunkhouse."

"A name?" asked Rae Ann. "Why? That's sort of stupid."

Madison hid a laugh. "I said the exact same thing when I was your age!"

"I still can't believe you came to Quartz Creek Ranch . . . you know, before," said Izzy.

Hanna couldn't imagine what someone like Madison had ever done wrong either.

"I know," said the horse trainer. "But let me tell you one thing: this place changes people. It changed me. And it will change you too. So as to commemorate the occasion and honor the tradition, we should give our bunk a name."

"Fine," said Izzy. "Like what?"

"Like . . . the Rockin' Ladies Cabin?" Madison suggested. "Get it? Like a rockin' horse?" Rae Ann let out a little snort. "Okay, maybe not."

Izzy raised an eyebrow. "It's not even a very good joke."

Madison pretended to look hurt. "Well, you come up with a better name, then."

"What about 'Pony Girls'?" said Rae Ann.

"But they aren't ponies," said Izzy. "They're horses. Ponies are small. Horses are not."

"Oh."

"No suggestions are bad," said Madison.

"Some are," said Izzy. "Like, 'Stinky Cabin' would be a bad name."

"Unless we were all sweaty and gross from being outside all day," said Rae Ann. "Then it might be a good name."

"Hanna?" asked Madison. "Do you have any ideas?"

Hanna shook her head.

"Cat got your tongue?" asked Izzy. Hanna said nothing.

"It's okay," said Madison.

"But how can we pick a name if she won't make any suggestions?" said Rae Ann.

"She can still vote."

So the brainstorming went on, until Rae Ann suggested Black Beauty's Cabin, because of the big black horse they'd seen galloping by in the pasture on the drive up, and everyone voted yes.

"All right," said Madison. "Time for bed. Go brush your teeth and get ready. Then it's time for lights-out."

Hanna waited until Rae Ann and Izzy were already inside the bathroom, giggling like hyenas, before she pulled her toiletries bag out of her duffel. Madison sat down on her bed beside it.

"Hey, Hanna," she said. "I know how you feel, you know. Us versus them? I've been through it too. I've felt like I'm the only one I've got. But do me a favor, please? Try and make friends. It's going to be a long six weeks if you don't even try."

"Okay," said Hanna automatically, but she knew it was going to be a long six weeks, no matter what she did or tried.

It was a horse ranch, after all.

CHAPTER THREE

The next morning was a flurry of activity. Madison told them to get dressed and get moving to breakfast, because they had a big day ahead. And breakfast went about the same as dinner the previous night: everyone else talked loudly, while Hanna sat quietly at the far end of the table.

Just the way she liked it.

Over scrambled eggs and bacon, Ma Etty addressed the kids.

"Who's ready to meet their horse?"

Cade threw up his hand and shouted, "Me!" Izzy laughed at him.

Ma Etty grinned at his enthusiasm. "Glad to hear

it, because we've picked out a special horse for each of you. You'll have a riding lesson with your horse every morning, under Fletch and Madison's instruction."

Every single morning? Hanna shrank lower into her chair, as if she could turn invisible and avoid her riding lesson altogether.

"Then, after lunch, we'll divide you up into pairs for other tasks the ranch needs done. And trust me when I say a ranch needs a lot!" She counted off on her fingers. "Weeding, mucking stalls, collecting eggs, feeding the chickens . . . We'll try to give you something different every day so you can have a go at lots of things, and you'll rotate partners as often as possible. After chores, you have free time until dinner."

"What do we do in free time?" asked Rae Ann.

Ma Etty grinned. "Whatever you want! Within reason, safety, and sight, of course."

After breakfast, the kids were led by a horse trainer out of the house, one at a time, until only Hanna was left, sitting alone at a graveyard of biscuits and eggs while Ma Etty and Mr. Bridle did dishes. Dread turned the food in her stomach to a roiling pulp.

"Hanna?"

At the sound of her name, Hanna glanced up. Madison smiled a wide, toothy smile and gestured for her to follow.

"Come on. It's time to go and meet your horse. The others are already out in the corral warming up."

This was the moment she'd known was coming since she got on the plane back in Michigan. A shiver slithered up her spine.

After clearing her place at the table, Hanna followed Madison's bouncing brown ponytail out into the warm summer morning. The ranch was alive in the sunlight, bright and green and bursting. As the two girls weaved among chickens pecking in the yard, Madison babbled about the horse she'd handpicked for Hanna. Gentle Lacey was a pony, she said—a little shorter than your average horse, standing at only thirteen hands high. A perfectly comfortable size for someone Hanna's age. Lacey was getting on in years but still knew how to run when Hanna was ready to run.

Hanna didn't have the heart to tell Madison she would never be ready to run.

They crossed a little bridge over the creek into a wide-open space clearly meant for horses. Closest to the bridge sat a small corral, with tall metal fencing;

behind it stood an old, weathered barn that was so big, it seemed to be peering down curiously over the rest of the ranch. An arena with a wood fence, big enough to pen in a whole cavalry, had been built to one side of the barn. In it, the other kids were already walking their horses around. Beyond the barn and the arena, a fenced-off pasture skirted the ranch and snaked off into the distance.

Madison led Hanna to the barn and opened the doors with a creak.

Inside, it smelled like old wood, leather, and manure—like horses. Hanna's hands were trembling in her pockets by the time Madison reached the stall on the far end of the barn and tapped the door.

"Here she is."

A brown nose reached over the top of the stall door, and Hanna took a step back. Madison patted the nose, crooning, "Hey, Lacey, pretty girl. How are you?" Lacey's furry head snorted and sniffled for treats, and Madison pulled a little brown biscuit from her pocket.

The pony's head was huge, even bigger than Hanna had expected—certainly large enough to bite off a hand. When Lacey's white teeth darted from her lips to eat up the treat, Hanna cried, "Watch out!"

Her yelp startled the horse and the trainer. "I'm fine, Hanna," said Madison, pressing a hand to her heart to slow it down. Lacey whickered on the other side of the stall door. "Come on over here and give Lacey a treat."

But Hanna was rooted to the spot. Lacey snuffled at Madison's arm again, looking for more treats.

"Hanna?" asked Madison. "Are you all right?"

Hanna tried to take a step forward, but she couldn't get any closer knowing the pony was there. Madison's smile faded.

"What's wrong?"

"I can't," Hanna said, and started backing away. "I can't."

"You can't what?"

Hanna swallowed. What could she possibly say? How could she tell a tough, cool girl like Madison she was plain afraid?

"I can't ride," said Hanna.

"What?" Madison frowned. "Of course you can. Not right now, of course, but that's why you're here—so we can teach you how to ride. As part of the program."

Hanna shook her head. "No, you don't understand. I can't ride. And I . . . I don't want to."

Madison's expression turned from confused to a little annoyed—the same expression Hanna's mom had whenever Hanna slouched at the dinner table or used the wrong past-tense version of *swim*.

"Well, now, that's a little different. But your parents said you love horses."

"Toy horses! When I was seven!" Hanna cried, exasperated. Those beautiful toys were all stuffed in a box in her closet now. "My mom forced me to come here, you know."

Madison's eyebrows went so high they disappeared under her brown bangs. "Forced you? That's not what she told me, Hanna. She said you've always wanted to ride horses."

"She's the one who wants me to want to ride," said Hanna. "But I don't. I don't even like horses."

Madison stood there, speechless. Then the barn door opened, and Fletch entered, leading a paint horse with Josh sitting on its back. He helped Josh off and said, "Find another helmet that'll fit you better in the tack room, and I'll tie her up over here."

"Fletch," said Madison. "I need your help."

Hanna's stomach dropped like a stone.

"What is it?"

Madison ran her hand over her forehead. "Hanna doesn't want to even get near little Lacey here. What do you think we should do?"

With a calm that reminded Hanna of old Mr. Bridle, Fletch stepped between them.

"All right. I've got it. Hanna, why don't you and I go outside and take a little breather, away from the horses? Madison, Josh's helmet is too small. Can you help out?"

"Sure." Madison turned and, without saying anything else to Hanna, trudged away. Hanna thought her face was probably purple with embarrassment. Madison must be furious with her.

"Hey, it's all right." Fletch's smile was broad and full of big, white teeth. She liked how genuine it was—and instantly felt guilty that she was going to disappoint him too. "Let's go talk outside."

Once they left the horse smell behind, Hanna could breathe better.

"There you go," said Fletch, reclining against the fence. On the other side, the kids walked their horses in figure-eight patterns around barrels in the arena. They were talking and laughing, already friends, already having a good time, already settled in with their horses.

"So, Hanna," said Fletch. "Can you tell me what you're thinking? Why don't you want to ride?"

She wanted to tell him—she really did. But how could Hanna admit she was terrified?

"Look," she said. "I really don't like horses, okay? I didn't want to come here. I even begged my mom not to send me."

Fletch studied her, and his gaze made her fidget. He looked right into her—and she could sense that he knew she wasn't telling the whole truth.

"I'm sorry you don't feel comfortable letting me in on what's really going on," he said. "But no one will force you to ride. We'll work up to it together. Why don't you watch the others for a while? When you're feeling less anxious, we can try again."

Hanna nodded. She didn't agree, but she didn't want to talk about it anymore either. Fletch patted her shoulder. "Don't worry so much, Hanna. There's no pressure. It'll work when it works." Then he turned and disappeared back into the barn.

Hanna felt even worse, having kept the truth from Fletch. So she did the only thing she could think of to do: she turned and jogged away, leaving the barn behind.

Running made sense when things got bad. When she ran, she could escape anything—including angry store owners who'd caught her stealing.

As her shoes hammered the dirt with a dull *thok, thok, thok*, Hanna felt the rush start at her throat and work its way down to her toes, calming her mind, letting her forget all about the barn and Lacey and Fletch and Madison, and about how she'd told her mom this place wouldn't work out.

Her mom hadn't listened. She never did.

Thok, thok, thok. Soon Hanna's thoughts were replaced completely by the steady beat of her feet.

They carried her away from the barn, away from the other kids talking and laughing in the corral. Her feet pounded the grass as she followed the fence line uphill. The air turned chilly as she ran through the shadow cast by a huge butte standing a hair east of the ranch. The butte was gently sloped and green on one side, then jagged and rocky on the other, like a giant had sliced off a chunk of it for buttering his toast.

After a while, Hanna's panic faded and she slowed down to a walk. Up ahead the pasture fence dipped abruptly. She stopped at the dip and gazed down, still breathing hard from her run.

She found herself standing at the top of a small crest. At the bottom of the slope, Quartz Creek bubbled along into a copse of nearby cottonwoods, the pasture fence trailing alongside it. The day was starting to heat up, and Hanna wished she could get closer to the creek, maybe dip her toes in it—but that would involve climbing over the fence and possibly coming face-to-face with a horse.

Besides, she'd have to climb over not one but two fences to get there. Another fence, constructed haphazardly with wood stakes and kinked wire, sectioned off a smaller pasture inside the larger one—and with it, a chunk of the creek.

What was this little pasture for? Were the Bridles keeping something separated from the other horses? Hanna didn't think she actually wanted to know.

Something moved in the trees. Hanna jolted. Whatever it was, it ambled around down by the creek, hidden by a low-hanging bough—and far enough away that Hanna could only hear the occasional rustle.

Then a white tail flicked.

A horse!

Hanna backed away from the fence. But the tail swished back and forth, as harmless and peaceful as a blade of grass blowing in a breeze. After a while the grazing horse turned around and emerged from the trees.

Hanna let out a loud gasp. It was beautiful—the prettiest horse she'd ever seen in real life, though from this distance, it looked like a toy. A white-flecked mane billowed down the powerful, faintly curved neck. Its coat was steel gray and shot through with white stars, like the horse had once been all white until someone dumped soot on it. Its barrel chest and sleek body reminded Hanna of a horse you'd see pulling a king's carriage in Victorian England.

Right then, it looked up—and spotted her. Hanna and the horse stared at each other, eyes locking across the pasture. Neither of them moved, each frozen in shock at the other's sudden appearance.

She should be afraid of it—what if the horse decided to come check her out?—but she found it impossible to look away.

Then the horse reared, flicked its silver mane

back, and galloped off into the trees.

Hanna stood there, awestruck, wondering if she had really seen what she thought she'd seen. Then she saw the horse's hooves had left holes in the grass. It had to be real.

What was that she'd seen in those wide, brown eyes? Fear? And . . . something else. Something dark, hidden, imperceptible.

Whatever it was, it made her chest ache. She felt like she'd seen a ghost.

"Hanna?"

She jumped at the sound of a girl's voice. It was Izzy, and her lips were twisted up with annoyance.

"What are you doing way out here?" Izzy said. "Everyone's been looking for you. Madison and Fletch told us you disappeared."

"I—I'm sorry." Hanna blushed purple again. "I didn't mean to."

"What do you mean you 'didn't mean to'?" Izzy crossed her arms and gave a huffy *pfft*. "How can you 'not mean' to run off?"

"It was an accident."

In the distance, voices called Hanna's name.

"She's over here!" shouted Izzy, waving her arms as people came down the road. "I found her!"

Madison ran up to Hanna, panting, looking both angry and worried. "Why did you run off like that?" Behind her, the other kids were whispering, until Fletch told them to keep quiet.

"I didn't mean to," said Hanna again. "I just started walking."

Madison let out a frustrated breath. "Well, I'm glad you're all right," she said. "So no big deal. But don't leave again without telling anyone where you're going, okay?"

"Okay," said Hanna. "I'm sorry."

Madison shrugged and shook her head. "Let's head back. It's lunchtime anyway."

Izzy rolled her eyes. "Great. I only got to ride for, like, five minutes."

"Come on," said Madison, giving Izzy a look. "Let's go help Ma Etty set the table. We'll discuss this later."

Izzy sighed and ran on ahead, joining the other kids in the front as they started walking back to the ranch.

Madison took up step next to Hanna like she was afraid Hanna might run off again. Hanna knew she should say something—apologize again for worrying her and Fletch, maybe—but all she could think about was the silver horse hiding in the trees.

So Hanna wasn't the only one on this ranch afraid of something. But what had made that beautiful horse so frightened?

CHAPTER FOUR

Before lunch could start, Ma Etty, Fletch, and Madison walked into the living room to talk, while Mr. Bridle got the kids seated at the table. Ma Etty's eyes occasionally flicked to Hanna. She knew by the sinking, nauseated feeling in her stomach that they were discussing her.

Would they send her home? That would be a relief, but her mother would be furious. *We spent all this money on that camp, and you couldn't even stick with it for one day?*

"So, Hanna, I'm just curious," Izzy said with a slight smile. "How do you 'accidentally' wander off?"

Rae Ann giggled.

"It's like, oops! How did I end up way out here?

Must have been an accident! Couldn't have been my feet or anything."

Cade reluctantly laughed too. Izzy was on a roll, and Hanna wanted to crawl under the table and die.

"I mean, seriously." Izzy's gaze pressed Hanna for a response. "Do your feet usually just do whatever they want?"

The laughter tapered off.

"Izzy," said Josh. "Leave it alone."

"What? I can't be curious?"

"He's right," said Cade. "Let it go."

"Jeez, guys." Izzy huffed. "Way to take all the fun out of everything."

Luckily, Ma Etty and the others returned just as lunch was served, and Izzy was forced to give up. Hanna tried to pretend that she hadn't even heard, but scarfing down green beans and tater tots at top speed didn't help calm her stomach. She wished she could be like that beautiful, frightened horse and gallop away into the trees.

\\\\\\\\\\\\\\\\\\\\\\\\\\\\\\\\\\\\\\\

In the afternoon, Madison handed out chores to everyone. Izzy and Cade helped Fletch move hay with Paul, the blond, mustachioed ranch manager, who reminded Hanna of Brad Pitt—if he were a cowboy from Colorado. Rae Ann fed and cared for the chickens with Ma Etty's help, and Hanna and Josh were put on garden duty.

Hanna let out a relieved breath to not be working with any of the animals after her disastrous morning with the horses. And an hour into mostly silent laboring on their knees in the dirt, Hanna decided she liked Josh. He was a fish out of water at the ranch, same as her; obviously from the city; and not a big talker. For a long while, the silence was comfortable.

"Fletch told me what that mountain's called," Josh said suddenly, nodding to the butte.

"Really?" said Hanna. "What is it?"

"Fool's Butte," he said. "I guess 'cause when prospectors started findin' quartz here, they thought they'd hit gold—they go together or somethin'. So they started up this whole town. Wasn't till they'd already dug up half the mountain that they realized there wasn't any gold at all."

"So that made them the 'fools'?" asked Hanna.

Josh shrugged. "Guess so."

She laughed. "I like your accent. Where are you from again?"

Hands black with dirt, he tossed a few more weed roots onto the pile. "Tennessee. Nashville. You?"

"Little place in Michigan called Sturgis." Hanna pulled out a weed, but only the leaves came off in her hand, leaving the rest of the stem stubbornly poking out of the ground. "Dang it. That keeps happening."

"You have to get it by the roots, and once you've got it, pull up slow-like." He showed her how to pinch the plant at its base and then tug out the entire thing, roots and all. Then he tossed the weed into the growing pile.

"You're good at this," said Hanna.

"Pull a lot of weeds in Nashville." Josh shrugged. "It's Mom's favorite thing to make me do when she grounds me."

"You get grounded a lot?"

"First four times she caught me smokin', I got grounded." Josh held up four fingers on one hand and then lifted the last one. "Fifth time, I got sent here."

Wow. Smoking? Josh couldn't be much older than Hanna, and she'd never even considered stealing a cigarette.

Hanna heard someone calling her name. She sat up and peered over Josh's head, and spotted Ma Etty waving at her from the edge of the garden.

Oh, no. She didn't know what Ma Etty wanted to say, but it couldn't be good. Hanna's spirits plummeted into the dirt.

"Hanna!" the old woman called again, shielding her eyes from the sun. "Can I speak with you? Josh, why don't you take a break inside and have some water. It's important to stay cool and hydrated when it's this hot."

Once Josh had gone inside, Ma Etty linked her arm with Hanna's, like they were old friends.

"Why don't we go for a walk?" she asked.

"Uh, sure," Hanna managed. Her mouth had suddenly dried up like a desert.

Leaving the garden behind them, Ma Etty led her out onto the gravel road that the van had come in on yesterday. She headed north, past the ranch house, toward the bunkhouses. Afternoon was in full swing and the sun beat down with all its June ferocity, making Hanna sweat even more.

Ma Etty adjusted her straw hat. "I heard what happened."

Tears burned their way from Hanna's throat, to her jaw, to the back of her eyes.

"I'm so sorry, Ma Etty. I told my mom not to send me here. I told her it was a bad idea, and she wouldn't listen. She wants me to be this great horse rider she can show off to her friends . . ." Then the tears broke through, despite Hanna's best efforts to keep them in, and filled her eyes so thoroughly the world became a blur. "I tried to tell her, Ma Etty. I did!"

Ma Etty didn't interrupt, but she turned Hanna to face her and settled a hand on her shoulder.

"I can't ride," Hanna managed between sobs. "I can't. Mom was wrong when she told you I love horses. She doesn't understand."

"Parents never do, do they?" Ma Etty's voice was so quiet, so soft and full of knowing, that it shocked Hanna into silence. "But that doesn't change that you're here now, Hanna. You're at this ranch, in my care, for a reason. And I see that reason right in front of me." Gently, Ma Etty reached out and tucked a stray lock of Hanna's long blonde hair behind her ear. Hanna couldn't look at her, too afraid of seeing disappointment on her face, too afraid of seeing pity there. But as the silence drew on, she finally did.

And Ma Etty was gazing at her with such kindness, such hope, and such . . . admiration? Hanna thought for a moment that maybe Ma Etty was looking at a mountain behind her.

"What's the reason?" asked Hanna, her voice trembling.

"I see such a kind, smart, sensitive girl here," said Ma Etty. "I see a girl with so much heart that sometimes, she's afraid. Sometimes things intimidate her." Her eyes crinkled when she smiled. It made her look years younger, not older. "That's not a bad thing. I don't think your mother intended to hurt you by sending you here, Hanna. I think she wanted something new and better for you. I think she wanted you to grow, and she knew you could do that here, with people who can listen and help."

"Except for Izzy," said Hanna with a sniffle.

Ma Etty gave a small chuckle. "Izzy's got a good heart. In fact, I think you two are more alike than you think." She took Hanna's arm again and resumed walking. They made their way toward the little path that bridged the creek. The musty old barn stretched up into the sky on the other side. "Hanna, what would you say to me giving you something else to do in place of riding lessons?"

It was so unexpected and so much more than Hanna could have hoped for, she couldn't respond at first.

"Yes!" she said. "Yes, please, oh please, yes."

Then she paused. "But . . . it's a riding camp. Can you do that?"

"Can I do that?" repeated Ma Etty. Then she broke out into a very un-old-lady-like giggle. "Of course. I can do whatever I want on my ranch. And if the idea of being near a horse is so frightening that it makes you run like a spooked horse yourself, well—I'm not in the business of forcing children to do things that bring them to tears."

Self-consciously Hanna wiped at her tear-streaked cheeks, but Ma Etty shook her head. "It's okay, Hanna. We all have our fears. Seeing a daddy longlegs has reduced me to tears more than once."

"Really? A spider?"

"Yep. Can't stand 'em. All those long, spindly legs and beady eyes and . . ." Ma Etty shuddered. "Having fears is part of being human. But we don't have to be slaves to them. We are capable of living relatively normal lives despite our fears. I mean, if I couldn't keep it together every time I saw a spider? Look where we are." She gestured at the huge old barn, the grass, and the trees. "Bugs everywhere! I'd be hopeless. So I had to learn how to manage my arachnophobia and work around it. I had to learn how to ask for help so I could get through the day."

"Who do you ask?"

"Mr. Bridle, of course. When I see a spider now, I call for him. He'll move the spider so I can get on with things. And knowing Will's there to back me up? It helps. Now I can even put a cup over the spider while I wait for him." She looked genuinely proud of this accomplishment and made Hanna feel less silly about the fear that had torn through her when she saw Lacey.

"But I don't know how to do that," said Hanna. "Who can I ask for help with a horse?"

"Growing up is about learning just that. I'll help you. Let me be your Mr. Bridle for now. I'm happy to rescue you when you're scared. Little by little, I'm sure we can find a way for you to be happy and healthy on this ranch. And we'll start by giving you jobs you can manage, okay?"

Hanna nodded almost imperceptibly.

"Tomorrow, when the others go to lessons, I'll show you some new things you can do. It'll be all right, Hanna." They turned around and headed back to the garden in silence. Josh stood drinking water by the pile of weeds.

"Remember," said Ma Etty, "dinner's in an hour."

Then she waved good-bye and went inside.

Hanna could feel that her eyes were red and puffy, but Josh didn't ask about them. Instead, he offered Hanna some water.

"Hydrate," he said and returned to weeding. As Hanna drank, she watched Ma Etty's strong back, trying to imagine how a little spider could make a woman like that cry.

CHAPTER FIVE

Izzy kept to herself that night in the girls' cabin, and Hanna was thankful. There was one thing Ma Etty had been wrong about: Hanna and Izzy were absolutely nothing alike.

In the morning, the other kids buzzed with excitement about their upcoming riding lesson. As Madison and Fletch herded them out of the dining room, Hanna stayed behind. Izzy cast her an indecipherable look as she slipped out the door.

Ma Etty appeared a few minutes later dressed in muddy overalls. "Ready for your new duties, Hanna?"

"As I'll ever be."

Hanna expected them to milk cows or maybe

feed the goats, but Ma Etty led her to the horse barn. Hanna's stomach performed a fabulous backflip.

Seeing her face, Ma Etty said, "Don't worry. I won't ask you to do anything you can't do."

Inside the barn, the scent of animal and leather made Hanna want to walk right back out again. She tried to visualize putting Lacey the horse under a cup, like a spider. It helped a little.

In the tack room, saddles of all sizes sat on racks, and halters and bridles dangled from hooks. Ma Etty opened a cupboard and pulled out a bottle of leather cleaner, a handful of rags, and a bucket.

"It's been a while since any of us had time to care for the tack," she said. "But good tack makes for safe horses and happy riders. Why don't you start with the saddles?"

Hanna nodded. Easy enough.

Ma Etty showed her how to pour cleaner on the rag and rub the saddle leather. Once Hanna got the idea, she took over.

This was a job she could do. A tremulous warmth seeped into her as Ma Etty left her to her work. The repetition of scrubbing made her think of running, of her feet pounding the ground as they carried her to safety.

Through the door, she could hear the horses eating and stomping, but it didn't frighten her.

\\\

That afternoon Madison took them to see the bees.

Everyone was excited except Rae Ann. She stood ramrod straight and refused to take another step toward the cloud of bees buzzing around the white bee boxes on the edge of the garden, even though the kids had all been outfitted in head-to-toe, bee-proof suits.

"They don't actually want to sting you," said Madison, who now waded into the swarm toward the first box. "And they won't unless you give them a reason to. They'll only sting when they're irritated."

Rae Ann adjusted her huge helmet and made an awful face.

"Won't they be irritated if you start stealing their honey?" said Izzy. She didn't appear to be afraid, though, and followed right behind Madison.

"That's what the gloves are for."

Hanna flexed her hands inside the thick gloves and picked up the empty cardboard box intended for hauling honeycomb. Collection was her assigned job, and after gulping air for good luck, Hanna waded after the others into the swarm.

The low hum of buzzing bees engulfed her. They landed all over her, tasting the suit's nylon fabric with their long, curled noses. No, not noses. Proboscises? Hanna remembered her sixth-grade science teacher calling them that.

"They're furry!" Cade cooed at one that had landed on his outstretched hand. "Like tiny hamsters."

"Tiny hamsters that will sting you!" cried Rae Ann, who still hadn't moved an inch.

"Cool," said Cade. "Let's keep one as a pet."

"A lot of people keep bees," said Madison as she opened the lid of the first bee box and set it aside.

"Who would put bees in their backyard?" asked Izzy. "Sounds dangerous."

"I'd rather have a cat!" called Rae Ann.

"Bees won't sting if you don't disturb them," said Madison. "Bees are pollinators. Without them, lots of plants don't reproduce. We wouldn't have fruits or vegetables without bees! Hanna, come over here with that empty box."

Hanna would have to venture deeper into the bee swarm, but with every inch of her covered in that dense, sting-resistant fabric, she was fine. She carried the box to Madison, who took frames full of dark orange honeycomb out of the beehives and began placing them inside it. If any bees were still clinging to it, she wiped them off, and they harmlessly buzzed away.

When the box of honeycomb was full and the beehive empty, Madison called for Josh. "The new frames, please!"

They did this for almost an hour, trading empty boxes for full ones as Madison made her way from beehive to beehive. There were six hives, and halfway through, Rae Ann suddenly spoke from her spot at the edge of the garden.

"You don't look stung," she said, surveying Hanna's suit.

Hanna smiled. "Nope. Not a single sting." Ma Etty was right. Everyone was afraid of something.

Rae Ann gazed out into the swarm. "I don't think my mom would like this," she said. Then she took a single, cautious step toward the buzzing swarm of bees. Inside her helmet her face was puckered and red, and she was biting her lower lip. After a step into the swarm, Rae Ann paused, as if waiting for something to happen. Nothing did.

Another step. Hanna offered her one thick, suited

arm, and Rae Ann seized it. A horde of bees on a mission to pollinate buzzed by, and Rae Ann let out a squeak, squeezing her eyes shut.

The bees passed, and when Rae Ann opened her eyes again, she was unharmed.

"Whoa," she said.

"Yeah, right?" Hanna picked up a box of empty frames. "Do you want to give these to Madison?" Rae Ann hesitated and then nodded. She let go of Hanna's arm and took the box. Expression resolute, she ventured into the humming cloud of bees like an explorer into an arctic storm. She stopped and paused a few times, shoulders shaking, but eventually made her way over to Madison.

In the mass of bees somewhere, Izzy yelled, "Glad you could make it to the party, Rae Ann!"

"My parents would never allow this," Rae Ann moaned.

Izzy barked a laugh. "Luckily, they aren't here!"

Hanna heard a squeaky voice in her ear. "I didn't see you during our riding lesson today." She turned to find Cade standing behind her.

"Yeah," Hanna said. "Ma Etty gave me, um, something else to do."

"Something besides riding? That's weird. I

thought everyone was supposed to ride. It's like our therapy."

Hanna forced out a laugh. "I guess I don't need therapy."

Cade frowned. "But isn't that why you're here? Because you stole stuff? Said so yourself."

Hanna swallowed. So far, none of the other kids had started this conversation. No one wanted to talk about what they'd done wrong, so nobody had asked. And she had preferred it that way.

"It's not a big deal," said Hanna evasively.

"Huh." Cade tilted his head. "Back in California, I beat a kid up."

What? This scrawny, freckled little guy couldn't be a fighter. He probably weighed half as much as Hanna, and she was pretty gangly herself.

"The horses are supposed to help me calm down," Cade went on. "'A healthy outlet' for my anger, or something."

"Is riding . . . helping?"

"No idea. But it's fun!" Cade shrugged. "So what are you doing instead of riding?"

"Polishing saddles."

"Hmm," he said. "Izzy was right."

Her name was like a paper cut. "What was

Izzy right about?" Hanna asked too quickly.

"That you're getting special treatment 'cause you're scared of horses." Cade tapped his chin. "Why are you here, then? I mean, it's a horse camp."

That familiar wave of hopelessness washed over her. "I've been asking myself the same thing."

"Maybe you could, like, get over your fear?" Cade said helpfully.

If only it could be that easy—as easy as walking into a cloud of bees.

CHAPTER SIX

Cade's question haunted Hanna over the next few days. *Maybe you could, like, get over your fear?*

Why couldn't she just "get over it"? What was holding her back? But even watching the other kids doing their riding lessons made her fear for them, as if the horses would suddenly stampede and they'd all get thrown off and trampled.

Over the weekend, the ranch schedule shifted, giving them more free time. But that meant more opportunities for Izzy to get on Hanna's case.

"Not coming on the trail ride today, Hanna?" Izzy asked as the other kids put on their helmets, their horses saddled and ready to go. They waited in front of the ranch house for Mr. Bridle to get his map and Fletch to check the riders' cinches for safety. At the front of the line, Madison rode her Appaloosa, Snow White, a mostly white horse with a mess of big, black spots on her rear.

"No," said Hanna. "I . . . I'm doing something else."

"Whatever," Izzy said, flipping some of her hair out of her face. "I'm sure going on a trail ride will be way more fun than anything you're doing here."

Behind her, Fletch's voice answered. "Actually, Hanna and I are working on a project together."

Great, thought Hanna. Now Izzy would really have some "special treatment" to hassle her about.

"Izzy," said Fletch, cocking his head, "your saddle's cinch is way too loose. Need me to show you how to tighten it properly again?"

"No!" Izzy led Fettucini a few steps away and checked the cinch herself. "I can do it."

Fletch raised his hands in mock surrender and went over to Hanna. "Hey. Are you ready?"

Hanna nodded. When Mr. Bridle arrived riding a muscular black beauty, Madison let out a little whoop. "Mount up, everyone!" she said. "It's time to go!"

Together, Hanna and Fletch stood out of the way as the trail riders got on their horses and strode off down the road.

Fletch closed his eyes and exhaled. "A few hours of peace. Whew."

Peace? Kind, quiet Fletch found her peaceful? She liked that.

"So what are we doing?" Hanna asked.

"You'll see. For now, go into the barn and grab two buckets. Fill one with water and the other with grain. Then go wait over in the small corral, next to the barn."

Hanna's heart skipped a beat. Those sounded like supplies for a horse.

"You want me to get what?" she asked in a small voice.

"It's all right, Hanna. I'm not going to ask you to do anything you can't do. Just meet me at the corral with those two things."

With that, Fletch tipped his hat and left.

Hanna did as she was told. Carrying the two buckets, she went to the corral and set them down. Then she waited.

Soon, on the other side of the pasture fence, Fletch appeared—leading the beautiful, silver horse she'd seen her first day on the ranch. Today he looked more like a horse in a movie than a figurine, with his snowy coat lightly dusted with speckles of ash, his silvery mane and tail flowing in the wind, and his powerful neck arched and taut.

He was beautiful.

But he didn't act at all like a horse in a movie. He stayed as far away from Fletch as he could, yanking against the lead rope with his huge head as the trainer urged him out of the pasture. The horse's ears lay flat against his skull and his nostrils flared.

When they reached the corral, where Hanna was standing, the horse stopped abruptly and pawed the ground. When Fletch tried to get near him, he backed away, ears flattening even more. His massive chest muscles bunched up underneath him like he might turn and bolt at any moment, and if Fletch didn't let go, he'd get dragged along behind.

This close to the horse, Hanna's blood rushed faster. He was the biggest, scariest animal she'd ever seen.

"Hanna," said Fletch, sounding strong and stern, "open the gate to the corral and put the grain inside. Make sure you shake the bucket."

"But . . . !" If she was inside the corral when the

horse came through, he might trample her.

"*Hanna.*" His voice left no room for objection. Shocked, Hanna grabbed the bucket of grain and went into the corral, shaking it as she went. The horse's ears tipped up and forward, and he stopped pawing. With Fletch moving out of the way, the horse edged toward the corral.

"Now put down the grain," said Fletch. "You're small enough—once he's about to go into the gate, I want you to slide out through the fence. Okay?"

Hanna's heart was pounding so hard she almost couldn't hear Fletch over the sound of it. She could get trapped inside the corral with a horse—a horse that appeared quite out of control, even with an experienced trainer.

Hanna set down the bucket, still shaking it to keep the horse's interest. The huge animal walked toward her, closer and closer to the corral's open gate.

At the threshold, he paused, and his ears perked forward. He was no longer looking at the grain on the ground but right at her.

Hanna froze, rooted to the spot, same as when they saw each other her first day at the ranch. His huge brown eyes stared through her, and she couldn't stop him. He took another step toward her, this time through the gate, and Fletch let the lead rope slide out of his hand.

"Hanna," whispered Fletch, "get out of the corral."

Her senses returning to her, Hanna squeezed out between the fence's metal bars. The horse, curious, walked after her into the corral—and Fletch closed the gate behind him.

When he realized what had happened, the horse turned, ears flat against his head again, and tried to go back out the way he'd come in. But the gate wouldn't budge. With deft fingers, Fletch reached over the gate and unhooked his lead rope.

The big, gray horse squealed, like a creature in a horror movie. Flinging his head from side to side, he pressed his entire weight against the closed gate. Hanna jumped back from the fence as the whole thing gave a metallic rattle. When he realized the gate wouldn't give, the horse turned and galloped back along the edge of the corral, knocking over the bucket of grain and scattering it across the dirt without a second look. Only one thing mattered to him: getting out.

Around and around the corral he went, ears pressed back against his skull, his huge nostrils flaring

as he looked for a hole or weakness in the craftsman-
ship. Sometimes the horse would stop and turn and
run back the other way, throwing his head over the
top of the fence and taking huge, rumbling breaths.

Every time he completed a circle, he stopped on
the other side of the fence from Hanna and stared at
her. Fletch stood beside her, and they both watched
in silence as the wild, terrible creature flung his head
to and fro, mane tangling up in itself, and continued
running in endless circles until he'd worked up a
foamy, brownish sweat.

"What . . . what is he?" asked Hanna.

"He's hopeless," said Fletch. "Paul, the ranch
manager, found him wandering around with the
cattle up on the north end of the ranch. Abandoned,
maybe, or escaped. Ma Etty wanted to find his owner
and return him, because we thought for sure it was a
mistake. By his head and conformation, we're pretty
sure he's at least part Hanoverian—a kind of German
sport horse—and we couldn't imagine anyone losing
a fine creature like this and not desperately wanting
it back. So we checked with the sheriff, but no one's
reported a horse missing."

"He's so beautiful," said Hanna. "Why would
someone intentionally abandon him?"

"I don't know," said Fletch. "After we started trying to work with him, though, we might not have returned him anyway, no matter who came forward. He was rail-thin when we found him, and he's obviously been abused. He had the saddle sores and was head shy to prove it."

"Head shy?"

"Don't raise a hand too close to his head," said Fletch. "He freaks out. It reminds him of being hit."

"So what did you do with him?"

"Nothing. Nobody could get him under a saddle without him biting or breaking loose. Madison, Paul, Ma Etty, and even Mr. Bridle tried—and Willard Bridle's the best horse trainer I know. He's worked with wild mustangs. But he had no luck, and no one around here has the time to start over from scratch with Shy Guy, what with camp going all summer."

"Shy Guy?"

"I gave him that nickname after he came to us, because he's so terrified of people." Fletch's voice dropped low, dangerously low, and his kind, almost sad face turned hard and cold. "Whoever owned him before really did a number on him."

Hanna glanced at the horse in the pen, still anxiously trotting in circles. Abandoned. Abused.

Afraid.

"Why did you put him in the corral?" asked Hanna.

"Shy Guy's back at square one, like he's never even been broken. No, worse—he's at square zero, because we can't even get close enough to trim his hooves. At least a green horse will let you do that." When Fletch leaned his weight against the corral fence, Shy Guy let out another terrible squeal and backed against the opposite fence. Fletch sighed and stepped away. "And if we can't trim his hooves," he said, "they'll grow out, break, chip, or even make him lame."

"I don't see what that has to do with the corral or me," said Hanna.

"Shy Guy needs to be socialized—just enough that we can trim his hooves, maybe get him into the barn again and off eating grass all the time, now that he's fattened up a little. Ma Etty hopes that if he spends enough time around people, in a safe, calm environment, we could work up to exercising him with a longe line. Even if no one can ever ride him again, he needs the attention and to not be alone all the time." He leveled his gaze on Hanna. "And that's where you come in."

"Me?"

"You. All I want you to do is feed him. Give him water and be near him. You don't have to touch him—you don't even have to get close. In fact, it might be better if you keep your distance. Just let Shy Guy get used to your presence. That's all I ask."

"But—"

Fletch held up a hand. "It's not the most glamorous job, but I think it will be good for both of you. And it's what Ma Etty wants. If you can't do it, you'll have to tell her yourself. You're the only one on the ranch with time to spare right now."

Hanna's whole body felt cold. Her job was to stay near that massive, powerful, unpredictable horse? He was way worse than little Lacey. He was wild. Out of control.

When she looked at him, Shy Guy stopped his pacing and looked back at her. His brown eyes roiled with fury. But under that, she saw something else—something familiar.

He was terrified.

Hanna knew exactly how he felt.

CHAPTER SEVEN

As morning turned into afternoon, the sun cooked Hanna like a fried egg on pavement. The high altitude made it worse—the sun never beat down this hot and bright back in Michigan.

Shy Guy had slugged down his water after all that running around and left the bucket bone-dry, so she'd have to fill it again. And she had to somehow get the empty bucket out of the corral—where a big, dangerous horse was currently tromping around.

Waiting until Shy Guy was distracted on the other side of the pen, Hanna edged closer to the corral fence. She snatched the bucket out from between the metal rails without him noticing. Whew. She wiped the sweat from her forehead and clutched the bucket to her chest.

First part completed.

Hanna had to use all her weight to push down the long, metal handle on the water faucet. As icy water shot out, she splashed some on her face and then finished filling the bucket.

When she got back to the corral, Shy Guy had stopped pacing and now leaned against the fence, looking as close to despondent as a horse could look. He shifted from one foot to the other and flicked an ear in her direction, but that was all.

Hanna set down the bucket. She'd have to get close enough to the corral again to slide it back under the fence, but she didn't want him to freak out and rear or kick when she got close. She walked around to the other side of the pen, hoping she could slip it under the fence without him seeing her, but as soon as she moved, he turned and followed her with his eyes. It was like a game of chicken—he wanted to keep an eye on her, and she didn't want to be seen.

So Hanna stood there, simply watching him, and Shy Guy watched her back.

Neither of them moved for a long time as she

thought about what to do. Shy Guy's tail lashed some flies that had landed on his rump, scattering them.

They were both baking in this heat. But he was a horse—he couldn't splash himself with cold water as she had. Hanna glanced down at the bucket of water.

He was calm, for now. But how long would that last?

Stuck between getting close enough to give him the water and keeping a safe distance, Hanna simply sat down and gave up her jeans to the dirt. Every time she moved, he flicked his ears at her, but the longer she sat still, the more he relaxed—and began to look bored.

And so, so hot. Hanna wasn't covered in hair like he was, but sweat still dripped down her face.

Finally, she stood up. Shy Guy glanced at her but didn't move. He looked more curious than anything.

She took a deep breath, picked up the water bucket, and edged toward him.

He focused on her, both ears flicked forward. Hanna took another step toward the fence. Dust rose from the edges of her boot.

Shy Guy's nostrils flared. He must be taking in the smell of her. Animals were sensitive to smell, she remembered. What if her human scent set him off?

What if it reminded him of all the humans who had done him wrong before?

Shy Guy readjusted his weight so he was standing on all four legs. Hanna could feel her pulse all the way up in her throat, in her hands, in her feet, pounding away like an out-of-control marching band. Water sloshed out of the bucket, surprising them both as it hit the ground.

Shy Guy retreated one step back, eyes wide, and stared at the wet spot in the dust as if it offended him. Hanna didn't move any closer, but she also couldn't look away.

He was majestic, no doubt about that. Majestic and terrifying.

And thirsty, she reminded herself.

Trying to steady her hands, Hanna took yet another step toward the corral fence. Shy Guy lifted one hoof, as if to match her step forward with one of his own back—but then set it down again. He focused on the water in her hands, his nostrils sucking in the smell.

One more step brought Hanna to the fence. Only a few rickety metal crossbars separated her from a thousand pounds of skittish muscle and hooves.

Panic welled up inside Hanna. Shy Guy's huge

head was so close she could smell him. He smelled like . . . horse. Sweat. Grass.

And he, undoubtedly, could smell her too. His neck arched and his sturdy, barrel-chested body poised to flee.

Hanna dreaded getting any closer, and she could tell Shy Guy was just as torn between his fear of her and his thirst. He wanted the water she had, but getting close—putting himself in a position where someone could hurt him—was too much for him.

She knew how he felt. When Hanna dropped something on the floor, slouched, or talked with food in her mouth, she'd panic like that. Had her mom seen? Would she be spending another evening balancing books on her head to "correct" her posture?

Hanna was always waiting for the other shoe to drop. After she'd started stashing under her bed the candy bars, energy drinks, trinkets, and even a pair of expensive sneakers she'd stolen, Hanna waited to be discovered. Her mom would blame Hanna's friends, her school, and everyone except herself— proving, yet again, how much she just didn't get it.

Shy Guy took a sudden step forward and Hanna jumped. He angled his head up and opened his mouth, exposing two rows of huge, square, white teeth. Hanna shrank back, almost dropping the bucket of water.

But he didn't lunge or snap with his jaws. He simply waved his lips around, open and closed, like a fish, in the silliest expression Hanna had ever seen a horse make. He reminded her of a frog prince trying to get a kiss.

A laugh burst out of her before she could stop it. Shy Guy leaned back, surprised by the sudden noise. Hanna covered her mouth.

"Sorry," she said to him. "Didn't mean to scare you."

Hanna was still holding the water, and again, Shy Guy waggled his lips at her. Well, if a horse was ever going to come right out and tell her he was thirsty, this was it.

Her fear dried up like that splash of water in the dust. She squatted down and pushed the full bucket under the fence. Shy Guy stepped back. His nostrils reached an impossible size and his eyeballs bulged, like he thought the water would bite him now that he'd finally gotten it.

The hard work was over. He had something to drink. But now Hanna's fear rose its massive head, and she realized how close she was to the fence—and the massive horse behind it.

Letting out a little wail, she skittered backward like a crab. Once she was a safe distance away, she let out a gasping breath and fell back in the dirt.

Shy Guy was startled too and stood uneasily a few feet from the fence. But the water drew him back, and with timid ballerina steps, he returned to it.

Hanna got up and dusted off her pants. The adrenaline finally caught up to her, and she drowned in a tidal wave of fear, happiness, and at the end of it . . .

Thrill.

She'd done it!

Shy Guy buried his muzzle in the bucket of water, scattering droplets everywhere. Hanna wrinkled her nose. She'd have to get him more water pretty quickly if he was going to be messy about it.

When he was done, Shy Guy looked up at her, ears perked—a thank-you, maybe? Hanna found herself nodding back to him.

It had never occurred to her how alike people and horses could be. Someone had hurt Shy Guy—and it had made its mark on him, the way hurt makes its mark on everyone.

Eventually, Hanna stood up. The horse watched her as she approached and put one hand on the railing.

He looked as if he might run; his entire attention was directed at her. But he didn't move.

"I'm sorry somebody did this to you," she said to him. His ears flicked back and forth, listening. "You didn't deserve it."

Something inside her—something alien and new and fearless—wanted to reach out and touch him. To comfort him. And to comfort herself.

\\

That night they had a free hour before lights-out while Madison drove into town to swim some laps. Cooking in the Colorado heat all day had drained Hanna, and she wanted nothing more than to read in peace.

"I can't believe Hanna is getting another special new chore," groaned Izzy, falling back on her bed with a *thump*.

Hanna turned a page of her book and pretended to read.

"What's up with that white horse all covered in splotches, Hanna?" asked Rae Ann.

"He's not white," Hanna found herself saying. "He's gray. White horses have pink skin under their hair. Gray horses like Shy Guy have black skin. And he's not 'splotchy'—Shy Guy is a dapple gray."

Rae Ann tilted her head. "Shy Guy? That's a weird name."

"No, it's not," Hanna said. "Fletch gave it to him." She pressed her lips together. She shouldn't be telling these two any of this.

Izzy squinted at her. "He didn't have a name before?"

"No."

"Why not?"

"I don't know."

"Come on, Hanna. Tell us."

Hanna didn't say anything and tried to keep her eyes on the book.

"Fine," Izzy said. "I guess since you think you're so special, we should give you special treatment, right?"

Rae Ann giggled. "So-o-o-o special!"

"Hey, Rae Ann," said Izzy, turning away from Hanna, "know what would make her feel real special?"

Rae Ann opened her mouth but sensed she was walking into a trap and closed it.

"Putting some spiders in her bed!"

Spiders? Please.

Rae Ann's smile faded. "Madison will get mad at us," she said.

"Come on, goody-goody. Madison won't find out." Izzy waltzed to the cabin door. "I'm sure there are a few cobwebs hanging out here."

"Izzy, stop," said Rae Ann, following her. "I'm not going to put spiders in Hanna's bed."

"Why not? It's funny."

"It's mean. And if you do it . . ." Rae Ann's voice dropped. She sounded dangerous and very unlike herself. "I'm going to tell on you."

Izzy halted mid-step, and they stared at each other. Hanna regretted the mean things she'd thought about Rae Ann. She had it where it counted.

"Fine. Tell on me, *tattletale*," hissed Izzy. "You sound like a dumb little kid."

Without replying, Rae Ann stalked back into the cabin and climbed onto her bunk. Izzy stood at the door like she wasn't sure what to do anymore. Then she stomped outside and slammed the door behind her.

Rae Ann didn't look at Hanna, but under her breath she muttered to herself, in her most childish voice, "Meanie head."

After that, Hanna gave up trying to read. She fell asleep imagining Izzy stuffing spiders under her mattress, but she was glad it was her bed, and not Ma Etty's.

CHAPTER EIGHT

The next day, the need to steal something and get away with it consumed Hanna. She could slip a hoof pick into her pocket right under somebody's nose, or maybe swipe that pink halter she liked and stash it in her bag. Something to remember this place by.

But she'd feel bad stealing from the Bridles—and her mom would definitely find it once she got home. After discovering the goods under Hanna's bed, her mom had started performing weekly room searches. Anything that Hanna couldn't prove was hers was another tally on the "I'm So Disappointed in You" scorecard.

"Same thing again today," Fletch told Hanna as the other kids finished breakfast and went out to get started on their ride for the day.

Right. Shy Guy. Hanna's heart skipped a beat. No, it was a hop, a skip, almost a dance. She felt . . . excited to see him, not afraid.

Well, maybe a little afraid.

When she reached the corral, there he was, shining in the morning sun—its rays weaving through the fine silver threads of his mane.

Shy Guy's head shot up when she appeared. His whole body angled toward her, short ears standing straight up like a rabbit's.

"Good morning," Hanna said in a low voice as she approached the corral fence. Shy Guy tensed up, like he might put some space between them, so she stopped where she was.

They stood like that, looking at each other, in what was becoming their ritual.

Hanna checked his bucket. Still full. Good. In one corner, stray bits of alfalfa were mixed in with the dirt. Fletch or Madison must have fed him earlier.

Good.

Hanna flopped down on the ground. Shy Guy

shook his head and snorted, like he was displeased with the sudden movement, but he didn't move away.

After a while, he grew bored and wandered off, nibbling in the dirt for the leftover alfalfa. Was this it? Was this really her job, to sit here all day? All she could do was gaze out at the landscape—the green mountains with distant snowcaps, the blue skies—or she could stare at Shy Guy.

She did a lot of staring.

An hour later, Madison came and sat down next to Hanna. She was out of breath and dusty. Shy Guy cast Madison a suspicious look from the other side of the corral.

"How's it going over here?" she asked.

"Uh, I don't know, fine? Should something be . . . happening? I'm just sitting here."

"Good! No, that's great. How's he doing?"

Hanna shrugged. "Also fine, I guess."

"Perfect. Keep at it."

"I don't really get how this is helping."

"Ma Etty hopes that if he's around people enough without stress, maybe he could trust us enough to let us trim his hooves without having to put him in a tilt and trim."

"A tilt and trim?"

"Shy Guy won't let anyone near his legs, but when we found him, his hooves were so long he couldn't walk properly. The farrier had to bring over a tilt and trim—a metal cage we usually use on mustangs to prevent kicking—and put Shy Guy inside it, so she could turn him sideways and get to his hooves."

Hanna gazed at Shy Guy with newfound awe. "That's scary." *He must have been frightened, crammed inside a metal cage like that.*

"I doubt he was always like this. Hanoverians are usually obedient and sturdy—the Germans used them in the military and to pull coaches. You couldn't fight on a horse that spooked easy, could you?" She sighed. "I think he's just been hurt so many times he's forgotten how to trust people. Ma Etty thinks you can teach him that again, and then trimming up his hooves doesn't have to be a big event."

Hanna's eyes widened. "Me? I don't know anything about trust or horses or trimming hooves. I'm the worst person to choose!"

Madison shrugged. "Not my call. This all surprised me just as much as it did you." She stood up and handed Hanna a water bottle. "You're not a prisoner, though. Go to the bathroom, take breaks. It's hot out here. You put on sunscreen?"

Hanna rolled her eyes. "Yeah, I did. Thanks, Mom."

Madison laughed. "Okay. Remember, don't get too close to him. I mean, give him water. But even though he's pretty, I don't want you to get hurt if he spooks."

Hanna couldn't believe they had put her, of all the kids, with the dangerous horse. What kind of crazy operation was this?

But, she supposed, it sort of made sense. She was the only one not participating in riding lessons. She was deadweight. Maybe she could put her time to good use.

"Okay," said Hanna. "I understand."

\\

So the afternoon dragged on. And the next. And the next.

Soon Shy Guy started waiting at the fence when she returned with the full bucket of water. This afternoon, he'd even stepped aside so she could push it under the bars—but when she stood back up again, he was so close that the wind blew his long, coarse forelock hair into her eyes. She didn't want to move backward too fast and surprise him, so she stood stock-still as his eyes locked with hers.

They were inches from each other, but Hanna didn't budge.

Shy Guy turned his neck so his lips brushed the metal bars. His head was so big that the space between his nostrils dwarfed her whole hand. But in his brown eyes she didn't see a horse that kicked or a horse that bit. She saw a horse that made funny faces when he wanted water and galloped through the trees at the bank of a creek for fun.

That feeling returned—that sensation of wanting to steal something, of breaking the rules, of making her own way and her own mistakes.

Remember, don't get too close to him.

Hanna raised her hand, slowly, steadily, all in Shy Guy's field of vision. He didn't move. His ears were still forward, attentive. She settled the hand on the bars, near his head. It felt right.

Safe.

His lips started to move, like he was feeling out the texture of the metal. Then his neck turned, and he ran his lips along her fingers. For a split second Hanna thought, *He could bite my fingers clean off.*

But some part of her knew that he wouldn't. So

she turned her hand to face palm up, and he ran his nose along that too.

It was velvety soft, softer than she could have imagined. Gradually, she moved her hand up his long face. He ducked his head so her hand landed on the spot between his eyes where the fur swirled like a whirlpool. Hanna rubbed under his forelock, and Shy Guy nuzzled her arm right back.

He was so soft. Each movement of his head was gentle, as if he was afraid of breaking her or scaring her off.

Hanna thought maybe they each saw the frightened creature inside the other, wanting to break out.

"I'm sorry," Hanna said to him. "I promise, whatever happened, I won't let it happen again."

\\\

It was getting late in the afternoon, and the sun was sinking behind the butte when a voice called her name.

"Hanna?"

Shy Guy's head snapped up, startling her more than Madison had.

"Hanna, get down from there."

Hanna realized how precarious her position must look and climbed off the fence.

Madison was standing with her hands on her hips when Hanna landed on the ground, sending up a little dust cloud. When Madison approached, Shy Guy's ears flattened to his head and he backed away. She stopped.

"Whoa. Sorry." She eyed Hanna. "I thought I told you not to get too close."

Hanna ducked her head. "Sorry. My butt hurt from sitting on the ground, and he . . ."

"You're all right, though?"

"Yeah, I'm fine. He had an itchy head and wanted me to scratch it."

"Did he?" Madison phrased it like a question, but the corner of her mouth turned up in a slight smile. "So head scratches are a thing now?"

"I guess so."

"Cool." Madison glanced at her watch. "Well, you're off the clock. You've got an hour of free time before dinner."

"I think I'll stay here," said Hanna.

Madison frowned. "You sure? Josh is setting up the bean bag toss. He said he thought you might want to play."

Josh had said that? Hanna glanced at Shy Guy over her shoulder. He stood dispiritedly on the other side of the corral, tail flicking the air.

"I think I'm still going to stay."

Madison shrugged. "Okay. Your prerogative. I'm going to go help with dinner, so come find me if you need anything." She turned to walk away and then stopped. "Oh, and Izzy is still out in the field with Fettucini, practicing the barrel race with her free hour. In case you see a horse running around."

So Izzy was using her free hour to ride? She must be doing really well for Madison to trust her alone with her horse. Maybe she was already running barrels like a pro.

Of course a girl like Izzy would be, Hanna thought.

"Thanks," she said, climbing back up on the fence. Shy Guy came back and rested his head against the bars near her hand. Madison watched them with a smile crawling across her face.

"Have fun," she said and waved good-bye.

CHAPTER NINE

From her perch on the top bar of the corral fence, Hanna was enjoying the way the late afternoon sun turned the low-hanging clouds all sorts of pink, orange, and purple. She sat at just the perfect height to scratch between Shy Guy's ears. When someone shouted off in the distance, she didn't think twice about it—probably the ranch manager, Paul, yelling at one of his ranch hands in the milking barn across the way.

Then the shout came again, closer. Shy Guy backed away and stared at something behind Hanna.

She turned around on the metal railing and spotted Izzy, galloping toward them on her big chestnut horse. Fettucini, lathered in sweat, bumped into Hanna's knees as Izzy sidled up to her. Hanna gasped and almost fell back into the corral. And now, with Izzy in the way, she couldn't get down off the fence.

"Well, hello again, Princess Hanna," Izzy said, her huge smile making her appear extra menacing. Shy Guy snorted nervously, his ears back. "I just beat my best time on the barrels."

Hanna puckered her lips. She didn't care an inch about Izzy's barrel time.

"How's your little 'vacation' going?" asked Izzy, urging Fettucini once again closer to the corral fence. With Izzy on her horse and Hanna on the fence, they sat at the same height, and Izzy's haughty gaze met Hanna's eyes. Shy Guy paced nervously inside the corral.

"Get out of here," said Hanna, swatting at Izzy and her big red horse. She couldn't do much else from up there. "You're scaring Shy Guy."

"Oh?" Izzy leaned closer, and Hanna leaned back, feeling her balance grow unsteady. "I don't think it's him who's scared of me. I think it's you." She covered her mouth in mock surprise. "But Hanna," she cried, "I'm half your size! What are you afraid of?"

"I'm not afraid," said Hanna, but the tremble in her voice gave her away.

Izzy's grin widened. "You big wussy." With that, she reached out, put her hand on Hanna's shoulder, and shoved her backward.

Hanna's arms pinwheeled as she tried to find balance or something to hold onto, but she only grabbed open, empty air. Her riding boots flew up in front of her, and somewhere behind her, Shy Guy let out a neigh.

Her back hit the ground hard inside the corral. A searing pain shot from her hips upward, and Hanna let out a cry that was horrible even to her own ears.

Worse, she was now inside the corral—with a potentially dangerous horse. Wincing, Hanna searched for Shy Guy. Just as she turned around, huge, black hooves swung past her head. She let out a scream and rolled out of the way. Shy Guy's hooves landed with a heavy *thump*, but quickly he was galloping around the corral again, ears flattened to his skull, every muscle as tightly wound as a spring as he searched for a way out of the enclosed space. On his second pass, he almost stepped on Hanna's legs—but she tucked them under herself and rolled away again.

There wasn't enough room for both of them in here with him out of control.

"Help!" Hanna shouted at Izzy, who was scrambling off Fettucini's back. "He's going to step on me!"

"Hanna!" Izzy shouted as she sprinted to the gate. She struggled with the latch, but her movements were too panicked and it wasn't giving. Shy Guy galloped back past Hanna again, neighing frantically. Then the latch clicked, and the gate swung open.

Izzy ran inside, heedless of the huge horse making panicked circuits of the corral. She grabbed Hanna's hand and yanked her up to her feet. Behind them hooves pounded dirt, and then came a metal crash.

They turned to find the gate hanging wide open, and Shy Guy galloping away.

"No!" Hanna shouted after his retreating shape.

"Uh-oh," said Izzy, as he leapt right over the creek separating the horse barn from the rest of the ranch and took off at full tilt down Bridlemile Road.

"He's headed toward the town!"

Izzy helped Hanna limp out of the corral. None of her bones were broken, at least, but she was pretty bruised, thanks to Izzy.

But right now, that stuff didn't matter. She had to get to Shy Guy. She could only hope the ranch's front gate was closed.

"I'm going after him," said Hanna, pulling away from Izzy and stumbling.

"Are you sure you can even stand up?"

"Yeah." Hanna grunted when she put her weight on her right hip. "No thanks to you."

Izzy didn't say anything, but with tear tracks running down her cheeks, she took Fettucini by the reins. Hanna felt no sympathy.

"I'll go after him," Izzy said. "It's my fault."

Hanna was already limping off in the direction Shy Guy had run. "And bring him back how?"

"I'll get help."

"We don't have time to get help. Look! He's gone!" Shy Guy's gray shape was already disappearing behind the ranch house. Running after him on foot was pointless. At this rate, he'd make it all the way down Bridlemile Road before Hanna could catch up to him.

That was when Hanna had an idea.

"I'm going to ride with you," she told Izzy. "Get on first."

"What? You want to actually ride a horse?"

"Yes!" Hanna cried, imagining her beautiful

gray horse getting hit by a car, his heavy body collapsing lifeless to the pavement. "Now get on!"

Izzy obeyed mutely and climbed onto Fettucini's back. Then she offered one of her stirrups to Hanna.

Hanna took one, two, and then three deep breaths before she stuck her foot in the stirrup and leapt onto the horse. She landed awkwardly on the back of the saddle, and a stinging pain shot through her bruised hip. But Izzy was already turning Fettucini the way Shy Guy had gone, and she made a kissing sound with her lips.

"Hold on!" she shouted. Hanna's arms wrapped around Izzy's waist as Fettucini leapt into a gallop, taking off after Shy Guy.

They sprinted down the gravel road, Hanna barely holding on as Fettucini bumped and bounced under her. Her stomach turned with every lurch, but all she could think about was getting to Shy Guy.

Then, up ahead, she spotted him. The ranch house whizzed past. Ma Etty stepped out onto the porch, sipping her coffee, and she stared after Izzy and Hanna as they galloped by.

"Will!" she yelled behind them. "Get your horse!"

Hanna had to admit that Fettucini was fast. The three of them roared down the drive, following

Shy Guy's dust trail. Part of her thought—no, knew—that she should be afraid. But there wasn't room inside her for fear for herself. Right now, she only had space for Shy Guy. What if a truck came barreling up Bridlemile Road too fast? She could hear his bones crunching . . .

No! All Hanna could do was grit her teeth and hold on as they flew down the road, toward the front gate—which now hung wide open, the QUARTZ CREEK RANCH sign hanging over it.

"No, no, no!" cried Hanna, visualizing Shy Guy making it all the way to Main Street in Quartz Creek. But he wasn't running as fast anymore, and Fettucini easily overtook him on the straightaway.

Then Izzy and Hanna were galloping alongside him, clouds of his dust filling the air. Maybe Hanna could jump from one horse to the other, like in the movies? But that couldn't work. She'd get herself killed. But if she got off Fettucini, she couldn't keep up with the horses on foot.

A diesel engine roared up ahead. A truck was coming! Dread settled in her chest as she imagined her worst fear coming true.

But Izzy let out a whoop. "Paul!" she shouted. "We've got a runaway horse!"

A blond head in a wide-brimmed hat leaned out the window of the truck.

"Runaway?" Paul slammed on his brakes, and the truck swerved. Shy Guy stopped and reared as the truck's metal body swung around in front of them. It fishtailed, rear wheels spewing gravel until it sat stopped in the middle of the road, wedged between the fence and the creek. It wouldn't stop a horse if he was determined, but it created a small barrier.

Shy Guy neighed like a demon and reared again, sending Fettucini dancing away. Shy Guy's head craned left, then right, searching for a way past this new blockade. There was enough room at the back of the truck to slip by—and as soon as Shy Guy saw it, he lunged.

"No way!" said Izzy, reining Fettucini around to get between Shy Guy and the tail of the truck. Shy Guy backed off, throwing his head from side to side in his panic.

Paul was getting out of the truck to try to catch him with a lead rope when Shy Guy broke past the barrier Fettucini had formed with his body, knocking their legs. He dashed toward the gap between the back of the truck and the creek bed.

"No!" Hanna couldn't let him run into town,

undeterred, in this frantic and frightened state.

She jumped off Fettucini, landing with an unceremonious *thud* and a cloud of dust. Every muscle in her back and hips ached, but she ignored them. She grabbed the lead rope from Paul and jogged toward Shy Guy, even as he reared up again.

"Hey, buddy," she crooned, keeping enough distance that his flailing hooves wouldn't hit her. He landed on all four feet again and turned to look at her, ears pinned back and panting. Sweat coursed down his chest.

"Hey there," Hanna said again, in her calmest, kindest voice. "It's okay, boy. Everything will be all right."

His ears pricked slightly toward her, and his eyes followed her every step. His entire body was tensed to run, even as he looked tired, breathing heavily.

"Hanna," warned Paul. "Don't go near him. Let me—"

"I've got this," she said, still using her kindest voice. Shy Guy's gaze flicked to a point behind her, probably Paul, and his ears flattened. "Don't either of you move," she said.

"I'd listen to her," whispered Izzy.

"Hey, Shy Guy," Hanna said, earning his

attention again. She took another step toward him. "Hey, you pretty boy. See? It's okay. I'm not going to hurt you."

Shy Guy's nostrils flared, and he lifted one foot as if he might take a matching step back, but she held her hands out palms up and he stopped.

After a long moment, the only sound was Shy Guy's heavy breathing, and she took another step toward him.

"It's just me." Hanna was so close now she could smell his terrified sweat. Shy Guy shook his head, mane swishing over his huge neck. If he bolted now, he'd trample her. But if she showed fear, she would only frighten him.

Hanna had to be brave for both of them.

One more step, and she was close enough to touch him. She reached out and gently ran a hand along Shy Guy's long nose, and he seemed too tired to pull away. He whuffed, his hot breath filling her hand. Slowly she moved her hand down his neck and, fingers shaking, wrapped the lead rope around it. She tied it off in a loose knot.

"Got him," she said. Shy Guy shimmied away as Paul appeared at her shoulder, carrying a halter. He stopped mid-step.

"Maybe you should lead him back," he said quietly, handing her the halter.

"Yeah." Hanna rubbed the exhausted horse's head and neck a few more times before he was calm enough that she could buckle it over his head. He tilted his head away, but seemed too tired to fight back. She clipped on the lead rope and finally let out the breath she'd been holding.

"You did it," said Izzy, her voice surprising Hanna. She'd forgotten anyone was there but her and Shy Guy.

"Knock on wood. We still have to get back." She turned toward the ranch. Shy Guy's head hung low beside her. He was too out of energy to pull away from her as he had with Fletch.

Grasping the lead rope tightly, Hanna said, "Let's go home."

CHAPTER TEN

Hanna and Izzy walked back up Bridlemile Road, Shy Guy on Hanna's left, following along uneasily, and Izzy leading Fettucini to her right. Mr. Bridle had caught up to them on his big black horse and rode up ahead of them to make sure the way was clear. After closing the ranch gate, Paul drove behind as a blockade in case Shy Guy tried to make a break for it again. That left the two girls and their horses alone.

"Hanna . . ." Izzy trailed off. When Hanna glanced over, Izzy was fixated on her feet. "I . . . I didn't know that would happen."

"What? When you pushed me off that fence?" Keeping her voice low to avoid startling Shy Guy,

Hanna halted suddenly and turned to Izzy. The fury she'd pushed down while she focused on the rescue bubbled up, hot and fiery, to the surface. "How did you think it would turn out?"

"I don't know," said Izzy, still not looking up. "I didn't think."

"Who even does that? Pushes someone from four feet up into a corral? I could have broken my neck. Shy Guy could have trampled me. I could actually be dead right now, Izzy."

Shy Guy pulled his head away, snorting nervously at the sound of her voice.

Hanna had never been so angry in her entire life. She had disliked Izzy before, with her teasing and mocking and prancing around like she was the queen of the world. But this time, she'd gone too far.

"I'm . . . I'm sorry." Izzy's voice was so quiet, Hanna almost didn't hear her. "I'm so sorry, Hanna. I really am. I didn't mean for you to get hurt. I . . . I don't know what I was thinking. Please don't tell."

The request surprised Hanna so much, her response was a question. "Don't tell?"

"Please don't tell Madison and Ma Etty what I did. I'm in so much trouble already, you know. That's why I'm here. If my parents find out . . . if they hear I can't even stay out of trouble at a rehab camp, I'm done for. They were already threatening to make me change schools."

"But . . ."

Izzy covered her face in her hands and tears dripped out, down her chin, onto the dirt. "Please! I'll make it up to you. I promise." Shy Guy fidgeted at her wail.

They needed to keep moving and keep it down if they were going to get Shy Guy home safely, so Hanna let out a sigh. "Okay, fine. I won't tell."

Izzy dropped her hands to her sides and relief flooded her face.

"But don't think it means I've forgiven you. You put my life at risk for a . . . what? A joke? That's hard to forget."

Izzy nodded. "I understand. I promise I'll make it up to you."

Hanna wasn't sure what to make of the determination in Izzy's voice, but as they approached the ranch house and she saw Ma Etty waiting for them, she felt a little hopeful.

Or maybe it was the adrenaline.

\\

After Hanna had returned Shy Guy to his corral, Ma Etty told her to come inside.

"That was incredibly reckless, Hanna Abbott," she said, hands perched on her hips.

Hanna winced at her full name.

The ranch house was abuzz with news of Shy Guy's flight—and the maneuver that saved him. But Ma Etty had ushered everyone out of the living room except for the two girls in question.

Before Hanna could say anything, Izzy pushed in, physically standing between Hanna and Ma Etty.

"Hanna did the best she could, given the situation," said Izzy. "If we hadn't done something, Shy Guy would be roadkill!"

This made both Hanna and Ma Etty flinch.

Still. Of all people, it was Izzy defending her. Hanna didn't know what to make of that.

Ma Etty surveyed them. "You could have asked someone for help," she said. "Leaping onto a horse when you've never received even basic riding lessons . . ."

"We had to act fast," said Hanna. "If we'd had time, I promise, I would've way preferred to ask for help instead."

Paul leaned his head out the dining room doorway. "I don't know what you're lecturing her for, Ma

Etty," he said, his bushy blond mustache twitching. "That girl handled that horse incredibly well in a difficult situation, especially for a newbie."

Ma Etty frowned. "I didn't ask you, Paul."

"Well, that's true," he responded good-naturedly, "but isn't she the one that's scared to even get near a horse?" He tilted his head at Hanna.

"Yes," Ma Etty allowed.

"Pretty remarkable what she did, then, isn't it? Riding double your first time on a horse!"

Ma Etty didn't say anything, but her gaze went to Hanna.

"She didn't want to do it," said Izzy, breaking the silence. "But she had to!"

"Now, now," said Ma Etty, putting her hands up. "There are always options."

"There wasn't one this time." Izzy crossed her arms. "Hanna's the only one Shy Guy will let anywhere near him. It was a good thing she was brave enough to ride after him with me, because nobody else would've been able to get a halter on him."

Even though she was the one on trial, Hanna didn't dare interject—Izzy was handling it better than she would've.

"It was still a pretty dangerous thing to do, for

someone who's never ridden before," said Ma Etty. "I don't want anyone to get hurt on my watch. You didn't even have a helmet!"

Izzy gaped at her. "What? You can't be mad at Hanna for that. The scaredy-cat actually rode a horse! You should be happy."

Now, Ma Etty looked more confused than angry. She tilted her head at Izzy.

"And that makes me wonder. How did all this happen in the first place?"

Izzy and Hanna exchanged a glance. It was Hanna's turn to hold up her end of the bargain. She wished she'd worked on an excuse earlier.

"Shy Guy got out," she said lamely.

"How?"

Hanna opened and closed her mouth. This was the same thing that had happened when her mom found the stash of stolen stuff under her bed and demanded to know what she was doing. Hanna wasn't imaginative enough for good excuses.

"It was an accident," chimed in Izzy. "The gate wasn't latched properly."

Hanna nodded along. "Yep. And when Izzy came over with Fettucini to say hello, Shy Guy got scared and ran."

"To say hello?" Ma Etty surveyed both girls like a detective examining two suspects.

"Right," said Izzy. "You know, because . . . because Hanna and I have been hanging out a lot!" She flopped on the couch next to Hanna and put her in a headlock.

"Have you?" said Ma Etty, her surprise genuine this time.

"Y-yeah," managed Hanna, forcing herself to smile as she pushed Izzy off. "We have. All the time."

"We even came up with a joke," said Izzy. "Why didn't the horse speak?"

Hanna gave her a blank look. "Uh . . . why?"

"Because he was a little hoarse!"

Nobody laughed at the lame joke except Izzy, but Ma Etty did crack a smile. "Well, that's good to hear. But I'm still not happy with how reckless you were—riding double, leaving the property without permission . . ."

"We had to think fast," said Izzy. "We made a snap decision, and I stand by it."

"A decision that could have saved Shy Guy's life," chimed in Paul. Ma Etty gave him an annoyed look for his continued interference. "Even if she did get a little beat up."

Ma Etty's eyes narrowed. "Yeah, Hanna. How are you feeling? Neither of you has explained how Hanna got all covered in dirt."

Paul gave them a sheepish look and withdrew back into the dining room.

"I fell," said Hanna. "It was . . . before Shy Guy got out."

"Mm-hmm." Ma Etty didn't sound convinced, but when no one opted to explain further, she let out a defeated sigh. She did look pleased, though, to see the two girls sitting on the couch together. "Well, nobody's in trouble here, I suppose. Everyone did what they could in a bad situation and made it work." She nodded in Hanna's direction. "But you should be more careful. Remember, Shy Guy has had a hard time in life. You can't always trust him."

Hanna closed her eyes. "I know. But I think . . . I think he could be trusted again. He's a good horse, Ma Etty, but he's been hurt a lot."

"He was letting you scratch him," said Izzy. "Nobody could do that before, right, Ma Etty?"

Hanna shrugged. "I think he just knows I won't hurt him."

Ma Etty's smile widened. "I'm glad we paired you two up, then. He needs someone like you."

CHAPTER ELEVEN

The next morning, Madison told them at breakfast that Fletch would be working with Izzy, Rae Ann, Cade, and Josh so she could give Hanna a private lesson. Hanna waited for a snide remark from Izzy about getting more special treatment. But Izzy kept eating, even catching Hanna's eye and smiling lopsidedly.

Dumbfounded, Hanna missed her mouth with a forkful of eggs and spilled it right down her shirt.

After they broke up for riding instruction, Hanna met Madison by the corral.

"Normally we start everyone with the basics," she said. "We call it 'groundwork'—you know, how to handle the horse, lead it, and ask it to wait. Like heeling a dog. I want to teach you how to do it correctly right from the beginning so Shy Guy knows he can't get away with any fooling around on your watch. Given we can even get that far." Madison held out a pretty green halter to Hanna. "I think green is Shy Guy's color," she said with a grin.

Hanna took it, put it over her own shoulder, and shivered. She'd had no problem putting a halter on Shy Guy yesterday, when his life was at stake. It had been instinct.

She'd felt superhuman.

But now, with the halter in her hand, fear whistled through her blood. Madison had . . . expectations. Groundwork? Bossing around a horse?

Hanna couldn't do that. Hanna didn't know how to boss around anyone. Who would listen to her, anyway? Certainly not a big horse like Shy Guy.

"One thing," said Madison. "Remember to listen to everything I say. If it feels like Shy Guy might act up, I want you to drop the lead rope and get away as quickly as possible."

"You think that might . . . happen?" Hanna shivered.

"I don't know," said Madison. "I really don't. But I'd rather be safe than sorry."

Shy Guy stood peacefully in the middle of the corral, facing away from the gate. When they approached him from behind, he raised his head and pinned his ears back—until he spotted Hanna. Turning completely around, his ears pricked toward her.

Hanna walked up to the fence, and slowly, he walked forward to meet her. She patted his nose through the bars, and he let out a soft whuff.

"All right," said Madison, sounding like she'd been holding her breath. "We'll start with opening and closing the gate. We want Shy Guy to wait behind the gate while you open it and go in."

"Go in?" said Hanna. She had thought they would work somewhere a little less . . . enclosed.

"Yep. Just say, 'wait,' and hold the halter and lead rope in your hand. Shake the rope at him to ask him to move back. Don't open the gate until he's standing at attention and giving you plenty of space."

Hanna stared up at Shy Guy. He stared back at her through the fence. Carrying the halter, she made her way around the corral to the gate. He followed her every movement with his ears. Once she was at the gate, she said, "Wait."

Shy Guy stepped up to the gate and poked his nose through it, wanting her to pet him again. "No, silly boy. Go back." His ears flicked up at the command.

"Shake the lead rope a little," said Madison.

"Go back," Hanna said again, giving the rope the tiniest of shakes, scared she might frighten him if she shook it too hard.

But Shy Guy, head lowering, took a step backward. A surge of pride rushed through her.

Madison made an impressed noise. "Wow. I guess he's been trained by somebody along the way."

"You didn't know?"

"Nope. We had a hunch because of his breed—Hanoverians are usually dressage and jumping horses—but no one's been able to tell until now. Okay, now unlatch the gate and go inside."

Hanna's heart sped up. Reaching for the latch, she lifted it, and the gate opened a little. "Make sure he stays back," Madison said.

But Hanna didn't have to tell Shy Guy. He stood patiently a short distance away as she went inside and closed the gate behind her. She could practically feel Madison's anxiety on the other side of the fence.

Hanna was inside the corral with Shy Guy again.

Last time they were here, he almost took her head off. But he didn't move a muscle as she approached him with the halter.

"Now put the front strap of the halter up and over his nose," said Madison, voice barely loud enough to avoid startling Shy Guy. "I wish I could be in there to show you, but I don't think he'd allow it."

"That's okay," said Hanna. "I did it the other day. I remember how." And something told her he wasn't ready to engage with other people yet. He still couldn't be trusted.

Could she even trust him?

The thought flitted through her head so fast it was gone before she could think too hard about it. Hanna focused on bringing the halter strap up behind Shy Guy's ears slowly, so he wouldn't spook, and then buckling it. When she was done, she gently patted the side of his head and he snorted.

"Great job," breathed Madison, unclenching her hands, which had been gripping the metal bars. Her knuckles were white. "Now take the lead rope and lead him around the corral."

To both of their surprise, Shy Guy not only obeyed Hanna's commands, but with Madison doling out instructions, he didn't shy or balk. For all Hanna's novice guiding, Shy Guy knew exactly what he was doing. He stopped when she stopped, maintaining a polite distance. When she turned, he followed, and never pushed or tried to get ahead of her. He backed up at the word *back*. She didn't even have to shake the rope.

"Wow," Hanna heard Madison mutter to herself. "I'm sorry I doubted you, boy."

Eventually, after what felt like a long lesson, Madison stopped her. "Let's call it good while we're ahead. Looks like the tables got turned on me today. Shy Guy gave us a schooling in manners." She shook her head in amazement.

"Do you think he's ready to go in the barn yet?" asked Hanna. The successful lesson left her feeling rather bold. "I feel sorry for him, sitting in this corral alone all day."

Madison's eyebrows rose to her hairline. "I don't know, Hanna. Last time we tried to take him in there, he almost took off Mr. Bridle's arm trying to get away."

Hanna glanced at Shy Guy's gray coat, which was dusty and brown in splotches after all his sweating and running. The locks of hair around his ankles were matted together with mud.

"He's also really dirty," Hanna pointed out.

"Oh man." Madison nervously retied her pony-tail, the same way Hanna did. A resigned sigh escaped her lips. "I suppose we could try. But if he spooks or tries to run, let him go. I made sure the ranch gate was closed this morning."

"Okay," said Hanna. "I will."

Madison shook her head, like she couldn't believe she'd given in. "All right, first things first. Bring him to the gate. Then ask him to wait while you open it. Once you're outside, ask him to walk through, and close it behind you."

Hanna led Shy Guy to the gate, where she lifted the latch and pulled it open. She stepped through and then gestured for Shy Guy to follow. He dipped his head and walked through and turned to face her as she closed the gate behind them. She felt so victorious at the smooth, clean way they moved together that after the gate latched closed, she swung one arm up in the air and clenched her fist.

"Yeah!" she cheered.

Shy Guy threw his head back violently, yanking the lead rope out of Hanna's hand. When Madison jumped over to try to grab the spinning lead rope, he let out a frightened squeal and danced out of her range.

"Wait!" Hanna held up a hand. Madison immediately stopped moving. When she did, Shy Guy settled back down on four legs, breathing hard. "Just wait," Hanna told her. "It's all right." Giving him a moment to calm down, she calmly stepped toward Shy Guy and took the lead rope again.

"I'm sorry," she said, offering the offending hand for him to smell, to remember it wouldn't hurt him. When he didn't move away, she gently ran her hand down his nose. "I didn't mean to frighten you."

But her swinging arm had reminded him—it had brought him back to a time when he was trained, when he had been perfect, and someone had hurt him anyway. Hanna's heart ached.

Madison, taking careful, small steps, came up beside her. Shy Guy eyed her but didn't retreat.

"It's going to be a long, slow road," Madison said, holding out her own hand for him to smell. He jerked his head back, but when Madison didn't fight him or try to tug him closer, Shy Guy eventually stuck out his nose to smell her. After many long seconds, he ran his lips over her hand. Madison jerked back at first but Hanna shook her head.

"Don't worry. He does that when he wants you to pet him."

Even Madison was frightened of Shy Guy? The horse trainer steeled herself, reached out, and ran her palm over the velvety skin of Shy Guy's nose. He nuzzled her back.

Madison's face melted. "Oh, wow. He's soft."

"Isn't he?"

The moments drifted past, the three of them standing in silence while Madison petted Shy Guy. As his eyes closed and he leaned in to her scratches, Madison's eyes filled with unshed tears.

"Let's wait to do the barn tomorrow," she said after a while, her voice catching. "One victory at a time."

CHAPTER TWELVE

After another lesson on groundwork the next day, Madison suggested they take Shy Guy into the barn.

"You're right," she told Hanna. "He could use a good grooming."

Shy Guy put up some resistance at first, but with a full bucket of grain luring him in and Hanna at his side, Shy Guy eventually gave in.

Once they had him in cross ties, Madison talked Hanna through brushing. Starting at his neck with a curry comb, Hanna worked her way down his side, sweeping it in a circular motion. Once she'd stirred up all the dirt, Hanna traded the curry comb for the softer bristle brush. One flick at a time, his muddy gray coat turned silver and glossy until, even under the dim barn lights, he simply glowed.

For a long while, the two girls stared at Shy Guy in awe.

"Dang," said Madison. "That is one fine-looking horse."

Next, it was time to pick his hooves. Hanna had seen the other kids pick their horses' hooves before, and it required holding the horse's hoof close enough to your body to dig out whatever was stuck inside it—which was right inside kicking range.

"You'll be fine," said Madison, with a confidence Hanna did not feel. "It's one of the most essential parts of grooming, as well as trust building. Plus, he needs it. I bet his feet hurt."

Well, then, Hanna decided—she'd do it. She followed Madison's coaching, running her hand down the back of Shy Guy's leg, which, surprisingly, he didn't mind at all. He nudged Hanna's back with his nose, startling her. Was he playing with her?

Sure enough, his hooves were packed full of mud, sand, and even a few large rocks. "Poor Shy Guy," Hanna murmured. She went from hoof to hoof, and to both her and Madison's amazement, he obeyed without question. Hanna hardly had to apply pressure to his ankle—Madison called it his fetlock—to get him to lift it.

When she was done cleaning the final hoof, she set it back down on the ground. Shy Guy put his weight on it, testing it. His body relaxed noticeably, and he nudged Hanna again, as if to say thank you.

"So well-mannered," breathed Madison. "Where did you come from, Shy Guy?"

\\\\\\\\\\\\\\\\\\\\\\\\\\\\\\\\\\\\\\\

Hanna floated on clouds the rest of the day. She hardly remembered the milking lesson that Paul gave them in the cattle barn. When they had free time, Josh invited Hanna to play the bean bag toss with him.

"How's the troubled horse rehab going?" he asked her.

Hanna couldn't help but laugh. "Troubled youth in rehab meets troubled horse in rehab. Never thought about it like that before. But Shy Guy's coming along."

"You make a good pair." He threw his bean bag and completely missed. "Dang," he said. "Didn't realize I was so bad at this when I invited you to play."

"No, it's great," said Hanna with a chuckle. "Keep making throws like that. I like winning."

Josh gave a sheepish smile.

"Usually, I'm a pretty good shot," he said, collecting the bean bags. "You'd never guess, but I play baseball."

"You're right! I wouldn't guess."

Hanna was glad Josh's big laugh showed he hadn't taken her seriously. In the waning afternoon sun, they played until Hanna thought her arm would fall off.

That night in the girls' cabin, they read on their bunk beds in silence until it was time for lights-out.

"Tomorrow we'll do something more exciting with Shy Guy," Madison promised Hanna.

"More exciting?" She wasn't sure she liked the sound of that. "I liked what we did today."

"Good. But there's so much more to horsemanship. From what I saw out there, someone has trained Shy Guy very well." Madison balled one hand into a fist and looked up at the ceiling, like a coach in a football movie who's just found inspiration. "I wish it could be me, Hanna, but you're the one he's chosen to open up to. I have a feeling that if we go slowly, you'll discover some amazing things about that horse."

The lights clicked off, but Hanna lay awake for some time thinking about what Madison had said.

Shy Guy had done so well today—he was obviously a great horse underneath his fear, and eager to please. But what would taking the next step require Hanna to do?

\\

They did more groundwork the next day. And the next. Then one morning, after the other kids had already saddled up and gone outside, Madison stopped Hanna before she could lead Shy Guy out of the barn.

"I want to try something new today," she said cautiously. "What do you say we get a saddle on him?"

Hanna's gut did a leapfrog over her heart.

"You want me to ride?" she asked, her voice more of a squeak.

Madison shook her head. "No, no. Don't worry— this is just a small step to get Shy Guy accustomed to the saddle again. We can't catapult straight into riding. Neither of you are ready for that, anyway."

Hanna could feel she was still making a worried face.

"Seriously," said Madison, half laughing. She patted Hanna's shoulder. "Let's start with a saddle blanket."

Madison vanished into the tack room and returned with a thick, green blanket that matched Shy Guy's green halter.

"It happens this one's the right size," she said, winking. Hanna liked him in that deep, emerald green. Standing a safe distance from the horse, Madison set the blanket on a saddle rack. "Now, this may be a bit tricky, Hanna, if he has bad associations with the saddle—which he likely does after the saddle sores we found on him."

Hanna understood. Lifting the blanket off the rack, she carried it over to Shy Guy.

His ears pricked toward her, and she held out the blanket for him to smell. His head jerked away, nostrils flaring, and the lead rope snapped tight.

Suddenly the space in the barn became very small. What if he tried to bolt?

"It's okay, boy," said Hanna, taking the blanket away again.

"Here," said Madison, dumping a handful of horse treats in Hanna's hand. "Try giving him one of these while you let him smell it. Positive reinforcement!"

It was worth a try. With a treat in one hand,

Hanna held out the blanket again for Shy Guy's inspection. He sniffed the blanket for only a second before smelling the offered treat and lipping it up.

"Now, slowly, touch his side with it," said Madison. "Get him used to how it feels. Stay by his shoulder."

Holding the blanket in clear sight, Hanna took a step down Shy Guy's side and held it out so the edge barely touched him. She moved the blanket back and forth a little, so he could get a good sense of the texture and fabric. His ears flattened against his head.

"Give him another treat," encouraged Madison. Shy Guy lipped Hanna's hand before eating the treat out of her palm. His ears relaxed, and Hanna lifted the blanket higher on his back.

"Can you give him the treat so I can use both hands?" Hanna asked. "The blanket's too bulky."

Again, the nervousness on Madison's face surprised Hanna. But she held out the treat to Shy Guy and he slurped it up as Hanna slid the blanket over his back. His ears flicked in her direction, but that was all.

Hanna let out a heavy breath. "Wow," she said. "All that to get the blanket on?"

"I know it doesn't look like much, but this is a big step for Shy Guy. We couldn't even get a brush near him before."

\\\

After taking the blanket off, they worked with Shy Guy in the corral.

"Trust building," Madison told her. "One step at a time."

Every day, they put the saddle blanket on and took it off again, until Shy Guy stopped putting up a fuss. Then Madison dragged a saddle out of the tack room.

First, she demonstrated putting a saddle on her smaller Appaloosa horse, Snow White, so Hanna could see how it was done.

Adjusting Shy Guy to the saddle was easier than adjusting him to the blanket. Even when the saddle settled on Shy Guy's back, he appeared only mildly irritated. It wasn't until she tightened the cinch that he went over the edge.

Shy Guy broke free of her grasp, and arching his back, he jumped a foot straight up in the air. Hanna yelped. Madison pulled her out of the way as he crow-hopped again, almost running into the barn wall.

"Shy Guy!" Hanna squeaked. She wanted to pet him, to calm him down, but Madison kept her back.

"Let him work it out."

Shy Guy hopped side to side, desperate to get the saddle off—but it wouldn't budge. Soon he gave up and settled for standing uncomfortably with his ears pressed back, his tail flicking in obvious irritation, like a cat.

"Well, that's good progress considering where we started," said Madison.

"Why did he do that?"

She shook her head sadly. "Someone worked him hard with a saddle that didn't fit—probably didn't brush him down properly either. Every time he wore that saddle, it rubbed until his skin was raw."

Hanna wanted to take the saddle off him right then. "Is it hurting him now?"

"Oh, no. But now he associates the cinch tightening with pain to come, even if there isn't any. We just have to show him we know what we're doing." Madison pointed off to the other arena. "Let's go walk him around a bit and see how those other goofballs are doing."

Leading Shy Guy in a halter, the saddle still

on his back, they walked along the outside of the practice ring where Fletch was working with the other four kids. "Izzy!" he shouted as Izzy galloped past him. "Stop running around. We're trying to do an exercise here."

"Poor Fletch." Madison shook her head. "Izzy's enough to handle all on her own." When the other kids spotted Hanna and Shy Guy, they stopped what they were doing.

"Hey, Hanna!" Josh waved. "Looking great."

Hanna had no idea if he meant her or her horse, so she just smiled and waved back.

Izzy and Fettucini jogged over, making Shy Guy dance away from the fence.

"Izzy, don't scare him," called Fletch.

"Sorry!" Izzy reined in Fettucini, and the gelding patiently stepped back from the fence. "That's cool that you got a saddle on him."

"Yep," said Hanna, running a hand down Shy Guy's neck to calm him down. Once he was settled, she continued walking him along the fence line.

"Izzy, can you leave them alone?" asked Fletch, not trying to hide the impatience in his voice. "They're doing important training."

Disappointment settled on Izzy's small features.

"Okay, fine," she said, turning Fettucini back toward the others and trotting over to where they had lined up to practice the keyhole event.

Taking her turn, Rae Ann slowly walked her horse over to the four poles arranged in a square, passed into the middle, turned around, and walked out again.

"Come on, Rae Ann," said Fletch, sounding exasperated. "You can trot through it, at least. You're allowed to trot."

"I don't like trotting." Her stocky bay horse didn't much look like it liked trotting either.

"Sorry, Fletch!" Madison called to him, though her grin didn't make her appear sorry. "I think Hanna and Shy Guy could be ready to join the group sometime soon."

Hanna's head shot up. "Really?" she asked as they headed back to the barn. Shy Guy snorted. "You think we'll be ready?" She half wanted to hear Madison say *yes* and half wanted to hear *no*.

"I sure do," said Madison.

CHAPTER THIRTEEN

Hanna got garden duty again that afternoon, but when she showed up with her water bottle and trowel at the garden, it wasn't Josh who was waiting for her.

It was Izzy.

When Hanna stepped into the dirt, Izzy shot up to her feet and shoved both her hands behind her back.

"Hey, Hanna!" she chirped, too brightly.

"Hey," Hanna said, putting down her water bottle. What was Izzy up to now? "What'cha got there?" she asked.

Izzy glanced around like Hanna meant something other than what she was holding behind her back. "What do you mean?"

"I mean, what are you hiding behind your back, Izzy?"

Izzy's eyes darkened and a shiver ran up Hanna's spine.

"Nothing," she said quickly. "Gotta go. I have to use the bathroom."

"But we just got here." They stared at each other for a long moment. Then, with a defeated sigh, Izzy extended her right hand and opened it.

Lying in her palm was a phone and a pair of tangled earbuds.

"You're not supposed to have any electronics," Hanna said.

"I know. That's why I was hiding it, dork." Izzy rolled her eyes. "It doesn't get service out here, but I really wanted to listen to the Lawn-chairs. I used to play them all the time when I gardened with my dad."

"The Lawnchairs?" Hanna took the player and earbuds before Izzy could hide them again. "You know them?"

"What? And you do?"

"Yeah. Of course." How could Izzy possibly know the Lawnchairs too? "They're a little band out of my hometown."

Izzy gaped at her. "You're from Sturgis?"

"Yeah. I didn't think anyone else outside of Sturgis knew they existed. It's the same band, right? Maybe there are two with the same name."

"Nope." Izzy fervently shook her head. "The two girls, right? One does keyboard and sings. The other does guitar."

"Oh man, Noelle can shred! You know that song by them, 'Bonfire'?"

Izzy's face lit up. "Yeah! 'Bonfire' is one of my favorites! I heard it at my friend's house once, and I've loved them since." She pointed at herself. "Diehard fan."

"No way," Hanna breathed. "That's wild. I didn't know anyone else had even heard of them."

"Well, I have."

Hanna popped in one earbud and offered Izzy the other. Surprised, she took it and put it in her ear.

"Press PLAY," Izzy said. "I was only on the first song of the album."

When she tapped the screen, lyrics belted into Hanna's ear. "Mariah has such a cool voice," she murmured.

"I know. She can go so low! She sounds like a dude sometimes."

"Right? It's awesome." The guitar swelled and then gave way to keyboard synths.

"Here," said Izzy, taking the phone and changing the song. "'Bonfire' is great, don't get me wrong, but this is actually my favorite song on this album."

A song came on that Hanna hadn't heard in ages—not since that first day she stole something, when she took that first stolen candy bar out of her pocket. Hanna hadn't even wanted to eat it. She just enjoyed getting away with it. She'd thought, *This is the worst thing I could possibly do. If Mom found out, she'd never get on my case for something stupid ever again.*

After that, she'd done it a second time. And a third. At the grocery store, in a gas station. What Hanna loved most was operating right under her mom's nose, knowing how much she'd flip if she found out.

Izzy was watching Hanna's face carefully when the song ended.

"You're not going to tell on me, are you?" she asked. "For having the phone?"

"Is that why you were hiding it?"

"Duh. You already have dirt on me from when I . . ." Izzy stopped, pressing her lips together in a hard line. "Well, you know."

Right. When she almost got Hanna killed.

"Please don't tell," said Izzy. "I'm sure Madison would tell my parents, and they'd shake their heads just like they do when I come home with a pink slip."

"You get in trouble a lot?" asked Hanna.

Izzy shrugged. "I guess. My teachers in Arizona are dumb and so is everyone else at school. So I tell them that. And sometimes follow it up with a punch. I mean, not the teachers. Yet."

"Wow," said Hanna, eyes widening. Izzy was small, but Hanna still wouldn't want a fist in the face from her.

"But why?" Hanna asked. "Doesn't punching someone kinda . . . hurt? And don't you get in trouble?"

"If you do it wrong, it hurts," said Izzy. "And whatever. I didn't mind the pink slips that much."

"You like getting in trouble?"

"Sure. Sometimes. I have three sisters. Sometimes putting a pink slip in front of my dad is the only way to get his attention for more than five seconds."

Hanna understood that feeling more than she was willing to admit.

She could tell on Izzy for the phone. Hanna liked Ma Etty and Madison and everyone else, and disobeying their rules didn't sit well. But something about Izzy smuggling this in, right under everyone's noses, to listen to her favorite band—well, it was brave.

Plus, Hanna really liked the Lawnchairs.

"Well," she said, tapping her chin. "I guess I won't tell. But only if you let me listen in while we pull these weeds."

Izzy's smile was huge and white and bright as the sun. Hanna couldn't help smiling back.

"Okay," Izzy agreed. "Keep an eye out for anyone coming to check on us, though."

"All right." They stooped in the dirt and scooted closer together so they could share the earbuds. Then Izzy pressed PLAY on the next song.

They listened to the album three times through before the sun dipped behind the mountains and Madison called them in for dinner.

\\\

Hanna and Madison repeated the process of getting Shy Guy used to the blanket—but with the saddle. They put on the saddle, tightened the cinch, and waited while Shy Guy bucked out his anxiety. Then they walked him around before taking it off again.

After a week of this, he endured saddling with far less fuss. The day that he accepted the saddle without even pinning his ears back, Madison suggested they start out learning how to put on a bridle with an easier horse.

"I want you to try it a few times on Lacey and get it right before attempting to put a bridle on Shy Guy," she told Hanna as they entered the barn. "Think you can handle it?"

Hanna considered it. Already this summer, she'd fallen into a corral with a huge, frightened, stampeding horse. She'd ridden emergency double with Izzy, of all people. Hanna could put a bridle on a little sleepy pony like Lacey.

Sure enough, Lacey practically slept through it. When Hanna had successfully gotten the bridle on and off twice by herself, she realized she'd done the whole thing without any trepidation at all.

Madison clapped her on the shoulder and said, "Great job. I think you've got the nuts and bolts. Let's try it on our guy."

Once they'd put Lacey away, Hanna went to Shy Guy's stall door and lifted the green halter off the hook. He snorted and excitedly thrust his head toward her over the door.

"He's always so excited to see us," said Hanna, giving in to Shy Guy's demands for scratches.

"It's probably been a long time since a human treated him as well as you do."

After Hanna took him out of the stall, they went through the saddle routine again. Then it was time for the bridle.

Hanna walked through the steps of removing the halter. She let Shy Guy smell the leather reins of the bridle before putting them over his neck. When it came time to put the bit in his mouth, Hanna faltered. Getting her hands close to Lacey's mouth hadn't bothered her—Lacey didn't have a history of biting.

"You can do it," urged Madison. What if he didn't open for it? She didn't want to put her fingers in his mouth to make him open.

Taking a deep breath, Hanna pressed the bit to Shy Guy's lips.

His mouth opened immediately.

Hanna pushed the bit inside and pulled the bridle up and over his ears. When it was secure, she buckled the chin strap.

"Whew," she said, wiping her forehead.

"See?" said Madison. "No problem. Let's walk

him around again. Then we'll do some exercises in the corral to get him moving a little. He could use it." Without thinking about it, Madison patted Shy Guy's belly.

He let out a squeal and swung his body away, knocking over the wooden saddle stand. Hanna jumped and Madison stepped back, saying, "Whoa! Whoa, boy."

Hanna was shaking when Shy Guy, breathing hard, finally settled down.

Madison looked positively ashamed. "Sorry about that," she said, righting the saddle stand. "It's easy to forget since you started working with Shy Guy that he's still afraid of most people."

When her heartbeat returned to normal, Hanna picked up the fallen reins.

"No problem," she said. They all stood quietly, letting the charge of the moment drain away.

"You know, though," Madison said quietly, "he's come really far." She turned to Hanna. "And so have you. Do you think you're ready for your first riding lesson tomorrow?"

Hanna's stomach sank like a stone tossed in a lake. "R–riding lesson?"

Riding was what they'd been preparing for, after

all. She imagined sitting astride magnificent Shy Guy, galloping down a quiet country road, his silver hair flowing in the same wind as her blonde hair.

But in the same daydream, something startled him, and he reared up, beating the air with his hooves, tossing Hanna from his back like a sack of potatoes.

Shy Guy wouldn't hurt her intentionally, she reminded herself. But could she trust him anyway?

Madison looked reassuring. "Your first few lessons won't be on Shy Guy, of course. We'll start you on Lacey till you're more comfortable in the saddle."

Hanna couldn't speak.

"Think about it, and you can decide tomorrow," said Madison. "That horse has made a lot of progress, but you're the only person he trusts. I don't mean to pressure you—it's your choice, Hanna—but if anyone's going to be able to ride him again, it'll be you."

No pressure, indeed. Hanna tried to swallow the tight lump that had formed in her throat, but failed.

Hanna!

It was her mom's voice.

Hanna, honey, why are you crying?

You've always loved horses. I don't understand.

Hanna, please. You're embarrassing me.
It's not time to get off the horses yet.
Hanna.
Please.
Stop crying.

CHAPTER FOURTEEN

Around the dinner table everyone but Hanna was in a good mood, swapping funny vacation stories over Mr. Bridle's "famous" eggplant lasagna. Hanna brooded as she picked apart the slippery layers of noodles.

Madison was right. Shy Guy didn't trust anyone else. And Hanna couldn't very well ask Madison to try him out first—she could get hurt. Hanna had to learn how to ride.

"Eggplant not your thing?" Ma Etty asked, startling Hanna.

"No, no," she said, and made a point of taking a big bite. "The eggplant's fine. I'm not that hungry."

"What are you thinking about?" Ma Etty asked.

Hanna let out a stuttering breath. "Madison wants me to ride tomorrow. But . . ." She dropped her fork to her plate. "I don't think I can do it."

"What do you mean?" Ma Etty shot her a look of pure surprise. "Of course you can."

"What if I get thrown? What if—"

"Did what-ifs stop you when Shy Guy got out of the corral?"

"No."

"Then why let nerves stop you this time? Shy Guy needs you as much now as he did then."

Hanna's brow creased. "Needs me?"

"Absolutely," said Ma Etty. "Everyone deserves a second chance—even Shy Guy. Especially Shy Guy. He has so much potential. How sad would it be if he was never ridden again? If he spent the rest of his days in a pasture—exercised occasionally in a pen and otherwise forgotten about?"

Hanna hadn't thought of it like that. She'd been so focused on herself, on her own fears and well-being, that she hadn't considered how Shy Guy must feel. He was so well-trained, so eager to please. What a shame to waste a great horse.

"I just don't know," said Hanna. The time she'd

ridden Fettucini had been an emergency.

This wasn't. And she was scared.

"Get a feel for the saddle with Lacey tomorrow," said Ma Etty. "And give it some thought. Seems to me that you're Shy Guy's best chance to be the horse we both know he can be."

\\\

The whole walk from the ranch house to the barn the next morning, Hanna kept reminding herself: *I'm giving Shy Guy a second chance. I'm learning to ride for his sake.*

"So let's talk about mounting," said Madison, once they'd gotten little Lacey out of her stall. "You always want to mount on the left. She should stand still for you—if she starts to move, stop and resituate her before you try getting on again. Put one foot in the stirrup and pull yourself up by the horn."

Trying to remember all of these instructions, Hanna walked around Lacey's front so she was standing on her left side. Taking a deep breath, she put one hand on the horn, one foot in the stirrup, and hauled herself up into the seat.

Lacey yawned.

Hanna settled into the saddle and was surprised to find the fear she'd expected had dulled and faded, like well-worn jeans.

Madison passed Hanna the reins. "Okay. Let's start real easy, with a walk, and we'll go from there."

\\\

The landscape of the ranch changed dramatically atop a horse. The sun shone brighter, and the pasture spread out even farther, like a green shag carpet. Even that big, lumpy butte took on a shimmery halo during Hanna's morning riding lessons.

Riding turned out to be far less stressful than she'd expected. Then again, riding Lacey was a bit like sitting in the car when her grandmother drove. Slow, steady, and kind of boring.

Madison never pressured her to do more than she could. Hanna could get off whenever she wanted. The first time they tried a trot, the fast bouncing frightened Hanna so much that she had to have Madison help her off the horse's back. She stood, shaking, until she grew calm enough to try again.

After another circuit of the corral, bouncing crazily, Hanna decided she didn't particularly like the trot.

"Don't hold onto the horn," Madison kept telling her. "You're not going to fall off!"

"I feel like I am!" Hanna would shout back.

Over the next few days, Hanna learned how to turn, back up, and ask for a trot and a canter, all while they worked on her posture and control. The lessons were intensive, but Hanna was determined to become the best rider she could for Shy Guy.

After her lesson every day, though she was tired from riding and brushing down Lacey and putting her away, Hanna and Madison would still tack up and work out Shy Guy in the corral. Madison taught her how to use the longe line to exercise him, and they discovered that Shy Guy understood every verbal command that Madison had stored up.

Madison shook her head. "I can't tell if it's him or the Hanoverian in him," she said.

"What?"

"He's perfectly obedient. He'll do whatever you ask, when you ask it." Madison shook her head. "I'll never understand why someone hit a horse like Shy Guy. Honestly."

Hanna didn't either.

After a week of longeing Shy Guy almost every day, Madison said, "How about tomorrow?"

"What about tomorrow?" asked Hanna.

"I think it's time to try riding him. So how about tomorrow?"

Right. The real test and the reason for all this.

"Think about it," Madison said. "But in my professional opinion, you're both ready to try."

Hanna made herself nod, but she couldn't even force out a *yes*.

\\\

Breakfast the next day was a blur. Rae Ann moaned about missing her cat back in Vermont. Josh and Cade were arguing about video games. Hanna wasn't listening. Instead, she was chewing one of her nails down to the bed when someone tapped her on the shoulder.

"You okay?" It was Izzy, collecting dishes. "You're white in the face. I mean, uh, whiter than usual."

Hanna couldn't help but laugh at that. It came out tremulous and shaky.

"I'm thinking."

Izzy scooped up her dish. "About what?"

Why did she want to know? "I'm going to ride Shy Guy today," said Hanna.

The dishes clattered as Izzy almost dropped them. "Whoa. That's a big step."

"I know."

"Here, I gotta go put these in the kitchen, but wait up for me." Before Hanna could say anything, Izzy twirled and flew away, making a ruckus in the kitchen as she deposited the dishes.

"It's your day to load the dishwasher, Izzy," Hanna heard Ma Etty say.

"Dang it!" A faucet ran.

"You have to get the food off them first!" A loud sigh. "Let me do it, Izzy. Go on. I know you're itching to ride."

Ma Etty was too nice to them. Izzy jogged back out of the kitchen.

"Come on," she said, grabbing Hanna by the arm and dragging her out ahead of the others, saying she wanted to talk in peace.

Talk? All they'd done was listen to the Lawnchairs together. For three hours. Okay, sure, they had laughed a lot about riding their horses and how cute Josh was. And sure, Izzy was a real joker, and most of the laughing was on Hanna's end as they pulled weeds to the thrumming of Noelle's guitar. But that didn't make them friends.

"You've already decided to do it, right?" Izzy prompted. "So why are you thinking about it?"

"What if he bucks? What if he rears?" Hanna rubbed her head. "What if I fall off?"

"So what? Wear a helmet. The worst that can happen is your butt gets a little bruised." Izzy shrugged as they approached the barn, and they opened the double doors together. "And Madison's helping you. What have you got to be afraid of?"

Everything, Hanna wanted to say. But for once, Izzy was right. She had Madison. This part was up to Hanna. No one else could ride Shy Guy for her.

And though she didn't want to admit it, she wanted to be the girl riding on his back with the wind flowing through her hair.

Eventually Fletch, Madison, Cade, Josh, and Rae Ann caught up to them in the barn.

"Change of plans, guys," said Fletch. "I know it's inconvenient, but I'm going to do a demonstration in the small corral today with my horse, Sawbones, so Hanna and Shy Guy can use the big arena." He glanced at Hanna. "That is, if you're still planning to ride today?"

Her throat had stopped working, and Hanna had to swallow three or four times before she could talk.

"Yes," she managed. "I am."

"Why does she get the whole practice arena?" asked Cade, puffing out his bottom lip.

Madison started, "Because—"

"Because she and Shy Guy need space, that's why!" Izzy glowered at Cade. He shrank back, even though she was probably a foot shorter than he was. "It's the first time he's been ridden by anybody in a long time, and the other horses make him nervous. Okay?"

"Okay, right, sorry!"

Madison and Fletch exchanged a look as Fletch led the kids out of the barn. Izzy was the last one to leave, and she flashed Hanna a thumbs-up on her way out.

"Before we do this," Madison said, getting a conspiratorial look in her eyes, "I want to give you something, Hanna."

She ducked into the tack room and rifled through a box of papers, pulling out a manila envelope. She handed it to Hanna and, like a kid who had worked hard on a homemade Christmas gift, said, "Open it!"

Hanna tore open the top and pulled out a heavy piece of metal. She turned it over. It was a gold nameplate with "Shy Guy" etched into it.

Her chest constricted. Madison's grin grew about as wide as her face.

"Will you do the honors of putting it on his stall?" she asked.

"Of course," Hanna whispered.

Together, they mounted the plate right in the middle of the door. It shimmered under the barn lights.

"Your patience and kindness brought Shy Guy to where he is now," said Madison. "So, are you ready to ride?" The look on her face was full of encouragement but underneath, a little trepidation.

Hanna nodded. "Ready as I'll ever be."

CHAPTER FIFTEEN

By the time Hanna was done with tacking up Shy Guy, he looked beautiful. Like a horse in a TV show.

He was ready to ride.

Madison led them out the back of the barn to the arena, where all the barrels and poles had been removed to leave an open, unthreatening space. Hanna swallowed and gripped the helmet in her hand tighter. She'd have to make sure that Madison put on the straps extra tight.

Just a bruised butt, she reminded herself. Walking beside Shy Guy, she was painfully aware of his massive size; of the muscles that rippled along his shoulders and his flanks; and of his heavy, sturdy hoofbeats.

But all that didn't frighten her anymore. When this thought made its way to the top, a surge of warm victory swept over her.

If Shy Guy did throw her, it wouldn't be on purpose. It would be out of fear or surprise or the multitude of other things that haunted an abused animal. She knew how unpredictable the ghost inside oneself could be.

Hanna put on the helmet, buckled the strap, and tightened it all on her own.

"Looks good," said Madison, rattling the helmet around on Hanna's head to test it. "Get on whenever you're ready. And please," she emphasized, concern seeping into her voice, "take your time. Stop if anything seems off."

Leading them over to a mounting block, Madison held the reins—though Shy Guy was suspicious of her at first—as Hanna picked up the stirrup in one hand.

"Here goes," Hanna said. She climbed up on the block and stuck her left foot in the stirrup. Shy Guy glanced back at her, ears perked, but he didn't move away.

Hanna reached for the horn and put all her weight in the stirrup. The saddle tilted slightly as she pushed up and swung her right leg over Shy Guy's back.

She settled back down, both feet in the stirrups. Shy Guy hadn't moved a muscle. Relief cascaded over Hanna.

"Wow," said Madison. "I can't believe it. We're really going to do this."

Frankly, Hanna couldn't believe it either. But the hard part was yet to come.

\\\

"Make sure you leave the reins a little slack," said Madison. "No, that's too much." She reached for the reins to adjust them, and Shy Guy's head swung away. Hanna let out a yelp as he jostled underneath her.

"Whoa," said Madison, backing away with her hands up. "Whoa, boy. Okay—you'll have to do all this on your own, Hanna. I can only give you instructions."

Hanna was still breathing hard from the shock of Shy Guy moving so suddenly. She tried to straighten her back and fix her posture to calm herself down. She would only frighten Shy Guy if she was afraid herself.

"Good," encouraged Madison. "Confidence will go a long way on a horse. Now ask him to walk."

Hanna lightly nudged Shy Guy with her heels,

and he started into a slow walk. Her breath caught in her throat.

He walked with a smooth, even gait, completely unlike Lacey's. Each step was controlled and fluid. It felt like floating.

She couldn't believe it. She was riding Shy Guy!

"Great job, Hanna," called Madison as they headed away. "Walk along the fence for a while, then try turning him."

When Hanna and Shy Guy had walked the entire circumference of the arena a few times, she pulled the reins across Shy Guy's neck to the left, to take him into the middle.

He balked for a second, as if he had forgotten what a bit in his mouth felt like. Hanna felt panic rise up in her, but she tamped it down and pulled the reins to the left again.

This time, his head followed. His whole body moved in the same direction, making him curve under her. He moved fluidly, like a snake, as she righted him again and they headed for the center of the arena. Madison stepped out of the way as they passed her.

Hanna had done it. She had asked him to turn, and he did. She was breathless with elation.

"Great!" Madison called after them, her voice laced with genuine surprise. "Looking really, really good. Keep on with the basic maneuvers."

Hanna and Shy Guy did another half of a lap, and then she turned him to the right. His right side was a little tougher than his left, but after a few tries, he turned and swept gracefully back into the center of the arena.

"Wow," said Madison. "He moves so smoothly. I wonder if he was trained in dressage."

"Dressage?" asked Hanna, as she and Shy Guy made another reverse figure eight.

"It's a high-level kind of English-style riding," she said. "It's mainly about the bond and communication between horse and rider, because they have to work together to do a series of complex movements. Requires a lot of skill. A good dressage horse is ultra responsive and graceful, so all the movements look effortless."

"Cool. So how do you know he was trained to do that?"

"I don't, but look at the way he responds to your cues," Madison said. "He's paying very close attention to you. So do you feel comfortable walking and doing basic turns?"

Hanna glanced down. She had forgotten she was even on a horse. Riding Shy Guy felt natural, easy. Like walking on her own two feet.

"I think so," she said.

"Great! Let's try taking him to a trot, then."

Hanna swallowed. She hated the bouncy trot and hoped she could keep it together.

Letting out some slack in the reins and leaning just the tiniest bit forward, she barely moved her feet before Shy Guy suddenly picked up his pace. Hanna held in a yelp, not wanting to frighten him.

But . . . his trot wasn't scary. And it certainly wasn't bumpy. Shy Guy simply slid into a longer walk, his legs reaching farther with each step— incredibly far, as if he were swimming through air.

"Holy cow," muttered Madison, watching them with golf ball-sized eyes as they passed her. "What even is that? An extended trot? How did you do that?"

"I don't know!" cried Hanna. They cruised, like a yacht on still water, around the arena. Whatever Shy Guy was doing, it didn't feel anything like Lacey's trot. Hanna's breaths grew shaky and uneven as she wondered what she'd done wrong.

But then a look of pure glee came over

Madison's face. "Here, Hanna—try this." She held out her hands. "Hold the reins tighter, and sit back a tiny bit."

"Tighter?" Hanna gathered up some of the slack in the reins and instantly, Shy Guy slowed down—but kept trotting. Hanna let out a squeak as she flew up on the saddle, her feet still tucked in the stirrups. She came back down, hard.

"Yowch!"

"Sorry!" called Madison. "Try matching his gait. Hanoverians are special-bred for smooth, predictable trots. When he goes up, let your natural bounce take you up too. Get in his rhythm."

Hanna had no idea what Madison meant, but as Shy Guy trotted around the arena, she tried to match her bounce to his. It took a few laps, but soon she wasn't hitting the saddle quite as hard—though she was sure she'd be bruised tomorrow.

Madison was shaking her head, and for a moment, Hanna thought she was disappointed or maybe angry. But when Madison looked up again, Hanna saw wonder on the trainer's face.

"I had no idea," she said, gesturing for the two of them to ride into the center of the arena. Hanna pulled the reins across Shy Guy's neck, and he immediately changed directions at a trot. "Now lean back to stop. You shouldn't even need to pull on the reins—sit back in your saddle and—"

Hanna adjusted her weight so she was sitting deep in the saddle, and Shy Guy ground to a complete halt. She was panting, and so was he.

The emotions came in a torrent. She had ridden Shy Guy. They had glided across the arena, together.

Before she could stop it, tears were rolling down her cheeks in big, messy streams.

Hanna collapsed forward on Shy Guy, wrapping her arms as far as they'd go around his huge neck. He turned his head slightly so she could reach his ears, and she rubbed behind them, not even caring about the saddle horn digging into her diaphragm. Her tears fell hot on his mane, disappearing in the silver-gray hairs.

"Oh, Hanna." Madison approached them slowly, but Shy Guy ignored her. Madison touched Hanna's knee reassuringly. "That was wild. I am so impressed. I can't believe how well you did. And you got him into an extended trot! I've never seen anything like that outside of dressage on TV. What did you do?"

"No idea," Hanna said. "He just . . . did it. I must have asked for it without knowing."

Carefully, Madison reached for Shy Guy's neck. He eyeballed her but didn't move away. With the gentlest of motions, Madison ran her hand through his long mane.

"What a horse," she said.

CHAPTER SIXTEEN

The rest of the day was a blur for Hanna. She couldn't stop smiling, and it was infectious. When the other kids heard the news, they clapped her on the back. At dinner, Mr. Bridle raised his water glass.

"Everyone," he said in his low, gravelly voice, "I'd like to propose a toast."

"A toast!" echoed Madison.

"To Hanna and Shy Guy. Congratulations on your first ride today."

Hanna felt her entire body turn red as everyone turned to look at her, also raising their glasses.

"To Hanna and Shy Guy," they repeated, clinking their glasses together. Rae Ann grinned at her.

Cade stopped studying his fingernails. Josh even brandished a rare smile. And everyone made a point of clinking Hanna's glass.

\\

In the girls' cabin late that night, after Madison had turned the lights out and gone into her room, Izzy whispered in the darkness.

"Hanna?" she said. "Are you awake?"

Before she replied, Hanna listened for Rae Ann's breathing. It was even and regular. She was asleep.

"Yeah?" Hanna finally answered.

"I . . ." She heard Izzy inhale sharply. "I'm sorry. I'm sorry I was mean to you. You're . . . you're actually pretty nice. And brave. And I kind of spied on you when you were riding today."

"You did?"

"You looked really cool out there. Way cooler than me. You . . . you're a natural."

Hanna swallowed hard.

"Thank you," she whispered into the dark.

"Whatever," said Izzy gruffly. "It's the truth."

\\

When Hanna and Shy Guy joined the other kids for their daily lesson a few days later, Madison warned them to keep some distance, just in case. But under a saddle, Shy Guy was confident. Sturdy.

Fearless.

Even when a barn cat got into the arena and frightened the other horses—especially Josh's horse, whom he hollered at in his Tennessee accent as it spooked and ran—Shy Guy stood his ground.

Hanna got him up to a canter that same day, and she couldn't hold back a shriek of excitement when they shot across the arena. Shy Guy's legs extended far out in front of him; it felt like they were flying.

"There it is again!" shouted Madison, grabbing Fletch's arm and pointing. "See? He can extend his canter too."

"Whoa." He took off his hat. "What in the name of . . .? Who trained him to do that?"

"Who knows," said Madison. Hanna blushed under their words, even though she knew it had nothing to do with her. It was all Shy Guy—a jewel hidden in plain sight.

When Hanna led Shy Guy through the barrel pattern, everyone cheered. Shy Guy strutted after that, like he knew he was a big shot.

Hanna could see she had a ham on her hands.

On Saturday, Madison and Fletch decided to let them skip chores and go on a trail ride into town for ice cream.

"Ice cream!" cried Izzy, flopping back on Fettucini as if he were a lawn chair. "I would kill for some cake batter ice cream. Or cookie dough."

"Hopefully you won't have to kill anyone," said Fletch, dropping his hat on Izzy's face as he rode past. "Because I'm pretty sure they have both."

"Woo-hoo!" Izzy turned to Hanna. "What's your favorite kind of ice cream? Do you think Shy Guy likes ice cream?"

Madison held up her hands. "I hate to break it to you, girls," she said, "but Hanna can't bring Shy Guy. If you want to come on the trail ride, Hanna, you'll have to ride Lacey."

"What?" asked Izzy. "But Shy Guy has been doing great in the arena."

Hanna understood, though. Trekking into a town full of cars and people would terrify Shy Guy. Could she handle him if something happened?

"I know, Izzy," said Madison. "It's not that I don't trust Hanna or Shy Guy. There are too many factors in play if we take him into town, and he's still so skittish . . ."

"From what I've seen, Maddie," Fletch offered, "Shy Guy is a different animal with someone in the saddle." Fletch leaned back, leaving Sawbones's reins hanging over the horse's freckled neck. "He's not faint of heart, and he listens to Hanna without question. Remember when Shy Guy didn't even blink at that cat?"

"That's true," Madison allowed.

"He's the kind of horse that respects confidence." Fletch looked hard at Hanna. "Whenever you tell him what to do and he listens, he's passing the authority to you. He's putting his life in your hands. He believes in you so much, Hanna. You could blindfold a horse like Shy Guy and he'd do whatever you told him, trusting you not to walk him over a cliff."

"I'd never do that," gasped Hanna.

"Of course not. But you see my point?"

"Yeah."

"You're in control. You decide what goes. Whether he spooks on this ride is up to you." Fletch arched one eyebrow and leaned forward. "Do you feel confident, Hanna?"

Was that all it took? Confidence?

"Yes," she said, her own certainty surprising

her. But she was—she had total confidence in Shy Guy now. She could feel the connection between them, the trust they'd forged, every time she sat in the saddle.

Fletch threw a grin at Madison and shrugged his shoulders, like he'd proven his point. Madison made an annoyed, thinking noise.

"Okay," she said eventually. "Fine. If you think you can handle it, Hanna, Shy Guy can come with us."

"I know I can," Hanna said. "And so can he."

"Awesome!" Izzy whooped. Every horse startled at the noise except Shy Guy. Madison just shook her head.

Getting out on the road with Shy Guy was a different tin of sardines from riding in the arena. But Hanna had trusted in Shy Guy so far, and look how far they'd come.

\\

Madison, riding her spotted horse, and Fletch, with his freckly red roan, led the group off Bridlemile Road and onto a special trail that crisscrossed the patchwork of farms and ranches of Quartz Creek, far from the highway. At its opposite end, the trail spilled out right onto downtown Main Street.

"Everyone rode horses here at one time," said Fletch, pointing out the tie poles scattered all over town. "You'd ride up to the General Store, tie up your horse, and do your grocery shopping."

People waved at them as they walked down the street. Cars slowed down and gave them a wide berth. Shy Guy walked with his head high, unperturbed by vehicles or people or pavement. As they arrived at the ice-cream shop and tied up their horses, Fletch winked at Hanna and said, "Told you."

Hanna and Fletch stayed with the horses while the others went in for ice cream. Izzy promised to get Hanna's order for her.

All the Quartz Creek Ranchers ate together outside. Rae Ann somehow managed to get ice cream on Cade's face, and Izzy practically inhaled hers.

"How on earth did you do that so fast?" asked Josh.

"I don't get brain freezes." To demonstrate, Izzy took Madison's leftover ice cream and sank her teeth directly into it. Everyone winced.

Hanna wasn't watching. She studied Shy Guy, who simply stood tied by the other horses, lazily swatting flies with his tail. As she finished her ice cream, she felt buoyant, like a balloon rising into the sky.

\\

During dinner that night, a car came grumbling down the driveway. Conversation at the table halted.

"Are we expecting anyone, honey?" Mr. Bridle asked his wife.

Ma Etty shook her head. "No—not that I know of. But it could be the Goodsteins."

Mr. Bridle rose to his feet and peered out the dining room window. "Not Jim's truck," he said.

No one spoke as the car pulled into the parking lot. Mr. Bridle and Ma Etty got up to answer it. The air buzzed with anticipation. No one had come to the ranch this late before, especially not unannounced.

After a long, loaded silence, a knock came at the door. In the other room, the door creaked as it opened.

"Hello," Hanna heard Mr. Bridle say. "What can I help you with at this hour?" He stressed *this hour*, as if to impress upon the visitor that the late visit was unwelcome.

Heeled shoes clicked on the wood floors. Izzy got out of her chair and scurried to look.

"Izzy!" Madison hissed, but Izzy ignored her, peering into the living room.

"My name is Elena Baxter," boomed a woman's voice, sharp and steely. "This is my husband, John Curry."

Josh followed Izzy, peering over her short head.

"Josh!" Fletch tried this time, but the kids couldn't be stopped. Eventually, Rae Ann and Cade got up too, and soon Madison and Fletch couldn't help their curiosity either. Hanna was the last to join them in the doorway, openly staring at the couple who had arrived on the ranch's doorstep.

The woman stood as tall as Mr. Bridle and thin, dressed in a white, billowy blouse and dark-washed jeans. Everything on her gleamed, from her flashy earrings to her faux crocodile skin boots. Her husband, a stout, older man with a deeply receded hairline, huddled behind her.

"What can we help you with this evening, Ms. Baxter?" asked Ma Etty, her politeness almost sounding genuine.

"We're here about our horse."

"Pardon me, but what horse?" asked Ma Etty. "I

don't know you, and neither do I know your animals."

"Yes, you do. You have my horse, Star Dancer."

Ma Etty shook her head. "Sorry," she said. "There's no horse here named Star Dancer."

Elena took another step into the house. Something about her made Hanna shrink back from the doorway. Her face was all sharp angles, no dimples—strange for someone her age. It was like she had never smiled in her life. "I think you do. In fact, I know you do."

"I'm sorry," Ma Etty repeated, taking a matching step closer. Mr. Bridle stayed put, as if his wife was more fit to handle this than he was. "We really don't have your horse."

"But I saw one of your girls riding him around town today. The big gray Hanoverian—that's our Star Dancer!" Elena Baxter clasped her hands in front of her. "I've been looking for him for so long."

There was only one big gray Hanoverian at Quartz Creek Ranch. Hanna's heart dropped. The woman had to be mistaken.

"I think you've made an error," said Ma Etty evenly. "That horse—*Shy Guy*—was abandoned on our property, and we took him in."

"No, no," said Elena. "I think you're the one

who's made a mistake. I went on a short vacation to Europe. When I returned, my beloved Star Dancer was gone. He must have escaped, or——"

"Then that was a different horse. When we took in Shy Guy, no horses had been reported missing to the sheriff."

The two women stared each other down, despite the immense height gap between them.

"Do you know who I am?" said Elena. "My mother was an Olympic dressage rider. She was known all over the world."

"No, I don't know you," said Ma Etty. "Or your mother. It's not going to change my opinion on the horse."

"I insist you return him to me. This is theft."

Hanna only felt total and complete horror.

"How dare you——!" Ma Etty stopped mid-sentence and took a deep, calming breath. "Ms. Baxter," she began again, squaring her shoulders. "Please refrain from making such unfounded accusations until you can prove it—with paperwork."

"If that's what it takes," Elena said. "You'll be seeing me again very soon. I promise you." Elena turned, grabbed her husband's hand, and yanked him out the still-open door.

Outside, the engine roared to life. The car veered at full speed back onto Bridlemile Road, the red taillights flickering in the window of the main room as the couple sped away.

Hanna burned from head to toe. She couldn't tell if it was fear or anger—all she knew was that she really wanted to grab one of that woman's crocodile skin boots and hit her with it.

"You okay?" Izzy asked her.

Hanna shook her head, unable to speak. Izzy hugged Hanna with one arm, frizzy curls brushing her face.

"Everyone back into the dining room," said Ma Etty. "That woman has a case of mistaken identity. I'm sure we've seen the last of her."

But a knot of dread had settled in Hanna's stomach. She didn't think Elena Baxter would go away that easily.

CHAPTER SEVENTEEN

A dreary silence settled over the ranch the next day. Clouds had rolled in overnight, and in the morning, they turned dark and angry. Riding lessons were canceled because of a storm warning. Ma Etty didn't even have the spirit to assign jobs that day, so when it started raining and thundering in the afternoon, she called everyone inside for board games and a movie instead.

It felt like a rainy Saturday when Hanna was little—when her dad didn't travel so much and her mom wasn't so anxious.

Paul came to the house as soon as he heard about the strange visitors. He and Ma Etty disappeared down the hall, talking in hushed voices.

Izzy got up and gestured at Hanna to follow her.

"What?" Hanna whispered.

"Come on. I want to hear." They made off like they were going to use the bathroom but stood outside the office door instead, listening to the conversation inside.

"Baxter, huh?" Paul was saying. "Yeah. I do know her. They moved here when I was in high school, from somewhere east. I never heard why, but I did meet her mother once—Juliet Baxter. She went to the Olympic Games in '68, I think. Came back with a bronze. Scary lady too, just like her daughter. I heard she left Elena a bunch of money, but she's blown most of it on having horses shipped over from Europe."

"Horses, plural?" asked Ma Etty.

"Yeah—gets a new one every few years. It's a big event when one of those fancy trailers rolls into town, you know? But I don't think she keeps them long."

"Probably because she ruins them, just like she did Shy Guy."

"I reckon you're right, Etty." He sighed. "She's going to come back with papers, you know. No way that big horse isn't hers. And she's gonna want him back, now that Hanna's fixed him up."

"I know," Ma Etty said with a sad sigh. "I know, Paul."

Izzy noticed Hanna's tears before she did. "It'll be fine," she whispered. "I'm sure of it."

\\\

The knock came around 5 p.m. Ma Etty rose from her spot on the floor playing the banker in Monopoly and went into the entryway. Everyone stood up to see what was happening, but Madison ushered them into the dining room to start setting the table. Izzy and Hanna lingered in the hallway, and no one hassled them.

When Ma Etty opened the door, Elena stood on the other side dressed in jeans and riding boots, her hair pulled back in a tight, high bun. Beside her stood a tiny older woman with glasses.

Ma Etty did not invite them in. "Hello again."

"This is my lawyer, Ms. Marcelle," Elena said. The lawyer did not extend her hand but, instead, held out a manila envelope.

"What's this?" asked Ma Etty.

"An injunction. To release my horse." Elena gestured to the gleaming white trailer sitting in the parking lot. "I trust you'll cooperate in bringing Star Dancer out so I can load him into my trailer, and I won't report to the sheriff that one of your hoodlums stole him."

Ma Etty's hands balled into fists. "They are not—" She stopped herself; took a long, calming breath; and took the envelope.

Hanna squeezed her eyes shut and then opened them again, hoping this was all a nightmare. Her pulse hammered as Ma Etty undid the clasp on the envelope and pulled out a piece of paper. She read for a short time, and Hanna wished she could see her face.

Then Ma Etty's hands fell to her sides.

"He's out in the barn," she said, her voice painfully quiet. "Will, can you—?"

Mr. Bridle set his hands on her shoulders and steered her back into the house. "Give us some time," he told the lawyer, not looking at Elena, and closed the door in their faces.

When Ma Etty turned around, her eyes met Hanna's.

"Hanna," she said, gesturing at her to come over.

She drew Hanna in for an embrace. "I think you know what this means."

Hanna could only nod, her whole face hot and swollen with tears. They hadn't broken through yet, but her nose felt like a volcano ready to burst. She didn't believe it. That woman really was Shy Guy's owner. His old, abusive owner. He'd tried to escape her once, but she'd found him again.

"I'm so sorry," Ma Etty said. "We'll do whatever we can to fight this, believe me. But for now, we have to let her take Shy Guy. Okay?"

Hanna nodded slowly. It would be temporary until they could get a scary-looking lawyer too. Right? Isn't that how these things worked?

"But . . . Hanna." Ma Etty looked her in the eye. "I can't promise anything. If that Baxter woman is Shy Guy's owner, if those papers are real, then we have to give him up. He's not ours."

"But she hurt him!" cried Hanna, pushing Ma Etty away. "She hit him so much he ran away from her! That woman is evil. She *can't* have him back."

"Hanna's right," said Izzy. "Elena Baxter is abusive. She'll send Shy Guy back to the way he was before."

"We can't prove that she's ever done anything

wrong," said Madison, who had followed Izzy. "There's no evidence. Not anymore."

Another knock came at the door. Mr. Bridle's face turned beet red.

"We're coming!" he roared, and everyone stood stock-still. He took a few deep breaths and then wiped his forehead under his hat and replaced it on his head. "Can't stand those impatient city people."

"There's nothing we can do right now," said Ma Etty in her calmest voice. "But we'll talk to the sheriff later and find out what options we have. That's all we've got right now." She turned away from Hanna. "Paul, Will—it's time to go out to the barn."

"I need to say good-bye!" cried Hanna, lunging after Paul and Mr. Bridle as they headed for the door. She couldn't let them take Shy Guy without getting to see him one last time. The tears that had threatened behind her eyes finally burst free, and they burned as they ran down her cheeks.

"You can go with them," assured Ma Etty. "But don't help them get Shy Guy into the trailer. We'll see then what this Baxter woman is about."

CHAPTER EIGHTEEN

Outside, rain pelted the ground in torrents and the sky was so muddy black that it was impossible to tell whether the sun had gone down. Even in the parka Ma Etty had put over her, Hanna shivered as she walked between Paul and Mr. Bridle out to the barn. The black shale roofing shuddered in a gust of wind.

When Mr. Bridle opened the barn door, a gale ripped it out of his hand and slammed it against the barn wall. The horses neighed in their stalls. As he reached to get the door back under control, Hanna and Paul rushed into the barn. Mr. Bridle followed them in, latching it closed behind them.

Inside, Hanna pulled down the hood of her

parka. The barn was quiet save for the gentle shaking of the walls in the wind and the occasional whinny of a horse. The air was electrified.

When Paul went to take the green halter off Shy Guy's stall, Hanna stopped him.

"Use a different one."

He gave her an odd look but grabbed a junky old one from the tack room anyway. Shy Guy's shiny new nameplate flickered as Paul opened the stall door.

When Shy Guy saw the strange man, he retreated a few steps back into the darkness, his eyes bulging and worried.

"Hanna," said Mr. Bridle, "can you help us get him out?"

Anger shot through her—not at Mr. Bridle but at Elena Baxter. At the whole world. Why should she help that horrible woman take Shy Guy away? She'd be complicit in betraying him.

"No," Hanna said, stepping back from the stall. "If she wants him, she can get him herself."

Mr. Bridle looked at her long and hard and then nodded. Instead, Paul strode into the stall with the halter hanging over one arm and reached to put the lead rope around Shy Guy's neck.

Shy Guy pressed himself against the far back wall, but Paul wouldn't give up. Despite Shy Guy tossing his head, Paul managed to get the halter over his nose and buckle it behind his ears.

"Shh," said Paul, trying to calm him. "It's only rain." He tugged on the lead rope toward the open stall door, but Shy Guy wouldn't budge. He'd put his ears so far back they were nearly flush with his head, and his frightened eyes flicked from Hanna to Paul and back to Hanna again.

He was terrified. Not of the rain—but of this strange person, of the tension and fear buzzing in the air. It felt like he could even see the tears on Hanna's soaked face and knew something bad was coming.

"Come on, boy," called Mr. Bridle, grabbing a bucket of grain. But even shaking the pail didn't help, and Shy Guy tried to make himself as small as possible in the back of the stall.

Hanna's heart crumbled. He was so frightened, and refusing to help only made it worse. Elena Baxter was going to take him away, no matter what.

She owed it to him to make it less painful if she could.

"Here," Hanna said, walking into the stall and taking the lead rope from Paul. Shy Guy's ears immediately pricked forward, and his silver head reached out toward her from the shadows. Hanna lifted her hand, running her fingers over his velvety nose. He took a step toward her and weaved his head through her arms.

Shy Guy's nostrils flared as she brushed his face. He could smell that she was afraid. He nudged her chest.

"I'm sorry," Hanna whispered, pushing his forelock out of his eyes. He blinked gentle brown eyes. "I told you I'd protect you," she murmured in his ear. "But I can't. It's only temporary, though. I'll get you back. We'll get you back, Shy Guy. I promise."

He snuffled her hand, hoping for a treat. She still had some stashed in her pocket, so she produced one, and he lipped her hand before eating it up. She was never afraid he'd bite her. He had the gentlest soul of any creature she'd ever met.

Elena Baxter didn't deserve him.

Shy Guy waited obediently as Hanna left the stall, then came out after her, turning around so she could close the door behind them.

Mr. Bridle had propped the barn door open, and a cold, wet wind stole inside, shuffling a paper tacked to the wall. Shy Guy's ears flicked back and forth, but not anxiously. He had no idea who was waiting to take him away.

Hanna felt like a traitor.

After ushering them outside, Mr. Bridle shut the barn door. The sudden noise startled Shy Guy, but at Hanna's side, he didn't spook.

"You did well with him," Mr. Bridle said.

"I didn't do anything," said Hanna. "It was all Shy Guy." She was glad for the rain because it hid the fresh tears that rushed down her face.

Paul pointed toward the gleaming white trailer in the parking lot. "Let's go."

Together, Paul, Mr. Bridle, Hanna, and Shy Guy crossed the little bridge over the creek onto the gravel road, which now ran black with mud. The closer they got to the white trailer, the more Hanna wanted to turn around and run away with Shy Guy, off into the woods, where there were no Elena Baxters who could hurt him.

They stepped into the parking lot and Hanna swallowed. Elena approached in a hooded, silvery raincoat, so not a hair on her head was wet. Hanna found an ounce of pleasure in the big splotch of mud staining the hem.

Elena extended one hand for the lead rope. Behind her, her husband lifted the latch on the back of the trailer and lowered the ramp.

"I know what you did to him," Hanna growled.

"I don't know what you mean." Elena shook her hand, emphasizing that she wanted the lead rope, and Shy Guy shied away—whether from the sudden movement or because he recognized Elena, Hanna didn't know. "Now, please, dear, hand him over."

"I know how you hurt him," said Hanna, clutching the lead rope tightly. "And even if we can't prove it—"

"Hanna," Mr. Bridle told her. "Now is not the time."

But she didn't let go. She pressed her hand to Shy Guy's cheek, and he watched her, eyes frightened.

"Yes," Elena echoed, "now isn't the time. The lawyers can fight it out later if you insist on it. Anyway," she leaned forward and patted Hanna's head, "what good would a horse like Star Dancer do an inexperienced child like you? He's been trained in Germany by the best in the business. He's a Grand Prix competitor. Who knows what damage your novice riding has already done to him?"

"Me? Damage him?" cried Hanna. "You—!"

Reaching out a third time for the lead rope, Elena plucked it right out of Hanna's hands. Hanna grappled to get it back, but Mr. Bridle took her by the shoulders and drew her away.

"No!" Hanna shouted, reaching for the lead rope, for Shy Guy, for anything. She couldn't let him go. She wouldn't. "No! Shy Guy!" Shy Guy neighed and yanked his head away from Elena, but her grip was iron strong. His eyes widened and his nostrils flared as she tugged him toward the open trailer door.

"Please control your hoodlum," Elena snapped at Mr. Bridle as Shy Guy pulled again. "She's frightening him. Whoa, boy. Whoa!"

"It's you who's frightening him!" Hanna couldn't control the sobs that tumbled out of her as Mr. Bridle led her away to where Ma Etty stood on the front step.

"We can't do anything right now," Ma Etty said, wrapping her arm around Hanna's shaking shoulders and positioning an umbrella over them both. "But I promise, tomorrow, we'll do whatever we can."

"You can't let her take him!" Hanna cried, but she had stopped struggling.

"I'm so sorry," was all Ma Etty could say.

When Shy Guy continued backing away from

the trailer, Elena's husband emerged with a whip. The whip cracked and Shy Guy reared up, hooves clawing the air. But Elena wasn't frightened. She simply yanked on the lead rope and yelled, "Get in!"

"Idiot woman," growled Mr. Bridle. "Didn't even open the windows inside. Who'd walk into a dark box?"

"He's so scared," Hanna said in a tiny voice.

Elena snatched the whip from her husband and, holding the lead rope in one hand and the whip in the other, smacked Shy Guy across the rump.

Lightning shot down from the sky, turning the black clouds bright white.

Shy Guy's ears flattened against his head, and he let out a horrible neigh. The third time the whip snapped, he jolted forward. Ears flattened to his skull and tail thrashing wildly, he finally hopped into the trailer.

"What a good horse," murmured Paul, as the trailer ramp went back up and Elena latched it closed behind him. She returned to the truck and climbed inside.

Her husband went around to the passenger side door, then paused, and closed it again. He approached Hanna and Ma Etty.

"You have to understand," he said quickly. "He's the last one. He's all she's got. She's not trying to hurt you, little girl. She just wants her horse back."

"I want him back too," said Hanna.

"Just, please." His lower lip trembled. "Please, don't blame her. Elena knows no other way."

A head leaned out the truck's window. "Come on, John!" Elena shouted. The squat man just shook his head and returned to the truck, getting in after her.

The truck's engine roared to life and the vehicle started backing out. When the headlights blazed on and it started to drive away, Hanna suddenly shrieked and ran after it.

This was her last chance.

"Shy Guy!" she cried. Everything they'd been through, everything they'd done together—it was all for nothing. Elena was going to ruin him all over again, and she couldn't save him, not this time. "Shy Guy!"

But it didn't matter. The truck roared off down Bridlemile Road, heedless of her. The last thing Hanna saw was Shy Guy's gray tail blowing in the wind as it vanished into the night.

CHAPTER NINETEEN

"**T**here must be something we can do." It was the third time Ma Etty had said that since she got on the phone with the sheriff earlier that morning, and Hanna's heart sank even further. "Can we file a counter injunction?"

There was noise on the other end of the line, and Ma Etty's lips pursed into a deep scowl. Hanna had never seen this side of her before. She and Izzy leaned forward in their chairs. For the first time, the Bridles had allowed ranch kids into their small office in the back of the house (the one with a paper sign reading *Internal Affairs* taped on it). But to Hanna, it wasn't a privilege. She couldn't think of anything but getting Shy Guy out of that awful woman's clutches.

"Well, I don't know these things, Doug," Ma Etty shot back at the phone. "Fine. I need to make a few phone calls, but I'll be calling you back." She hung up and turned to Mr. Bridle. "Will, I need you to call Ron."

When Mr. Bridle took the phone, Ma Etty explained that Ron was their lawyer, and he should be able to help. But a few minutes later, Mr. Bridle returned, his face lined with defeat.

"Ron says there's nothing he can do. Elena Baxter has purchase papers for Shy Guy—*Star Dancer*—and he fits the bill, markings and all. He's all hers."

That was it. They were out of options.

Hanna desperately needed some air. She walked out of the office and left the house. Izzy followed, not saying anything. But it helped just knowing she was there.

The wind and the rain had died down since the previous night, leaving the sky overcast and gray. The downpour had filled the creek to overflowing, leaving the driveway and pasture wet and muddy.

It was past time for riding lessons to start.

"Hey, girls," Madison called to them, as if on cue. She walked over, swinging a halter and forcing a smile. "Ready to join the rest of us for lessons?"

Hanna shrugged, and they followed Madison back to the arena, where the other kids were working with Fletch. Rae Ann trotted over when she saw them.

"How did it go?" she asked. "Is Shy Guy coming back?"

Josh, Cade, and Fletch joined her. Hanna was so shaken that she realized she couldn't speak, but luckily, Izzy stepped in.

"Elena has papers proving she owns Shy Guy," she said. Her eyebrows lowered dangerously. "She even told the sheriff that she thinks one of us stole him."

"What?" cried Rae Ann. "How could she?"

"She has no proof," growled Josh.

Cade sat back abruptly. "That's a crock."

Hanna nodded, helpless. "There's nothing we can do," she said.

Everyone was silent, not sure what to say.

"Tomorrow's another day," said Fletch eventually. "I'm sure the Bridles will figure something out. Come on, everyone. We've got a lesson to finish."

After lights went out that night and Madison closed her door, Izzy didn't even wait for Rae Ann to fall asleep before whispering to Hanna in the dark.

"We have to get him back," Izzy said.

"How?" asked Hanna wearily. "What can we possibly do?"

"What if we broke in and stole him? Maybe camouflaged him or hid him somewhere on the property where Elena couldn't find him?"

"And what, get arrested? She'll know we took him. And so will Paul when he finds him, not to mention the sheriff . . ." Hanna sighed. "Sorry, Izz. I don't mean to shoot you down. I've just thought of all this before."

"We understand," said Rae Ann. "You love him. Like I love my Sadie."

Hanna's chest ached. She felt a lot more strongly about her horse than about a cat. "Yeah," she said. "Like Sadie."

Rae Ann plowed on. "We should ask the boys. I bet they have some good ideas. Josh is really smart."

"Together we can think of something," said Izzy, her voice steady and sure. "I know we can. We have to, for Shy Guy's sake."

Hanna didn't want to talk anymore. She was

tired and her head hurt and her mind swam with images of Elena hitting Shy Guy—sometimes with the whip, sometimes with her bare hands. Every time Hanna heard the same cracking sound.

She wanted to fall asleep and never wake up again.

"Let me know when you've all come up with your great idea," Hanna said, curling into a ball on her bed.

"Don't worry," Izzy replied, without an ounce of doubt in her voice. "We will."

\\

The next day, Madison asked Hanna to ride Lacey during the lesson, and she agreed without thinking about it. It was all the same to her.

In the ring, Lacey was . . . well, a horse. She did everything that Hanna knew how to ask for—and she did it completely placidly, without any of Shy Guy's smooth grace or spirit. Hanna and Lacey were both robots, doing what they were told.

Lacey was a fine horse.

Hanna didn't really care.

"Good work, Hanna!" Fletch called from the edge of the arena as she completed the keyhole.

"Lacey's really responding to you."

"Thanks," she muttered and walked to the back of the line behind Josh.

"Hey," he said. "Since we have free time this afternoon, you want to play bean bag toss?"

"Isn't it a little muddy still?"

He glanced around at the trenches their horses had carved in the arena, thanks to the rain.

"I guess so. Well, maybe Monopoly? You owe me a rematch."

Hanna shrugged. "Sure."

Josh's slight smile faded. "I'm really sorry about Shy Guy. That was such . . ." He sounded like he was about to say a curse word, but Madison was standing right near them, so he coughed and went on. "I can't believe the nerve of that lady."

"Yeah," she said as Cade finished his turn. "Nothing I can do now but try and forget."

He furrowed his eyebrows. "Forget?"

"Josh!" Fletch was trying to get his attention. "Your turn."

The rest of training, Hanna didn't speak to anyone. As they were putting the horses away, Cade came over to help her close up Lacey's stall.

"Hey, Hanna," he said. "I know you're really sad

right now. We all are. But I hope you know . . . we're here for you. And I hope you don't actually forget about Shy Guy and what you did for him. I'm sure he won't forget you."

Hanna's throat tightened. "Thanks, Cade." She bowed her head. "You're right. I could never forget him."

"Remember the good things. And, well," he looked around and lowered his voice, "if you do come up with a plan to get him back, I'll be the first to help you. I have over four hundred hours of experience as a tactician in my Team Strike Ops guild! Undercover missions are my specialty."

Hanna cast an annoyed glance at Izzy, who gave a sheepish shrug.

"Seriously," Cade said. "Josh and I are standing by, ready to assist."

The dedication in his voice made Hanna pause. He sounded so confident that it could be done, that there was no reason to give up hope.

She started to wonder if maybe there was something they could do.

\\

The day Hanna realized she'd been at Quartz Creek Ranch for more than a month was the day she realized she hadn't once missed home. Or her mom, for that matter. Mom was probably itching to call, but she knew the ranch rules: no visits, no letters, and no phone calls. One of the few things Hanna could appreciate.

It had been a week since that rainy night, and her thoughts were still consumed with Shy Guy— with the feeling of total freedom she'd felt as they flew together across the arena, the wind whipping her hair back.

What was he doing now? How was Elena treating him? Each day Hanna felt worse, rather than better. She thought, unfortunately, it was probably the same for Shy Guy.

She had to save him, but she didn't know how.

One evening during free time, Hanna took Izzy's elbow and pulled her aside.

"I don't have an idea yet," she whispered, "but I want to see if the Internet can help us."

"What do you want to find?" Izzy asked, her brown eyes lighting up with hope and curiosity.

"Where Elena Baxter lives. What she does. Anything we could use against her."

Izzy's smile was devilish. "Yeah!"

Hanna asked Ma Etty if they could use an hour of their free time to look something up online.

"Sure," she said, not even putting down her newspaper. "I'll come get you when your time's up."

Once they had the computer to themselves, they looked up Elena Baxter's name, hoping they could find her house, anything about her that might be helpful.

But it wasn't Elena's name that brought up search results—it was her mother, the Olympic athlete, who kept appearing.

Honoring Our Coloradan Olympians.

Dressage Hall of Fame: Great Olympic Goofs that Cost a Medal.

Olympian Juliet Baxter's Legacy Lives On—Daughter Announces Entry Into Olympic Competition.

"That's her," said Izzy, pointing at the screen. It was dated over five years ago. Hanna clicked on it, but after scanning the article, didn't find any useful information about Elena besides a heavily doctored photo of her face.

"She looks way too old to be going to the Olympics," said Izzy.

"Ugh," said Hanna. She started writing an angry comment at the bottom of the article. "I hate her."

"Don't." Izzy deleted the text before Hanna could post it and navigated back to the search screen. "Come on. Let's look for something else."

The next result was for Elena's dubious-looking real estate business. It listed an office address and phone number but nothing else. Hanna closed the window in frustration.

Even if they had found Elena's address, what would they have done with it? Stolen Shy Guy for real, only to end up in jail? It was a pointless exercise, Hanna realized, and got up halfway through their hour. She went out to the garden to pull weeds instead.

Izzy came out to find Hanna later and crouched in the dirt next to her.

"You're pulling weeds. With your only free time." She said it as a statement, rather than a question.

"So?"

"So that's pathetic."

"Thanks," muttered Hanna. "That makes me feel so much better about it."

Izzy's mouth opened to make a retort, but they

were interrupted by Paul calling their names. Izzy shot up, her crush on the handsome blond ranch manager blatantly obvious. Hanna thought it was kind of gross.

"He's, like, thirty," Hanna had said.

"So?" Izzy shrugged. "He looks exactly like young Brad Pitt. Swoon!" Hanna had to agree about the Brad Pitt thing.

"Hey, girls!" Paul greeted, leaning up against his truck. He gestured with his thumb to the cab. "I need some helpers to come with me and pick up feed. I know you're on free time, but if you come with me, we can get subs at the sub shop."

Neither of them had eaten out since getting to the ranch, so Izzy jumped to her feet.

"Subs and ice cream, and you've got a deal."

"Done," said Paul, and opened the back doors of his four-door truck. The girls hopped in, and they roared off to Quartz Creek.

CHAPTER TWENTY

At the feed store, Paul got sidetracked by a work boot sale, so Izzy said, "Let's go look around out back while Brad gets his shop on."

Outside, the feed store lot was piled high with stacks of hay bales, bags of grain, and rusted farm equipment. "Check it out!" Izzy pointed past tractors with no tires and a dismembered Caterpillar claw to a graveyard full of old cars.

Before Hanna could stop her, Izzy clambered over the equipment in a way that Hanna was sure Paul would not approve of and vanished.

"Izzy!" Hanna called after her, but she was gone. With a sigh, Hanna followed.

On the other side of the junk pile, Izzy roamed through rows of old, broken-down cars, *oooh*-ing and *ahh*-ing. "Look at this, a '51 Mustang!"

"You like junky cars?" asked Hanna.

Izzy shrugged. "My dad collects scrap cars like this, and I used to help him fix them up." She laughed. "My mom hates it, though. Takes up a lot of space."

"You don't help him anymore?" Hanna asked.

Izzy paused next to an old Chevy truck. She patted the domed hood. "No. Not since I started getting in trouble at school."

She stopped and gave Hanna a calculating look, like she was trying to decide whether to trust her with more. After a moment, Izzy went on.

"My parents figured they needed to spend more time with me. And that was what I wanted! But they treated me so differently. When my mom and I used to garden together, we'd listen to music and she'd tell me about the different instruments and styles. But after things at school got bad, she'd make me stay inside to do my homework and look over my shoulder the whole time. Dad used to ask me to help him with the cars, but now he lectures me about why school's important or why fighting won't get me anywhere. Instead of looking at me like his helpful assistant, he looks at me like I'm the thing that needs fixing. And maybe I am."

She stopped talking and walked around the old Chevy, opening the rusty door. She climbed inside and leaned back in the seat.

"Careful," said Hanna. "There could be mice."

Izzy shrugged. "I'm not scared of mice. But sounds like you are."

"I'm not!"

"You're scared of horses," said Izzy. "And I don't see how horses could possibly be scarier than mice. I mean, those long, scaly tails! And they're diseased."

"Are you kidding?" said Hanna, climbing in the passenger seat to prove her wrong. "Horses are totally scarier. They're huge, for starters."

"Of course."

"And you never know what they're going to do. They could kick you, and *bam*, you're done."

Izzy narrowed her eyes. "Has a horse ever tried to kick you?"

"Well, no."

"Then what's your deal? You know, way back when, I heard Madison say you liked horses."

Hanna rolled her eyes. "When I was, like, seven!

My mom told her that because I used to collect little toy horses."

"So what's the difference?"

"Well, there's a big difference. One's a toy. One's big enough to kill you."

Izzy narrowed her eyes and leaned over the middle seat toward her. Hanna leaned away. "What happened?" Izzy asked. "Did something happen?"

"No," Hanna said automatically.

"Come on, Hanna. Tell me. I told you my secret. What made you so freaked out about horses?"

Hanna swallowed. Izzy was right. Fair trade.

"Mom took me to the county fair," Hanna said. "I was seven. I'd been collecting toy horses forever, so when we got to the pony ride, she insisted I do it." Remembering it, her pulse jumped. "But the horses were so much bigger in real life, and I didn't want to ride. But Mom made me. As soon as I got on that pony, I started crying."

"Did it throw you or something?"

Hanna slowly shook her head. "No. We walked around in a circle for twenty minutes. That's it. But it felt like forever, Izz. I wanted down more than anything, but Mom kept saying, 'Hanna! You love horses. Come on, I bought this ride for you. Why can't you have fun? Why are you making a scene?' And I kept crying and crying, but I didn't want my mom to get mad at me, so I stayed on the horse."

Izzy let out a breath. "And I thought my mom was a piece of work."

"Sometimes I think she wishes I was somebody else. Like, wishes she'd had a different daughter."

"I feel that," Izzy said, sighing. "Me too. I still don't understand what that has to do with stealing or how you, of all people, ended up at QCR. You're scared of ponies walking around in a circle. Nice white girls like you don't get sent to rehab camp just for stealing a candy bar."

Hanna didn't know how to put it into words.

"I guess I wanted to stick it to her," Hanna said finally. "Show her I could be horrible too. Make her miss the old me."

"Still don't get what that has to do with stealing," said Izzy.

"She's always getting on my case about everything!" The venom in Hanna's voice surprised even her. "If I get an A instead of an A-plus, she flips out. She says my friends talk too loud or I eat too fast or my piano should be better, but I've only been playing for a year! I practiced every single day. But nothing is ever enough for her." Something dark crept into her tone. "So I decided to do something she'd hate."

Izzy looked genuinely worried.

"At first, I took stuff right where Mom could see. Then, when I got away with it, whenever I could. But . . . it was impossible to stop." She collapsed back in the ripped leather seat. "She finally figured it out when she cleaned under my bed and found everything."

"Everything?" prompted Izzy.

"Candy, lipstick, an iPod . . ."

"Dude," said Izzy, whistling. "You were hard-core."

"I guess." That unsettled Hanna. She didn't want to be good at stealing. After a moment of quiet, she said, "We should go back, in case Brad Pitt is looking for us."

"Good call," said Izzy.

Together they climbed out of the car and shut the doors, leaving their puddle of spilled secrets behind. But when Hanna glanced past the feed store lot fence, she spotted a familiar gray horse trotting past.

Her entire body went white-hot.

"Izzy," she hissed, pointing. "Look, Shy Guy!"

Elena Baxter, dressed in high leather riding boots, rode Shy Guy past on a little black English saddle. He performed a long, canter-like gait along the perimeter of the fence. He was lathered in sweat. Elena hit him with the whip every time he slowed down or missed a step, and Shy Guy pressed his ears back but obeyed nevertheless.

"Come on," she growled. "Stop messing up that lead change!" Angrily she yanked on the reins, and Shy Guy stumbled over his own feet.

Hanna's face burned. She wanted to strangle that woman. Shy Guy worked and worked, and Elena Baxter didn't appreciate an ounce of it. Hanna had never hated someone so much in her life.

As if he knew Hanna was nearby, Shy Guy ground to a halt. Elena tried to make him trot, but he wouldn't budge. His ears flicked forward, searching for something.

"Come on, you dumb horse," she said, hitting him again with the switch. "We're not even close to done yet." But it had no effect. When she jerked the reins to the side, Shy Guy threw his head up, clocking her right in the chin.

"Oooh," Izzy said, wincing but smiling a little. "That looks like it hurt."

Elena, startled, put a hand to her damaged face. Her shoulders trembled. Then she climbed off Shy

Guy's back, grabbed the reins, and hit him.

He tossed his head to the side, trying to get away, but she held the reins fast—and Shy Guy was too gentle to try to hurt her in his effort to escape.

He was a prisoner.

Rage filled Hanna to the brim. "Hey!" she shouted. Izzy grabbed her by the arm, but Hanna was already crawling over the old Chevy toward the fence. Shy Guy's ears perked forward. "HEY!"

Elena looked up, eyes wide, thinking she'd been caught. But when she saw Hanna and Izzy, the fear evaporated.

"Why, hello," she said, holding Shy Guy back when he tried to walk toward the fence to greet Hanna. He tossed his head again, but she tugged the reins down. "You really did a number on my horse. He refuses to collect on his canter."

"You messed up your own horse," said Hanna.

"He'd probably listen to you if you didn't hit him all the time," said Izzy.

Elena's face reddened. "The problem is you, not me. Bad behavior warrants punishment. It worked for my mom, and it works for me. He wouldn't be acting this way if you hadn't gotten your delinquent paws all over him. "

"We're not delinquents," snapped Izzy. Now she was mad.

"Oh, aren't you?" said Elena as she got back on Shy Guy. "Then how did you end up at a place like Quartz Creek Ranch?"

"You . . . you . . . !" Izzy probably would have climbed over the fence if it weren't for the barbed wire.

"Now, thanks to your distraction, he gets no dinner tonight," said Elena.

"That's messed up," said Hanna. "Not feeding him won't make him respond to you better."

"Bad behavior," Elena repeated, "warrants punishment."

Hanna's eyes turned blurry as angry tears started squeezing out of the corners of her eyes. "Give him back!" she cried. "You didn't even want him. You abandoned him."

Elena nudged Shy Guy with her knee and obediently, he turned around. "A temporary flaw in judgment," she said. "But a mistake is a mistake. Everyone makes them."

"You're the worst," said Hanna.

"Another thing you have wrong," she said. "With Star Dancer's help, I'm going to qualify for the Grand

Prix this year. Because I am, in fact, the best." She glanced up at the sky. "And unlike my mother, when I get to the Olympics, I'm not going to mess up on the piaffe. I'm going to bring home the gold."

"Fat chance," said Izzy. "You haven't been an Olympic hopeful in five years."

Elena huffed. "How dare you. I really ought to press charges against those Bridles for how you horrible kids kidnapped Star Dancer." She clicked to Shy Guy and nudged him with her heels, and reluctantly he started walking away. "But it's not worth my time."

Hanna and Izzy stood, speechless, as Elena rode off. Shy Guy twisted his neck around to look back at Hanna, but Elena yanked his head back again. Soon he was nothing more than a vague gray shape disappearing into the trees.

When he was gone, Hanna broke down.

"She can't do that!"

"I think she just did," said Izzy.

Hanna furiously wiped her face with her arm as they walked back to meet Paul. They found the ranch manager ogling a new pair of Wranglers. He dropped the jeans when he saw the tears running down Hanna's face.

"What happened?" he asked.

"Elena Baxter," she said, sniffling.

Paul took off his hat and pressed it to his chest. "You should stay away from that woman," he said. "She's disturbed."

"Evil is more like it," said Izzy.

He shook his head. "I talked to a few folks in town after she took Shy Guy," he said, nodding at the feed store owner. "Her mother, Juliet Baxter? As an old lady, she was no walk in the park either—an even worse woman than her daughter, or so Mark told me. Real hard on her animals and real hard on her family. Elena Baxter maybe hasn't had the easiest life."

"So what?" demanded Hanna between hiccups. "That's no excuse for what she's doing to Shy Guy."

"Not saying it is," agreed Paul. "But I wouldn't doubt that the late Mrs. Baxter treated Elena much the way Elena treats her horses."

In the back of the truck on the way home, as Paul blared country music from the stereo and the girls ate their ice cream, Izzy leaned over.

"At least we know where she lives now," she said, just quiet enough that Paul couldn't hear. Hanna's eyes widened. She was about to say something when, in the front seat, Paul turned the music down.

"How's the ice cream, ladies?" he called back to them.

"Hooo grrd!" replied Izzy, her mouth suddenly full of ice cream. How she'd done that, Hanna couldn't guess.

Paul laughed at Izzy's answer. "Okay, I'll take that as an *excellent*."

So Izzy was pretty sneaky too? Hanna filed that information away for later.

CHAPTER TWENTY-ONE

After dinner that night, when Madison left them alone to go for her biweekly swim, Izzy and Hanna filled in Rae Ann on what they'd seen near the feed store that day.

"Poor Shy Guy!" she said, covering her mouth. "That woman's so horrible. You have to tell Ma Etty what you saw."

"And then what?" said Izzy. "Ma Etty already tried everything she could."

"Elena Baxter is smart. Too smart." Hanna flopped on her bunk bed, arms spread-eagle to keep the heat off her sides. "We have to outsmart her."

"How?" asked Rae Ann. She crossed her legs on

her bed and stared down at her toes. "I can't out-smart anyone, even my folks—and they usually have their noses buried in Bibles. The only thing I can do is sound like someone's mom on the phone. Need me to pretend to be anyone?"

No one had an answer to that. Izzy suddenly sat up.

"I think we need some fresh ideas. We're spinning our wheels in here. Why don't we ask the guys?"

"It's late," said Rae Ann.

"So? Let's say we're bored with Madison gone and challenge them to a game of dice. Fletch won't care. Josh says he's always in his room reading anyway."

Hanna agreed, and the three of them got up and left the girls' bunkhouse. They knocked on the door to the boys' cabin, and Cade answered.

"Whoa, hey. What's up?"

"Hey. We're, uh, bored. And thought you guys might want to play dice."

Fletch came out of his room, and sure enough, he was holding a book in his hand. He was in sweatpants and still had his cowboy hat on. It had partially slipped down over his face.

"Dice?" he said, peering out the door looking for Madison. "Oh, I guess Maddie went swimming.

Well, okay. Come on in. But only for half an hour, okay?"

"Okay," the kids agreed.

Fletch, yawning, went back into his room but left the door cracked. When they were all set up for dice on the little table, Josh lowered his head and narrowed his eyes at the three girls.

"What's really going on?" he whispered.

"We found out where Elena Baxter lives," Izzy whispered back. Cade and Josh exchanged a surprised look.

"How?"

"We saw her near the feed store today," said Hanna. "She was abusing Shy Guy again."

"No!" Cade bared his teeth. "So it's all true. And the Bridles let her take him?"

"What could they have done?" demanded Josh.

"Shh," said Rae Ann, glancing around fearfully. "Fletch."

"Right, sorry."

"That's why we need your help," said Izzy.

"How can we possibly help?" said Cade. "Don't get me wrong, I want to. But . . ."

"But nothing," interrupted Josh. "We'll help however we can."

"We need a plan," Hanna said. "We know where she lives. We know what she's doing. But how do we prove it?"

"The sheriff has to see it," said Josh, with total certainty. Everyone at the table turned to him. "What? Seriously. That's it. That's all you have to do."

"How do you suggest we do that?" said Rae Ann, voice dripping with sarcasm. Everyone looked surprised at that.

"I don't know, Little Debbie," said Josh, rising to her tone. "He needs to catch her in the act. Maybe we can get a recording of it, something you can show to him."

But before Josh could say anything else, Hanna glanced at Izzy knowingly.

The phone.

"No way," said Izzy. "If they find out I brought it . . ."

"So what?" said Hanna. "This is bigger than that."

Now the others looked confused. "Brought what?" asked Cade.

"Hanna . . ." Izzy trailed off, looking frightened for the first time. "That was our secret!"

But Hanna plowed on. "Izzy brought a phone to

camp," she said. "Sorry, Izzy." Rae Ann gasped, but the boys didn't look surprised.

"Big whoop," said Josh. "Cade snuck in an MP3 player." Then understanding dawned on him. "The camera in the phone!"

"Shh!" said Rae Ann again. She grabbed the dice and threw them just as Fletch opened the door to check on them.

Cade pretended to write down a score. Josh said, "Dang it! I should have cashed out while I was ahead."

When the door was closed again, Hanna leaned forward, feeling a rush now that they finally had an idea.

"So we sneak in," said Izzy, "and wait until we see what we're looking for, then film it?"

"Sneak in?" squeaked Rae Ann, sinking back in her chair as if the physical distance would keep her from getting involved—and getting in trouble.

Hanna agreed. "We can't. If we break the law, we're as bad as she is."

Izzy arched an eyebrow at her. "Oh, all about not breaking laws now?"

Josh and Cade watched them curiously.

"Yeah," said Hanna, narrowing her eyes. "I am. This is trespassing, Izzy. That's kind of a big deal."

"But if we can get video, Hanna—if we can prove that Elena is mistreating Shy Guy, it won't matter. We can sneak in and sneak out without her seeing us. I know we can." She shot Hanna a look. "And I know *you* definitely can."

Rae Ann covered her ears. "I can't believe I'm hearing this."

"Then stay out of it," snapped Izzy.

"Whoa, whoa," said Josh. "Okay now, take it easy. We're all in this together to save Shy Guy. At least we have a plan, even if it bends a few rules."

He was right. It would have to do.

"All right," said Hanna, shoring up her resolve. "Let's do it. But how?"

CHAPTER TWENTY-TWO

Over the next few days, the five of them put the finishing touches on their plan. Hanna was glad they'd brought in Josh and Cade, because it was easier to plug up the holes with everyone involved.

On the day they'd picked, they waited until after lunchtime to put their plan in motion.

"Free time starts at two today," Madison told them over lunch. "Everyone know what they want to do?"

Izzy's hand shot in the air. "Free ride," she said.

"Me too," chimed in Hanna.

Madison looked surprised. "Okay, sure," she said. "I can work with you two."

"Actually," said Rae Ann, "Madison, I was hoping we could go swimming this afternoon and you could show me some things. I know you're really good at it, and I was thinking I'd join my school's swim team next year."

Madison's eyes lit up. "Well, yeah! Of course, Rae Ann. Ma Etty will need to coordinate getting you a temporary gym pass, but . . ."

"Not a problem," said Ma Etty, putting a fresh bowl of salad on the table. "Rae Ann expressed interest the other day, so I made sure we had some."

"Ma Etty," piped up Cade, "are you still planning to pick up baby chicks this afternoon?"

She glanced up. "Yes, I think so. Paul already set up a spot for them in the cattle barn."

"Can I go with you during free time? They're so cute. I want to help pick them out."

"I don't see why not," she said, then glanced at Fletch. "Weren't you and Josh going to go help Paul brand some new cattle? No one will be around to watch Hanna and Izzy."

"That's still the plan," said Fletch. "Since Josh says he wants to get into cattle ranching someday."

Mr. Bridle, who'd kept quiet until now, shrugged. "I think Izzy and Hanna will be fine, as long as they stay in the arena. They've both become excellent horsewomen. And I'll be in the house doing paperwork anyway, if something comes up." He smiled at both of them, and Hanna felt a pang of guilt. But it was quickly swept away by the memory of Elena working Shy Guy to the bone.

"All right then," said Madison. "It's settled."

And the plan was under way.

\\

Once Fettucini and Lacey were tacked up, Hanna and Izzy made a point of making a few circuits around the arena. Madison and Rae Ann left for the pool, and Ma Etty and Cade drove off in her truck. When they were alone, Hanna took Lacey back inside and put her away. They'd already doubled once, and hiding one horse was easier than hiding two.

"Plus," Hanna said, "Fettucini's a faster getaway vehicle."

Izzy beamed proudly at that.

They pulled out the copy of the town map they'd drawn, based off the one tacked up in the barn, and Hanna opened the arena gate.

The hardest part would be getting all the way down Bridlemile Road, down to the spot where the trail diverged from the road, without anyone seeing them. They decided to walk Fettucini instead of riding him, to appear less conspicuous if Mr. Bridle happened to glance out the window.

According to the map, the trail split before it joined Main Street, its upper fork curving northeast behind the feed store lot. They weren't sure of the exact location of Elena's property, but it would get them close enough.

Hopefully.

They took the north fork and encountered no one besides a farmer driving his tractor through a field. Soon the skeletal remains of cars and tractors appeared to their right, behind a barbed wire fence.

At the edge of the feed store lot's scrapyard, a new fence started that had to be Elena's. Hanna's stomach turned over. It was a lot to hope that Elena Baxter would be on the same schedule today as before, but hope was all they had. There was a spot in the fence that had been broken and recently, it looked like, repaired.

"We should get off here," Hanna said as they rounded a grove of trees on their left. To their right was the open field where they'd seen Elena and Shy Guy riding.

Izzy and Hanna dismounted, and Izzy led Fettucini into the trees, where she tied him to a hefty branch. When she reappeared, she brandished her camera phone.

"Ready?" she asked.

"Ready," said Hanna.

She put on a pair of thick leather gloves she'd slipped off a hook in the tack room and held the barbed wire fence open so Izzy could slip through. Hanna passed the gloves between the wires and Izzy did the same for her.

Her heart beat faster. The bushes hid them for now, but if Elena was close by, she'd see them for sure.

Once both girls emerged safely on the other side, they snuck around the pasture's perimeter, pushing through the low brush. Up ahead, the ground sloped up to a corral, a small white barn, and a beige farmhouse.

"Let's take the back fence," said Izzy, pointing to the far north side of the pasture, which was lined with greenery. "We can at least stick to the trees and bushes there."

It was slow going. Bushes with thorns snagged

their jeans as they went, and they still hadn't spotted Elena or Shy Guy yet.

Then they heard a door creak, and Hanna pulled Izzy behind a small tree. Up ahead of them, the barn door opened, and Elena led out Shy Guy. He was covered in dirt and mud, and his head hung low. Hanna's heart reached out to him, but they had to stay hidden.

Elena walked Shy Guy away from Hanna and Izzy's hiding spot, over to the corral, where she attached a long longe line to his halter. She began shouting commands at him and held out the whip. Seeing it, Shy Guy's eyes widened, and he jumped into a trot.

"Ugh, that's all wrong," Elena said, stopping him. She batted his ears with her hand, and he yanked his head away. *No wonder he'd been head shy*, thought Hanna, fury boiling up inside her.

Elena tossed out the longe line again and shook it. "Come on now," she called, smacking Shy Guy with the whip so hard the noise echoed. "Trot!"

At the command, Shy Guy leapt immediately into a trot, his eyes bulging with fear that he'd done it wrong.

"Get out the phone," whispered Hanna. Izzy

fumbled for it, and it almost fell to the ground. She saved it mid-air. But when she turned on the video camera, she let out a little moan.

"We're too far away for a decent video!"

Hanna ducked under the tree, and when Elena's back was turned, she jogged across the open expanse of field to the next tree, closer to the barn, upwind of the corral. On Shy Guy's next circuit, Izzy did the same. They kept moving this way until they were close enough that they could dash across to the barn itself and get a close-up view of the corral.

"Behind the barn," hissed Hanna, pointing.

"Check!" whispered Izzy.

The next time Elena was facing away from them, they sprinted across the largest expanse of field and ducked behind the side of the barn as she started coming back around.

They were still a good twenty yards off but close enough to get a decent shot.

"There. Got it," Izzy said, holding up the phone and pressing the button to record.

Watching Elena's cruelty unfold without being able to say or do anything made Hanna's body shake. She stood, covering her mouth, as Elena hit Shy Guy.

When Elena hit him the third time, a sob escaped Hanna's throat.

Elena spun and spotted them.

"You!" She threw the whip down, and Hanna knew only one thing—the same thing she'd known the few times store clerks and shopkeepers caught her stealing.

It was time to get out of there.

"Run!" Hanna yelled.

In her panic Izzy dropped the phone, and Hanna scrambled to pick it up. Izzy was already sprinting back the way they'd come when Hanna looked up again. Now outside of the corral, Elena was dashing after Izzy.

But Izzy's short legs couldn't stay ahead. Elena caught up in no time and seized Izzy by the arm.

"No!" cried Hanna. "Izzy!" But she also knew the top priority was getting the video footage to safety. Turning, she dashed the opposite direction from Elena Baxter: into the open barn door. Once inside, she slammed it closed behind her. That would buy her a few extra seconds.

Inside, the barn was dark, but the smell of horse manure overpowering. Hanna gagged.

This was where Elena Baxter was keeping Shy Guy.

Three stalls lined the right wall, and knowing she didn't have much time, Hanna peered in the first one. This was where she kept Shy Guy, she could tell—there was manure piled almost a foot high. Taking out the phone, which was still recording, she surveyed the catastrophe. She recorded mound after mound of manure and old, rotting hay.

Hanna thought maybe it had been true about Elena blowing the last of her money on Shy Guy. When she was rich, she paid someone to do her dirty work for her—but now there was no one.

Behind her, the door Hanna had come through banged opened.

There stood Elena, silhouetted by the afternoon sun, a howling Izzy clutched in one of her strong hands.

Hanna threw open the opposite door.

"Stop!" Elena screeched, but Hanna dashed out and sprinted as fast as her long, gangly legs could carry her, the phone still clutched in her hand.

CHAPTER TWENTY-THREE

Elena hadn't bothered chasing Hanna, with Izzy already her captive. But that didn't stop Hanna from running as fast as she could, back the way they'd snuck in, frightened, angry tears streaming down her face.

She squeezed through the fence, tearing her shirt on the barbed wire, but she didn't care. Back where Fettucini was still tied up, Hanna threw his reins over his neck and climbed on his back. He was harder to control than Lacey, but Hanna trusted him to get her home safe.

And he did, galloping home to Quartz Creek Ranch like the wind.

"Mr. Bridle!" Hanna shouted as she and Fettucini cantered up Bridlemile Road, passing the ranch house. "Ma Etty! Fletch! Madison!"

Ma Etty and Cade were climbing out of the truck when Hanna raced up to them.

"Whoa," said Ma Etty, holding up her hands. "What's going on? What are you doing riding out here? And why are you on Fettucini?"

"Can't explain," said Hanna, panting. She jumped off and handed Fettucini's reins to Cade. "It's Izzy. Elena Baxter has Izzy." Fumbling in her pocket, she took out the phone.

"What on earth is that?" asked Ma Etty as the ranch house's front door banged open.

"Who's callin' my name?" said Mr. Bridle. He took in the scene cautiously. "Someone going to explain to me what that horse is doing all lathered up?"

Hanna held out the phone, the video queued up. "Just watch," she said.

Ma Etty and Mr. Bridle peered at the screen. In tinny low-fi, Hanna could hear Elena shouting. Ma Etty covered her mouth, and a deep crease appeared in Mr. Bridle's brow.

"Elena has Izzy," Hanna said again, trying to impress upon them the urgent nature of their predicament. "She caught us filming her. We have to go help Izzy!"

Ma Etty and Mr. Bridle exchanged a long look. Then, without any words passing between them, Mr. Bridle nodded.

"Cade, go find Fletch. Tell him what's going on." He looked at Hanna. "Get in the truck. We're going to get our girl back—and our horse too."

\\\

Hanna directed them to Elena's property, but this time, instead of taking the back way, the Bridles roared up the front drive. Up ahead, blue and red lights flashed—it was the sheriff, and as they pulled into the driveway, Hanna saw him putting tiny Izzy in the back of his car. Elena stood behind him with her arms crossed over her chest.

"Let her go!" Shouting, Hanna jumped out of the truck before it was completely stopped and raced toward the sheriff's car. "She didn't do anything wrong."

When the truck was parked, the Bridles hustled out after her. Right as he was about to slam the patrol car door, the sheriff looked up and his mouth dropped open.

"Mr. and Mrs. Bridle," he said, giving them each a nod. "I was about to call you. This girl's one of yours?" Izzy's head poked out of the door, and Hanna's chest twisted at the terrified look in her usually confident eyes.

"Of course she is," said Ma Etty, walking up to the car and helping Izzy out of it. The sheriff stepped back, clearly knowing better than to get between Ma Etty and one of her ranch kids.

"Hey," snapped Elena. "I'm pressing charges against that girl for trespassing."

Ma Etty glared at the other woman. "Sheriff Handy, you're arresting the wrong person." She pointed directly at Elena. "That woman neglects and abuses her horses."

"That's quite an accusation, Etty," the sheriff said, glancing between them.

"I have proof," said Hanna, pulling the phone out. "She hits Shy Guy. I've seen her do it twice now, but this time I recorded it." She pressed PLAY on the video and passed it to the sheriff. "And she punishes him by withholding food."

"Those hooligans were trespassing on my

property," said Elena, trying to grab the phone away.

The sheriff held up a hand. "Let me watch," he warned her.

As the video played, his eyebrows drew together and his mouth slowly parted. When it was over, he stared long and hard at Elena, who no longer looked quite so certain that things would work out her way.

"This is truly atrocious, Ms. Baxter," he said, giving the phone back to Ma Etty. He not-so-subtly patted his badge. "Show me the barn, please."

"You can't use that as evidence," Elena said, growing frantic. "They were the ones who broke the law."

"I won't ask again, Ms. Baxter. Show. Me. The barn."

Hanna, Izzy, and the Bridles waited as Sheriff Handy looked inside the barn. When he returned, his face was ashen.

"It's obvious to me what's going on here," he said, taking off his hat. He rubbed his face. "And it is in my authority as county sheriff to reclaim and foster abused animals. But we both know I don't have the kind of room or resources for that. Etty, could you foster Ms. Baxter's horse for me?"

Hanna couldn't believe her ears. She and Izzy turned to each other and hugged.

"You can't give away my horse," roared Elena. "He's mine! I bought and paid for him! He's taking me to the Olympics!"

"Keep it down," snapped the sheriff, turning to her. "You better watch it, Ms. Baxter. The only reason I haven't thrown you into the back of my car is I think you're quite sick. But give me a reason to, and I'm happy to do it. And we all know that Olympics story is a crock—you've been telling everyone that for years."

"I'm calling my lawyer." Elena pulled out her phone and began dialing, but Sheriff Handy looked unconcerned.

"We'll let the lawyers work out the details," he said with a shrug.

The Bridles both nodded. "Of course," said Ma Etty gratefully. "Of course we'll take in the horse, Doug."

"Then go get your Shy Guy," he said to Hanna and Izzy. "Go take that poor horse home."

Elena was yelling angrily into her phone as Hanna walked to the corral where Shy Guy was standing, still attached to the longe line. Izzy opened the corral gate and waited outside while Hanna stepped in.

Shy Guy looked startled when she approached, and for a moment, she wondered if he was lost again—if everything they'd done together was washed away by Elena Baxter. But then his nostrils flared, and his ears pointed toward her. He took a step and then two in her direction, and she matched them, until her arms wrapped around his neck and his head curled over her shoulder.

"Good boy," she said, leaning her cheek against his soft throat, running her hands through his mane. "Oh, you good boy. I'm so sorry. No one's going to hurt you again. Not ever."

He let out a long sigh, as if he understood.

\\\

Elena's squat husband came home while they waited for Paul to arrive with the trailer. Hanna led Shy Guy past where they stood by the police cruiser, answering Sheriff Handy's questions.

"How?" Elena demanded, startling girl and horse. "I don't get it. How did a talentless kid like you fix him? How did you get him to perform?"

Hanna blinked at her.

"I only loved him," she said. "I love him just the way he is."

Elena had no response. Her husband sighed.

"I hope you can understand," he said, putting an arm around Elena's shoulders. Hanna was surprised to see tears in Elena's eyes. "My wife has always tried so hard. But it was never enough, you know."

"Actually," Hanna said, "I do understand."

Soon the trailer came up the drive, and Paul parked the truck and let the ramp down. When Hanna led Shy Guy toward it, he jerked his head back, straining against the lead rope, eyes wide.

Hanna knew what he was remembering: the rain pelting the ground, Elena Baxter shouting and whipping him as she forced him into the trailer.

"Can I just ride him back?" Hanna asked.

Paul grinned and rubbed his hands together. "Just so happens I brought a saddle just in case."

"Perfect."

Hanna led Shy Guy away from the trailer and ran her hand down his neck for a long time.

He was fearful, but not lost the way he used to be. She still recognized Shy Guy in there, and Shy Guy still recognized her. Hanna knew they had some ground to make up.

Once he was calm again, Hanna saddled him and mounted. Izzy rode shotgun in the truck as she and Paul followed Hanna and Shy Guy home.

The sun was setting as they passed under the sign reading QUARTZ CREEK RANCH. Everyone had gathered out front of the ranch house, and a cheer went up as they walked up Bridlemile Road. Shy Guy hesitated at first, but with Hanna stroking his neck, he was convinced to approach the crowd.

After she got off and hugs were exchanged with everyone, Hanna led Shy Guy back to the barn. He had to smell it first to know it was their barn—the good barn—before he'd go in.

Inside, she slowly took off his bridle and saddle, and spent almost an hour cleaning him up. When she was done, she led him back to the stall with the nameplate reading "Shy Guy" and gave him two flakes of hay and a full bucket of grain.

CHAPTER TWENTY-FOUR

The last week at Quartz Creek Ranch was surprisingly somber. They would all have to leave soon—to go home and return to their regularly scheduled lives.

But it was especially so for Hanna. Every day she got to spend with Shy Guy was more valuable than diamonds. The kids and their trainers went on a trail ride together, and Shy Guy relished the climb up into the hills behind the ranch. They even had an impromptu race around the little lake they found in a secluded valley.

Shy Guy and Fettucini finished neck and neck. They weren't really sure who won.

Hanna was grateful to find Elena hadn't undone

all the ground she'd gained with Shy Guy. They fell back into their old pattern, and soon he even started letting Madison work with him. He didn't even seem to mind other people, as long as they kept their hands where he could see them.

As the final day approached, the idea of leaving Izzy and Rae Ann and Madison and everyone twisted Hanna's heart. She didn't know when she'd come to care about them all so much.

"There are always airplanes," Izzy said one night after lights-out, when Rae Ann was already asleep. They'd snuck out of the cabin and were sitting on the front stairs, talking in hushed voices. "You could come visit me in Phoenix. Or I could visit you in Michigan. And we could go see the Lawnchairs together!"

"Yes!" But Hanna knew it was unlikely either of their parents would foot the bill for a plane ticket. "They play Sturgis a lot. Home turf and everything."

They both knew this was probably good-bye, but they didn't say it. Popping in the earbuds, one each, they played the album all the way through one last time.

On the last day of camp, there were no chores and the kids were given free time to do whatever they wished around the ranch. Most of them chose riding, but Josh wanted to play bean bag toss with Paul. Hanna went and played with him during lunch and won four games in a row.

"Dang it, Hanna," he said in his lilting southern drawl. "When did you become so good at this game?"

"When you made me play it every day," she said, and he gave her one of his rare, lopsided smiles. She kind of hoped she'd see Josh again too.

At dinner that evening, Rae Ann started the waterworks when Ma Etty mentioned it was the last night, and Cade made sure everyone knew his e-mail address. Then they went back to their cabins and packed up their things. While Hanna was shoving clothes haphazardly into her duffel bag, a knock came at the door.

Madison opened it, and Ma Etty stepped inside.

"Hanna?" she asked. "Can we talk outside?"

Hanna nodded and followed her out onto the porch, and the door closed behind them.

"I called your mom." Hanna's stomach soured. Her mom? Had she done something wrong?

"Why?" asked Hanna.

"Because I wanted to tell her what a privilege it's been having you here at the ranch this summer. I explained a little about Shy Guy and how brave you were, and I suggested that if she could, she should come pick you up in person."

"In . . . person?" Her mom, here at the ranch? Hanna wanted to see her mom even less than she wanted to leave.

"She's flying in tomorrow. I thought I'd give you a heads-up. She's looking forward to seeing you."

Hanna's head drooped. Ma Etty put a hand on her shoulder.

"I know you and your mom have had a rocky relationship. But I think it's important she see how much you've grown here and what a great thing you've done working with Shy Guy."

"I don't know . . ."

"Trust me, Hanna. She's your mom. She loves you, and I know she wants to understand you. I think that seeing what you've done here will help."

She nodded. There wasn't anything she could do about it now. "Okay."

"Don't worry," said Ma Etty, smiling. "It will be fine. I promise."

\\

The next morning, while the other kids loaded their things into the old Econoline van to head to the airport, Hanna saddled up Shy Guy and did a few exercises with him in the arena. Izzy appeared outside the fence and leaned against it.

"Looking good, killer," she said. "You guys are awesome together."

Hanna and Shy Guy sidled over, and Hanna dismounted. Izzy slipped through the bars and, without a preamble, wrapped her up in a hug. "Don't you forget about me."

Hanna laughed, thinking about spiders crawling around in her bed. "It would be impossible to forget you."

"Your mom's here." With that, Izzy affectionately punched Hanna's shoulder, turned, and climbed back out. Then she was gone, and Hanna blinked back tears.

Sure enough, her mom walked around the side of the barn and paused when she saw Hanna. She didn't say anything as Hanna led Shy Guy over and opened the gate to the arena. Her mom cautiously stepped through, her shoes already muddy from walking around.

"Hi," said Hanna.

Her mom smiled a cautious smile, but her eyes were happier and brighter than she'd ever seen them.

"Oh, my Hanna." Her mom leaned forward and

put her arms around her. She kissed the top of Hanna's head, then stepped back to observe Shy Guy. "Wow. He's so gorgeous. Like one of your toy horses."

"Yeah," said Hanna. "I thought the same thing." Slowly her mom reached out one hand toward Shy Guy, who, surprisingly, didn't flinch away. She petted his soft nose, and Shy Guy blew out a gust of air.

"Tell me everything," her mom said. "Everything. Please."

\\\

When Hanna was done, her mom was crying. She hugged Hanna again and held onto her tightly. Hanna felt tears land on her hair.

"You're incredible," her mom said. "You're such an incredible girl. Ma Etty told me how proud she is of you. How frightened you were and how hard you worked anyway. It's all thanks to this guy?"

Hanna nodded. Her mom released her, and Hanna patted Shy Guy's strong neck. He dipped his head as if to say, *Yes, that's me.*

"I guess," said Hanna. "He's the one who's incredible. You wouldn't believe the things he knows, Mom. He's smart. He's sweet. He's kind."

"Sounds like a girl I know," her mom said.

"And he's so eager to please. But to Elena . . . it was never enough." Hanna paused, choosing her words carefully. "I know how that feels, you know. For nothing you do to be enough."

Her mom sucked in a breath, then gave a slow nod.

"Hanna," she said, voice shaking a little, "I . . . I think we have some things to talk about."

"I think so too."

"The stealing. It has to stop."

"I know." Hanna swallowed back tears. "I didn't do it because I like it, Mom. I did it because I . . . I was so angry at you. Because I tried my hardest to be the best, to be the daughter you wanted, and you kept telling me it wasn't enough. That I wasn't good enough for you. So I thought stealing would show you how good I'd been. That I could also be an awful daughter, if I wanted."

"Oh, Hanna." Her mom's eyes turned glossy. "I'm so sorry. I'm sorry I ever made you feel that way. You are exactly the daughter I want. More than! You're perfect." She stroked Shy Guy again, and he leaned into her hand. His brown eyes observed them both with a gentle kindness.

"If I promise to be better," her mom began, sniffling, "will you promise not to steal anymore?"

"Of course!" Hanna felt something inside her break. "Of course, Mom."

This time, her mother's embrace was a bear hug. When she was finished, her mom let her go and said, "And what about Shy Guy, here? You must be so sad to be leaving him behind. After what you told me, I'm sure he'll be sad to see you go. You know, there are some horse barns near our house. Maybe we could ask Ma Etty if we could take him with us?"

Hanna's heart nearly exploded out of her chest. Keep Shy Guy? Oh, how she wanted to! Shy Guy understood her in a way only Shy Guy could, the same way she understood him.

But she shook her head.

"I can't," she said quietly. "I can't ever ask him to get into a trailer again—not after what Elena did to him."

Her mother's eyes shone with unshed tears. She wiped them and nodded.

"I understand," she said. "You are so brave." Summoning a smile, she added, "Now show me what you two can do! I hear good things."

Taking a deep breath, Hanna stuck her foot in

the stirrup and pushed herself up. Once she was on Shy Guy's back, everything was perfect.

As they walked along the fence, Hanna let out just enough rein for him to glide into a trot, and then more rein until they fell into a sweet, smooth extended trot.

Then they were sailing—no, *flying*—together around the arena. Shy Guy's powerful hooves pounded the dirt, and his shoulders rippled, all silver muscle and shine. And the wind had never felt better as it raced through Hanna's hair.

ABOUT THE AUTHORS

KIERSI BURKHART grew up riding horses on the Colorado Front Range. At sixteen, she attended Lewis & Clark College in Portland and spent her young adult years in beautiful Oregon—until she discovered her sense of adventure was calling her elsewhere. Now she travels around with her best friend, a mutt named Baby, writing fiction for children of all ages.

AMBER J. KEYSER is happiest when she is in the wilderness with her family. Lucky for her, the rivers and forests of Central Oregon let her paddle, hike, ski, and ride horses right outside her front door. When she isn't adventuring, Amber writes fiction and nonfiction for young readers and goes running with her dog, Gilda.

ACKNOWLEDGMENTS

We have to thank our superhero agent, Fiona Kenshole, for suggesting that we write this series in the first place, for encouraging us to work together, and for championing us all the way to publication. Huge thanks to Anna and our wonderful team at Darby Creek for bringing Quartz Creek Ranch to life. Thank you to Heidi Siegel for all her horsey expertise; to Cesca for letting us use her band name; and to Whitney for dropping everything to make sure this book became a reality.

We also want to remember Spring, the wonderful gray horse who serves as the real-life inspiration behind Shy Guy. When Kiersi was a young girl, she was entrusted with rehabilitating an abandoned horse named Spring—from foundered to healthy, from forgotten to loved. You went through so much, and were still so full of heart.

Wherever you are, Spring, this one's for you.